Pioneers of the Field

Focusing on the crucial contributions of women researchers, Andrew Bank demonstrates that the modern school of social anthropology in South Africa was uniquely female-dominated. The book traces the personal and intellectual histories of six remarkable women through the use of a rich cocktail of new archival sources, including family photographs, private and professional correspondence, field-notes and field diaries, published and other public writings, and even love letters. The book also sheds new light on the close connections between their personal lives, their academic work and their anti-segregationist and anti-apartheid politics. It will be welcomed by anthropologists, historians and students in African Studies interested in the development of social anthropology in twentieth-century Africa, as well as by students and researchers in the field of Women and Gender Studies.

Andrew Bank is a professor in the History Department at the University of the Western Cape, South Africa. He was commissioning editor of the journal *Kronos: Southern African Histories* from 2001 to 2015 and is a member of the editorial board of the *South African Historical Journal*. He is also the co-editor of *Inside African Anthropology: Monica Wilson and Her Interpreters* (Cambridge University Press, 2013). His previous monographs are on slavery in Cape Town (1991) and the Bleek-Lloyd Collection of Bushman folklore (2006).

THE INTERNATIONAL AFRICAN LIBRARY

General editors

LESLIE J. BANK, *Human Sciences Research Council, South Africa*
HARRI ENGLUND, *University of Cambridge*
DEBORAH JAMES, *London School of Economics and Political Science*
ADELINE MASQUELIER, *Tulane University*
BENJAMIN SOARES, *African Studies Centre, Leiden*

The International African Library is a major monograph series from the International African Institute. Theoretically informed ethnographies, and studies of social relations 'on the ground' which are sensitive to local cultural forms, have long been central to the Institute's publications programme. The IAL maintains this strength and extends it into new areas of contemporary concern, both practical and intellectual. It includes works focused on the linkages between local, national and global levels of society; writings on political economy and power; studies at the interface of the socio-cultural and the environmental; analyses of the roles of religion, cosmology and ritual in social organization; and historical studies, especially those of a social, cultural or interdisciplinary character.

For a list of titles published in the series, please see the end of the book.

Pioneers of the Field

South Africa's Women Anthropologists

Andrew Bank
University of the Western Cape

International African Institute, London
and

CAMBRIDGE
UNIVERSITY PRESS

University Printing House, Cambridge CB2 8BS, United Kingdom

One Liberty Plaza, 20th Floor, New York, NY 10006, USA

477 Williamstown Road, Port Melbourne, VIC 3207, Australia

4843/24, 2nd Floor, Ansari Road, Daryaganj, Delhi - 110002, India

79 Anson Road, #06-04/06, Singapore 079906

Cambridge University Press is part of the University of Cambridge.

It furthers the University's mission by disseminating knowledge in the pursuit of
education, learning and research at the highest international levels of excellence.

www.cambridge.org
Information on this title: www.cambridge.org/9781107150492

© Andrew Bank 2016

This publication is in copyright. Subject to statutory exception
and to the provisions of relevant collective licensing agreements,
no reproduction of any part may take place without the written
permission of Cambridge University Press.

First published 2016

A catalogue record for this publication is available from the British Library

Library of Congress Cataloging in Publication data
Bank, Andrew, author.
Pioneers of the field : South Africa's women anthropologists / Andrew Bank.
International African library.
New York : Cambridge University Press, 2016. | Series: The international
African library | Includes bibliographical references.
LCCN 2016026286 | ISBN 9781107150492
LCSH: Women ethnologists – South Africa – Biography. | Ethnologists –
South Africa – Biography. | Ethnology – Study and teaching (Higher) –
South Africa – History – 20th century.
LCC GN20 B34 2016 | DDC 305.80092/268 [B]–dc23
LC record available at https://lccn.loc.gov/2016026286

ISBN 978-1-107-15049-2 Hardback

Cambridge University Press has no responsibility for the persistence or
accuracy of URLs for external or third-party internet websites referred to in
this publication, and does not guarantee that any content on such websites is,
or will remain, accurate or appropriate.

To my wife Anja

Contents

List of figures		*page* viii
Acknowledgements		xii
	Introduction: rethinking the canon	1
1	Feminizing the foundational narrative: the collaborative anthropology of Winifred Tucker Hoernlé (1885–1960)	15
2	An adopted daughter: Christianity and anthropology in the life and work of Monica Hunter Wilson (1908–1982)	64
3	Anthropology and Jewish identity: the urban fieldwork and ethnographies of Ellen Hellmann (1908–1982)	104
4	'A genius for friendship': Audrey Richards at Wits, 1938–1940	151
5	Historical ethnography and ethnographic fiction: the South African writings of Hilda Beemer Kuper (1911–1992)	189
6	Feminizing the discipline: the long career of Eileen Jensen Krige (1904–1995)	239
	Conclusion: a humanist legacy	272
	Bibliography	284
	Index	309

Figures

1.1: Winifred Tucker in her matric year at Wesleyan Girls' High School, Grahamstown, 1902. *page* 20

1.2: Winifred Tucker and the South African College's first SRC, 1905. 21

1.3: 'Breakdown of our waggon near Sendeling's Drift', Richtersveld, Northern Cape, 1912. 27

1.4: This portrait of a Nama woman photographed on Winifred Tucker's first field expedition of 1912 is reproduced from the only glass negative to have survived a devastating fire in Wits University Library that would destroy all of her field-notes and other materials. 28

1.5: Winifred and Alwin as a young baby, Boston, 1915. 31

1.6: Winifred (front row, second left) was photographed with her family on her return to Johannesburg in 1920. 33

1.7: Winifred Hoernlé around the time that her intellectual 'daughters' first encountered her, August 1927. 48

1.8: Winifred Hoernlé as photographed by Leon Levson in 1944. 62

2.1: Monica Hunter as a teenager, Edinburgh, 1922. 68

2.2: Monica at work in the Stanley Library, Girton College, Cambridge, 1930. This was the year in which she completed her undergraduate degree, having earlier switched from history to social anthropology, and won an Anthony Wilkin Scholarship which funded her fieldwork in Pondoland and the Eastern Cape from 1931. 74

2.3: 'Nosente, the Mother of Compassion', Auckland Village, 1931. Nosente was a Christian convert whose testimony about the rapid social changes in the Eastern Cape between the time of her birth in the late 1860s and that of Monica's fieldwork in the 1930s was the subject of an autobiography that Monica recorded, edited and published in Margery Perham's *Ten Africans* (1936). 77

List of figures ix

2.4: The trading store run by Mary Soga and her husband at Ntibane, Western Pondoland (south-east of Mthatha) where Monica spent seven highly productive months doing fieldwork. She claimed to have developed her understanding of Pondo culture through sitting on mealie sacks in the store and listening to the gossip of clients, like the young Pondo women in the foreground. 79

2.5: The first of the page-spread features published in the *Illustrated London News* of 22 August 1936 in 'appreciation' of *Reaction to Conquest*. The photographs were selected from the twenty-eight plates that featured in the book. 83

2.6: Members of the African Studies Department and senior students, Fort Hare Native College, 1946. Monica is in the centre of the middle row. Her friend and colleague Z.K. Matthews is seated on her left. Her talented graduate student Livingstone Mqotsi is seated at the end of the middle row, far left. 98

2.7: Monica Wilson on a hike during her retirement, with the Hogsback Mountain in the background. 102

3.1: 'The Family, 1922': Bernard and Chlothilde Kaumheimer with their daughters, Ellen (left, aged 14) and Inez (right, aged 10) at a public swimming pool in Johannesburg. 111

3.2: 'No. 4 Alleyway'. This was one of nineteen photographs that featured in the appendix to the belatedly published *Rooiyard* (1948). The large barrels were used for beer-brewing. 118

3.3: 'No. 17 John Chafimbira'. Ellen's research assistant and bodyguard in Rooiyard, 1933. 119

3.4: Ellen and Ruth, aged two, 1938. 127

3.5: Photographs from the appendix to Ellen Hellmann's doctoral thesis (1939). 132

3.6: Ellen Hellmann, 1945. 135

3.7: Ellen Hellmann addressing a public meeting during the 1950s, possibly at Entokozeni, a clinic in Alexandra with which she was actively involved. 141

4.1: '*Shilusako citimene*, Audrey!' ('Don't worry about *citimene* [tree-cutting], Audrey!') Audrey researching methods of agriculture in the field, Bembaland, c October 1933. 162

4.2: 'The Hockey Team!' Audrey and Lorna after a hockey match at Shiwa Ngandu. Audrey is standing with her stick in her left hand. Lorna is kneeling in front of the trophy, c 1933. 163

x   List of figures

4.3: 'In Swaziland. Rock climb (staged) with Biesheuvels (lecturer
in psychology here [at Wits University]).' An outstretched
Audrey with Dr Simon Biesheuvel (1908–1991) and two
students on their vacation fieldtrip to Swaziland, July 1938.   172

4.4: 'With Biesheuvels and the prettiest student.' Further
adventures on the Swaziland fieldtrip, July 1938. Audrey is on
the right.   173

4.5: 'Descending ravine to a native village. (Ainslie trying to show
that there is *no* need to be alarmed).' Audrey, a colleague
and their students on yet another adventurous vacation
fieldtrip, 1939.   174

5.1: 'Princess Topi and Hilda Beemer outside her house at
Lobamba.' This photograph was probably taken by
Malinowski during his fortnight in the field with Hilda in
late July and early August 1934.   200

5.2: 'Photo of Hilda Kuper in the field.' This photograph was
probably taken by Leo Kuper when he visited her field-site on
the eve of her departure for her three-month tour of
Swaziland, beginning in September 1934. From left to right:
Sobhuza II, Hilda Beemer and her guide-cum-research
assistant, standing alongside her car with its TJ (Transvaal,
Johannesburg) registration number.   201

5.3: 'Recruits for the gold mines of the Rand lined up with their
papers and bundles, ready to get on the bus for the first stage
of their long journey out of Swaziland.' Photographer Hilda
Beemer, c 1935.   209

5.4: A photojournalistic sequence capturing an incident in the
Johannesburg city centre in the mid-1940s. It involved
a young milkman falling off a bicycle followed by animated
pavement discussion about the incident between a young
white teenager and a group of stylishly dressed township
youth. It is her eye for the unusual incident, for the personal
and the particular that made her such a gifted story-writer.   210

5.5: 'Dolly's wedding.' Hilda Kuper's photograph of her
daughters, Mary (right) and Jenny (left), at a Hindu wedding
celebration in Durban, 1954.   220

5.6: The Kuper family on a visit to Chatsworth House in
Derbyshire in 1958. Hilda was on a Simons Fellowship at
Manchester University organized by Max Gluckman. Jenny is
on the left alongside Leo, Mary on the right alongside Hilda
and their cousin John Beemer is in the middle.   224

List of figures

5.7: Hilda's research assistant and later UCLA graduate student, Thoko Ginindza, doing tape-recorded interviews in the field for Hilda's biography of Sobhuza II, c 1973. The project almost derailed when the tape and a mass of other field materials went missing in Johannesburg in 1974 before they could be posted to Los Angeles.   233

5.8: Hilda Kuper and Sobhuza II at the Reed Dance in Lobamba in September 1981.   237

6.1: Eileen and her university friends, Johannesburg Training College Hostel, c 1922. From left to right: Louise Jongbloed, Maisie Eaton, Cato Smuts and Eileen Jensen.   243

6.2: Envelope labelled 'July 1926 [sic]: Holiday with Lennie Impey at W.N.L.A., Zoekmakaar [sic].' Left to right: Valda Inglis, Lennox Impey, Eileen Jensen, Cato Smuts.   246

6.3: Eileen and Jack at the time of their engagement, 1926.   247

6.4: Deputy South African Prime Minister Jan Smuts visiting Eileen and Jack at their field base, 1937. He later wrote the Foreword to their book. From left to right: Cato Clark (née Smuts), Jack Krige, Eileen Krige, Bancroft Clark, Jan Smuts, two local men and three children (unidentified).   255

6.5: Eileen and baby Thor, Durban, 1946.   259

6.6: Eileen at Modjadji in the early 1980s. She is greeting the late Mantwa Modjadji who was one of the wives of Modjadji III.   269

Acknowledgements

All books are thoroughly collaborative products, a collective biography probably more than most. Sustaining long-term research projects involves patience, curiosity and determination, but also a great deal of emotional and psychological support. For this I owe a major debt to my wife Anja Macher. She not only created the conditions that have allowed for steady creative engagement over a long period, but joined me on archival trips to Los Angeles, Johannesburg and a fieldtrip to Swaziland, and patiently listened to pages and pages of text readings, simply and dispassionately identifying them either as 'lively' or 'boring'.

Intellectual friends have played a particularly supportive role. My brother, the South African anthropologist Leslie J. Bank, spent years working collaboratively on an edited collection on Monica Hunter Wilson, one of the six women who will feature in this study. He has helped me retain a sense of enthusiasm and perspective on the long road. Diana Wylie read a draft manuscript at a stage where I was veering off course and commented with warmth, insight, openness and enthusiasm. Karen Tranberg Hansen helped me formulate my publication proposal and read the entire manuscript with a trained critical eye. Elizabeth F. Colson got in touch with me after reading the collective edition on Monica Wilson and not only provided the most incisive of commentaries on all my chapters, but convinced me that bringing to life these women intellectuals was a worthwhile and relevant endeavour. Adam Kuper, Michael W. Young and Nancy Lutkehaus added generous endorsements, while Kuper and John Sharp provided generous reviews of the book in manuscript form. They inspired me to produce a more stirring and fitting conclusion.

I own a special debt to my research assistant Sue Ogterop whose long experience of accessing data at the African Studies Library of the University of Cape Town enormously enriched all six biographies. I am also grateful to her for meticulous copy-editing. I sent each of the chapters to specific readers and have acknowledged them individually in each case, but thank them collectively here. My long-time visual and design guru, Jenny Sandler, has assisted me with the choice of visuals and has patiently managed their arrangement and archiving.

Acknowledgements

In her remarkable self-reflective sounding on the biographical constructions of Sylvia Plath, Janet Malcolm identified living descendants as the biographer's sworn enemy. 'They are [she declares] like the hostile tribes an explorer encounters and must ruthlessly subdue to claim his territory.' Fortunately, my own experience of relations with relatives has been far more benign; in fact, positively charmed. Eileen's granddaughter and daughter-in-law, Emily-Ann and Dulcie Krige, have selflessly copy-edited and meticulously corrected not only the chapter on their beloved forebear, but the entire manuscript in final draft forms picking out scores of errors in each chapter. This is quite apart from their sharing of deeply private papers on Eileen, including love letters between her and Jack, and Emily-Ann's expert guidance through her grandmother's extensive archive based on her own 144 page index! Jenny and Mary Kuper have shared memories, family photographs and patiently read and reread sundry draft chapters on Hilda. Their disarming honesty about Hilda as a surprisingly doting wife and dedicated mother has profoundly reshaped my appreciation of her life and work. I have likewise been deeply moved by Dame Ruth Runciman's openness in sharing often painful details about her mother Ellen Hellmann's difficult life, and have been touched by her gratitude for my efforts to tell an alternative and more appreciative story about Ellen. Diana W. Higgs allowed me to use photographs from the Winifred Hoernle Papers. Francis and Tim Wilson gave permission for reproduction of visuals from the Wilson Collection.

My main intellectual debt is to my selfless friend, the historian and editor Russell Martin who has vastly improved each of the narratives that make up this book. He has taken my bloated, baggy draft chapters, one at a time, and knocked them into readable shape. He has made accessible stories of my typically long-winded excursions into the personal lives of my cast, trimming away side characters, unnecessary detail and cumbersome qualification. After all, it is not everyone who will casually enquire over a hand of bridge whether you, too, happen to be in the habit of reading and rereading, from cover to cover, the 1965 Onions edition and more occasionally the 1996 Burchfield edition of Fowler's classic *Modern English Usage*.

Finally, I am grateful to the midwives from CUP and the International African Institute who have nursed this book to life. Stephanie Kitchen remains a model of warmth, efficiency and enthusiasm. Sarah E. Green was patient and generous regarding my ever-expanding wish list for last-minute visuals, while Velmurugan Inbasigamoni injected a welcome energy in seeing the book through to copy-editing, layout and printing. Margie Ramsay is responsible for the multi-layered and enticing Index.

Introduction: rethinking the canon

> The question now inevitably asks itself, whether the lives of great men only should be recorded.   Virginia Woolf, 'The Art of Biography' (1939).[1]

Along the main wall of the hallway in the Social Anthropology Department at the University of the Witwatersrand in Johannesburg, there is an exhibition of the department's intellectual forefathers. This fictitious lineage, which graduate students and professors pass daily, has been on display, unchanged, for two decades. The exhibition consists of a row of ancestors presented, in each case, in large glass-bound framed portrait form with a paragraph-length caption explaining their significance, with particular emphasis on their theoretical contribution to 'the British school'. Those on display are Alfred Reginald Radcliffe-Brown, Winifred Hoernlé, Isaac Schapera, Max Gluckman, David Webster, David Lewis-Williams, David Hammond-Tooke and David Coplan.

The problem with this narrative is that the founding intellectuals and heads of this truly remarkable department were, without exception, women.

This silence regarding women's contributions to the history of anthropology is not specific to South Africa, although the dominance of women in establishing and then developing the field in South Africa does make the bias in this case particularly revealing. In the introduction to the landmark collection *Women Writing Culture*, the feminist anthropologist, Ruth Behar, points to the heightened awareness in American anthropology of the late 1980s and early 1990s of the power of a conservative male-dominated canon.

Anthropologists have belatedly begun to realize that we, too, have a canon [like literary scholars], a set of 'great books' that we continue to teach to our students, as dutifully as they were taught to us in graduate school. That these books just

---

[1] Virginia Woolf, *Collected Essays, Vol. 4*, ed., Leonard Woolf (London: Chatto and Windus), 1967, 222. Thanks to Deborah James for editorial advice on this chapter.

2   Pioneers of the Field

happen to be the writings of white men is an idea that can never be brought up. It seems somehow impolite.[2]

The questioning of this gendered and racially exclusive canon in American anthropology began, in her analysis, with the outrage of feminist anthropologists following the publication of the 1986 volume *Writing Culture*. While this initiated a self-reflexive turn in the discipline, and a greater appreciation of the complexity of cultural knowledge production, the collection featured just one female scholar, and its editor, James Clifford, explicitly defended the male canon by suggesting that feminist anthropologists were not experimental writers. In the fallout and then ferment that led to their alternative feminist history of the discipline, Behar was led to ask:

> Why is the culture concept in anthropology only found through Sir Edward Tylor, Franz Boas, Bronislaw Malinowski, Claude Lévi-Strauss, and Clifford Geertz? Could the writing of culture not be traced, as the essays in this volume suggest, through Elsie Clews Parsons, Ruth Benedict, Margaret Mead, Ella Doloria, Zora Neale Hurston, Ruth Landes and Barbara Meyerhoff to Alice Walker?[3]

Let us return to the photo gallery of founding fathers that graces the hall at Wits. The first head of department, Winifred Hoernlé (1885–1960), does feature. The story of her role in establishing the discipline of social anthropology in South African universities between 1923 and 1937 will be at the heart of this study. She was, however, not preceded by Radcliffe-Brown. He had worked for a brief time as temporary lecturer in the psychology department at the Transvaal School of Mines before founding the social anthropology department at the University of Cape Town in 1921. Her successor as head of department was not Isaac Schapera, whose place on the wall relates to a single semester he spent as Hoernlé's stand-in when she travelled to London to visit Malinowski, but Audrey Isabel Richards (1899–1984), then a far more senior figure in the British school of social anthropology. Richards spent three highly productive, and hitherto almost entirely unacknowledged, years at Wits between 1938 and 1940. She consolidated Hoernlé's legacy in teaching excellence, departmental resource development and, above all, active promotion of a new generation of young researchers, almost all of whom were women. We should note in passing that the eldest of this cohort, Eileen Jensen Krige (1904–95), would have as much right as Schapera to a spot on the

---

[2] Ruth Behar, 'Introduction' in Ruth Behar and Deborah A. Gordon, eds., *Women Writing Culture* (Los Angeles and London: University of California Press, 1995), 11.
[3] *Ibid.*, 12.

Introduction: rethinking the canon 3

wall, given that she too served as a substitute lecturer for Winifred Hoernlé for a semester, this time in 1936.

Audrey Richards was not succeeded by Max Gluckman. He did apply for a post in the Wits Bantu Studies Department but was rejected, partly at Richards' prompting.[4] Instead, Richards ensured that the university put aside its misgivings about appointing Jews and ensured that Hilda Beemer Kuper (1911–92) served as her successor, as she would do from 1941 to 1946. If one were to consider research contribution then Ellen Hellmann (1908–82) would surely also deserve a place on the wall. She published two monographs that pioneered the field of urban anthropology and was the first woman in the university to be awarded a doctoral degree, for the second of these studies completed in 1939. If contribution as a public intellectual were the yardstick, then Beemer Kuper's undergraduate and graduate student, the radical journalist and anti-apartheid activist Ruth First, would have a case for consideration. If the criterion remained narrowed down to leadership and senior teaching, Monica Hunter Wilson (1908–82) would have been the *fifth* successive woman head of department (after Hoernlé, Krige, Richards and Kuper) had the University Appointments Committee not turned down her application in 1946 in favour of a transparently weaker male candidate, Mervyn Jeffreys.[5]

We should note that women scholars would continue to play a leading role in the Wits department in subsequent decades from a second generation of urban anthropologists, Laura Longmore and Mia Brandel-Syrier researching and publishing in the 1950s, 1960s and 1970s, to talented ethnographers and ethnographically oriented historians who began their long careers in the 1980s and 1990s, most notably Deborah James and Carolyn Hamilton. But it is the six founding foremothers associated with this department, and indeed social anthropology in South Africa – Winifred Hoernlé, her one-time informal student Monica Hunter Wilson, her successor Audrey Richards, and her three most dedicated disciples, Ellen Hellmann, Hilda Beemer Kuper and Eileen Jensen Krige – who are the central protagonists in this revised narrative about the discipline's history.

Before giving an overview of how, in more detail, I propose to reconstruct their hidden contributions, I would highlight that the Wits

---

[4] University of Cape Town Libraries, Manuscripts and Archives Department, BC880 Monica and Godfrey Wilson Papers [Wilson Collection, WC], Correspondence, B4.7 [GW] To and from Audrey Richards, MSS & TSS, Audrey Richards to Godfrey Wilson, 2 February 1939.

[5] WC, Correspondence B6.14, [MW] To and from Audrey Richards, Audrey Richards to Monica Wilson, 25 June 1946.

4   Pioneers of the Field

exhibition is a fair and accurate reflection of how social anthropologists in South Africa have told, and continue to tell, the story of their past. In this regard it is instructive that the standard overview history of the discipline by David Hammond-Tooke, published by Wits University Press in 1997 and reissued in 2001, devotes no more than one page in ten to the work of women scholars. He devotes more attention to the alleged contributions to South African social anthropology of two pro-segregation, German-trained linguists-turned-'tribal' ethnographers, the Afrikaner nationalist and later architect of apartheid, Willi Werner Eiselen, and the official Native Affairs Department anthropologist, Nicolas van Warmelo, than to the full collective of women scholars cited above, whose writings, as the chapters that follow will indicate, are consistently undervalued, marginalized and sometimes misread in Hammond-Tooke's study.[6]

There are dozens of journal articles or book chapters on the work of 'The Founding Fathers'. Scholarly writings on South African women anthropologists, by contrast, have been few and far between. There has been surprisingly little curiosity regarding the lives, works and intellectual legacy of the women pioneers who form the core cast of this study. The recent upsurge of interest in Monica Hunter Wilson, beginning with a centenary conference held in July 2008 and culminating in two book-length biographies, makes her a notable exception.[7] Apart from their respective obituaries and relatively brief appreciative retrospective essays written two or three decades ago, women anthropologists have received short shrift. Indeed, in those rare instances where they have been the subject of any attention by the current generation of social anthropologists, as in Kelly Gillespie's essay on Winifred Hoernlé's work in the field of social welfare in the 1940s, the argument has been a rehearsal of the somewhat well-worn case for the ambiguities and limitations of the racial ideology of South African liberalism.[8] Even in the case of Audrey Richards, who has had the benefit of gifted and eloquent students and

---

[6] On Eiselen and Van Warmelo, see W. David Hammond-Tooke, *Imperfect Interpreters: South Africa's Anthropologists, 1920–1990* (Johannesburg: Witwatersrand University Press, 1997), 57–69, 108–18. On the six women anthropologists cited above, see 35–8, 77–90, 143–4.

[7] See Andrew Bank and Leslie J. Bank, eds., *Inside African Anthropology: Monica Wilson and Her Interpreters* (New York: Cambridge University Press in association with the International African Institute, 2013); Seán Morrow, *The Fires Beneath: The Life of Monica Wilson, South African Anthropologist* (Johannesburg: Penguin South Africa, 2016).

[8] Kelly Gillespie, 'Containing the "Wandering Native": Racial Jurisdiction and the Liberal Politics of Prison Reform in 1940s South Africa', *Journal of Southern African Studies*, 37, 3 (2011), 499–515. For the original Marxist critique, see Paul B. Rich, *White Power and the Liberal Conscience: Racial Segregation and South African Liberalism, 1921–1960* (Johannesburg: Ravan Press, 1984).

Introduction: rethinking the canon

friends to showcase her work and charisma, the lack of a book-length biography to rival those of her male mentors and peers remains a striking silence.[9]

Why, we might ask following Ruth Behar, is the concept of culture traced only through a male lineage? Could the writing of culture in southern Africa not be tracked instead through a female line, from Winifred Hoernlé and Audrey Richards through Hunter and Hellmann, Kuper and Krige, to new generations of women ethnographers including those mentioned earlier? Following this lineage one could make a powerful case for these foremothers having invented a, or *the*, 'great tradition' during what has rightly been seen as 'a golden age' of creative fieldwork and internationally acclaimed ethnographic production by South African anthropologists. These women ethnographers led the way in documenting and analysing the then still much-derided cultures of African peoples in the kind of meticulous detail that subsequent generations of ethnographers have seldom been able to replicate, for reasons I will explore in concluding this study.

A graduate course on women writing southern African culture would have to begin with the three essays written in the early to mid-1920s by Winifred Hoernlé, the 'mother of South African anthropology', as her devoted students warmly acknowledged. Here students would explore her first fieldwork-based case studies for understanding African social systems, beginning with the Nama communities of the southern African interior, in relation to their histories, as well as their interrelated cultural 'elements', with the concept of ritual rites of passage centre-stage. The course would continue by examining how a path-breaking cultural theory of biological needs was developed by Audrey Richards in her 1930 study *Hunger and Work* and then ethnographically applied at field-sites in southern Africa by all of the women scholars mentioned earlier, but most fully of course by Richards herself in the case of Bemba society in *Land, Labour and Diet* (1939). One would proceed by highlighting the sustained attention to sexuality and gender in the work of each of these women who, unlike their male counterparts who wrote about sexuality (like Schapera), gathered their field data, in the main, from women informants. This allowed them, inter alia, to foreground the political power of women in southern African societies, from the Swazi Queen

[9] In 1978 Adam Kuper asked Audrey whether he could write her biography. She rejected his 'startling suggestion', enquiring: 'Have you special associations with Routledge [publishers of his controversial 1973 history of the British school] that enable you to do this?' She never did 'get first shot' at writing her life history as she was too busy completing her Elmdon village histories. Audrey Richards to Adam Kuper, 13 June 1978, London, Private Papers of Adam Kuper.

6   Pioneers of the Field

Mother and Lovedu Rain-Queen down to the Bemba matriarch and Pondo mother-in-law. Their women-centred fieldwork allowed them to provide richer and more textured accounts than those of their male counterparts of the agricultural work, family relations and ritual lives of southern African women.[10]

One could then track these three central themes in the understanding of traditional cultural systems in the region, those of ritual, nutrition and gender relations, through to the more mature writings of these women scholars. Here students would read Kuper on the *Incwala* rituals associated with Swazi kingship (1947) and later on the rituals associated with Hindu worship in Durban (1960), by Hunter Wilson on the communal and family rituals of the Nyakyusa (1957, 1959), by Richards (if we may extend our interest in her beyond her time at Wits) on the Chisungu puberty ceremonies (1956), and articles by Krige on Zulu women's songs (1968) and Lovedu 'woman-marriage' (1975). In all these cases there was a new emphasis on ritual symbolism, creatively interpreted in ways that prefigured the work of the male scholars, notably Victor Turner, who is conventionally credited with having initiated African anthropology's 'symbolic turn'.[11]

Surely the most distinctive feature of their body of work, however, the latter section of the course would reveal, was their opening up of the study of cultural change in southern Africa. This involved entering new kinds of ethnographic field-sites beyond the 'native reserves' studied by their male counterparts like Schapera and Gluckman. Whether or not one chose to track the roots of urban fieldwork in the region right back to Hoernlé's two months in Windhoek in 1922–3, as I later propose, all would surely agree that they collectively pioneered urban anthropology during the early to mid-1930s. Whether emphasizing the straining of traditional cultures in urban settings, as all of them did, or the resilience of a female-dominated working class subculture, as Hellmann did so richly in 'Rooiyard' (1935), theirs were the first ethnographies of Africans in South African cities: in East London and Grahamstown (Hunter), Pretoria (Krige) and Johannesburg (Kuper and especially Hellmann in two full monographs). One might also reflect more deeply than is usually the case on how one of them (Hunter) opened up the anthropological study of white farms, a field South African women scholars have taken

---

[10] On Audrey Richards' achievement in this regard, see Henrietta L. Moore and Megan Vaughan, *Cutting Down Trees: Gender, Nutrition, and Agricultural Change in the Northern Province of Zambia, 1890–1990* (Portsmouth, New Haven: Heinemann, 1994).

[11] Victor W. Turner, significantly, devoted his famous *The Forest of Symbols: Aspects of Ndembu Ritual* (Ithaca, NY, and London: Cornell University Press, 1967) to Monica Wilson who had influenced him during time at the University of Cape Town in 1954–5.

Introduction: rethinking the canon

forward in recent years,[12] as part of a multi-sited ethnographic method that anticipated the work of the next generation.[13] Another (Kuper) produced the first historical ethnography of Indian communities in South Africa, in this case in Durban of the 1950s.

One would also need to feature a seminar on the late historical turn in the careers of Hunter Wilson and Beemer Kuper, whose writings had always been historically sensitive in their attention to African oral tradition. They now also drew extensively on documentary sources, especially in the *Oxford History of South Africa*, in which Wilson rather than Leonard Thompson played the dominant role as planner, co-editor and most prominent author,[14] and in their biographies of the African leaders Sobhuza II (1978) and ZK Matthews (1981).

Given the literary turn in the discipline, one would surely also need to feature a seminar on the narrative gifts of all these women. Here one would examine their skill as ethnographers, an aspect of their craft that has received less attention than it should. A study of carefully crafted narrative could usefully be explored in relation to their dozen excellent monographs: in chronological order of completion, *Hunger and Work* (1930), 'Rooiyard' (1935), *Reaction to Conquest* (1936), *Land, Labour and Diet* (1939), *The Realm of a Rain-Queen* (with Jack Krige, 1943), *The Analysis of Social Change* (with the late Godfrey Wilson, 1945), *An African Aristocracy* (1947), *The Uniform of Colour* (1947), *Good Company* (1951), *Chisungu* (1956), *Communal Rituals of the Nyakyusa* (1957), *Kinship Rituals of the Nyakyusa* (1959) and *Indians in South Africa* (1960) with a case to be made for *Langa: A Study in Social Groups* (with Archie Mafeje).[15] One would certainly need to explore the precocious ethnographic experimentation with new forms of creative writing by Hilda Kuper, whose female- and African-centred short stories, plays and novel anticipated by some decades the literary turn in social anthropology world-wide, let alone in the region.

Why has the story of these women's contributions to 'theory', as well as fieldwork innovation and ethnography, not been fully appreciated?

---

[12] See, for example, Susan Levine, *Children of a Bitter Harvest: Child Labour in the Cape Winelands* (Cape Town: HSRC Press, 2013).

[13] Jean Comaroff, 'Monica Wilson and the Practice of "Deep Ethnography": Roundtable on South African Women Anthropologists and Ethnography' (unpublished paper presented at the Anthropology Southern Africa Conference, University of the Western Cape, September 2008).

[14] Seán Morrow and Christopher Saunders, '"Part of One Whole": Anthropology and History in the Work of Monica Wilson' in Bank and Bank, eds., *Inside African Anthropology*, 291–8.

[15] See Andrew Bank with Vuyiswa Swana, '"Speaking from Inside": Archie Mafeje, Monica Wilson and the Co-Production of *Langa: A Study of Social Groups in an African Township*' in Bank and Bank, eds., *Inside African Anthropology*, 253–79.

8   Pioneers of the Field

The answer is partly because historians of anthropology have highlighted the achievements of male rather than female ancestors. There is, however, more to it than the privileging of male at the expense of female mentors. It relates to how the narrative of the origins and development of South African anthropology, a tradition on the periphery, has been subordinated to a narrative about the metropolitan tradition, the wider story about the origins and development of the British tradition of social anthropology. And here of course Adam Kuper has played the central role as the author of the foundational text, currently running into its fourth edition. The fact that Radcliffe-Brown, Schapera and Gluckman all became significant figures in anthropology in Britain, at Oxford, London and Manchester, respectively, and founders of schools, those of structural-functionalism and the Manchester School in particular, accounts for the prominence given to their contributions to South African anthropology at the expense of women scholars. The latter, with the partial exception of Hilda Kuper who emigrated in 1961 (and of course Richards who returned to England in 1940), stayed in South Africa and courageously sought to develop the discipline from within under increasingly oppressive intellectual and political circumstances.

A comparison with the way in which American sociology came to construct the canon in its own image is instructive. Adopting a definition of a 'canon' as 'a privileged set of texts, whose interpretation and reinterpretation defines a field', Raewyn Connell demonstrates how a narrowed-down cast of Founding Fathers, here the unholy trinity of Durkheim, Weber and Marx, and a stripped bare core theory, that of dealing with disorder and deviance in the making of the modern Western state, came to displace what had been a much more complex intellectual tradition in the decades before the First World War. The earlier, richer, turn-of-the-century tradition had been more internationally collaborative, here between Europe and the United States, and more diverse and eclectic in scope.

Connell too readily dismisses the value of challenging these male-dominated metropolitan narratives of disciplinary origins and development on the grounds that it 'does nothing to change the terms of intellectual production in the present'.[16] Her pessimism derives perhaps from the difficulties of rethinking the discipline of sociology in a more open and inclusive way. While Harriet Martineau is among the only candidates to have been proposed as a 'foremother' of sociology, the situation is different for social and cultural anthropology, where women

---

[16] Raewyn Connell, *Southern Theory: The Global Dynamics of Knowledge in Science* (Cambridge: Polity, 2007), xi.

Introduction: rethinking the canon

did play a much more active role from the outset. This was in part due to the newness of the discipline as well as the greater difficulties in policing fieldwork as compared with laboratory or library knowledge. The enhanced presence of women in allied field sciences, like botany, suggests that the spatial dispersion of the anthropological method, at least as practised from the 1910s and 1920s in the mainstream British and American traditions and beyond, allowed for the enhanced participation of women. From the very outset, even the relatively conservative evolutionary anthropologists like the Oxford professor Edward B. Tylor, who occupied the first chair in anthropology in Britain from 1888, explicitly promoted the idea that women could play an important role as researchers given their enhanced access to the women's sphere in 'primitive cultures'.[17] This idea continued to have currency through the interwar years and beyond. As many scholars have noted, these two mainstream traditions enjoyed the benefits of two gatekeepers from the 'outside', the German Jew Franz Boas and the Polish aristocrat Bronislaw Malinowski. They were both unusually welcoming to students from the margins, whether ethnic minorities, colonials or women, and trained and promoted the leading women scholars of the pioneering generation, notably Margaret Mead and Ruth Benedict in cultural anthropology and Audrey Richards in social anthropology. Indeed, Mead (1901–78) became the face of the discipline in twentieth-century America, publishing more than 1300 books, biographical articles and reviews in the second and third quarters of the century and becoming 'an American icon', highly adept at garnering radio and television in service of both self- promotion and that of the discipline, as Nancy Lutkehaus so vividly demonstrates.[18]

It was, after all, Mead who coined the concept of anthropology as 'The Welcoming Science'. In an essay written in 1960, she reflected that 'Anthropology, a new science, welcomed the stranger ... [A]nthropology was kinder to women, those who came from distant disciplines, to members of minority groups in general ... to the "over-mature", the idiosyncratic, and the capriciously gifted or experienced, to refugees ... '[19] It is certainly true that women entered anthropology from an early stage in all traditions, metropolitan and marginal. Again the trend was particularly pronounced in American anthropology

---

[17] Lyn Schumaker, 'Women in the Field in the Twentieth Century: Revolution, Involution, Devolution?' in Henrika Kuklick, ed., *A New History of Anthropology* (Oxford: Blackwell Publishing Ltd., 2008), 280.

[18] Nancy C. Lutkehaus, *Margaret Mead: The Making of an America Icon* (Princeton: Princeton University Press, 2008).

[19] Nancy Parezo, 'Anthropology: The Welcoming Science' in Parezo, ed., *Hidden Scholars: Women Anthropologists and the Native American Southwest* (Albuquerque: University of New Mexico Press, 1993), 3.

10   Pioneers of the Field

where feminist theory and the long-established history of women in institutions of higher learning opened the flood-gates for women field-workers and researchers, especially from the period of 'the explosion of anthropology in the 1960s'.[20]

Louise Lamphere revisited this question in her seminal centenary address to the American Anthropological Association meeting of 2001, later published as 'Unofficial Histories: A Vision of Anthropology from the Margins'. She goes on to identify important areas in which women and minorities have made an unacknowledged impact on American anthropology, three of which have direct application to the pioneering generation of South African women scholars whose work is showcased in this study. First, these 'scholars on the margins' contributed to 'the transformation of field research through problem-oriented participant observation' as exemplified in the early fieldwork of Margaret Mead. Second, they developed more diverse and 'dialogical forms of ethnographic writing'. Third, they typically had a much more strongly 'applied', engaged or socially committed orientation than their male counterparts. She highlights the combination of anthropology and activism, as exemplified by Anita McGee and Alfonzo Ortiz as well as Mead and Benedict.[21]

If women's contributions to American cultural anthropology have been dumbed down, this is all the more so in the case of the British social anthropological tradition out of which South African social anthropology emerged from the 1920s. There are many ways of illustrating this, but perhaps the strongest index is how women in the British anthropological tradition feature in biographies or biographical dictionaries. For a current example we might take the fascinatingly diverse Routledge collection on *Fifty Key Anthropologists* published in 2011. The three co-editors, based in North America and Canada, indicate that they canvassed widely and found a large measure of consensus about the core figures in the history of the discipline, which would have included those mentioned above as male founding fathers by Behar and Gordon, but that there was more dispute about the remaining places. In the end, though, only ten of their top fifty are deemed to have been women and fully half of their cast comprises American cultural anthropologists. There are a further eleven British social anthropologists and six French scholars. While representative voices from other parts of the empire are lacking, South African anthropology features rather generously with six representatives. Yet all

[20] Nancy Parezo, 'Preface' in Parezo, ed., *Hidden Scholars*, xii.
[21] Louise Lamphere, 'Unofficial Histories: A Vision of Anthropology from the Margins', *American Anthropologist*, 106, 1 (2004), 126–39.

Introduction: rethinking the canon

but one, Monica Hunter Wilson, followed careers in England or the United States (where they had obtained their doctoral degrees) rather than in universities within South Africa.[22] While different scholars will have their particular quibbles about who has most unjustly been excluded, my own view is that Audrey Richards is a regrettable omission, for reasons that should be apparent from my later chapter on her African years, particularly her three years at Wits University, within the context of her long and richly productive career.

While there are advantages in having anthropologists dominating the way in which their discipline gets documented, and to having disciples documenting the contributions of mentors, whether in festschrifts, book-length biographies or later edited collections, there are also drawbacks. An insider view yields insufficient critical distance, a potentially incestuous reading of colleague contributions and an overly invested commitment to portraying a teacher, and often friend, in a particular light. Here I would make a case for my relatively unusual and distanced position in relation to the subjects of my study, both as a male scholar writing about a cast of women intellectuals and as a somewhat traditional, strongly empirically oriented historian writing about the lives and works of anthropologists.

How does a deeply historical approach differ from the anthropological approach of the majority of practitioners in the subfield of the history of anthropology as it has emerged since the 1970s? The first obvious distinction relates to the greater priority given to texts by anthropologists. Their interests have typically been in how classic texts get circulated and relate to one another within increasingly international circuits of co-production, distribution and consumption. As formulated by the anthropologist co-editors of *Fifty Key Anthropologists*, how did they 'forge original ideas that can be used by other scholars'? The emphasis in this model of knowledge production is on individual inspiration and creativity, on the flair and the genius if you like. Richard Fardon's biography of his former mentor, Mary Douglas, provides an incisive case study. While he demonstrates in the opening section of the book that her interest in the history of Christian and Jewish theology and associated notions of 'purity and danger' were rooted in her own childhood immersion in a Catholic convent, the central section of his study provides an extended structuralist analysis of her two best-known texts with close attention to particular features of her writings from paragraph links to

---

[22] Robert Gordon, Andrew P. Lyons and Harriet D. Lyons, 'Introduction' in Gordon, Lyons and Lyons, eds., *Fifty Key Anthropologists* (London and New York: Routledge, 2011), xviii–xix.

12   Pioneers of the Field

chapter outlines. He proposes, in effect, that the historian of anthropology should read from texts to lives rather than vice versa, that 'an in-depth knowledge of the work explains the person'.[23]

My own approach, by contrast, has been to start with the lives of the women anthropologists as revealed to me in their usually incredibly rich collections of personal and professional papers. These have been lodged by their children, or spouse in the case of Ellen Hellmann, in university libraries across three continents between 1982 and 1995. I have supplemented this information, where possible, with interviews with the children of these women scholars, who have provided the kind of insights and texture of person that no archival document can duplicate. Any biographer's ability to reconstruct a story about a life, 'the biographical illusion' as Bourdieu termed it,[24] is framed in the first instance by the kinds of source materials that afford access to the inner and outer worlds of the biographical subject, like letters or diaries. As many scholars of biographies have highlighted, the biographical genre is a deeply partial one. It is biased towards the literate and the professionally affirmed, like those considered worthy of having papers lodged in university collections. Whatever the degree of institutional discrimination experienced by the six women scholars featured in these chapters, and this should certainly not be underestimated, they were all relatively privileged subjects who left extensive paper trails over the course of their productive and fulfilling lives. While there is much that could be said about the differences between these respective collections of private and professional papers,[25] and the ways in which they have shaped the kind of stories I have been able, or chosen, to tell in each case, the most striking feature is their bounty. All six collections contain a rich cocktail of personal photographs, private and professional correspondence, field-notes or notebooks, drafts and final versions of published and other public writings, information about wider institutional affiliations, even in three cases love letters between the woman anthropologist and her (future or current) husband. This has allowed for an unusual degree of access to the personal and 'the

---

[23] Richard Fardon, *Mary Douglas: An Intellectual Biography* (London: Routledge, 1999). For an incisive review of this and four other books he associates with 'a new burgeoning of biographical interest in the lives and experiences of our anthropological forebears', see Patrick Laviolette, 'Anthropology in the UK: Never Mind the Biographies, Here's the Reflexive Symbols', *Reviews in Anthropology*, 37 (2008), 231–58.

[24] Pierre Bourdieu, *The Biographical Illusion*, trans. Y. Winkin and W. Leeds-Horwitz (Paris: Centre for Transcultural Studies, Working Paper No. 14, 1987).

[25] For a preliminary overview of the particular richness of the Wilson Collection in relation to the Hoernlé, Hellmann, Kuper and Krige Collections, see Andrew Bank, 'Introduction' in Andrew Bank and Leslie J. Bank, eds., *Inside African Anthropology: Monica Wilson and her Interpreters* (New York: Cambridge University Press, 2013), 31–4.

Introduction: rethinking the canon

intimate', especially when supplemented with the information shared by children to whom the memories of their hard-working mothers remain vivid.

The second distinctive feature of the historian's approach is a heightened attention to detailed reconstruction of what is best termed 'the micro-politics of knowledge production in the field'. Here I have been influenced by the re-orientation towards fieldwork in the study of field sciences, initiated in the mid-1990s by the late Henrika Kuklick,[26] and then applied most fully in the case of African anthropology by Lyn Schumaker in her path-breaking study of the collaborative field methods of the anthropologists associated with the Rhodes-Livingstone Institute in Central Africa.[27] As will become apparent across the chapters that follow, it was, above all, the extent, depth and empathetic nature of the fieldwork of this cast of women scholars that made them such excellent ethnographers. Their studies were internationally acclaimed not primarily because of theoretical innovation (though, as we will see, they did also make significant contributions in this regard). Rather it was the meticulous, systematic and thoroughly collaborative form of fieldwork that allowed for such rich empirical documentation of specific African cultures based, in all cases, on years rather than months in the field. This is what lends the kind of texture and weight to their ethnographic monographs that have allowed them to stand the test of time. If fieldwork is indeed the distinctive feature that explains their collective contribution, one that was much more fully recognized by their peers than by latter-day historians of anthropology, then it is necessary to examine the micro-social worlds of the field in particular detail as well as the methods that they brought to their different field-sites.

The swift creation of a fieldwork-based ethnographic tradition across southern Africa during the interwar years was, to a greater extent than has been acknowledged, the determined work of one woman scholar: Agnes Winifred Hoernlé. She embarked on the first fieldwork expeditions in the region in 1912 and 1913, co-founded and applied the sociological theory of African social systems from her base in the social anthropology department of Wits University during the mid-1920s, and proceeded to train the four southern African-born women (Monica Hunter, Ellen

---

[26] Henrika Kuklick, 'Introduction' in Kuklick, ed., *Osiris: Special Issue: Science in the Field*, 11 (1996) 1–16.

[27] Lyn Schumaker, *Africanizing Anthropology: Fieldwork, Networks, and the Making of Cultural Knowledge in Central Africa* (Durham, NC and London: Duke University Press, 2001). For an extended application of this collaborative, field-based model to southern Africa with a strong biographical orientation, see Bank and Bank, eds., *Inside African Anthropology*.

14   Pioneers of the Field

Hellmann, Hilda Kuper and Eileen Krige) who, in my retelling of the history, came to dominate the discipline during the 1930s. The chapters that follow will track, through richly detailed biographical case studies, her energetic promotion of their undergraduate studies, their postgraduate research and their published work, re-affirming her status as 'the mother of Social Anthropology in South Africa'.[28]

[28] This title was first bestowed on her by Eileen Jensen Krige and Jack Krige in the dedication of their celebrated study, *The Realm of a Rain-Queen: A Study of the Pattern of Lovedu Society* (London, New York and Toronto: Oxford University Press in association with the International African Institute, 1943).

1 Feminizing the foundational narrative: the collaborative anthropology of Winifred Tucker Hoernlé (1885–1960)

> Your suggestion of the possibility of our collaboration together [in the field of African sociology] opens up the most enticing vision of possibilities.
>
> Alfred Reginald Radcliffe-Brown to Winifred Hoernlé, 31 July 1925.[1]

According to the standard narrative of the history of anthropology in South Africa, it all began in January 1921 when one of 'the founding fathers' of the British anthropological tradition, Alfred Reginald Radcliffe-Brown (1881–1955), established social anthropology as a modern, professional, university-based discipline during his five years as professor and head of the social anthropology department in the newly created African School of Life and Languages at the University of Cape Town (UCT). This was the first such chair in the British Commonwealth.[2] 'Brown', as he was known, gave social anthropology in South Africa a theory: that of structural-functionalism. Although he did no fieldwork in South Africa, he provided an analysis of the understanding of society derived largely from Durkheim, and an associated set of concepts, mostly concerning kinship. He championed his 'sociological method' to missionaries, administrators doing vacation courses, undergraduate students in growing numbers, the wider public in newspaper articles and, indeed, whoever else was willing to listen. He advertised anthropology as a science akin to chemistry, insisting that the role of the anthropologist was to ascertain 'general laws' which could 'lead to results

---

[1] A.R. Radcliffe-Brown to Winifred Hoernlé, Cape Town, 31 July 1925 reproduced in Peter Carstens, Gerald Klinghardt and Martin West, eds., *Trails in the Thirstland: The Anthropological Field Diaries of Winifred Hoernlé* (Cape Town: University of Cape Town African Studies, Communication Series, No. 14, 1987), Appendix B, 184. Special thanks to Diana Wylie for warmly engaged and constructive commentary on multiple drafts, as well as to Patrick Harries and Isak Niehaus for critique and clarification. Thanks to my UWC colleague Riedwaan Moosage for collecting the materials from the J.D. Rheinallt-Jones Papers at Wits University cited in this and subsequent chapters.

[2] Isaac Schapera, 'The Appointment of Radcliffe-Brown', *African Studies*, 49, 1(1990), 2.

15

16   Pioneers of the Field

of practical value to South Africa'.[3] He was an outspoken opponent of the developing government policies of segregation in the early to mid-1920s and his applied anthropology has justly been read as an 'immanent critique of apartheid'.[4]

His founding theory, according to this standard account, was carried forward by others. One of these was his 'student', 'follower' and 'disciple', Winifred Tucker Hoernlé (1885–1960).[5] As the first lecturer in social anthropology at Witwatersrand University from 1923 to 1937, she loyally spread the message of her mentor. The more important lineage, however, is said to have been that of his star student, Isaac Schapera (1905–2003), who after having completed his undergraduate and master's studies under Radcliffe-Brown at UCT, proceeded to do his doctorate at the London School of Economics. He returned to UCT in 1929 to launch a fieldwork tradition in the region and, after a few years, took over his former mentor's position as professor and chair.

He is credited with having initiated that decisive shift in social anthropological method that allowed for the inclusion of colonial agents within the analytical framework. His one-time student, Max Gluckman (1908–1975), retrospectively identified Schapera as the main influence behind his explicit theoretical challenge to the Malinowskian 'tribal' model, which came to be encapsulated in that famous series of essays known as 'The Bridge'. This text became the training manual for Gluckman's research teams at the Rhodes-Livingstone Institute in Zambia, after he had become its second director in 1942, succeeding Godfrey Wilson, and later for his disciples in the famous Manchester School which is alleged to have pioneered the study of ethnicity and urban anthropology.[6] Gluckman and Schapera were thus the true heirs of Radcliffe-Brown's 'one-society model'.

The contribution by the alleged 'disciple' was, with few exceptions,[7] relegated to the margins. She was seen to have played a limited role in the

---

[3] Adam Kuper, 'South African Anthropology: An Inside Job' in Kuper, *Among the Anthropologists: History and Context in Anthropology* (London and New Brunswick, NJ: The Athlone Press, 1999), 147.

[4] Robert Gordon, 'Early Social Anthropology in South Africa', *African Studies*, 49, 1 (1990), 15–48 and in fuller form Isak Niehaus, 'Anthropology at the Dawn of Apartheid: Radcliffe-Brown and Malinowski's South African Engagements, 1919–1940' (unpublished paper presented at the workshop 'Reimagining Alterity and Affinity in Anthropology', University of Cambridge, 2015).

[5] Adam Kuper, *Anthropologists and Anthropology: The British School, 1922–1972* (London: Routledge, 1973), 177.

[6] Hugh Macmillan, 'From Race to Ethnic Identity: South Central Africa, Social Anthropology and the Shadow of the Holocaust' in Megan Vaughan and Patrick Harries, eds., *Social Dynamics: Special Issue: Essays in Commemoration of Leroy Vail*, 26, 2 (2000), 87–115.

[7] Peter Carstens, 'Introduction' in Carstens, ed., *Nama Social Organisation and Other Essays* (Johannesburg: Wits University Press, 1985), xi–xxiii, republished in slightly amended

Feminizing the foundational narrative 17

founding of South African anthropology. Her racial politics were also tainted by her association with the liberal segregationist ideology espoused by her husband, the liberal philosopher and public intellectual R.F.A. (Alfred) Hoernlé (1881–1943), in his Phelps-Stokes lectures of 1940 as well as by her friendship with R.D. (David) Rheinallt-Jones, the first director of the South African Institute of Race Relations (established in 1929). According to some, she too was a 'paralyzed conservative'.[8]

The silencing of Winifred Hoernlé is nowhere more apparent than in Hammond-Tooke's *Imperfect Interpreters*, where her contribution is confined to two blandly biographical pages.[9] She features in passing, wedged between fourteen pages of detailed analysis of the theories of 'the founding father' and thirty-two pages on the alleged twin 'consolidators of the discipline', Schapera and, astonishingly, Willi Werner Eiselen, the architect of apartheid who built a *volkekunde* department at Stellenbosch University from 1926 to 1936. As I have argued elsewhere, Eiselen's Berlin Mission Society background, German linguistic training under the racist cultural nationalist Carl Meinhof and already strident Afrikaner nationalist politics produced a detached form of 'tribal ethnography' driven by a quest to classify which was emphatically in the service of segregation from the outset. The anthropological method and the racial ideology of this all-male Afrikaner nationalist school of *volkekunde* diverged radically from the anti-segregationist, left-liberal tradition of social anthropology advocated by Winifred Hoernlé, whose women students spent years involved in immersed participant observation through long-term residence among African peoples.[10]

form in Carstens, 'Introduction' in Carstens, Gerald Klinghardt and Martin West, eds., *Trails in the Thirstland: The Anthropological Field Diaries of Winifred Hoernlé* (Cape Town: University of Cape Town African Studies, Communication Series, No. 14, 1987 1–17).

[8] See Hugh Macmillan, '"Paralyzed Conservatives": W.M. Macmillan, the Social Scientists and "the Common Society", 1923–1948' in Hugh Macmillan and Shula Marks, eds., *Africa and Empire: W.M. Macmillan, Historian and Social Critic* (London: Institute for Commonwealth Studies, 1989), 72–90.

[9] Hammond-Tooke, *Imperfect Interpreters*, 37–8.

[10] For a series of three articles dealing with consecutive stages of Eiselen's early ethnographic career, see Andrew Bank, 'The Berlin Mission Society and German Linguistic Roots of *Volkekunde*: The Background, Training and Hamburg Writings of Werner Eiselen, 1899–1924' in Andrew Bank and Nancy Jacobs, eds., *Kronos: Southern African Histories, Special Issue: The Micro-Politics of Knowledge Production in Southern Africa*, 41 (November 2015), 166–92; Bank, 'Fathering *Volkekunde*: Race and Culture in the Ethnological Writings of Werner Eiselen, Stellenbosch University, 1926–36', *Anthropology Southern Africa*, 38, 3–4 (2015), 163–79; Bank, '"Broederbande" [Brotherly Bonds]: Afrikaner Nationalist Masculinity and African Sexuality in the Writings of Werner Eiselen's Students, Stellenbosch University, 1930–36', *Anthropology Southern Africa*, 38, 3–4 (2015), 180–97.

18   Pioneers of the Field

It was, in fact, Winifred Hoernlé rather than Werner Eiselen, as this androcentric mythology has it, who co-founded and then jointly consolidated social anthropology in South Africa. This was perfectly apparent to the internationally acclaimed scholars who knew her personally and, in many cases, studied under her. In retrospective accounts written in the mid-1950s and early 1960s, Monica Wilson, Ellen Hellmann (with Quinton Whyte), Eileen Krige, Audrey Richards, Max Gluckman (with Isaac Schapera) and Hilda Kuper (in a later autobiographical essay) all wrote in what was truly one spirit about the enormous significance of Hoernlé as a foundational figure in their discipline, along with Radcliffe-Brown.[11] They drew attention to her formative contributions as author, teacher and social activist. Collectively, they argued that she was indeed 'the mother of social anthropology in South Africa' during the 1920s and 1930s. They highlighted her role as an inspiring lecturer with a broad vision and an openness to viewpoints other than her own (Hilda Kuper), as a selfless graduate mentor (Krige), as a leader who assisted in building the discipline (Schapera), as a deeply committed and socially engaged scholar, greatly respected for her welfare work and race relations activism. They characterized her as a generalist whose breadth of interests, intellectual rigour and curiosity about anthropology in all its branches was highly unusual. In fact, Isaac Schapera described her (in 1935) as 'the only all-round anthropologist we have in this country'.[12]

Building on this forgotten tradition, I argue that Winifred Hoernlé was a central figure in the establishment and consolidation of social anthropology in interwar South Africa. Indeed, if we consider this period as a whole she was *the* central figure in the development of the discipline. Her significance is not due to her having founded 'modern fieldwork' in 1912, as Peter Carstens suggested in his otherwise incisive biographical essays.[13] Rather it was due to her having introduced a series of methodological innovations that led to the creation of a professional, scientific

[11] Ellen Hellmann and Quinton Whyte, 'Introduction' and Monica Wilson, 'Development in Anthropology' in *Race Relations Journal: Special Issue: Homage to Winifred Hoernlé*, 22, 4 (1955), 1–6, 7–15; Eileen Jensen Krige, 'Agnes Winifred Hoernlé: An Appreciation', *African Studies*, 19 (1960), 138–44; Max Gluckman and Isaac Schapera, 'Dr Winifred Hoernlé: An Appreciation', *Africa*, 30 (1960), 262–3; Audrey Richards, 'Obituary: Agnes Winifred Hoernlé: 1885–1960', *Man*, 61 (1961), 53; Hilda Kuper, 'Function, History and Biography: Reflections on Fifty Years in the British Anthropological Tradition' in George W. Stocking, ed., *Functionalism Historicized: Essays on British Social Anthropology* (Madison, Wisconsin: University of Wisconsin Press, 1984), 192–213.

[12] Wits University William Cullen Library, AD843/RJ/Kb18.4 (file 2), Box 174, Inter-University Committee for African Studies (April–June 1934), Schapera to Jones, 21 April 1934.

[13] Carstens, 'Agnes Winifred Hoernlé (1885–1960): The Mother of Social Anthropology in South Africa', *Anthropology Today*, 1, 6 (1985), 17–18.

Feminizing the foundational narrative

and, then during the 1930s, a field-based ethnographic tradition, what we might call 'modern ethnography'. My central argument is that her development of this modern anthropological method in South Africa was collaborative at every stage: indeed, it could only be so given the thoroughly male-dominated nature of the enterprise in the formative decades of her anthropological career.

Given the centrality of Hoernlé in this history of social anthropology in South Africa, not least as the primary mentor of the internationally famous women scholars whose biographies feature in the chapters that follow, I shall dwell a little longer here on family background and education than I do in subsequent chapters.

From South African segregationist to Cape liberal, 1885–1907

Born in Kimberley on 6 December 1885, Agnes Winifred Tucker was the second eldest of the eight children of a self-made mining pioneer and surveyor, William Kidger Tucker, and a descendant of the 1820 settler, Sarah Bottomley.[14] Soon after gold was discovered on the Rand, he moved his family to Johannesburg, which had risen as a city from the veld. During the next forty years he became one of the city's most prominent citizens, serving as mayor in 1906 and 1907, and then spending two decades as a Transvaal Senator in the new Union Parliament.[15] From his testimony before the South African Native Affairs Commission as representative of the Rand Pioneers, it is clear that her father held strongly racist views of Africans, whom he believed should be controlled in segregated locations and mining compounds.[16]

Fortunately for Winifred, her father's attitude towards the education of women was more open than that regarding the education of Africans. She matriculated at Wesleyan Girls' High School, having developed a passion for what would be her true vocation. 'I love teaching more than anything.'[17] Against the advice of his family, her father encouraged her to enrol in 1903 at the South African College in Cape Town, later known as the University of Cape Town, presumably with a view to becoming

---

[14] Eileen Jensen Krige, 'Winifred Hoernlé', *Dictionary of South African Biography, Vol. 4* (Pretoria: Government Publishers, 1968), 238–9.
[15] On William Tucker as one of Johannesburg's first surveyors in 1886–7, see Gerhard-Mark van der Waal, *From Mining Camp to Metropolis: The Building of Johannesburg, 1886–1940* (Pretoria: H.S.R.C. Press, 1987), 8.
[16] *South African Native Affairs Commission, 1903–5, Vol. IV: Minutes of Evidence* (Cape Town: Cape Times Limited, 1904), esp. 808.
[17] WHP, Box 2: Personal Papers, Winifred Tucker to William Tucker, Grahamstown, 20 March 1901.

Figure 1.1: Winifred Tucker in her matric year at Wesleyan Girls' High School, Grahamstown, 1902.[18]

a teacher. Although women students had been admitted to the college since 1887, the gains had been painfully slow. She was one of only 16

---

[18] WHP, Box 2: Personal Papers, Photographs.

Feminizing the foundational narrative 21

women out of 299 registered students. The numbers of women students in the new university colleges that would open upcountry were even lower.[19] In short, university education in South Africa was still in its infancy with no more than a few dozen women enrolled countrywide at the time of Union in 1910.

Winifred was a star student. She won the class prizes for most of her undergraduate subjects, including those for her majors, English and Philosophy. Her college friend, Edith Stephens, who was training as a

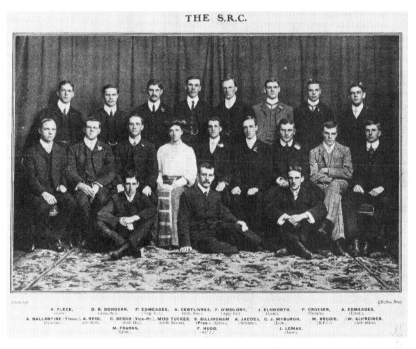

Figure 1.2: Winifred Tucker and the South African College's first SRC, 1905.[20]

---

[19] Fourteen women enrolled at Victoria College (later Stellenbosch University) in 1905, nine at Transvaal University College (later Pretoria University) when it opened in 1908, eight at the University College of Natal (later Natal University) when it opened in Pietermaritzburg in 1910. Cherryl Walker, *The Women's Suffrage Movement in South Africa* (Cape Town: UCT African Studies Centre, Communications Series, No. 2, 1979), 72.
[20] UCT Libraries, Manuscripts and Archives Department, BUSV: South African College, Students, Photographs.

22   Pioneers of the Field

botanist and would be the first woman to be appointed as a lecturer at UCT, recalled their Oxford-trained Chair of Philosophy, H.E.S. Fremantle, confessing that he had been 'deeply shocked' when he found out that Winifred Tucker's final year examination script had been the work of a woman.[21] She also showed an early gift for leadership, serving in her final year as the only woman member of the College's first Student Representative Council.

Thomas Loveday, another of her Oxford-trained philosophy professors, proposed that she continue her studies at Cambridge.[22] She would later identify his advice as the turning point in her career. 'There seemed, at that time, very few openings for a woman wishing to teach philosophy, and so I was very wisely advised to study psychology and anthropology, since a wide field lay open to all who would use their knowledge, among the native races of South Africa of whom we know so little, and of whom we need to know so much.'[23]

Before following her to Cambridge, there are other legacies of her South African College years that warrant mention. The first is that she probably developed her taste for fieldwork on the botanical expeditions of William Welch Pearson, another influential and supportive mentor. Pearson took his students on expeditions up Table Mountain and his taste for adventure later took him to the desert regions of German South West Africa, something that may well have influenced her to choose the Richtersveld and Namib deserts as her first field-sites. Second, she became part of an educated network whose ideas about race were located within the alternative liberal tradition of the Cape. Most of her friends were from prominent Cape liberal families like the Schreiners and the Fullards. That Winifred Tucker soon became a 'Cape liberal' is evident from her correspondence with her father. Already by the end of her second year in Cape Town, he had grown concerned about her changing racial politics. He sternly wrote that he was 'not prepared to accept' her liberal view that educated Africans should have the vote, as was still the case in the Cape Colony.[24]

---

[21] Wits University Archive, AU8 Winifred Hoernlé Papers [henceforth WHP], Box 2: Correspondence, Personal Details, Diaries of Expeditions [henceforth Personal Papers], Folder on Eileen Krige's Obituary Essay, Edith Stephens to Eileen Krige, 5 May 1960.

[22] WHP, Box 2: Personal Papers, Thomas Loveday, 'Academic Reference to South African College', 2 October 1911.

[23] WHP, Box 2: Personal Papers, Newspaper clippings, 'A Great Woman Worker in a Great Field', *Rand Daily Mail*, 24 August 1927.

[24] WHP, Box 2: Personal Papers, William Tucker to Winifred Tucker, 9 October 1904, Johannesburg.

Training in A.C. Haddon's 'field school', Cambridge University, 1908–1910

Winifred Tucker was given an extraordinarily privileged induction into the social sciences during the five years that she studied at Cambridge University (1908–10) and then Leipzig and Bonn Universities (1911–12), having attended lectures at the Sorbonne in Paris for some months between (1912). Her list of teachers reads like a roll-call of the founding fathers of the social sciences. Her main mentors at Cambridge, A.C. Haddon and W.H.R. Rivers, played decisive roles in the transition of anthropology from an armchair evolutionary theory to a rigorous discipline based on intensive fieldwork.[25] During her Cambridge years, she also attended lectures by James Frazer and Radcliffe-Brown. She worked in the laboratory of Charles S. Myers, a member of Haddon's famous Cambridge Torres Straits Expedition of 1898 who co-founded the field of British psychology along with Rivers.[26] In Germany she studied under Wilhelm Wundt and Oswald Kulpe, the co-founders of Gestalt psychology, before rounding off her training at the Sorbonne with the founder of modern sociology, Emile Durkheim.[27]

Her letters from Europe, though frustratingly sparse, do reveal that one of these teachers had the dominant influence: Alfred Cort Haddon (1855–1936) whose reputation as the grandfather of the British school of anthropology derives mainly from his organization and leadership of the Torres Straits Expedition.[28] She would certainly have heard his stirring address in Cape Town in 1905 before the members of the newly founded South African Association of the Advancement of Science at their joint meeting with the British Association. Haddon was President of the Anthropological Section. The future of South African anthropology, he declared, now lay in 'very careful and detailed studies of definite or limited areas ... rather than [in] a general description of a number of peoples', along the lines of the older Victorian anthropologists. Following

---

[25] The literature is extensive, but on Haddon, see esp. Anita Herle and Sandra Rouse, eds., *Cambridge and the Torres Strait: Centenary Essays on the 1898 Anthropological Expedition* (Cambridge: Cambridge University Press, 1998) and on Rivers' role in the transition to modern fieldwork, see Henrika Kuklick, 'Personal Equations: Reflections on the History of Fieldwork with Special Reference to Sociocultural Anthropology', *Isis*, 102, 1 (2011), 1–33.

[26] On the role of Myers, Rivers and the Torres Straits expedition in the discipline of psychology, see Graham Richards, 'Getting a Result: The Expedition's Psychological Research, 1898–1913' in Herle and Rouse, eds., *Cambridge and the Torres Strait*, 136–57.

[27] Krige, 'Winifred Hoernlé', 140; Carstens, 'Agnes Winifred Hoernlé (1885–1960): The Mother of Social Anthropology in South Africa', 17–18.

[28] See Herle and Rouse, eds., *Cambridge and the Torres Strait*.

24   Pioneers of the Field

his Torres Straits model, he presented anthropology, above all, as a science of salvage. 'What judgement will posterity pass upon us if, while we have the opportunity, we do not save the memory of these primitive folk from oblivion?' Salvage logic dictated that future students, like Winifred Tucker, would need to begin their work among 'those that will disappear first', namely 'the Bushmen and the Hottentots'.[29]

She would follow to the letter his model of fieldwork as a series of data-collecting activities, the foremost of which involved the measurement of bodies. Indeed, her training under Haddon was predominantly one in the study of 'racial types'. He had spoken in Cape Town of 'an urgent need for physical anthropological data to be acquired through the measurement of living subjects [in South Africa]'. This would prompt Louis Peringuey, then director of the South African Museum, to launch a Bushman body casting project and what has more recently been uncovered as an extensive traffic in human remains across almost two decades.[30] Winifred spent much time at Cambridge attending Haddon's three courses on physical anthropology and working in his laboratory. Her letters home give a lively sense of his sociable manner, warmth towards women students and, as his biographer put it, his 'boyish impulsiveness in speech and action'.[31]

Life up here is very amusing sometimes. You should see us down at Dr Haddon's Lab in the afternoons. We go down to measure skulls before the ordinary lecture commences. Then at about four we boil the kettle and make coffee ... Then we all sit round amongst the skulls in the full view of any passers-by and drink our beverage.[32]

He set her to work on anthropometric data in the laboratory of his colleague Myers, with whom she also enjoyed a warm relationship. They prompted her to read widely in the field of physical anthropology. She was first author of a joint paper with Myers, published in the *Journal of the Royal Anthropological Institute* in 1910, which had involved hundreds

---

[29] Alfred Cort Haddon, 'Keynote Address', *South African Society for the Advancement of Science: Report of 1905: Transactions of Section H*, 524–5. The literature on 'salvage anthropology' is vast. For a useful early account which traces the concept right back to the Report of the British Select Committee of Aborigines in 1837, see Jacob W. Gruber, 'Ethnographic Salvage and the Shaping of Anthropology', *American Anthropologist*, 61 (1959), 379–89.

[30] Patricia Davison, 'Human Subjects as Museum Objects: A Project to Make Life-Casts of "Bushmen" and "Hottentots", 1907–1924', *Annals of the South African Museum*, 102, 5 (1993); Martin Legassick and Ciraj Rassool, *Skeletons in the Cupboard: South African Museums and the Trade in Human Remains* (Cape Town: South African Museum, 1999).

[31] Allison Quiggin, *Haddon, The Head Hunter: A Short Sketch of the Life of A.C. Haddon* (Cambridge: Cambridge University Press, 1942), 121.

[32] WHP, Box 2, Winifred Tucker to William and Sarah Tucker, 12 October 1909.

Feminizing the foundational narrative 25

of measurements on skulls which he had obtained from Sudan in earlier years.[33] In a later testimonial, Myers commented on the 'accuracy, thoroughness and care' with which she went about her laboratory work as well, more generally, as her 'keen psychological insight'.[34]

Psychological experiments were the second most important activity of the field anthropologist in this laboratory-oriented model. Anthropology was very closely allied to psychology in these transitional years, as the careers of Rivers and Myers attest. Haddon had spoken in 1905 of the 'need for [South African] data in the "large field" of experimental psychology, data based on tests conducted on individual native subjects'.[35] Rivers and Myers had conducted a veritable barrage of tests on the sense impressions of 'native subjects' in the Torres Straits for the purpose of cross-cultural comparison.[36] Here again Haddon ensured that Winifred Tucker got the very best training. He arranged for her to work with Rivers, who was testing the theory that colour perception differed significantly across cultures,[37] and had now begun to enquire whether it also might differ by generation. He got Winifred to administer colour vision tests on Cambridge primary school children. She described it as her first 'taste of fieldwork'. Her findings were published in a sole-authored article in the *British Journal of Psychology* in 1911 with grateful acknowledgement to Rivers.[38]

The final activity of the field anthropologist was the collection of cultural artefacts. This was a branch of their 'Cinderella science' in which Haddon excelled, as Winifred and her fellow students could attest from their weekly visits to his home, which was eccentrically decorated with ethnographic objects from the Pacific, whether 'decorative arts' or 'native toys'.[39] He also employed her for some months as his research assistant on the fourth and penultimate volume of the *Reports of the Cambridge Expedition to Torres Straits*.[40]

---

[33] A. Winifred Tucker and Charles S. Myers, 'A Contribution to the Anthropology of the Sudan', *The Journal of the Royal Anthropological Institute of Great Britain and Ireland*, 40, 1 (1910), 141–63.

[34] Hoernlé Papers, Box 2, Charles S. Myers, Reference for Winifred Hoernlé at Wits, 4 April 1926, London.

[35] Haddon, 'Keynote Address', 524.

[36] Graeme Richards, 'Getting a Result: The Expedition's Psychological Research, 1898–1913', 141.

[37] See, for example, W.H.R. Rivers, 'The Colour Vision of the Natives of Upper Egypt', *Journal of the Anthropological Institute of Great Britain and Ireland*, 31 (January–June 1901), 229–47.

[38] A. Winifred Tucker, 'Observations on the Colour Vision of School Children', *British Journal of Psychology*, 4, 1 (1911), 33–43.

[39] Quiggin, *Haddon, The Head Hunter*, 110.

[40] WHP, Box 2: Personal Papers, Winifred Tucker to William Tucker, Newnham College, 15 October 1909.

26   Pioneers of the Field

Her letters from Germany express no comparable sense of excitement about being inducted into a new field of study. From Leipzig she reported on the rigours of work in the psychology laboratories of Wundt and Kulpe. In Bonn she was distracted by a passionate affair with an older man, probably a university lecturer, to whom she was briefly engaged.[41]

A laboratory in the desert: Richtersveld and German South West Africa, 1912–1913

Winifred Tucker set sail from Cape Town to Port Nolloth in September 1912 for what was supposed to have been the beginning of three years of fieldwork studying Nama and Bushman 'tribes' along the Orange River. Haddon sent her an enthusiastic letter with pages of detailed instructions about how and when to record field-notes, the necessity of the phonograph and the possibilities that a recently published book of rock art copies would afford for eliciting new information about the meaning of Bushman paintings. 'You will be the first woman to do real fieldwork and you must not miss the chance.'[42]

She worked among Nama communities in three regions in 1912 and 1913: those in the Richtersveld, on the Khuiseb River south of Walvis Bay, and at Berseba Native Reserve north of Keetmanshoop. On reading her published field diaries, most of which record her daily experiences on the first expedition, I am struck by the yawning gulf between Haddon's great expectations and her own dismal experiences, between an ambitious vision concocted in Cambridge and the messy, frustrating and depressing matter of attempting to carry it through on the ground. She was not working on a small and isolated Pacific island. This was a sprawling subcontinent with a century-long history of long-distance migration and inter-ethnic contact, more than half a century of missionary influence, and three decades of German colonial rule from 1884. At all of her field-sites there had been a government presence from before the turn of the century, beginning with land surveyors and extending to the establishment of police posts near each of the mission stations. German colonization had become particularly brutal in the decade preceding her arrival. While none of the

---

[41] Details of this affair only come to light in the letters that she wrote to her future husband Alfred from the field. Sadly, only his side of the correspondence has survived. Wits University Archive, R.F.A. Hoernlé Papers, Closed Access Letters 1912–1915 [henceforth RFAHP, Letters]. Thanks to the then Deputy Vice-Chancellor of Wits, Belinda Bozzoli, for granting me permission to consult them in 2007.

[42] WHP, Box 2: Personal Papers, Alfred Cort Haddon to Winifred Tucker, 12 August 1912, Cambridge.

Feminizing the foundational narrative 27

Figure 1.3: 'Breakdown of our waggon near Sendeling's Drift', Richtersveld, Northern Cape, 1912.[43]

communities among whom she worked had been direct victims of the German genocide of the Nama and Herero during and after the protracted colonial war of 1904–8, the indirect consequences of the violence were obvious.

Nama subjects resisted being turned into laboratory objects at every turn. 'They did not like my having all the measurements of their heads and limbs to make what dreadful use of I might wish.'[44] Her attempts to conduct psychological experiments beginning with tests for colour perception and colour blindness using 'Helmholz wools', proved equally fruitless, as did the more abstract psychological tests derived from her training in Gestalt psychology. 'Tried to explain mental imaging to them, by asking them to describe a family member who was absent.

---

[43] This image features as an illustration in Winifred Tucker, *Richtersveld: The Land and Its People* (Johannesburg, Public Lecture of March 1913), 21.

[44] A. Winifred Tucker, *Richtersveld: The Land and Its People* (Johannesburg, Public Lecture of March 1913), 12.

Figure 1.4: This portrait of a Nama woman photographed on Winifred Tucker's first field expedition of 1912 is reproduced from the only glass negative to have survived a devastating fire in Wits University Library that would destroy all of her field-notes and other materials.

Explained that dream-imaging was the same. They understood little of what I said.'[45] Even the simple matter of deriving general information about traditional customs met with non-compliance partly because, as she soon was forced to concede, she was 'fifty years too late'. Her informants were constantly feigning ignorance, incomprehension and complaining of an inability to concentrate, something she rather too readily took as evidence of laziness.[46] This was quite apart from the considerable practical obstacles involved in traversing inhospitable deserts with a ramshackle ox-wagon, inexperienced drivers and inexpert travelling companions in the form of a female friend and her

---

[45] Carstens et al., *Trails*, 56.
[46] See her diary entries for 27 October, 10, 21 and 22 November 1912 in Carstens et al., *Trails*, 38, 48, 55, 56.

Feminizing the foundational narrative 29

twelve-year-old brother Victor. Her daily record is one of donkeys gone missing, donkeys exhausted, broken axles, days stranded short of supplies, days spent thirsting in the debilitating heat of the Northern Cape summer.[47]

On her two expeditions to German South West Africa between March and October 1913,[48] lengthy love letters between her and her future husband, Alfred Hoernlé took the place of the field diary as a channel for the expression of daily frustrations. Although we only have his side of the correspondence, the letters are a rich source on the fieldwork trials of Winifred Tucker. Her woes are perhaps best encapsulated in Alfred's reply to an increasingly despairing series of missives from Sandfontein, the windswept dunes south of Walvis Bay inhabited by the Topnaar Nama.

My poor darling! So you have had a very bad time, deprived of your proper interpreter by the fatal illness of her baby, with an inefficient substitute; an indisposed companion; cantankerous witnesses refusing to give you information; and sand seasoning all your food! It is a formidable list of grievances against providence.[49]

A professor's wife, Boston, 1914–1919

Despite Haddon's claims to the contrary, the most productive outcome of Winifred Tucker's early expeditions into the desert was her engagement by correspondence to Alfred Hoernlé in April 1913. It had been an unusual courtship. They had met in Cape Town in 1908, the year of his appointment as philosophy professor at the SAC. The son of a well-known Oriental scholar who was born and schooled in Bonn, R.F.A. Hoernlé (1880–1943) trained in a liberal, idealist school of philosophy at Oxford University before lecturing in Moral Philosophy at St Andrews College, Scotland. He has been described during these Cape Town years as 'a self-conscious and somewhat solemn young man, but ... neither eccentric not unduly insecure'.[50] Theirs was not love at first sight. A mutual friend recalled: 'After their first meeting, each of

---

[47] For the most despairing among many examples, see her diary entries for 23 October and 4 December 1912 in Carstens et al., *Trails*, 35, 62.

[48] There are only six pages of diary entries relating to her second fieldwork expedition of 1913. Most of these relate to her journey into the field and her discomfort with wind and sand at her first field-site south of Walvis Bay. See Carstens et al., *Trails*, 70–6.

[49] RFAHP, Letters, Alfred Hoernlé to Winifred Tucker, Oxford, 15 August 1913.

[50] Andrew Nash, 'Colonialism and Philosophy: R.F. Alfred Hoernlé in South Africa, 1908–1911' (unpublished M.A. thesis, Political Philosophy, University of Stellenbosch, 1985), 7.

30   Pioneers of the Field

them was distinctly "sniffy" about the other to me in private.'[51] Alfred, it must be said, was clueless when it came to matters of the heart.[52] He was certainly taken with Winifred when they met for a second time at his parent's home in Oxford in March 1912.[53]

The circumstances of their renewed acquaintance were unusual. She had applied for a post as his successor as Chair of Philosophy at the South African College. Although he was now based at the University of Durham, the SAC Appointments Committee had tasked him with explaining to her the reasons for her rejection. There were no women lecturers at the College, let alone professors so the Committee 'felt . . . that it would, under present circumstances, be too great an experiment to appoint a woman . . . '.[54] Would she be willing to consider the possibility of 'an [unpaid] Honorary Lectureship in Anthropology' instead?[55]

She had scarcely turned this offer down when he put another one on the table. This time it was for marriage. 'It is now or never for me', he wrote to her the following month, sounding desperate.[56] While she found his proposal 'precipitate', breaking off correspondence for a time, she wrote to 'renew friendship' in January 1913 and a few months later accepted his second marriage proposal, agreeing to cut short her southern African fieldwork to Haddon's annoyance.[57]

After marrying Alfred in Oxford in April 1914, she accompanied him to Harvard University where he took up a highly prestigious post as a professor of philosophy. Her years in Boston were dominated by 'the care of a house' as Alfred put it.[58] The birth of what would be their only child in September 1915 brought her great joy, but increased domestic responsibility. Alfred turned out to be a traditional father rather than

---

[51] WHP, Box 2: Personal Papers, Papers relating to Eileen Krige obituary article, Edith Stephens to Eileen Krige, Cape Town, 5 May 1960.

[52] For a lively account of his ill-judged pursuit of Vera Ritchie, his undergraduate student and the daughter of a senior professor, see Nash, 'Colonialism and Philosophy', 253–9.

[53] RFAHP, Letters, Alfred Hoernlé to Winifred Tucker, 20 April 1912, Oxford.

[54] RFAHP, Letters, Alfred Hoernlé to Winifred Tucker, 3 February 1912, Oxford. The South African College employed thirty full time members of staff in 1910, all of whom were men. See South African College Calendar (Cape Town: South African College, 1910).

[55] RFAHP, Letters. Alfred Hoernlé to Winifred Tucker, 3 February 1912, Armstrong College, University of Durham, Newcastle-upon-Tyne.

[56] RFAHP, Letters, Alfred Hoernlé to Winifred Tucker, Good Friday, [April] 1913, Armstrong College, Durham University.

[57] On her father's reaction, see WHP, Box 2: Personal Papers, Papers relating to Eileen Krige obituary article, Kathleen Risbeth (nee Haddon) to Eileen Krige, [n.d.], c. May 1960.

[58] RFAHP, Letters, Alfred Hoernlé to Winifred Tucker, 13 August 1913, Armstrong College, Durham University.

Feminizing the foundational narrative 31

Figure 1.5: Winifred and Alwin as a young baby, Boston, 1915.

a modern parent.[59] It would be two-and-a-half years after her return from the field that she was able, for the first time, to 'pick up the threads of anthropological literature'.[60]

---

[59] WHP, Box 1: Correspondence, Winifred Hoernlé to William Tucker, 2 November 1915, Cambridge, MA.
[60] WHP, Box 1: Correspondence, Winifred Hoernlé to William Tucker, 24 March 1916, Cambridge, MA.

32   Pioneers of the Field

It took Winifred a further two years to find the time to see through to publication her first article on Nama ritual and belief. She applied the theoretical model of the Swiss sociologist, Arnold van Gennep,[61] to four surviving rituals of transition among the Nama that she had encountered in the field: those relating to puberty, marriage, illness and death. In each case, she traced the ritual process by which the individual-in-transition, or 'crisis' in Van Gennep's terms, was isolated from society, then treated and tutored by elders to protect them from the dangerous potency associated with their liminal status, before being ritually prepared for their reintegration into society with a new social status. Her application of Van Gennep's model to southern African ethnographic data was pioneering, even if her data was less complete than she would have liked.[62] Her applied sociological analysis of African rituals as involving the resolution of life crises and liminal identity through stages of ordered and protective social management remained the dominant approach towards the analysis of ritual in the southern African ethnographic literature of the interwar years. This was because the most significant studies of ritual would be penned by her Wits students, for whom her 1918 essay and a further trilogy on African ritual published in 1923 and 1925 would be core undergraduate texts. Before turning to this trilogy, we need to consider the new sociological approach to anthropology that she developed in collaboration with Radcliffe-Brown.

A historic meeting: Hoernlé and Brown in Cape Town, November 1922

1922 is the year Adam Kuper chose as the starting point for his history of the modern British school of social anthropology. It was 'the year in which Rivers died and both Malinowski and Radcliffe-Brown', the two founding fathers, 'published their first major field studies', *Argonauts of the Western Pacific* and *The Andaman Islanders* respectively.[63]

The origins of South African anthropology can also symbolically be associated with the same year, arguably even with a single event: the meeting of Winifred Hoernlé and Alfred Reginald Radcliffe-Brown in Cape Town in November 1922. Fortuitously, for the history of South African anthropology, Brown and Hoernlé both suffered from forms of

---

[61] Patrick Harries, 'Arnold van Gennep' in Robert Gordon, Andrew P. Lyons and Harriet D. Lyons, eds., *Fifty Key Anthropologists* (London and New York: Routledge, 2011), 239–43.

[62] Winifred Hoernlé, 'Certain Rites of Transition and the Conception of !Nau among the Hottentots', *Harvard African Studies*, 2 (1918), 65–82.

[63] Kuper, *Anthropology and Anthropologists*, 9.

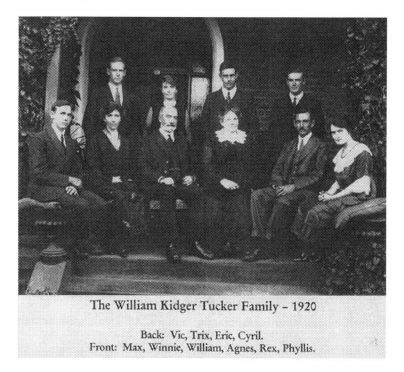

Figure 1.6: Winifred (front row, second left) was photographed with her family on her return to Johannesburg in 1920.[64]

ill-health that required them to relocate to warmer climes. Just as Brown chose to move from Tonga to South Africa for medical reasons in 1919, Winifred relocated to her native Johannesburg in October the following year after a series of severe New England winters had brought on a recurrence of a serious bronchial condition she had suffered from since childhood.

In the two years between her return and her historic meeting with Brown, she had lived with her parents in what would immediately have struck her as a dramatically changed city. The most obvious difference was the presence of Africans: there were now more than 100,000 Africans living in Johannesburg, a figure that would grow to a quarter of a million over little more than a decade. In this period she would also witness the rise of skyscrapers that evoked comparison with New York in the imaginations of patriotic white residents. The experience of watching the

[64] Diana Higgs, Family Photograph Album, Johannesburg.

34   Pioneers of the Field

transformation of that mining town in the veld of 1890 into what was already by 1920 the largest metropolis in sub-Saharan Africa surely accounts, to some degree, for her decision to pioneer urban fieldwork on her third and final expedition in December 1922.

It was, in fact, this pending expedition to South West Africa, which brought her to Brown's UCT office that November. The South African government in the recently acquired colony of South West Africa was in quest of an ethnographer. They approached Brown as the senior anthropologist in the country. He recommended Winifred Hoernlé. They were long-standing friends, having known each other from Cambridge days. He was four years her senior. They had worked under the very same mentors, Haddon and Rivers. He was more influenced by the kinship-oriented 'genealogical method' of Rivers and had completed his Cambridge doctoral thesis in 1908. While both would be deeply influenced by Durkheim, it was only while working with Brown in South Africa that Winifred engaged fully with Durkheim's sociological theory.[65] We can only guess as to the degree of warmth of their Cambridge friendship. It is perhaps fair to assume that Winifred would have recognized that she was dealing with a rather peculiar man. He seems to have regarded himself as 'a bit of a superman' and was oddly self-conscious. 'He aspired to be conscious of every gesture; had even thought out the best position in which to sleep.' After doing fieldwork in Western Australia in 1910–11, he had married an Englishwoman in 1912, spent the next two years as a school-teacher in Sydney, and three years as director of education in Tonga before relocating to Johannesburg where he gave lectures in psychology at the School of Mines and served as the curator of the ethnological collection of the Transvaal Museum. In January 1921 he had taken up the post as professor of social anthropology at UCT where he is said to have continued to play 'the rather archaic part of the eccentric English gentleman abroad'.[66]

Winifred may have met him in Johannesburg immediately on her return, but they probably renewed their friendship by correspondence from October 1921 when she joined him on the 'Publication Committee' of the newly created journal *Bantu Studies and General South African Ethnology*, which was simplified to *Bantu Studies* the following year.[67] If

---

[65] There is, for example, no reference at all in her earlier published writings, notably in her 1918 article on Nama ritual, to suggest earlier sustained engagement with Durkheim. Here I differ from Carstens who suggests otherwise. See Carstens, 'Introduction' in Carstens, ed., *Nama Social Organisation and Other Essays*, xii.

[66] Kuper, *Anthropology and Anthropologists*, 39.

[67] The editor was J.D. Rheinallt Jones. Her eight male colleagues on the journal's initial 'Publication Committee' were Rev. A.T. Bryant, Prof. C.M. Drennan, Principal

Feminizing the foundational narrative   35

there is one aspect of Brown's legacy that has been overlooked, and one of the many aspects of her legacy that has been forgotten, then it is their contribution as co-founders of what would become, along with *Africa*, the leading outlet for the publication of social anthropological knowledge about the region. In what was a familiar role for her from her undergraduate days, she would be sole woman representative on the journal's editorial board until her retirement from Wits in the late 1930s.

When they met again in person in Brown's office in Cape Town, he gave her a copy of *The Andaman Islanders*. It would provide the theoretical framework that they would jointly apply to ethnographic data in southern Africa. This provided the theory that she took into the field on her third and only successful expedition. He showed her a draft of what would be his famous essay on 'The Mother's Brother in South Africa' (first published in 1924). This much is clear from her frequent references to it in her field diary, as well as to his 'marriage theory', his theory about 'joking relationships', as well as his newly coined theories regarding the 'sib [clan] group' and 'social value'.[68] Where Haddon had encouraged her to measure and test bodies, Brown encouraged her to collect data about 'kinship terms and usages'. These were presented in two lengthy family case studies as an appendix to her later report. Like Haddon, Brown encouraged her to collect ethnographic objects. He must have been very pleased when she presented him, on her return in April, with dozens of artefacts of Nama material culture for his UCT Ethnological Museum.[69] She kept numerous artefacts for the establishment of her own ethnographic museum at Wits.

Pioneering urban fieldwork: Windhoek location, December 1922 to March 1923

When Winifred Tucker set off in December 1922 on her third expedition, she had a much more useful concept of fieldwork than that which Haddon had imparted a decade earlier. The context of this mission was more political than had been the case on her previous fieldtrips. Where

---

Jan H. Hofmeyr, Prof. J. Macmurray, Prof. L.F. Maingard, Rev. W.A. Norton, Prof. A.R. Radcliffe-Brown and Prof. H.J.W. Tillyard.

[68] See, for example, Carstens et al., *Trails*, 112; Winifred Hoernlé, Letter to the Secretary for South West Africa, '14 April 1923 in Carstens et al., *Trails*, Appendix A [henceforth Letter to the Secretary], 180.

[69] A list of the thirty-three items she donated to Radcliffe-Brown is provided in Carstens et al., *Trails*, Appendix H. In 1961 Monica Wilson arranged for all of these artefacts to be transferred to South African Museum. They were later used in the reconstructed Nama diorama which has featured in the African Cultures Gallery for some decades.

36   Pioneers of the Field

the 1912–13 fieldtrips had been jointly funded by the Royal Society of South Africa and the Witwatersrand Council of Education,[70] the current expedition was sponsored by the South African government in South West Africa. After five years of military administration, following their 1915 conquest over the Germans, South Africa was granted formal control over South West Africa as a 'C class mandate' under the League of Nations. The day-to-day administration of the new colony was under white South Africans, working within the framework of South African law, including the extending network of laws to entrench racial segregation. The South West African Native Reserves Commission had recently recommended that the colony establish a policy of 'native reserves', as they had done in South Africa with the passing of the Land Act of 1913. In this context, her brief was explicitly political: she was meant to conduct studies among the remote Nama 'tribes' that could be used as evidence to motivate for the development of Nama reserves. While this policy was indeed passed in 1923, her report had very little to contribute to its rationalization. In fact, she chose to subvert directly the intentions of her sponsors by spending most of her time in Windhoek location rather than in the remote rural areas where she had been encouraged to gather data.

The focus of her final report was oriented to her urban fieldwork and its tone was out of keeping with the official government policies. She sought to expose the appalling living conditions of the diverse Nama communities living in Windhoek location. She documented Nama grievances about new charges introduced by missions, schools and marriage officials, all of which weighed heavily on the minds of her informants.

One man put it tersely as follows, 'under the Germans our backs knew no rest, but this government does not know how to keep its hands out of our pockets.' Another said, 'yes, the money is put into our hands, but it slips through our fingers, and the hand of the government is waiting underneath to catch it as it falls.'[71]

Her findings did not sit well with the South African officials, one of whom, rather ironically, scribbled across her final report: 'Politics not Science'.[72]

In general, this South West African expedition of 1922–3 was more productive than her earlier expeditions. Even when she revisited her old

---

[70] WHP, Box 2: Personal Papers, Newspapers Clippings, 'Native Problem. What Has the White Race Done? What Should It Do? Miss Tucker's Conclusions', *The Star*, n.d. [March 1913].

[71] Winifred Hoernlé, Letter to the Secretary, 176.

[72] Cited in Robert Gordon, 'Review of *The Social Organisation of the Nama and Other Essays*', *Social Dynamics*, 13, 1 (1987), 75.

Feminizing the foundational narrative 37

field-site at Sandfontein in January and February of 1923, she was able to collect much more data about Nama ritual than had been possible a decade earlier. This was partly a function of her more modern methods. It was also a function of a changed attitude towards her informants. As the above analysis suggests, she was now more empathetic towards the hardship experienced by her Nama informants than she had been a decade earlier. I am struck by the reference in her report to her desire 'to get into as intimate a touch with the people there [in Windhoek location] as possible'.[73] This quest for 'intimacy' was radically different from the earlier approach which treated Nama informants as laboratory subjects. Communication with Nama communities in Windhoek location would presumably also have been easier than had been the case in the remote desert regions, as more informants would have been able to communicate in English, German or Afrikaans, the languages in which she was fluent. Under these more favourable circumstances, she witnessed four Nama rituals in the location at first hand: a funeral service, a reed dance, a rain-making ceremony and a girls' initiation ceremony. These would provide the basis for two further articles about Nama ritual.

Building a theory of African sociology, 1923–25

In January 1923 Alfred returned from Boston to take up a post as head of the philosophy department at Wits University. His letter of acceptance from the Vice-Chancellor, Jan Hofmeyr, mentioned her appointment as an afterthought. It was certainly conditional on the university having secured his services.[74] Brown may well have played a role behind the scenes. She later explained to Haddon that it was initially a research post.

I was appointed research fellow at the University of the Witwatersrand three years ago [in 1923] and was supposed to do field work. This I did for one year, and then this University decided to start classes in Social Anthropology, as Cape Town was doing it, and I was asked to do the teaching on the Cultural side, in spite of the research appointment I had ...[75]

During these three years, she and Brown developed a thoroughly collaborative vision which could serve as the foundation of social anthropology as a new discipline in South Africa. It was conceived as a discipline in the true sense of the term, one that would be based on what they

[73] Winifred Hoernlé, Letter to the Secretary, 175.
[74] Wits University Archive, RFA Hoernlé Papers, Box labelled 'Personal, Genealogical Papers, Family Testimonials etc.', Jan Hofmeyr to Alfred Hoernlé, 20 December 1922, Johannesburg.
[75] Haddon Papers, Cambridge University Library, Hoernlé to Haddon, 3 February 1926, Johannesburg reproduced as Appendix D in Carstens et al., Trails, 190–2.

38   Pioneers of the Field

considered to be professional and rigorously scientific lines. They saw their task as an effort to systemize, theorize, to 'make science' out of what had formerly been an unprofessional, unsystematic, eclectic and antiquarian field of enquiry. This involved drawing clear lines between the properly trained scientist, on the one hand, and the missionary, the government official or the amateur ethnographer, on the other.

For the most part, this was a project by correspondence.[76] They did meet occasionally, as at the annual South African Association for the Advancement of Science conferences, including the conference in Bloemfontein in November 1924 where Brown presented his famous paper on 'The Mother's Brother in South Africa'. Her influence on the redrafted version was evident. He cited her Nama data no fewer than six times and explicitly acknowledged the extent of his reliance on her field materials.[77] As is well known, his essay argued that kinship relations in social anthropology had been misrepresented by earlier ethnographers working with the hitherto dominant 'historical method'. He illustrated this by means of an extended case study. He explained that the Swiss missionary ethnographer Henri-Alexandre Junod, author of what was the most extensive ethnography in southern Africa, the two-volume *Life of a South African Tribe* (1912–13),[78] mapped social customs along an evolutionary model of stages of societal development. He argued that the reconstruction of earlier stages of development was purely speculative. Instead he advocated a structural-functionalist method for social anthropology, one that analysed social relationships as they existed in the field at present. He called for the anthropologist to forego their hypotheses about the distant past in favour of paying close attention to social structures, especially kinship structures, which they could actually observe in the field. He also called on anthropologists to explore the deeper meaning, the social functions, behind these observed structures and systems.[79]

We should read this seminal article, as well as the other strongly methodological essay he had published in 1923,[80] alongside the three

[76] The Isaac Schapera Papers, BC1168 in UCT Libraries, Manuscripts and Archives Department contains '8 letters from A R Radcliffe-Brown to Winifred Hoernlé, 25.03.1924–27.17.1927'. There are two further letters in Winifred Hoernlé Papers, University Archive, Wits University. For published versions of the letters dated to 31 July 1925 and 11 August 1925, see Carstens et al., *Trials*, Appendix B-C.

[77] Carstens, 'Introduction' in Carstens et al., *Trials*, 8.

[78] On Junod, see Patrick Harries, *Butterflies and Barbarians: Swiss Missionaries and Systems of Knowledge in South-East Africa* (Oxford: James Currey, 2007).

[79] A.R. Radcliffe-Brown, 'The Mother's Brother in South Africa', *South African Journal of Science*, 21 (1924), 542–55.

[80] A.R. Radcliffe-Brown, 'The Methods of Ethnology and Social Anthropology', *South African Journal of Science*, 20 (1923), 124–47.

Feminizing the foundational narrative 39

articles Winifred published in the 1923–5 years which I discuss in detail below. They were clearly seen as part of a single collaborative project. In this regard it is instructive to note Brown's response when she proposed that they work as a team.

Your suggestion of the possibility of [further] collaboration together opens up the most exciting vision of possibilities. Would it be possible for us to collaborate at the distance that we are from one another [Cape Town-Johannesburg]? If it were possible, the field that it would be best to work in would be that of African sociology . . . [81]

Their project was striking for its intellectual ambition. Brown provided most of the theoretical guidelines and was certainly the senior partner. She agreed to gather more data, through her own fieldwork and through active correspondence with other researchers. Before their meeting in Bloemfontein, he asked her to send him the notes that she made on Herero kinship terminology when she was in Windhoek. But sometimes the roles of data provider and analyst were reversed. In November 1924, after having commented at length on her courses and exam scripts in his role as external examiner in her first year anthropology course, a class that included Eileen Jensen (later Krige), he addressed their joint project.

I will write a paper on animal sacrifice for the Oudtshoorn meeting [of the SAAS in November 1925]. I am glad that you have now been paying attention to the subject, for it will certainly give us important results in connection with Bantu sociology. If you definitely decide to deal with marriage customs [as she did in her paper at the Oudtshoorn meeting], let me know. I can give you some help, and can let you have material collected by [his research assistant, John] Goodwin from the literature, and I can perhaps set him on to collect more material for you. With kind regards and best wishes . . . [82]

The tone of this letter should give us pause. This degree of warmth on Brown's part was highly irregular. Indeed, it was unique in his relationships with his colleagues in South Africa. He is best remembered for his animosity towards those he regarded as amateurs and inferiors rather than for his intellectual friendships with those he regarded as peers. His relations with his fellows in the School of Life and Languages at UCT had been severely strained from the start. By 1923 he had famously hounded the Rev. A. Norton from his post as Chair of Bantu Languages, evidently being of the view that this former missionary's 'laborious grubbing after

---

[81] Radcliffe-Brown to Hoernlé, 31 July 1925, Cape Town in Carstens et al., *Trails*, Appendix B, 184.
[82] WHP, Box labelled 'Bantu', Radcliffe-Brown to Winifred Hoernlé, 3 November 1924, Cape Town.

40   Pioneers of the Field

folklore and history smacked of unscientific dilettantism'.[83] His actions and arrogance left a bitter legacy. The university's vice-chancellor, James Beattie, would describe Brown as 'a careerist' and commented, some years after his departure: 'I look upon the school [of African Life and Languages] as our worst effort.'[84] Although coloured by a personal dislike for Brown, this insider's assessment of the state of UCT's School in 1933, when Isaac Schapera had taken over Brown's post, warns against any easy narrative of the history of anthropology in South Africa, which privileges the Radcliffe-Brown-Schapera-UCT lineage at the expense of what will be shown in coming chapters to have been the far more dynamic Johannesburg school of social anthropology established and developed by Winifred Hoernlé.

Brown was sufficiently enthused by his work with Hoernlé to propose a joint monograph. It would be organized around the concept of kinship. This, he insisted, would be 'the best basis for building up a theory of African sociology'. His essay on 'The Mother's Brother in South Africa' was 'only a small portion' of their monograph-in-planning, if she was agreeable. The tone of his letters, and sadly we do not have her side of the correspondence, is interactive with frequent requests for new materials and constant enthusiasm about her ideas.[85] By September 1924 a joint paper on ancestors and marriage was well advanced. Brown referred to it as 'our paper'. 'We will find some method of publishing it, whatever its length.' Extended treatment would 'be to the best advantage for [our] students'. He thanked her for further data on kinship terminology and for new books that she had sent down to Cape Town. He sent a draft of another essay-in-progress.[86] They also planned to write joint chapters on 'the cattle complex', rituals of sacrifice and joking relationships. While this was ambitious given the underdeveloped state of the ethnographic data from southern Africa in the early 1920s, their shared vision of an 'African sociology' based on wide-ranging regional cross-cultural comparison of kinship structures anticipated 'the turn from function to structure' in the British anthropological tradition from the 1940s. This

---

[83] Cited in Howard Phillips, *The University of Cape Town, 1918–1948: The Formative Years* (Cape Town: UCT Press, 1993), 25.

[84] Cited in Phillips, *The University of Cape Town*, 26.

[85] These are some sample extracts across the letters: 'I am looking forward to your paper, and expect it will be the most interesting and important of the session [at the Bloemfontein conference of the SA Association in 1924].' 'Can you spare me a copy of your Hottentot paper?'; 'I am sending the first draft [of my ancestor paper] ... you may want to add to it'; 'Follow up that idea of yours ... There is, as you noted ... '; 'We should keep our eyes open, I think, on this ... You are quite right that ... ', 'I quite agree with you that it is useless to try and explain it with reference to property ... ', and so on.

[86] UCT Libraries, Manuscripts and Archives Department, BC 1186 Isaac Schapera Papers, Radcliffe-Brown to Hoernlé, 15 October 1925, Cape Town.

Feminizing the foundational narrative 41

was largely, of course, because that turn was led by Brown himself during his years at Oxford from 1938.[87]

Three seminal essays, 1923–1925

My case for 'co-production' requires detailed analysis of the way in which Winifred applied their new theory of structural-functionalism to southern African data in three incisive essays, one published in 1923 and two in 1925. I read her essays as the siblings of Brown's article on 'The Mother's Brother' rather than as poorer relations to it. Indeed, this was how they were read by Winifred's students like Monica Wilson,[88] if not by scholars in more recent times.

The first of her 'trilogy' was a sustained attempt to apply Brown's theory of 'social value' to Nama ideas about water. She set the scene by describing her experience of seeing dry land transformed by rains after attending a traditional Nama rain ceremony in Windhoek in January 1923. She then defined the concept of 'social value', quoting from Radcliffe-Brown's *The Andaman Islanders*. 'By the social value of anything, I mean the way in which that thing affects, or is capable of affecting, social life. Value may be either positive or negative, positive value being possessed by anything that contributes to the well-being of society, negative value by anything that can adversely affect that well-being.'[89] She proceeded to demonstrate that the concept of water in the cultural system of the Nama was deeply ambivalent, something she explored in relation to belief and ritual. On the one hand, the Nama saw water as having great protective power against antisocial forces. On the other, water was a potential danger to individuals. Here she provided an extended case study, again from her fieldwork in Windhoek location, of the way in which female Nama elders used water to protect a young girl undergoing menstruation. Here too she applied Arnold van Gennep's model of a 'rite of passage' from seclusion to reintegration. She concluded by insisting that African beliefs and rituals were 'intelligible' if subjected to scientific scrutiny. She described Nama beliefs and rituals as 'wholesome', given that they functioned to the benefit of individuals and communities within an interrelated cultural system.[90]

---

[87] See Kuper, *Anthropology and Anthropologists*, 'Chapter 3 The 1930s and 1940s – From Function to Structure'.

[88] See the discussion of 'The Mother's Brother' and 'The Social Organization of the Nama' in Wilson, 'The Development of Anthropology', 6–7.

[89] A.R. Radcliffe-Brown, *The Andaman Islanders* (Cambridge: Cambridge University Press, 1922), 264.

[90] Winifred Hoernlé, 'The Expression of the Social Value of Water among the Nama of South-West Africa', *South African Journal of Science*, 20 (1923), 514–26.

42   Pioneers of the Field

While Winifred and Brown's structural-functionalist theory may have produced too harmonious a view of traditional African cultures, as subsequent generations of critics have emphasized, there has been much less appreciation in modern scholarship of the fact that a model of African society as 'intelligible', 'rational' and 'cohesive' was deeply subversive in the political context of the time, especially in South Africa. White attitudes towards black people in South Africa were, in general, replete with racist stereotypes and underlying assumptions about innate biological difference.[91] The dominant discourse, whether among Afrikaner nationalists or English-speaking South African nationalists like Winifred's father, was that African societies were conflict-ridden, riddled with irrationality, or 'superstition' as it tended to be called, and at a very much more 'primitive' stage of evolutionary development than the modern, progressive societies exemplified by 'civilized' white settlers in South Africa and contemporary European cultures. The subversive potential of a positive and more complex representation of African cultures which called for respect for cultural difference and encouraged a view of those societies from their own internal perspectives was perfectly apparent to Winifred's students.

There is little to support the charge that her ethnographic writings show a lack of interest in history.[92] The best known essay in the trilogy, 'The Social Organization of the Nama Hottentots of South West Africa', published in the *American Anthropologist* in 1925, begins with an extended discussion of Nama history. She drew a clear distinction between Nama groups with 'acknowledged chiefs and acknowledged fountains' whose 'boundaries ... were not marked in a very clear manner' and nineteenth century 'invaders'. She argued that Nama culture was disrupted not by a single event, but by a series of incursions. The process began, as she was the first to highlight, not with the formal German annexation of South West Africa in 1884, but with the incursion of acculturated Nama newcomers known as 'Oorlams'. They had come from the south from the early nineteenth century onwards. This wave of conquest was followed in the mid-nineteenth century by the advances of the Herero from the north. The Germans who formally annexed South West Africa in 1884 were thus the last but most devastating of a sequence of

---

[91] See Saul Dubow, *Illicit Union: Scientific Racism in Modern South Africa* (Johannesburg: Wits University Press, 1995).
[92] Hugh Macmillan, '"Paralyzed Conservatives"', 77–8.

Feminizing the foundational narrative 43

'incoming tribes'.[93] Her narrative has been refined rather than overturned by historians.[94]

Her main argument was that the kinship system of the Nama was cohesive. In this sense it was similar to, rather than different from, the structured social systems that characterized the cultures of Bantu-speaking groups in the region. The social structure of the Nama was based, she demonstrated, on a kinship system in which age and gender were the most important determinants of relative status. Like the Bantu-speaking societies of southern Africa, Nama societies were also typically patriarchal with a complex structure of kin relationships expressed in a distinctive terminology.[95] Again, we should not underestimate the extent to which the very claim that the Nama had a cohesive, complex and 'rational' social structure profoundly challenged long-standing white settler stereotypes of 'Hottentots' as leaderless, restless wanderers, ever prone to strife and alcohol-addiction.[96]

The third essay in the series applied structural-functionalist theory to the marriage customs of the south-eastern Bantu. She explained that her paper was meant to have been 'read [at the 1925 Oudtshoorn conference] in conjunction with one by Professor Radcliffe-Brown on "Animal Sacrifice among the Bantu"'.[97] Brief though it was, this essay is remarkable on many counts. To begin with, it was the first systematic attempt to compare a single custom across a wide range of Bantu-speaking societies based on the literatures in relation to each. Radcliffe-Brown's paper on the mother's brother had been a rereading of evidence in relation to a single Bantu-speaking group previously studied by Junod. She had

---

[93] Winifred Hoernlé, 'The Social Organization of the Nama Hottentots of South West Africa', *American Anthropologist*, 27 (1925), 1–24.

[94] Collectively, this scholarship has given us a much more detailed picture of the Oorlam invaders and their Cape frontier origins, their mid-nineteenth century conflicts over land and water with local Nama groups, the rise to prominence of a centralized Herero polity which spread through the region often using violence, the destabilizing role played by traffic with the Cape Colony in indentured labour from the 1860s through to the 1880s, in which traders and missionaries played a significant part, but, above all, of the extremely brutal nature of the German colonial conquest in South West Africa from 1884 through to the Nama-Herero genocide of 1904–8. The best account is still Brigitte Lau, *Southern and Central Namibia in Jonker Afrikaner's Time* (Windhoek: Windhoek Archives Publication Series No. 8, 1987).

[95] Hoernlé, 'The Social Organization'.

[96] For detailed analysis of the consolidation of long-standing 'Hottentot' stereotypes in British and Dutch settler writings of the 1820s and 1830s, see Andrew Bank, 'The Great Debate and the Origins of South African Historiography', *Journal of African History*, 38, 1 (1997), 261–81.

[97] Radcliffe-Brown never completed this paper, but continued to lecture on this topic right through to his early seventies when he presented a series of talks to undergraduates at Rhodes University during a brief period back in South Africa. (Carstens, ed., *The Social Organisation of the Nama and Other Essays*, 115, note 1).

44   Pioneers of the Field

mastered the latest literature on the Pondo (Goodwin), the Zulu (Bryant), the Herero (Irle and Meyer), the Thonga (Junod), the Valenge (Earthy) and the Ronga (Roscoe). She presented a compelling case for the centrality of cattle in this south-east African 'cultural complex'. She argued that there was an intimate relationship between humans and cattle across these cultures, and that cattle were 'the most important medium of ritual relations between groups'. She insisted on the need to understand the African view of cattle, 'a point of view which differs radically from our own'. It was only once understood from this perspective that 'we can gain a proper appreciation of the original significance of customs which owe their function to this point of view'.

The core section of the article challenged 'the old view' that *lobola* was a system that involved 'transfer of cattle as a bride price'. The woman does not, she insisted, become the man's possession. She proposed instead that *lobola* be understood in relation to a 'whole complex of ceremonies wrapped up with cattle' and a view of marriage as a relationship between groups rather than individuals. Across all of these south-eastern Bantu-speaking cultures, marriage was a process involving a set ritual sequence. At the first stage, a man and a woman are transferred from the group of the unmarried to the group of the married, a change in social status. At the second stage, the woman is 'loosened from her own group' and incorporated into her husband's group. Third, and most importantly, a series of actions take place 'between the group of the man and the group of the woman in order to produce a relationship of friendship and stability between them'. She remarked in concluding that 'the marriage ritual [among south-eastern Bantu-speaking cultures] has profound human secrets to reveal, if only we are wise enough to unravel them'.[98]

The collective import of these three essays has been obscured, partly because they were never worked up into a doctoral thesis or monograph. At the end of the report on her South West African expedition, she had indicated that she had in mind a further fieldtrip 'to the southern [Nama] tribes' and anticipated that the combined data would then be sufficient for the production of 'a monograph on the Nama under the guidance of Professor Radcliffe Brown'.[99] In the event she produced two introductory background chapters for the thesis, which remained unpublished,[100] along with the two essays on Nama ritual discussed above, but no single field-based monograph (or co-authored study with

---

[98] Winifred Hoernlé, 'The Importance of the Sib [Clan] in the Marriage Ceremonies of the South-Eastern Bantu', *South African Journal of Science*, 22 (1925), 481–92.

[99] Hoernlé, 'Preliminary Report', 16.

[100] WHP, Box 3, Typescript chapters headed 'Introduction' and 'Background'.

Brown) which may have secured her an international reputation as an ethnographer.

We can now appreciate why Winifred considered Brown's sudden decision to leave for a post as head of social anthropology at Sydney University in December 1925 as 'a dreadful loss'.[101] She told Haddon in February 1926 that 'Brown has done a great deal for African sociology. He has really made anthropology a subject of which people take notice in this country ... '. It was she and Brown, rather than Brown alone as she claimed with typical modesty, who had 'put anthropology on the map in South Africa'[102] in the space of three intense years of social scientific collaboration and co-production.

Building an anthropology department at Wits University, 1926–1929

Winifred was only formally appointed to a full-time post at Wits in January 1926. Her official title was now lecturer rather than researcher in social anthropology. Eileen Jensen (later Krige) was part of the first social anthropology undergraduate class of 1924. She remembered this as an exciting time 'for anthropology, African studies and race relations in South Africa'.[103] Part of the dynamism was the political urgency of a form of African studies in these years that offered an alternative vision of society to that which informed the policies of racial segregation being introduced by the Pact government led by the National Party of General Hertzog. Liberal scholars at Wits were at the very forefront of what Edgar Brookes would later refer to as 'the Johannesburg school of liberalism'.[104] Most disciplines in the Arts Faculty and its newly created Department of African (Bantu) Studies were liberals outspokenly opposed to segregation, although a minority of liberals would later come to support a 'protectionist' version of the ideology of separate development.

The anti-segregationist liberal intellectuals occupied the senior positions in newly established disciplines across the Arts Faculty in the mid-1920s. At the forefront was the historian William Miller

---

[101] Haddon Papers, Cambridge University, Hoernlé to Haddon, 3 February 1926, Johannesburg in Carstens et al., *Trails*, Appendix D, 192. He felt that Sydney provided a better base from which to pursue his studies on Australian peoples and envisaged expanding his ethnological interests to China and Japan. The new post also paid better and allowed him to reconnect with old friends. Radcliffe-Brown to Haddon, 23 October 1926 cited in Niehaus, 'Anthropology at the Dawn of Apartheid', 15.

[102] Haddon Papers, Cambridge University, Hoernlé to Haddon, 3 February 1926, Johannesburg in Carstens et al., *Trails*, Appendix D, 190.

[103] Krige, 'Agnes Winifred Hoernlé: An Appreciation', 138.

[104] Cited in Bruce K. Murray, *Wits: The Early Years*, 126.

46   Pioneers of the Field

Macmillan who had now begun to immerse himself in the papers of the controversial abolitionist campaigner and London Society missionary John Philip. His research would culminate in the publication of a famous trilogy between 1928 and 1930 that profoundly challenged the dominant racist settler narrative of South African history. These books established the outlines of what we can identify as the modern liberal school of South African historiography with its sharp division between the British assimilationist tradition of missionaries like Philip and the racially exclusive ideology of Afrikaner nationalism embodied in the Boer Republics of the nineteenth century.[105] Most of Hoernlé's star anthropology students of the 1920s, including Eileen Jensen, Hilda Beemer and Max Gluckman, studied history with Macmillan at the height of his career. The rewriting of South African history by Wits liberals would be carried forward by I.D. Maccrone, who was appointed as the head of the psychology department in 1924. In the interwar years he developed what has become known as 'the frontier thesis': the argument that the insular, defensive and pious psychology of the Cape Dutch frontier settlers of the eighteenth century was the true origin of modern Afrikaner nationalism. Margaret Hodgson was also appointed at this time as one of the only other women lecturers at the university. From the late 1920s she became a liberal welfare activist and would later serve as a member of the Native Representative Council after being fired in 1936 for having the temerity to marry: in this case the trade unionist William Ballinger.[106] The more cautious liberals in the Bantu Studies Department included R.D. Rheinallt-Jones who had been actively involved in forming the first Joint Councils of Europeans and Africans from 1922 onwards. He would be appointed first director of the South African Institute of Race Relations, formed in 1929 and, significantly, based on the university campus. A.T. Bryant and Clement Doke began developing the field of Bantu linguistics and phonetics. Raymond Dart, the professor of anatomy, discovered the Taung skull in the year that Hoernlé taught her first class, which put South African physical anthropology on the international map. In the late 1920s the engineer C. van Riet Lowe was appointed as head of the department of archaeology, and, along with

---

[105] The trilogy consisted of *The Cape Colour Question* (1927), *Bantu, Boer and Briton* (1929) and *Complex South Africa* (1930). For an excellent overview of Macmillan's contribution as researcher, teacher and founder of the history department at Wits, see Bruce Murray, 'W.M. Macmillan: The Wits Years and Resignation', *South African Historical Journal*, 65, 2 (2013), 317–31.

[106] On this liberal scholarly community, see Murray, *Wits, The Early Years*, 127.

Feminizing the foundational narrative

his UCT colleague Goodwin, developed the new discipline in South Africa.

Alfred Hoernlé was a central figure in this intellectual community. He arrived with an established international reputation as a liberal scholar in philosophy and ethics, but soon took on a position of seniority in the university. He was the Dean of Arts from 1925. Winifred played a more significant role as an activist rather than an ideologist. She was said in obituaries never to have joined a political party.[107] In the mid-1920s her energies went into building an anthropology department from the ground up. She began by establishing a library for her gradually increasing body of students. Her grant application to the Bantu Studies Publication Committee in May 1926 indicates just how urgent this matter had now become.

Records of work done in the field constitute the working tools of a social anthropologist, and it is just as impossible to teach social anthropology adequately without such books and periodicals as it is to teach any other science without the necessary equipment. At present my own private library is, to a very large extent, the sole source of reference for the students, and this is a most inconvenient arrangement and is bound to break down in the near future; indeed, with twenty students taking the course this year [1926], and with the more detailed reading required for course two, this arrangement is stretched to breaking point.[108]

The Committee granted her 217 pounds and would grant a further 223 pounds the following year for the acquisition of journals and books for what she termed her 'Anthropological Research Library'.[109] Her journal wish list is striking for its comprehensiveness and multilingualism, featuring the leading anthropological journals in English, German and French. Her student numbers increased 'considerably' in 1927. She wrote to her UCT colleague and friend, John Goodwin, that 'I hope to get a real grip on the students and get the subject finally established.'[110] In 1929 she must have begun to feel that her subject had indeed arrived. Her most talented student, Eileen Jensen, had begun writing up the findings of her fieldwork and a new star trio of first years, Hilda Beemer, Ellen Hellmann and Max Gluckman, had begun what she

[107] Krige, 'Agnes Winifred Hoernlé: An Appreciation', 144.
[108] Wits University, William Cullen Library, SAIRR Papers [henceforth SAIRR Papers], AD843/RJ/Kb 32.2.1.1, Bantu Research Affairs Committee, Box 182, Winifred Hoernlé to Max Drennan, Chairman of the Bantu Studies Research Grant Committee, 2 May 1926.
[109] SAIRR Papers, AD843/RJ, Kb32.2.1.5, Box 182, 'Allocation of Research Grants by the Department of Bantu Studies', 1926–1927.
[110] UCT Libraries, Manuscripts and Archives Department, BC290 Goodwin Papers, Correspondence, Hoernlé to Goodwin, 27 March 1928, Johannesburg.

Figure 1.7: Winifred Hoernlé around the time that her intellectual 'daughters' first encountered her, August 1927.[111]

could scarcely have predicted would be internationally acclaimed careers as social anthropologists.

The other foundation stone of her department was its ethnological museum. When Hilda Beemer began her studies she was impressed by the 'wonderful little museum', recalling that Mrs Hoernlé used it as a

[111] WHP, Box 2: Personal Papers, Folder 'Newspaper Clippings', 'A Great Woman Worker in a Great Field', *Rand Daily Mail*, 24 August 1927.

Feminizing the foundational narrative

teaching tool and that it drew admiration from visiting international scholars including Melville Herskovits, Leo Frobenius and L'Abbe Breuil.[112] This was a period in which she worked closely with archaeologists Goodwin and van Riet Lowe. She spent her winter vacations visiting archaeological sites across the country, gathering new objects for her flourishing museum and publishing occasional articles in this allied discipline.[113] In 1931, for example, the Bantu Studies Research Committee agreed to refund '10 pounds for expenses incurred in [archaeological] research in Sekukuniland [in the Western Transvaal] during the May vacation; also 2 pounds, the cost of re-arranging and splicing native films prepared for the University by the Rev. Jacques [a missionary with whom she was in regular correspondence], and 12/-, the cost of photographic materials in connection with her research.' Alfred proposed 'purchasing for the Museum, for 50 pounds, the exceedingly valuable collection of native utensils and instruments formed by Mr. Barnard of Sekukuniland'.[114]

One can scarcely imagine the devastation that Winifred must have felt on hearing that the museum, including all of her own field-notes, had been burnt in a fire that completely gutted the central section of the Wits Main Block on Christmas Eve of 1931.[115] She wrote to Goodwin: 'The loss is horrible, worse than I had pictured it. The retrieved specimens are useful only for teaching purposes; their scientific value is gone, for not one culture is fully represented.'[116] It must have been with a heavy heart that she set about rebuilding the collection. After many years of enticement, she secured hundreds of 'Bushman artefacts' from Dr Louis Fourie, a friend from her Windhoek fieldwork days, the former medical officer and senior administrator in South West Africa who relocated to Johannesburg in 1933.[117] This revived museum would be opened in a room in the

---

[112] Kuper, 'Function, History and Biography', 194–5.

[113] R.F.A. Hoernlé and Winifred Hoernlé, 'The Stone-Hut Settlement on Tafelkop, near Bethal', *Bantu Studies*, 4, 1 (1930), 33–46; Winifred Hoernlé, 'A Note on Bored Stones among the Bantu', *Bantu Studies*, 5, 3 (1931), 253–6.

[114] SAIRR Papers, AD843/RJ, Kb32.2.1.5, Box 182, Bantu Research Affairs Committee, 1930–1931, 'Minutes of a Meeting of the Bantu Studies Research Committee', 9 June 1931.

[115] For a sense of the scale of the destruction, see the photograph taken after the fire reproduced in John R. Shorten, *The Johannesburg Saga* (Johannesburg: John R. Shorten Ltd, 1966), 300.

[116] UCT Libraries, Archives and Manuscripts Department, BC290 Goodwin Papers, Correspondence, Hoernlé to Goodwin, 20 January 1932, Johannesburg.

[117] For correspondence that allows us to track her successful acquisition of the Fourie Collection in 1932–3, see Wits University Archive, AU659 Fourie Papers, Hoernlé to Fourie, 27 April 1927, 8 April 1928, 4 June 1928, 10 June 1932, 2 August 1932, 18 August 1933, Johannesburg.

50   Pioneers of the Field

newly built William Cullen Historical Library.[118] It is fair to assume, however, that the new museum was no more than a shadow of the wonderful original display room that had enthralled undergraduate students and international visitors.

The creation of a South African fieldwork tradition

The development of a field-based South African ethnographic tradition needs to be located in relation to the history of white politics in South Africa. In 1929 the Afrikaner-dominated National Party, which would rule South Africa throughout the apartheid period, had come to power as an independent party for the first time in what has become known as the 'black peril election'. General Hertzog defeated General Smuts' South African Party, this time on the basis of 'a programme of Afrikaner cultural revival, ethnic mobilization in politics, job reservations for whites and racial segregation'.[119]

In this climate a field of study concerned squarely with promoting an appreciation of the complexity and richness of traditional and changing African cultures could scarcely avoid being seen as political, both by its own practitioners and by its detractors in the government or elsewhere. Here one should note the marked contrast between the National Party government's attitude to social anthropology in 1929 and that of the moderate South African Party coalition government which won the election of 1920. Where Smuts had actively assisted in working towards the establishment of the School of African Life and Languages at UCT, Hertzog was hostile to what he regarded as a politically dangerous field of study. He cut off all government funds for research in African Studies in 1929, closing down the post of government ethnologist that had been occupied by the linguist G.P. Lestrade. As we will see, this decision encouraged the anthropologists to form their own organization, an Inter-University Committee for African Studies.

Winifred's students, for their part, had no doubt whatsoever about the underlying political implications of her teaching and of their new discipline. The contemporary politics of the left-liberal anti-segregationist

---

[118] On the history of this collection, now housed at Museum Afrika in Johannesburg, see Ann Wanless, 'The Silence of Colonial Melancholy: The Louis Fourie Archive of Bushman Ethnologica' (unpublished Ph.D. thesis, University of the Witwatersrand, 2007).

[119] Adam Kuper, 'Isaac Schapera (1905–2003): His Life and Times' in John L. Comaroff, Jean Comaroff and Deborah James, eds., *Picturing a Colonial Past: The African Photographs of Isaac Schapera* (Chicago and London: The University of Chicago Press, 2007), 25.

Feminizing the foundational narrative 51

social anthropology of the 1930s was most eloquently articulated by Max
Gluckman in an essay published the year that he died.

And the way in which people made their history, how and with whom they
collaborated and struggled, how they thought about the past and present, in
both urban and rural areas, were problems for us [social anthropology students
at Wits] not only as scholars, but as citizens. Anthropologists in Europe and
North America could, and can, concern themselves abstractly with differences
in patterns of culture and alleged differences in the mentality of people: for us it
was a matter of the here-and-now of our own lives.[120]

In focusing on the official story of the establishment of university
departments at English- and Afrikaans-speaking universities in South
Africa and the texts associated with the scholars in those departments,
the standard narrative has given limited recognition to the fieldwork
revolution in South and southern African social anthropology in the
decade from 1929. The 'golden age of ethnography' that Hammond-
Tooke associates with the four decades from 1920 to 1960 was, in reality,
the work of a single decade of fieldwork. Between 1929, when Hoernlé's
star trio of Gluckman, Hellmann and Beemer began their university
studies, and 1947, when Beemer published her war-delayed Swaziland
monographs, social anthropology in South Africa had been radically
transformed. Almost all of what are still today regarded as the foundational texts in the discipline had been published in the first of their many
editions. My case, in this study, is that women scholars were at the very
centre of this revolution and none more so than Winifred Hoernlé.

What did this revolution involve? First, it involved the production of
a wide body of fieldwork-based ethnographic documentation about the
cultures of the different African societies in South Africa, as well as on
its borders. It was a revolution fuelled by fieldwork of the modern
Malinowskian kind; indeed all of the young scholars of the new generation
were influenced by Malinowski. Second, it involved a theoretical turn
from an abstract 'African sociology' concerned with relatively dry cross-
cultural comparisons of kinship structures across sub-Saharan Africa to
a much more intense and highly localized investigation of the themes of
cultural tradition and social change in African societies within a rapidly
modernizing South Africa. These investigations involved a process of
immersion and participant observation that was far more sustained and
systematic, indeed professional and 'scientific', than anything that had
gone before. The sites for this process of engagement were urban as well

---

[120] Max Gluckman, 'Anthropology and Apartheid' in Meyer Fortes and Sheila Patterson,
eds., *Studies in African Anthropology: Essays Presented to Professor Schapera* (London, New
York and San Francisco: Academic Press, 1975), 26.

52   Pioneers of the Field

as rural, and in some cases researchers adopted a multi-sited approach. Third, the outcome of these studies was also distinctive. They led to the production of a dozen or more scientific monographs on African cultures, again with the central emphasis on the dual themes of tradition and social change. No longer was the journal essay of the kind authored by Hoernlé and Brown the repository of the latest research in the discipline, but ethnographies running into hundreds of pages.

The best way of illustrating the transformation of the field is by comparing Winifred Hoernlé's brief overview of the state of ethnography in South Africa in 1931 with Monica Wilson's essay on the 'Development of Social Anthropology' in South Africa in a special journal issue dedicated to Hoernlé in 1955. *The Bavenda with an Introduction by Mrs A. W. Hoernlé* would be the first in that internationally famous series of ethnographic monographs published by the International Institute for African Languages Cultures in association with Oxford University Press. The study is even more remarkable for the severe disability of its author. Hugh Stayt was a young South African soldier who had been blinded during the First World War at the age of seventeen. His future wife, Evelyn Dyson, nursed his wounds in a hospital in Chelsea and shortly after their marriage in 1922 she assisted him in attaining a degree in social anthropology from Cambridge. We could scarcely ask for a clearer illustration of the way in which the male-dominated structures of knowledge production in interwar South Africa silenced the anthropological contribution of women fieldworkers and ethnographers. When Stayt embarked on fieldwork in Vendaland in the northern parts of South Africa in the mid-1920s, he had to depend almost entirely on his wife. She then helped him write the material up into a UCT doctoral thesis. He did dedicate the thesis to her, though without mentioning her by name, but the book was neither dedicated to Evelyn Dyson, nor so much as mentions her role in the field nor in the writing up process.[121]

Like so many other anthropologists of the interwar years, Stayt had stayed for a time with the Hoernlés in Johannesburg and had his manuscript, initially the UCT doctoral thesis, examined by Winifred Hoernlé. As in so many other cases, she actively championed its publication, now using her friendship with Malinowski to promote it as the first study in a new series. In her introductory comments, she hoped that it would mark the opening up of an entirely new field: the ethnography of South African tribes.

---

[121] The information above is taken from Patricia Davison, 'Women Anthropologists in South Africa' (Exhibition at the Iziko South African Museum, Cape Town, 2002).

Feminizing the foundational narrative 53

[Hitherto] no adequate monograph on any of the South African tribes has been written in all the years in which White and Black have been in contact in the sub-continent ... No-one has found it possible to give a full picture of the life of these tribes nor the whole background of belief on which their culture rests. The Union of South Africa has no monograph to compare with Henri Junod's *Life of a South African Tribe* which portrays the whole cultural background of the BaThonga of Portuguese East Africa.[122]

Wilson's article, which I read as the first essay on the history of social anthropology in South Africa, highlighted the extent to which the understanding of African cultural tradition and social change had developed in South Africa within a relatively short space of time.

[W]e have had Schapera's classic studies of the Tswana, analyzing tribal law and government, kinship relationships, and land tenure, published between 1938 and 1943; detailed studies of the Venda [Stayt], the Lobedu [Eileen and Jack Krige, 1943] and the Basuto; the Valenge [Dora Earthy, 1932], the Pondo [Hunter Wilson, 1936], the Swazi [Hilda Kuper, 1947, 1947], the Zulu [Eileen Krige, 1936] ... Taken by and large our material on the traditional societies [of South Africa] is now very considerable ... These studies show an increasingly systematic approach ... Along with, and very closely associated to, the study of social varieties – social morphology – has gone the study of social change ... It has been the strength of anthropology in South Africa that studies of tribal life and of the growing towns have gone along hand in hand, and a constant attempt has been made to throw a bridge between the two – to watch what happens to the peasant when he migrates to town, and to the industrial worker when he retires to his home village – to observe the process of revolution.[123]

Here she was referring to the urban anthropological work on Rooiyard by Ellen Hellmann (1935), Marabastad and Bethulie by Eileen Krige (1932), who also did fieldwork in Grahamstown (1942), as well as the seminal work on East London that she herself had done (1936).[124] In a sense I am merely following Wilson in crediting Winifred Hoernlé as being the founder figure in this bridge-formation. Wilson mentions her work in Windhoek which pioneered the field of urban anthropology, the theoretical import of her early essays notably that on 'The Social Organization of the Nama', which she places alongside Radcliffe-Brown's article on 'The Mother's Brother' as a foundational theoretical

---

[122] Winifred Hoernlé, 'Introduction' in Hugh A. Stayt, *The Bavenda with an Introduction by Mrs A.W. Hoernlé* (London: Oxford University Press for the International Institute for African Languages and Cultures, 1931), vii.

[123] Wilson, 'Development in Anthropology', 7. Her comments could as easily have been made in 1947, the date of the publication of Hilda Kuper's two war-delayed studies on tradition and social change in Swaziland.

[124] The new wave of urban anthropological studies, including her own co-authored book with Archie Mafeje, had yet to appear.

54   Pioneers of the Field

text, but especially her ability to encourage a new generation to bridge the gap between the rural and the urban, between the study of tradition and the study of social change.

Winifred Hoernlé knew a small-scale society at first hand – she had lived primitive in Namaqualand – and she was a citizen of Johannesburg with a lively concern for her neighbours. Therefore she was keenly aware of the double task of understanding both small-scale societies and the attitudes of men bred in them, and the structure of urban 'locations' and townships, and stressed both in her teaching.[125]

Working with Schapera, 1929–1937

At the heart of this transformation was the collaborative work of Isaac Schapera and Winifred Hoernlé after Schapera's return to South Africa in 1929. Schapera was twenty years younger than Winifred. He would later attribute his interest in Khoisan peoples to his origins in the small Namaqualand town of Garies. The youngest child of turn-of-the-century Jewish immigrants from Belarus, he moved to Cape Town with his family when he was six, but frequently returned to Namaqualand during school holidays.[126] He began studying social anthropology at UCT at the tender age of sixteen, the year of Radcliffe-Brown's arrival in 1921.

Winifred's correspondence with 'Mr. Schapera', as he was then known to her, dates back to December 1925. She had been the external examiner for his M.A. thesis on the relationship between 'the Bushman' and 'the Hottentots', as they were termed in the scholarly literature. She wrote to tell him that she had found the thesis 'a very good piece of work'. She encouraged him to publish it, which he did in 1927, including her suggested revisions based on her Nama work. 'I most sincerely hope that you will get a scholarship overseas and that you will come back to make Social Anthropology your life's work'.[127] This is exactly how things turned out. Schapera won a scholarship. He began his doctoral studies at the London School of Economics in October 1926 and completed his thesis in less than three years. His supervisor was Charles Seligman rather than Bronislaw Malinowski with whom he had a fraught relationship.[128]

---

[125] Wilson, 'Development in Anthropology', 8.
[126] Jean Comaroff and John L. Comaroff, 'On Founding Fathers, Fieldwork and Functionalism: A Conversation with Isaac Schapera', *American Ethnologist*, 15, 3 (1988), 554.
[127] UCT Libraries, Manuscripts and Archives Department, BC 1186 Isaac Schapera Papers, Hoernlé to Schapera, 3 December 1925, Johannesburg.
[128] For details, see Kuper, 'Isaac Schapera: His Life and Times', 23–4.

Feminizing the foundational narrative 55

His doctoral dissertation, published in the first of many editions by Routledge and Kegan Paul of London in 1930, under the title *The Khoisan Peoples of South Africa: Bushmen and Hottentots*, was an impressively wide-ranging synthesis of a vast body of literature on the country's earliest inhabitants from the earliest travellers to the most recent ethnographers and anthropologists, covering the fields of both social and physical anthropology. His study and the many articles that he had precociously published on Bushman culture from his late teens showed an impressive degree of familiarity with historical sources in German, Dutch, French and English. As the book's title suggests, this was the first social scientific study to make a comprehensive case for treating the San and the Khoi peoples of South Africa within a single analytical framework, something that remains one of his foremost contributions to southern African anthropology and African history.

What is less fully appreciated is the extent of his reliance on Winifred Hoernlé's work in this study. Indeed, the central and lengthiest section of the book, 'Part III Culture of the Hottentots', is little more than a meticulously detailed summary of the findings in her three published essays on the Nama with additions from her unpublished materials. His analysis echoed her arguments and evidence at every point. To be fair, he did admit something of the extent of his indebtedness to Winifred in the book's acknowledgements, as well as to Dorothea Bleek, Reader in Bushman Languages at UCT. His history likewise followed hers, highlighting in particular the impact on Nama society of the mid-nineteenth century Oorlam invasions. He analysed the 'social organization' of the Khoi, taking his chapter title from her 1925 essay, and rehearsed, argument by argument, her case for the centrality of kinship with particular attention to the primacy of divisions of clan, sex and age. 'Except where otherwise stated, this [Hoernlé's 1925 essay] is the principal authority for the facts recorded [in this chapter].'[129] His supporting evidence was also drawn almost entirely from her studies on the Nama. The core central section of his book is peppered with references to her field-sites and to the data that she had gathered in the Richtersveld, Sandfontein, Rooibank, Berseba, Windhoek and Franzfontein.[130]

His subsequent chapter (chapter 10) on the 'Social Habits and Customs' of the Khoi was, if anything, more derivative. Here again he

---

[129] Schapera, *The Khoisan Peoples*, 223.

[130] A few examples can serve here for many. On the Richtersveld, see Schapera, *The Khoisan Peoples*, 266; on the Topnaars of Walvis Bay, see *The Khoisan Peoples*, 223, 262–3; on Berseba, see *The Khoisan Peoples*, 225, 226; on Franzfontein, see *The Khoisan Peoples*, 227, 262–3. Interestingly he made the least reference to her most successful fieldwork, that in Windhoek in December 1922, and January and then March 1923.

56   Pioneers of the Field

followed her analysis argument-by-argument: in this case of her two articles on 'the life crisis' rituals of the Nama (1918, 1923). He followed her in paying attention to the rituals of birth, female initiation, marriage and remarriage, and death. He cited her application of Arnold van Gennep's concept of 'rites de passage' to each 'life crisis' ritual, her applied model of analysing Nama ritual as a process, a rite of passage, involving separation from society, ritual preparation of the initiate who was now in a dangerous and liminal state, and then their ritual reintegration into society. In relation to the intermediate phase he featured a subsection on 'The conception of !nau', echoing the title of her 1918 article, again with acknowledgement. 'The following description is taken almost verbatim from the analysis made by Mrs Hoernlé in her important paper ... '.[131] He made extensive use and reference to her article on 'the social value' of water, quoting her evidence about the complex and ambiguous nature of Nama beliefs and rituals associated with water. He cited with approval her newly coined phrases as, for example, when he wrote, '[after a ritual] the person, as Mrs Hoernlé expresses it, must be reborn'.[132] The textual references to her unpublished materials are extensive.[133]

In short, although he did reference his borrowings from her published and unpublished materials quite meticulously, the extent of his reliance on her arguments and evidence was pronounced. At least seventy pages of his book were, if not paraphrased, then at least directly summarized from her work.[134] Another scholar might have taken exception to their work being 'appropriated' in this way. Dorothea Bleek, for example, was privately aggrieved that her own work had been used without full acknowledgement.[135]

At the very time he penned his preface, symbolically from his home town of Garies in August 1929, she was raising a grant for him to begin what would be his ground-breaking fieldwork project. The following month she wrote to him to recommend a promising field-site. Here again he took her advice very seriously, as Adam Kuper explains.

Mrs. Agnes Winifred Hoernlé ... had at her disposal some government funds for research. She had been intrigued by reports of an initiation ceremony due to take place among the Kgatla in the Transvaal; she had also heard that a new chief was being installed among the Kgatla at Mochudi in the Bechuanaland Protectorate. Schapera was dispatched to Mochudi.[136]

[131] Schapera, *The Khoisan Peoples*, 256.   [132] *Ibid.*, 257.   [133] *Ibid.*, 263–6, 270, 273.
[134] *Ibid.*, 227–300.
[135] Kimberley Public Library, Maria Wilman Papers: Correspondence, Dorothea Bleek to Maria Wilman, 25 April 1934, Cape Town. Thanks to José de Prada for this reference.
[136] Kuper, 'Isaac Schapera: His Life and Times', 24.

Feminizing the foundational narrative

This three-month fieldtrip was the beginning of his studies of Tswana culture, which, according to his friend Meyer Fortes, would produce 'the most complete and comprehensive body of knowledge relating to the history, social and political life and the contemporary situation of any single group of African peoples as yet assembled', 'a body of work that is unique in the literature of African sociology'.[137]

Six months after his return from the field, Schapera came to Wits to take over teaching Winifred's star class for the second semester of their final year of undergraduate study. She was attending Malinowski's seminars in London. He recalled that: 'She thrust her teeth into me as soon as we met' and came to regard her as 'one of the most stimulating critical minds'.[138] When she left to tour archaeological sites in France, he donated a copy of his first book, *The Family among the Australian Aborigines* (1913) with the inscription: 'In token of the social identity of functional siblings'.[139] This referred to their joint commitment to functionalist theory, but was also a warm reminder of their 'sibling' status as fellow anthropologists. She would later persuade Malinowski to stay with them in Johannesburg for some weeks in July 1934 as the star guest at the New Fellowship Conference on African education. Her friendship with Malinowski was an important one in the history of South African anthropology in that she sent all of her star students to round off their induction into fieldwork methods and functionalist theory by working under him at the London School of Economics. His warmth towards the Hoernlés is best illustrated by this letter of thanks to Alfred dated October 1934.

I have quite a contingent of South African students in my study now – Hellmann, Gluckman, [Jack] Simons, [Pieter Johan] Schoeman and a South African Bantu named Matthews. I enclose a few stamps knowing your interest in them. Will you give my kind regards to the Missis and tell her that I am writing to her quite soon – a long and very anthropological letter.

May I thank you for what you have done for me in Johannesburg . . . Honestly I think that there is something transcendental about the quality of your (dual) kindness and hospitality . . .[140]

---

[137] Meyer Fortes, 'Isaac Schapera: An Appreciation' in Fortes and Patterson, eds., *Studies in African Anthropology*, 3. For fuller analysis of its import and degree of rigour, see Kuper, 'Isaac Schapera', 24–35.

[138] WC, B4.4 GW to and from Bronislaw Malinowski, Malinowski to Godfrey Wilson, 20 January 1935, London.

[139] Carstens, 'Introduction' in Carstens et al., *Trails*, 10.

[140] Wits University Archive, RFA Hoernlé Papers, Box labelled 'Correspondence 1930–1939', Malinowski to Alfred Hoernle, London, 31 Oct. 1934.

58   Pioneers of the Field

Winifred's friendship with Schapera blossomed after her return from London in 1930. She now addressed her letters 'My Dear Schapera'. His work on the Tswana made a deep impression on her and, along with her friendship with Malinowski, pushed her in a fresh intellectual direction. Her and Schapera's collaboration in promoting a field-based school of social anthropology is evident from their joint work on the Inter-University African Studies Committee. He had been a founder member in January 1932. She was elected onto the Committee in July 1933. As usual, she was the first and only woman representative.[141] Their correspondence with the Committee indicates that they saw themselves as working jointly towards the development of a national project. Of course, Schapera's own work was in the Bechuanaland Protectorate and that of Hilda Beemer in Swaziland, but the connections between South Africa and these protectorates beyond her borders were very close. Their emphasis was typically cast in national terms, as the titles of his three important publications of the 1930s would confirm: 'The Khoisan Peoples of South Africa', 'Western Civilization and the Natives of South Africa' and 'The Bantu-Speaking Tribes of South Africa'. The latter was conceived as a university undergraduate textbook with Winifred as a proposed co-editor.[142] Schapera pointed out in a letter to the Secretary of the Committee in April 1934: 'My impression is we submit nominees [for fellowships] to the [African] Institute for work in South Africa only, and not beyond its borders.'[143]

The call for South African fieldwork by a new generation had been the central theme of her Presidential Address to Section E of the South African Association for the Advancement of Science in July 1933. Entitled 'New Aims and Methods in Social Anthropology', the first part of her address provided a restatement of Brown's famous 1923 essay on method, which championed the inductive sociological or functionalist method at the expense of outdated evolutionist and diffusionist approaches to the study of culture.[144] She selected Schapera's first major article on the Tswana, a study of sexuality and premarital pregnancy among the Bakatla, as an illustration of the value of this new

---

[141] This is aside from a single (and to judge by the minutes, silent) guest appearance by Audrey Richards at the second Committee meeting of July 1932.

[142] Isaac Schapera, 'The Present and Future Development of Ethnographical Research in South Africa', *Bantu Studies*, 8 (1934), 258.

[143] SAIRR Papers, AD843/RJ/Kb18.4, Box 174 Inter-University Committee for African Studies, File 2 April–June 1934, Schapera to Rheinallt-Jones, 21 April 1934, Cape Town.

[144] Radcliffe-Brown, 'The Methods of Ethnology and Social Anthropology'.

Feminizing the foundational narrative 59

approach.[145] The latter section of her essay made a case for a fieldwork revolution driven by the Rockefeller-funded International African Institute under Malinowksi. 'This Institute is revolutionizing, not only the scientific work which is being done in Africa, but also the whole outlook of Social Anthropology.' She highlighted the role of the journal *Africa* (in which her students would publish their best work) and the seminal importance of the re-orientation of the discipline towards the study of 'culture contact'. 'It is proposed therefore that the enquiries fostered by the Institute should be directed towards bringing about a better understanding of the factors of social cohesion in original African society, the way these are being affected by the new influences, tendencies towards new groupings and the formation of new cultural bonds, and forms of co-operation between African societies and Western civilization.' She concluded with a clarion-call for the urgency of the scientific study in South Africa of these new themes of 'culture-integration, culture contact and, above all, culture change'.[146]

She and Schapera worked together on the Committee up to her retirement from Wits in 1937, the year in which she contributed two essays to his landmark collection on *The Bantu-Speaking Tribes of South Africa*, persuading her students to do likewise. Her essays are about tradition rather than 'culture contact', focusing respectively on African religious beliefs and the underlying patterns in the social organization of Nguni and Sotho-Tswana peoples of South Africa. What is most striking about the 1937 volume is its emphatic announcement of a changing of the guard, of what I regard as the feminization of South African social anthropology. While Schapera's edited collection of 1934 had not featured a single essay by a woman scholar,[147] five essays in this new collection were written by women anthropologists: two by Hoernlé, three by her students: 'Eileen Jensen Krige, M.A.', 'Monica Hunter, M.A., Ph.D.' and 'Ellen P. Hellmann, M.A.'.[148] The latter were undoubtedly the most significant contributions as we will see in the chapters that follow.

Winifred retained a warm friendship with Schapera after her retirement from Wits in 1937. The most touching evidence of this was her willingness to donate to him, in 1947, the eight letters that his first teacher,

---

[145] Isaac Schapera, 'Premarital Pregnancy and Native Opinion: A Note on Social Change', *Africa*, 6, 1 (1933), 59–89.

[146] Winifred Hoernlé, 'New Aims and Methods in Social Anthropology' [1933] reproduced in Carstens, ed., *The Social Organisation of the Nama and Other Essays*, 1–19.

[147] Isaac Schapera, ed., *Western Civilization and the Natives of South Africa: Studies in Culture Contact* (London: George Routledge and Sons Ltd., 1934), vi–vii.

[148] Isaac Schapera, ed., *The Bantu-Speaking Tribes of South Africa: An Ethnological Survey* (London: Oxford University Press, 1937), vi–ix.

60   Pioneers of the Field

Radcliffe-Brown, had written to her in the early-mid 1920s,[149] the very letters which have formed the basis of my reconstruction of her equally collaborative relationship with Brown.

Conclusion

The standard histories of anthropology tend to prioritize individual achievements and sole-authored monographs. This approach offers very little by way of understanding the anthropological contribution of a scholar like Winifred Hoernlé whose greatest gift was her ability to collaborate with others. Indeed, it was her social conscience, her desire to contribute to wider society and the welfare of others that, along with additional family commitments, led her to resign from her post as senior lecturer in social anthropology in December 1937. Her second and partially overlapping career as a liberal social welfare activist, beginning in 1932 and effectively continuing until her death in 1960 at the age of seventy-five, also awaits balanced and historically informed analysis.[150] The bare details are well known: she emerged as the leading activist in social welfare campaigns for collaboration between white, Indian and African women, for the provision of clinics for township mothers, for welfare services for township children, for improved schooling for township youth and later for penal reform and educational reform in reaction to the apartheid government's repressive Bantu Education Act of 1953. She also worked at a national level in organizations promoting the rights of women and the ideology of liberalism, notably the National Women's Organisation, of which she was President in 1938–9 and the South African Institute of Race Relations, succeeding her husband Alfred as President after his sudden death in 1943.[151] It is significant that when Wits awarded her an Honorary Doctorate in 1949, it was in the field of law rather than social anthropology.

The role of Christianity in this welfare work, and indeed in her life history more generally, is a theme that warrants closer attention. Her letters home are frustratingly silent on the subject, perhaps because her Christian commitment was taken for granted in correspondence with her devout parents who were founder members of the Wesleyan community

---

[149] UCT Libraries, Manuscripts and Archives Department, BC1186 Isaac Schapera Papers, D Letters from Radcliffe Brown to Winifred Hoernlé.

[150] For a narrow analysis of her work in the field of penal reform in the mid-late 1940s, here simply as yet another expression of the ambiguities of South African liberalism, see K. Gillespie, 'Containing the "Wandering Native"', 499–515.

[151] For a brief overview of the range of her welfare activism, see Krige, 'Agnes Winifred Hoernlé', 143–4. The Winifred Hoernlé Papers at Wits include five untapped boxes of material on this, her second career.

Feminizing the foundational narrative 61

in Kimberley, where she was baptized as an infant,[152] and then of the Wesleyan community in Johannesburg.[153] Her husband was also a devoted Christian, the son and grandson of London Missionary Society evangelists in India, where he spent five years of his early childhood. While the relatively sparse paper trail allows for little sense of her inner life as a Christian, the fact that Christianity and its message of equality underpinned her liberal humanism can be glimpsed from occasional religious references in her published writings,[154] her active institutional involvement in interfaith dialogue between Christians and Jews during the 1930s,[155] and numerous references in Alfred's letters of this period to the fact that their vision of a multi-racial South Africa was founded on Christ's teachings.[156]

Fortunately, historians of science have begun to recognize the thoroughly collaborative nature of knowledge production, not least cultural knowledge production in Africa.[157] In keeping with this shift in emphasis, I have sought to highlight the extent of Winifred Hoernlé's collaboration with other anthropologists, beginning with her training under 'the founding fathers' of the British school. While her induction into anthropology by A.C. Haddon proved to be unpromising preparation in terms of field method and ethnographic empathy, he encouraged a broad outlook, cross-cultural curiosity and, most importantly, a thoroughly collaborative concept of knowledge creation, whether in her work in his laboratory, in that with his gifted Cambridge peers Rivers and Myers, or that while serving as his research assistant on the Torres Straits report. His encouraging attitude towards woman anthropologists was highly unusual for its time.

It would, however, be her collaboration with her fellow Cambridge graduate student Brown that effectively established the discipline of social anthropology in South Africa between 1922 and 1925. Her essays

---

[152] WHP, Box 2, Folder 'Personal Details', Baptism certificate dated 31 January 1886.
[153] RFA Hoernlé Papers, Box 3, Lecture Notes, Tucker Files, Obituaries to Joseph Tucker entitled 'Notable Pioneer's Death' and 'A Veteran Gone' in *The Transvaaler*, [n.d. 1914].
[154] See, for example, the concluding lines of her published lecture of 1913, *The Richtersveld: Its Land and Peoples*, 13.
[155] On the Hoernlés' involvement in the Society of Jews and Christians formed in 1937 and the associated journal *Common Sense*, see I.D. Maccrone, 'A Memoir' in *Race and Reason, Being Mainly a Selection of Contributions to the Race Problem in South Africa by the late Professor R.F. Alfred Hoernlé* (Johannesburg: Wits University Press, 1945), xxv.
[156] For a few references among many, see RFA Hoernlé Papers, Box labelled 'Correspondence 1930–1939', Alfred Hoernlé to J. Reyneke, 19 November 1934, Johannesburg; the obituary notice by E.G. Malherbe, 'Friend of the Springbok Soldier', *The Digest*, August 1943.
[157] See esp. Schumaker, *Africanizing Anthropology*.

Figure 1.8: Winifred Hoernlé as photographed by Leon Levson in 1944.[158]

on the Nama deserve recognition as foundational texts, along with those of Brown. We should think of their work as 'the co-production of scientific knowledge' in the full sense, especially given their scientific conception of their craft. We should also not underestimate the radical challenge that their 'African sociology' posed to the segregationist politics of the time as Brown explained in his essays and speeches. I also made a case for regarding her fieldwork in Windhoek as the pioneering example of a new field, that of urban anthropology which she developed through the work of her women students from the early 1930s. Equally important was her generous work with Isaac Schapera, initially supporting his graduate studies, then decisively shaping the

[158] WHP, Box 2, Folder 'Photographs'.

central section of his first major monograph on the Khoisan and even directing him, in 1929, to the field-site in British Bechuanaland which he revisited across the next two decades resulting in a remarkably rich body of ethnographic work. She and Schapera (rather than, say, Schapera and Eiselen as the male-dominated mythology has it) played the decisive role on the Inter-University Committee for African Studies in supporting funding for a new generation of South African fieldworkers who would be centrally concerned with 'culture contact', or 'social change' as it soon became known, rather than simply with 'tribe' and 'tradition'.

Her gifts as a collaborator were as, if not more, evident in her work with women students than they had been in her work with male mentors at Cambridge and male colleagues in South Africa. Indeed, it was her women students who were at the very forefront of what she, like Malinowski, liked to describe as 'a revolution' in social anthropology. Her relationships were warm and mutually productive, but differed in each case according to the time in which she worked with them, the personalities involved and the career trajectories they followed. The chapters that follow explore her research collaborations with them, beginning with the creative relationship she forged with Monica Hunter in the course of what is increasingly acknowledged to have been her ground-breaking fieldwork and ethnography in Pondoland and East London between 1931 and 1936.

2 An adopted daughter: Christianity and anthropology in the life and work of Monica Hunter Wilson (1908–1982)

> Mrs. A.W. Hoernlé of Witwatersrand University found time, among her many duties, to correspond with me in the field, read draft notes, and the manuscript of the book, and I owe much to her encouragement and stimulating suggestion.
>
> Monica Hunter, *Reaction to Conquest: Effects of Contact with Europeans on the Pondo of South Africa* (London: Oxford University Press in Association with the International Institute of African Language and Cultures, 1936), xvii.

There is a striking continuity in the life and career of Monica Hunter Wilson, one that has its roots in her missionary origins, Christian upbringing and life-long commitment to a liberal humanist vision of racial relations.[1] Wilson was a Christian in the first instance, and then an anthropologist, even if her anthropology has been far more celebrated and scrutinized than her Christianity. In fact, I will demonstrate that she chose anthropology as 'a vocation' that would best allow her to realize her religiously-grounded vision of her personal and social commitment to a more open and racially harmonious South African society, a vision that was profoundly in opposition to the racial policies of the segregationist government in South Africa.

I foreground the theme of Christianity in her background, training and work because it seems to me *the* most distinctive feature of her identity as a social anthropologist when compared with her women peers. Her life history is amongst the most obvious counterpoints to the arguments of those scholars who question the extent of the importance of the personal and the private in shaping anthropological work, preferring to see the history of anthropology more in terms of great moments of theoretical innovation by gifted ancestors (usually men). I make the case that Christianity was a source of inspiration and powerful resource in Wilson's life and work, quite apart from the missionary social networks that facilitated access to field sites, interpreters and informants during her

---

[1] Thanks to my father Louis Bank, Elizabeth F. Colson, David Gordon, Nancy Jacobs and Pamela Reynolds for incisive comments on a draft version.

An adopted daughter   65

first period of fieldwork in Pondoland and the Eastern Cape. As a subplot in keeping with the central theme of this volume, I reveal how Monica corresponded with Winifred Hoernlé during her Pondoland fieldwork. I also document the role that Hoernlé then played in securing funding for further fieldwork, for the publication of her famous book *Reaction to Conquest* and in promoting the study in an extended review as the leading contribution to the understanding of African culture and social change in South Africa.

Christianity remained central during Monica's second extended field study, among the Bunyakyusa of south-west Tanzania, conducted between 1935 and 1938. Here again her networks with Christian interpreters were crucial as the Christian communities were now more squarely her focus of study. Her passionate marital and anthropological partnership with an equally deeply religious and socially committed Christian, Godfrey Wilson (1908–44) whom she married the month before entering the field, cemented this bond between anthropology and Christianity in her life and early work. I then highlight the continued significance of Christianity in her mature writings about religion and ritual from the late 1950s through to the early 1980s.

In general, my approach challenges those of her 1970s critics who saw her Christian beliefs as a limitation on her ability to achieve social scientific 'objectivity', or as a middle class ideology (even an 'expression of false consciousness') that inhibited proper appreciation of worker and peasant radicalism in apartheid South Africa. These criticisms were particularly vocal following the publication of her deeply personal Scott Holland lectures at Cambridge, which were published in 1971 and sought to achieve a philosophical reconciliation between her personal commitment to Christianity and her professional commitment to anthropology.[2] With 'the cultural turn' in historical studies and 'the spiritual turn' in the humanities in recent decades,[3] dismissals of religion

---

[2] See Monica Wilson, *Religion and the Transformation of Society: A Study of Social Change in Africa* (The Scott Holland Lectures, Cambridge: Cambridge University Press, 1971); Archie Mafeje, 'Religion, Class and Ideology in South Africa' in Michael Whisson and Martin West, eds., *Religion and Social Change in Southern Africa: Anthropological Essays in Honour of Monica Wilson* (Cape Town: David Philip, 1975), 164–84; Mafeje, 'A Comment on [Falk Moore's] *Anthropology and Africa*', *CODESRIA Bulletin*, 3&4 (2001), 15–21.

[3] Both literatures are extensive. For a critique of materialist and post-colonial theorists' lack of empathetic engagement with spirituality as a theme in the social sciences, and an emphasis on the importance of religion as a central theme in South African history and that of other societies of the South (Latin America and Asia) in the context of the growing secularization of the West, see Duncan Brown, 'Religion, Spirituality and the Postcolonial: A Perspective from the South' in Brown, ed., *Religion and Spirituality in South Africa: New Perspectives* (Scottsville: University of Kwazulu-Natal Press, 2009), 1–26.

66   Pioneers of the Field

as a distorting influence on objective social science, even a form of dominant class ideology or 'false consciousness' in Marxist formulations, seem woefully inadequate. Religious beliefs and identity were another aspect of the affective, the personal, in shaping creative work, social interactions and the spirit with which these were negotiated.

Tracing the role of Christianity in Monica Hunter Wilson's background and fifty-year career as a social anthropologist and historian, from 1931 when she entered the field until 1981 when she published her edited and expanded autobiography of her Christian friend Z.K. Matthews, is an ambitious undertaking. The sections that follow highlight aspects of this relationship. For a deeply spiritual person like Monica, Christianity was very much more than an ideology; one that, in her case, encouraged her to view people from different cultural and racial backgrounds with tolerance and mutual understanding. It was a lived inner journey, a path that was constantly being reshaped and developed as one moved through different life stages, including life crises. In short, Christianity was for Monica a lived experience rather than a rational worldview, although her love of gardening and nature does perhaps suggest an affinity with the theology of the joy and design in creation. This inner world is of course complex and difficult to access for any outsider, let alone a researcher of a later generation. Private diaries and letters do, however, offer a partial engagement with this world, particularly during her youth.[4]

From Lovedale and Collegiate Girls' High, Port Elizabeth, to Cambridge, 1908–1927

Monica Hunter was born in Victoria Hospital on the mission station of Lovedale to missionary parents, David and Jessie Hunter (née McGregor). She was home-schooled until the age of ten, when she attended classes at Lovedale. 'The whole atmosphere of the house was one of the deepest reverence and an awareness of the presence of God.' She grew up as an only child following the tragic death of her brother Aylmer from a bronchial illness when she was just four. In later years she would recall the awful experience of her brother's funeral and overhearing her mother's whisper: 'But it's *the boy*!' She reflected

---

[4] Monica did record a deeply personal private diary across her years as a university lecturer at Fort Hare Native College, and then as a professor at Rhodes University and the University of Cape Town. This record is kept in the family and is, unfortunately, not openly accessible.

An adopted daughter 67

that 'I think this was important in my later life because I always wanted to be a boy.'[5]

Monica retrospectively identified her schooling at Lovedale in her preteen years as the formative moment in planting the seeds of her later anthropological and historical interests. In a well-known essay written in 1973, the year of her retirement as a Professor of Social Anthropology at the University of Cape Town, she proudly identified herself as 'a daughter of Lovedale'.[6] She provided a richly detailed account of the dynamic cross-cultural and multi-ethnic educational environment of her Lovedale childhood and recalled classroom debates in which her Xhosa mates challenged their teacher's settler-centric views about the British–Xhosa frontier wars. Janet Maqoma, great-granddaughter of a famous Xhosa chief, opened her eyes to the Xhosa interpretation of the wars, while Peggy Mbilini and other Xhosa girls challenged her inherited ideas about *lobola* and other cultural practices.[7] On the other hand, Monica tended to downplay the significance of her schooling at the whites-only Collegiate Girls' High in Port Elizabeth, where she attended high school for four years, and that of her three years as an undergraduate student at Girton College in Cambridge. In late-life reflections she seems to have credited her Cambridge training with having encouraged her to think more critically but little more than that.

In this section I will challenge this retrospective construction based on a close reading of a unique source: some one hundred handwritten letters, mostly of four to eight pages, that she wrote to her father from Collegiate Girls' High School between 1922 and 1925, the year in which she matriculated, and then some fifty letters that she wrote to her father before and for the first eighteen months after she enrolled for a B.A. at Cambridge in October 1927.[8] I have written elsewhere of what might be described as the cognitive benefits of her Cambridge experience, making a case in particular for the importance of her involvement in a Labour Study Circle and suggesting that her lecturers in African anthropology did play a role in introducing her to a new literature and method.[9] Taking this

---

[5] University of Cape Town Libraries, Manuscripts and Archives Department, BC880 Monica and Godfrey Wilson Collection [henceforth WC], Uncatalogued materials, CD: Monica Wilson interviewed by Francis and Lindy Wilson, Hogsback, Eastern Cape, 'Childhood', 10 January 1979 [henceforth Monica Wilson interview: 'Childhood'.].

[6] Monica Wilson, 'Lovedale: Instrument of Peace', 4; on her self-image as missionary's daughter in her Pondoland monograph, see Monica Hunter, *Reaction to Conquest*, 12.

[7] Monica Wilson, 'Lovedale: Instrument of Peace', 4–5; WC, Monica Wilson interview: 'Childhood'.

[8] WC, B5.1 Letters MW to her father (David Hunter).

[9] Andrew Bank, 'The Making of a Woman Anthropologist: Monica Hunter at Girton College, Cambridge, 1927–1930', *African Studies*, 68, 1 (2009), 29–56.

Figure 2.1: Monica Hunter as a teenager, Edinburgh, 1922.[10]

as read, I am interested here in making a case for her Cambridge undergraduate experience as formative in her religious life, for the significance of Cambridge at the level of affect, emotion and inner motivation, in addition to its role in introducing her to a new field of study and a more left-wing politics.

In the most general sense I have been struck, on re-reading these letters yet again, by the difference in the sense of self she projected in her letters from high school (14–17 years of age) from that in the letters written from Girton College, Cambridge, just a few years later (19–21 years of age). The school letters make very limited reference to her religious life and identity. In fact, one has to scour them closely for reference to church attendance or school prayers, let alone for a deeper sense of the inner life

---

[10] WC, N1, Portraits of Monica Wilson. There are, unfortunately, no surviving portraits that date to her undergraduate years.

An adopted daughter   69

and orientation of a committed Christian girl. Certainly she formed a friendship circle with the other 'Presbyterian girls'.[11] She did attend church on Sundays and was friendly with the Scottish Presbyterian minister Revd MacRobert, who admitted her to full communion in the Presbyterian Church of South Africa in 1926 at the Hill Church in Port Elizabeth.

What looms much larger than her religion or inner life in these letters is her love of reading.[12] The letters leave no doubt that she received an excellent, albeit strongly anglo-centric, education at Collegiate.[13] They had a very good school library and she reported excitedly on her English literature textbooks. There is a sense of lightness in her attitude to reading and a willingness to experiment. In general her attitude to learning is marked by an abiding sense of curiosity and an outspoken willingness to express her tastes or distastes about subjects, events or people. There is also clear evidence of what I would term a well-developed 'historical imagination'. At the age of fifteen she was already passionate about the subject.

History is interesting. When I start reading it I want to go on and on. It's fatal if I have to look up something [in the library] and spike on a well written history of England. I get deep in it and forget to do my looking up. I would like to specialize in History one day.[14]

She spent the year after matric preparing for her admission examination for Girton College. She ground her way through a ten-volume *Cambridge History of England* and remembered enough to be offered an oral exam in Cambridge. She and her mother sailed on the *Union Castle* in March 1927 and three days after her interview on 20 April she proudly telegrammed her father with a single-word message: 'Girton!'[15]

What of the Cambridge letters written from the time of her acceptance to study at Girton College in October 1927 at the age of just nineteen? I have written elsewhere of the importance of her participation from the first month after 'going up' in a Labour Study Circle led by the South African Communist Party member Eddie Roux and attended by a number of her college mates including her closest friend, a 'rabid Egyptian nationalist' named Munira Sadek.[16] They explored issues of political economy in the British colonial world with a strong interest in

[11] WC, B5.1, Letters MW to her father, Monica Hunter to David Hunter, 26 February 1923, Port Elizabeth.
[12] *Ibid.*, 29 May 1923.   [13] *Ibid.*, 8 November 1923.   [14] *Ibid.*, 3 March 1923.
[15] *Ibid.*, 20 April 1927 with attached telegram 23 April 1927, Glasgow to Lovedale.
[16] *Ibid.*, 20 March 1928. For a fuller account of the influence of the Labour Study circle, and of her friendships with Sadek and Roux, see Bank, 'The Making of a Woman Anthropologist', 40–6.

70   Pioneers of the Field

Africa. Roux introduced her for the first time to a more radical critique of South African segregation than anything she had read at home or at school: texts like Lord Olivier's *Anatomy of South African Misery* led her to muse whether she was not beginning to become a socialist.[17] She and her Girton friends learnt first-hand of Roux's experiences of visiting Russia in 1928,[18] and also about his earlier experiences of working for the Communist Party in Johannesburg. He presented papers to their study group on the radical Industrial and Commercial Workers Union (ICU) and the wider trade union movement in South Africa from a position that was deeply sympathetic towards the workers, and was strongly African nationalist. He introduced her to African history in his talks on subjects like the Asante and the Golden Stool.[19]

This Labour study circle had an immediate impact. While she wrote in her first month in college in apologetic tones about her decision to get involved in politics via the study circle – something her father had seemingly warned her against – four months later her affiliations were clear. 'I, like all the other intelligent people in Girton, am wearing scarlet and vote Labour!'[20] She was nominated as the College's Labour Party secretary at the beginning of her second year, but declined due to the extent of her other commitments.[21] Her Labour connections soon went beyond college, and at a series of international conferences which she attended between terms she engaged in conversation and debate with prominent left-wing critics of imperialism and segregation. I have suggested that this left Labour political influence played a significant role in her decision to switch from 'that wretched constitutional stuff'[22] (English history) to African anthropology.

On Friday, I went along to Miss Jones [her college tutor and undergraduate mentor] and rather in fear and trembling broached the subject of doing anthropology in my third year, instead of history. She leapt upon the proposal ... In anthropology the skull measuring wash is mostly being cut out now, and [if I took African anthropology] I would be able to concentrate on social anthropology, which would give me a very good background for beginning to study Bantu social customs, and could well be combined with teaching in a native school, or (if I am lucky) at Fort Hare.[23]

We must remember that social anthropology was still a marginal field of study in the late 1920s. Monica joined a class of no more than a dozen students, all but one of whom were men. Significantly, she associated

---

[17] WC, MW A2.2 Pocket Diary 1927, entry for 2 November.
[18] WC, B5.1, Letters MW to her father, Monica Hunter to David Hunter, Cambridge, 21 October 1928.
[19] *Ibid.*, 30 October 1927.   [20] *Ibid.*, 24 January 1928.   [21] *Ibid.*, 15 October 1928.
[22] *Ibid.*, 13 November 1927.   [23] *Ibid.*, 6 May 1928.

anthropology with future research as well as teaching. 'I am sure I shan't want to teach for always and always, and anthropological research is a thing I can do on my own ...'[24]

I have also indicated that her two lecturers in African anthropology, the former colonial officials Jack Driberg and Thomas Callan Hodson, influenced her to a greater degree than has been acknowledged. Driberg had studied under Malinowksi and taught her about functionalist theory and fieldwork methods. He was working closely with Isaac Schapera on publishing a series of ethnographic studies in African anthropology at the time of her studies, and the first book in this series (subsequently discontinued) was Schapera's *Khoisan Peoples of South Africa* (1930), the main textbook for her course. Thomas Hodson gave her advice about anthropological method (here the need for case studies) and also introduced her to the regional literature, in this case to Junod's *Life of a South African Tribe* (1913), a copy of which she took with her into the field.

The intellectual benefits of Cambridge were also of a more general kind. Apart from Constitutional History and African anthropology, she took courses in Economic History and Political Science. In fact, her reading of leading philosophers of the Enlightenment like Adam Smith, Jean-Jacques Rousseau, John Locke and Thomas Hobbes, about whom she enthused in her letters, may have been as important in her training as her reading of the southern African ethnographies mentioned above. The importance of a general induction into critical thinking was most concisely formulated in a letter written during her first year exams. 'I feel that in three terms I have collected enough ideas to keep my brain busy for at least ten years. To me, it is not what you actually learn that is important, but they teach you to think, and work out things for yourself and make you so keen.'[25] She later wrote of 'hav[ing] got the proper thirst for knowledge now' and expressed appreciation to her father for giving her the opportunity to study at Cambridge.

Here I wish to extend my case for the significance of her undergraduate experience, by arguing that her correspondence from Cambridge also provides evidence of an inner transformation, one that was as important in shaping her later career path as the other factors outlined above. This process began in the months before she 'went up'. She recorded in her personal diary experiences of discomfort, even inner turmoil, while staying with relatives in Scotland in June and early July 1927. 'Dreadful attack of homesickness. Aching longing for sun. Sense of the uselessness

---

[24] *Ibid.*, 24 May 1928.   [25] *Ibid.*, 28 July 1928.

72   Pioneers of the Field

of my life.'[26] She wrote of sleepless nights and being dogged by a sense of failure.

Then on the 26 July 1927 she had a 'religious experience' akin perhaps to that which her father had had at Keswick in 1893, one that had led to his inner resolve to become a missionary in Africa. She recorded in her diary: 'Cycled up moors ... alone. Absolute misery of soul but found God in the mountains. Great, great happiness.' This profound inner experience was directly associated with a sense of future mission. 'It will be worth my while to dedicate my life to training Native girls – it's not the book work that matters but the training of character.' The Presbyterian and Reformed Churches were distinctive in the degree of theological emphasis they placed on the concept of 'vocation', typically seen in terms of 'the election of people to salvation and service', and on an individual's 'commitment to transform the world in obedience to God'.[27] 'Do not be discouraged [she continued] by the vastness of things – this life is but the beginning ... Religion no longer a duty but a necessity + joy.'[28] Her diary entries for August and September 1927 are filled, for the first time, with extensive biblical quotes, expressions of ardour and yearning, a sense of deepened commitment to prayer and other forms of religious practice, and a clear conviction about the existence of the afterlife,[29] a belief she would retain to her dying days.

Against this background I read her Cambridge letters as the story of the development in her of a cross-cultural, international and thoroughly ecumenical sense of Christian identity, one that would become the hallmark of her religious orientation in her adult life. Her Christian identity, in this sense, was not merely the transmission of a compassionate, liberal and politically engaged sense of mission from father to daughter, although her father's influence was clearly important. Nor was it primarily a matter of her inheritance of an intellectual tradition of 'rational divines' from the Scottish Enlightenment, even though the United Free Church of Scotland's liberal theology played a role.[30] It was an identity forged through Christian fellowship and common practice. Initially, this fellowship was with family and with the family's missionary networks in Britain. Her Hunter relatives in

[26] WC, MW A2.2 Pocket Diary for 1927, entry for 9 July.
[27] 'The Presbyterian Churches' in Daniel Patter, ed., *The Cambridge Dictionary of Christianity* (Cambridge: Cambridge University Press, 2000), 1006.
[28] WC, A2.2 Pocket Diary for 1927, entry for 26 July.   [29] *Ibid.*, 11 September 1927 ff.
[30] Hugh Macmillan, 'From "Rational Divines" to the Northern Rhodesian Mines: Christianity, Political Economy and Social Anthropology in Southern Africa' (unpublished paper presented at the Monica Hunter Centenary Conference, Hogsback, 24–6 June 2008).

Scotland were devout Presbyterians. Her father's brother, Ian, was a lay preacher who 'always travel[led] armed with a sermon'. When journeying around Scotland with her mother, who accompanied her overseas for the early months, she wrote that it was 'raining missionary breakfasts'[31] and reported on visits with 'Mumsie' to the Women's Missionary College and foreign mission evenings with lectures and discussions.[32] A number of her college friends were the children of missionaries and at least two members of her 'family' (her Girton friendship circle) wanted to become missionaries themselves.

During her first term at Girton her closest bonds were with her Presbyterian sisters. They attended chapel together after dinner and said prayers together twice a week. She emerged as a religious leader among her peers, being elected at the beginning of her second year as the head of the Student Christian Movement in college. There were some forty active participants in their SCM. She led bi-weekly prayer meetings and discussions in their study group, which, significantly, took 'comparative religions' as the subject for successive seminars.[33] They discussed Islam, Hinduism and Gandhi's religious philosophy at meetings, although they all remained committed Christians. Her outward-looking Christian identity was fostered by international religious conferences between terms. Her letters home after each of these meetings bubble over with a sense of excitement about lessons learnt from engaging with those of different religious, national and cultural backgrounds. At the Second Annual Conference of British and Dominion students at Geneva in September 1928, she noted that the 'colonials' included 'a lot of Indians, several Canadians, a Burmese girl and at least one representative from Australia and New Zealand'. The only other South African delegate told her that 'he's quite losing his colour prejudice over here'.[34] Here she met a young Englishman called Godfrey Wilson, who was studying 'Greats' (classics) at Oxford.

'I love England now', she wrote early in her second year, noting that she was beginning to develop an English accent, 'but you can't help belonging to South Africa when you have been born there.'[35] While reading Sarah Gertrude Millin's *South Africans* she commented: 'I had never realized quite how South African (and how proud of the fact) I was until last night, when everything she said seemed to strike a chord with one.'[36] When she saw the new South African flag for the first time, she 'got so excited over it that all the other people on top

---

[31] WC, B5.1, Letters MW to her father, Monica Hunter to David Hunter, 19 May 1927.
[32] *Ibid.*, 2 June 1927. [33] *Ibid.*, 28 October 1928. [34] *Ibid.*, 9 September 1928.
[35] *Ibid.*, 25 November 1928. [36] *Ibid.*, 3 May 1928.

Figure 2.2: Monica at work in the Stanley Library, Girton College, Cambridge, 1930. This was the year in which she completed her undergraduate degree, having earlier switched from history to social anthropology, and won an Anthony Wilkin Scholarship which funded her fieldwork in Pondoland and the Eastern Cape from 1931.

An adopted daughter 75

of the [London] bus stared [at me]'. She asked her father for more information about the new national anthem (*Die Stem*).[37]

What was it about being South African that she had come to consider important? The letters from Cambridge suggest that her sense of national identity had become bound up with her desire to challenge the current segregationist direction in South African politics and contribute to a multi-racial society in South Africa based on sound Christian moral values. In this sense her much more robustly independent political and religious identity at Cambridge, her new left-Labour political views, her transformed inner sense of self and her more thoroughly ecumenical Christian identity were channelled into a vision of her future. As she put it in one of her letters, 'it would make a very great difference if some of our generation of students in South Africa could honestly tackle the Native Question from a Christian point of view'. Where some of her peers attributed switching to anthropology in their graduate years to chance events like meeting the dynamic Malinowski on a train journey,[38] her decision to study African anthropology was taken un-usually early – in just her second year of university study – and was motivated by her long-standing but now much more independent and dynamic identity as a South African Christian devoted to a vision of social service.

Christian networks in Pondoland and the Eastern Cape, 1931–1932

Given that Christianity was so important in the childhood and under-graduate years of Monica Hunter, what role did it play in her life and work during her first and, ultimately most famous, anthropological study, *Reaction to Conquest* (1936), which was based on fieldwork conducted in Pondoland and the Eastern Cape in 1931 and 1932, and substantially reworked from her Cambridge University doctoral thesis of 1934?[39]

In 1930 in my last term [as an undergraduate] at Cambridge the professor [Thomas Hodson] asked me what I was going to do. I had no idea. I was told by Hodson to apply for a research grant [the Anthony Wilkin scholarship] ...

---

[37] *Ibid.*, 13 June 1928.
[38] Meyer Fortes, 'An Anthropologist's Apprenticeship', *Annual Review of Anthropology*, 7 (1978), 3.
[39] Compare Monica Hunter, 'Effects of Culture Contact on the Pondo of South Africa' (Ph.D. thesis, Cambridge University, 1934) with the more clearly structured, regionally comparative, and professionally produced text of 1936. Most of the reworking was done in Lovedale in 1934.

76 Pioneers of the Field

I thought this was rather a way out idea, but I did what I was told. I left Cambridge [after the May exams] without knowing what was going to happen. The scholarship was granted. Hodson said, 'Write and tell us when you begin work and what you are doing.' That was his idea of supervision.[40]

Audrey Richards confirms that Monica lacked the proper formal training in fieldwork method that she and Isaac Schapera, the other pioneers of extensive and intensive professional fieldwork in the region, had been given in London while working with Malinowski in the late 1920s.[41] Monica only attended Malinowski's seminar in 1933 while back at Cambridge writing up her doctoral thesis. Given this lack of clear guidance, she was forced to rely on South African networks during her eighteen months in the field. As we shall see below, Winifred Hoernlé acted as her informal supervisor. Here I explore how her family's Lovedale networks allowed her to establish a foothold and a sense of legitimacy in the field.

In February 1931 she set out for the field, choosing to begin in Auckland Village (e-Hala), 'a village of 583 inhabitants ... just on the border between the old Cape Colony and what was Kaffirland [Xhosaland]'.[42] As I have documented elsewhere, she was driven back and forth from her family home in Alice to this first field-site in her father's new Buick. She only occasionally journeyed on horseback, the mode of transport she would use extensively in Pondoland reserve.[43] She had seen Auckland Village dozens of times before while driving past to their holiday home Hunterstoun in the Hogsback mountains.[44] She boarded for the three months between February and April 1931 with family friends, the local shopkeeper and his wife Mr and Mrs Argyle. Women were the focus group for her early interviews as she set out to study 'the effects of contact with Europeans on the life of Bantu women'.[45] Indeed the status and family life of African women in the region would be the subject of her first two published journal articles

---

[40] WC, Uncatalogued materials, CD: Monica Wilson interviewed by Francis and Lindy Wilson, Hogsback, Eastern Cape, 'Pondoland', July 1979 [Monica Wilson interview: 'Pondoland'].

[41] Audrey Richards, 'Monica Wilson: An Appreciation' in Michael Whisson and Martin E. West, eds., *Religion and Social Change in Southern Africa: Essays in Honour of Monica Wilson* (Cape Town: David Philip; London: Rex Collings, 1975), 3.

[42] Monica Hunter, 'Methods of Study of Culture Contact', *Africa*, 7, 1 (1934), 336.

[43] See Andrew Bank, 'The "Intimate Politics" of Fieldwork: Monica Hunter and her African Assistants, Pondoland and the Eastern Cape, 1931–1932', *Journal of Southern African Studies*, 34, 3 (2008), 560–1.

[44] Monica Wilson interview: 'Pondoland'.

[45] Monica Hunter, 'In Pondoland', *The Girton Review*, 92 (Easter Term 1933), 27.

An adopted daughter 77

Figure 2.3: 'Nosente, the Mother of Compassion', Auckland Village, 1931. Nosente was a Christian convert whose testimony about the rapid

78   Pioneers of the Field

and her first published book review.[46] She wrote of her reliance on Lovedale connections, on 'a number of the people I had known since childhood ... ' and her acceptance into this Christian community. 'I spent days chatting in their huts. I played with their children, sat through their all-night concerts in the school house, and joined the women when they went to build the hut for the boys to be circumcised that year.'[47] Given her initial lack of fluency in Xhosa, she (or rather her father) employed 'the woman teacher at Auckland Village [primary school], a girl of twenty-two' to teach Monica to speak the language fluently,[48] but also to act as her intermediary in establishing contacts with older women in the location who were her primary informants.

After three months in Auckland Village, Monica wanted to study in a more remote rural area with more limited 'contact' influence. She chose the Pondoland reserve. Here again her Lovedale networks were crucial. 'Uncle Kenneth' (Hobart Houghton), the husband of her mother's sister, suggested that she would be safe at Ntibane, a mission station in the Ngqeleni District, 35 kilometres south-east of Umtata and 15 kilometres inland from the sea. There was a store opposite the mission station and, on his rounds as a School Inspector for the Transkei, Uncle Kenneth had established that the German storekeeper's wife was a member of the famous Soga family from Lovedale. She was the granddaughter of the Edinburgh-trained Lovedale minister and linguist Tiyo Soga. Like Monica, Mary Dreyer (née Soga) (1886–1950) had Scottish ancestry and had grown up on

---

Caption for Figure 2.3: (cont.)

social changes in the Eastern Cape between the time of her birth in the late 1860s and that of Monica's fieldwork in the 1930s was the subject of an autobiography that Monica recorded, edited and published in Margery Perham's *Ten Africans* (1936).[49]

---

[46] Monica Hunter, 'Results of Culture Contact on the Pondo and Xosa Family', *South African Journal of Science*, 29 (1932), 681–6, and especially Monica Hunter, 'The Effects of Contact with Europeans on the Status of Pondo Women', *Africa*, 6, 3 (1933), 259–76. See also Monica Hunter, 'Review of *Valenge Women* by E. Dora Earthy', *Africa*, 7, 1 (1934), 110–12. For discussion of the focus of women anthropologists on 'women's issues' in this early period of fieldwork, see Andrew Bank, 'Chapter 1: Family, Friends and Mentors' in Bank and Bank, eds., *Inside African Anthropology*, 60–1.

[47] Hunter, 'Methods of Study of Culture Contact', 336.

[48] On her initial lack of fluency in Xhosa, see Hunter, *Reaction to Conquest*, 12.

[49] Monica Hunter, 'The Story of Nosente, the Mother of Compassion' in Margery Perham, ed., *Ten Africans* (London: Faber and Faber, 1936), after page 135.

An adopted daughter

a mission station (Willowvale). She may well have been schooled at Lovedale, though twenty years earlier than Monica. She played a decisive role as interpreter and intermediary during Monica's highly productive period at Ntibane between May and November 1931.

I was not fluent in Xhosa when I began work, and at the first store [Ntibane] was greatly helped by my hostess who was a skilful interpreter. As time went on I began to speak easily... The women [purchasing cloth at the store] were in the habit of chatting to my hostess, who was extremely popular. I was accepted as her sister, and shared the goodwill shown towards her.[50]

Through Mary Soga's networks Monica attended seventy-three beer drinks, eight girls' initiation ceremonies, three weddings, two feasts for diviners and a number of ritual killings, most within an 8-kilometre

Figure 2.4: The trading store run by Mary Soga and her husband at Ntibane, Western Pondoland (south-east of Mthatha) where Monica spent seven highly productive months doing fieldwork. She claimed to have developed her understanding of Pondo culture through sitting on mealie sacks in the store and listening to the gossip of clients, like the young Pondo women in the foreground.[51]

---

[50] Hunter, *Reaction to Conquest*, 12.
[51] WC, Uncatalogued negative formerly contained in a brown box containing Monica and Godfrey Wilson's fieldwork photographs. See Hunter, 'Methods of Study of Culture Contact'.

80   Pioneers of the Field

radius of the store.[52] Mary also put her in contact with fellow converts. 'I made friends [through Soga's network] with members of the Christian community, and went to women's meetings, prayer meetings, school concerts, weddings, and funerals, as I did to the festivals of the pagan community.'[53] In later life Monica recalled that 'I thought nothing of working nine or ten hours a day … I was *completely swallowed* by the excitement of doing this research.' Mary was forty-five years old as opposed to Monica's twenty-three. 'She kept a very motherly eye on me. She didn't like my going round alone [on visits in the countryside].'[54] Mary sent young women to accompany Monica on these visits if she was unable to go along herself, guiding Monica in matters of etiquette and taking an active part in conducting the interviews.[55] She doubled up as Monica's main informant, especially on the changing status of women in Pondo culture. There are scores of handwritten field-notes from Ntibane that reveal that Monica's information on this subject, the theme of her first major published article on Pondoland,[56] had been gleaned from 'Mrs D' or 'M.D.'.[57]

In working from four stores and a mission hospital in Eastern Pondoland to the north of Ntibane between July and November the following year, she relied on a Christian 'clerk' named Michael Geza. He acted variously as her protector, sometimes being referred to as her 'bodyguard' in her notes, guide, facilitator of contacts, tutor on the male world of the Pondo and recorder of some 200 pages of field-notes on *iintsomi* (traditional tales), *ukubusa* (gifts), *iingoma* (songs), traditional medicine and so on. He was, she revealed, 'a retired policeman' who owned a motor-car, lived in a well-built brick house and whose six sons were all school teachers.[58] Like her later 'clerks' in Bunyakyusa, Michael Geza was a man-between, 'educated and a Christian, but [one who] came of a pagan family …' In his case this was a family 'of doctors, his ancestors having been doctors to the imiZizi chiefs [those of a Pondo clan] for nine generations'.[59] A letter she wrote to Winifred Hoernlé in October 1932, one of surprisingly few surviving letters from the field, gives a clear

---

[52] Hunter, *Reaction to Conquest*, 356.   [53] *Ibid.*, 11.
[54] Monica Wilson interview: 'Pondoland'. Her emphasis.
[55] WC, B5.2, Correspondence between Monica Hunter and Jessie Hunter, Monica Hunter to Jessie Hunter, 2 November 1931, Ntibane.
[56] Hunter, 'The Effects of Contact with Europeans on the Status of Pondo Women'.
[57] For further details about Mary Soga and her relationship with Monica, see Andrew Bank, 'The "Intimate Politics" of Fieldwork', 561–5.
[58] Hunter, *Reaction to Conquest*, 11.
[59] *Ibid.*, 12. For more detail on Michael Geza and Monica's relationship with him, see Bank, 'The "Intimate Politics" of Fieldwork', 568–71.

An adopted daughter 81

indication of the continued importance of her Lovedale network to her work in Pondoland.

> I was at Holy Cross mission the weekend before last. I particularly wished to meet Archdeacon Leary, who was born, and has worked all his life in Pondoland, and whom I was told could help me much with Pondo history (as he did) and I went visiting in the kraals round the mission ... I dropped into a hut for shelter the other day, when riding to Holy Cross, and was promptly given tea, and treated as a friend – Fingo immigrants from the Cape and some of them educated at Lovedale.[60]

It was especially during her fieldwork in the 'native locations' of East London, conducted between these periods of research in Western and then Eastern Pondoland, that her Lovedale contacts proved invaluable. East Bank location in East London was extremely volatile when Monica began working there in March 1932. There had been extensive strike and trade union activism led by a newly formed off-branch of the ICU named the Independent Industrial and Commercial Workers' Union (IICU).[61] Her field-notes confirm that some township residents felt a deep-seated hostility towards whites. 'Why do you come and ask these things? You have never been ruled and ill-treated by foreigners.'[62]

Her father was sufficiently concerned for her welfare to employ a male 'bodyguard'. As with Geza, her East Bank bodyguard doubled up as an interpreter. He too was a Christian, in this case a Wesleyan church elder and prominent political leader, R.H. Godlo.[63] It was, in fact, only because the leader of the IICU, Clements Kadalie, vouched for her at a specially arranged public meeting that she was permitted to conduct interviews. 'He said that he had had a meal in my father's house and he could vouch for me.'[64] She also relied on an ANC veteran and Location Advisory Board member, the 74-year-old Walter Benson Rubusana, and his wife Mrs Rubusana (formerly Kashe), who 'came from Tyumie' and was yet another 'daughter of Lovedale'. Where Mary Soga had accompanied Monica to distant beer-drinks, or on visits to elderly men, Mrs Rubusana took her to teas in Christian households. Here again her field-notes are a surer indication of presence and influence than the later

---

[60] WHP, Loose letter in Box 3: 'Bantu', folder labelled 'Bantu Religion', Monica Hunter to Winifred Hoernlé, 4 October 1932, Ntontela.

[61] For a fuller account of the political radicalism, see Leslie J. Bank, 'City Dreams and Country Magic: Re-reading Monica Hunter's East London Fieldnotes' in Bank and Bank, eds., *Inside African Anthropology*, 95–116.

[62] WC, Uncatalogued materials, Fieldnote in Folder 'East London'.

[63] Godlo was an elder in the Wesleyan Church, a Location Advisory Board member and would later serve on the regional Native Representative Council.

[64] Monica Wilson interview: 'Childhood'.

82   Pioneers of the Field

published texts.[65] It is difficult to disaggregate her views from those of her father and the Rubusanas in that pioneering section of her published work, 'Part III The Bantu in Town', given the extent to which the moral condemnation of a materialistic and sexually promiscuous youth was part of their shared Christian liberal discourse.[66]

Even in the case of her final two months of fieldwork in November and December 1932 visiting farms in the Adelaide, Bedford and Albany districts closer to home, before returning to Cambridge to write up her doctoral thesis, her family and Christian networks were essential.

For farms I could only get access if I could get a personal introduction. So again it was dependent on Uncle Kenneth who used to inspect in all of those areas and he sent me to the various farmers. And then I picked up with a lot of old school friends and managed to go from one farm to another.[67]

In short, Monica's fieldwork at each of her successive sites – in Auckland Village, Ntibane, East Bank, Western Pondoland and Eastern Cape farms – was reliant on the mediation of her Lovedale connections.

What of the analysis of Christianity as a theme in her published study? The Christian community in Pondoland numbered only around 10,000, or 4 per cent of the reserve's population, and her discussion was cut back in the published text to a brief overview chapter outlining its history, the influences of the different missionary societies, and what she regarded as the relatively separate communal identity of Christians in Pondoland.[68] The impact of Christian beliefs on 'pagan' culture was, however, a central theme across the study, as indicated by this entry in the index.

Christians: and ancestors, 268–9, 502–3, 536. Attitude of pagans towards, 353–4, 560–1. And cattle, 66. And childbirth, 150, 158. And circumcision, 477, 529. And death, 349–51. And festivals, 373–6, 468–9, 523. And girls' initiation, 174, 214–6, 530. And influence of, 351–3, 355, 504, 548. And inheritance, 121. And magic and witchcraft, 79, 84, 274, 280–1, 293–4, 302, 313, 318, 347, 489–93, 502–3, 531, 539–40. And marriage, 129, 183–4, 213–22, 483–5, 531–3. And social groups, 60–1, 351, 46.[69]

Christianity also features prominently in the most political of her chapters, an extended concluding essay entitled 'Tendencies', which offers a vivid account of African nationalism in South Africa of the mid-1930s. This would be the chapter which evoked the greatest interest from

---

[65] WC, Uncatalogued materials, Fieldnote in Folder 'East London'.
[66] For more information about the influence of the Rubusanas and these other cultural brokers on her East London fieldwork, see Andrew Bank, 'The "Intimate Politics" of Knowledge', 565–8; Leslie J. Bank, 'City Dreams, Country Magic', 101–10.
[67] Monica Wilson interview: 'Pondoland'.
[68] Hunter, *Reaction to Conquest*, Chapter 8: Christianity, 349–55.   [69] *Ibid.*, 579.

Figure 2.5: The first of the page-spread features published in the *Illustrated London News* of 22 August 1936 in 'appreciation' of *Reaction to Conquest*. The photographs were selected from the twenty-eight plates that featured in the book.[70]

---

[70] WC, H1.3, Reviews of *Reaction to Conquest*.

84   Pioneers of the Field

reviewers in what I have elsewhere termed 'the media event' that followed the publication of the first edition of *Reaction to Conquest* in July 1936.[71] She wrote the chapter back home in Lovedale *after* the submission of her Cambridge doctoral thesis in January 1934, along with the two other sections of the book which foregrounded social change (Part II Bantu in Town and Part III Bantu on Farms).[72] Her tone suggests that she anticipated that some readers might find her account of African nationalism and the growth of anti-white sentiment disturbing. 'I can merely give my impressions of their attitude [those of Africans], quote comments made to me, summarize the points made by Bantu writers in such publications as are available, and describe the organized action taken.'[73]

Her essay presented a summary of nationalist sentiment in the African press and in African literature, an outline of the history of African political resistance from the Eastern Cape frontier wars and Xhosa cattle-killing in the nineteenth century to the rise in recent decades of the African National Congress and the trade union movement led by the ICU and IICU. She ended with an analysis of the emergence of African independent churches during the previous half century and of other African religious movements that had reacted to conquest, notably the 'Israelites' and the 'Wellington movement'.[74]

It was, in fact, this new theme of African Christianity and religious movements that she had envisaged pursuing after completing her Pondoland study. In May 1933 she applied to the International African Institute for a 36-month fellowship beginning in January 1934 to 'make a study of native movements, such as the "Cattle-killing" of 1857, the "Israelites", and the "Wellington movement" ... important expressions of the reaction of the native mind to European political and religious ideas,' as well as of 'the effect of Christian missions on the community, among Pondo, Xosa and Fengu.' Her application was successful, only because of the vigorous support of Winifred Hoernlé, backed by Isaac Schapera and Alfred Hoernlé. These three were the most influential figures on the Inter-University Committee for African Studies that assessed the applications of the South African scholars who applied

---

[71] See Bank, 'The "Intimate Politics" of Knowledge', 571.

[72] Compare *Reaction to Conquest* with the relatively brief and unprocessed analysis in Hunter, 'Effects of Culture Contact on the Pondo of South Africa' (Ph.D. thesis, Cambridge University, 1934), Chapter 16 An Urban Community. Her thesis and book were not the same text as has been suggested by, amongst others, Francis Wilson, 'Monica Hunter Wilson: An Appreciation' in Monica Hunter, *Reaction to Conquest: The Effects of Contact with Europeans on the Pondo of South Africa* (Berlin: LIT on behalf of the International African Institute, 2009: Classics in African Anthropology Series, 4th edn.), 1.

[73] Hunter, *Reaction to Conquest*, 554.   [74] Hunter, *Reaction to Conquest*, 557–74.

An adopted daughter   85

for African Institute fellowships. One committee member felt that her Pondo work was not of sufficient quality to warrant further funding, while others felt that her application was compromised by the (independently acquired) news of her engagement to Godfrey Wilson. In view of the government linguist Lestrade, her engagement 'seems to weaken her case since if she does marry it might very well happen that she would be lost to anthropology soon after'. Winifred Hoernlé was annoyed. 'Since the man to whom she is engaged is also an anthropologist, it is possible that her marriage would make her very much better fitted for her task than she is now ... To bar her simply on the ground of her engagement, which may be a very great point in favour of her usefulness, would be ridiculous.'[75]

In the event, her engagement to Godfrey Wilson in 1933 did lead to a change in direction: that of taking her from South to Central Africa rather than that of swapping the field for the kitchen as her male elders seemed to anticipate. Before examining Monica's fieldwork and findings on African Christian communities in south-west Tanganyika, it is necessary to say something about the hidden story of the influence of Winifred Hoernlé on her Pondoland study, as well as the relationships of both women with 'the founding father of British anthropology', Bronislaw Malinowski.

A Christian connection: Hunter and Hoernlé

A shared commitment to Christianity and to a discipline respectful of African cultural difference lay at the heart of what would become a warm intellectual friendship between Monica and Winifred Hoernlé. It began during her two years of fieldwork in Pondoland in 1931 and 1932 as Monica later recalled.

I got a lot of help from Mrs Hoernlé who was so shocked at the idea of a girl going into the field on her own without proper supervision as she would have said ... [S]he said to me in an offhand way that if I would like to write in once a month to her, she would be happy to answer. So I used to write letters about what I had seen and she would ask all sorts of questions ... And then I would send her half a dozen cases ...[76]

---

[75] Witwatersrand University, William Cullen Library, Rheinallt-Jones Papers, Box 174: AD843/RJ/K6.18.1, File for the Inter-University Committee for African Studies, Letters from Schapera and Oldham to Rheinallt-Jones, 1933–1934; Applications for funding from Monica Hunter, June 1933. Thanks to Robert Gordon for providing me with scanned photocopies of the relevant letters in this debate.

[76] Monica Wilson Interview: 'Pondoland'.

86   Pioneers of the Field

Their correspondence intensified towards the end of Monica's time in the field. Take, for example, these letters written in October and November 1932. Monica wrote on 4 October from the trading store at Ntontela in Eastern Pondoland with detailed information across three single-spaced typed pages on Pondo tribal and clan-naming practices, medicine, witchcraft and institutions of chieftainship. She assured Mrs Hoernlé that she would take her advice and 'collect cases'.[77] A fortnight later she wrote again requesting 'permission' to leave her field-site. 'If you approve I think I shall return to Lovedale ... '[78] Mrs Hoernlé encouraged her to take a break from fieldwork. 'One needs to get away and look at one's information in perspective; one gets stale and needs [the] stimulus of collected thinking about one's notes.'

I have been thinking a great deal about sacrifice lately ... What I would like to know from you is the emotional reaction of the [Pondo] people to a sacrifice. I take it that there is at the least a release of tension e.g. on the part of the sick person. Is there more than this? What type of emotional reaction is there? What type of comment do you find? Is there *ululating* [jubilant throat-singing] and *giya-ing* [dancing in isiZulu]? Do watch carefully for these reactions.

On 27 November she sent Monica a thesis written by a UCT student who had been in Pondoland for a month and encouraged her to collect information about *ukumetsha*, the custom of sexual relations between boys and girls before marriage. As ever, her questions were meticulously detailed.

How many such *ukumetsha* relationships would a girl or a boy normally have? What is the relationship between persons who have had such relationships after the marriage of both of them? You mentioned once that the lover of a woman was sometimes called in to influence her when nothing else could ... Are love matches rather resisted but sometimes allowed, or would you say that normally within reason a man and a woman are allowed to find one another sexually and through mutual understanding?[79]

Monica warmly acknowledged Mrs Hoernlé's support on the opening page of *Reaction to Conquest* as indicated by the epigraph to this chapter. Mrs Hoernlé assisted Monica in securing additional funding for her study, something which caused great anxiety as the manuscript got

---

[77] WHP, Box labelled 'Bantu', Folder labelled 'Bantu religion', Typed letter, Hunter to Hoernlé, Ntontela, 4 October 1932.

[78] WC, Uncatalogued materials, MW Fieldnotes, Box 8 *Pondo Iintsomi Linguistic* [original label], Hunter to Hoernlé, Ntontela, 18 October 1932: Opening line of draft of typed letter recorded on reverse side of the field note.

[79] *Ibid.*, Hoernlé to Hunter, Johannesburg, 27 November 1932.

An adopted daughter 87

closer to publication. The International African Institute's Director, Dr Dietrich Westermann, had written to Monica suggesting that she abbreviate her manuscript, something she emphatically refused to do. 'I am not at present prepared to publish portions only.'[80] She turned for support to Mrs Hoernlé.

> Professor Hoernlé asked when we were in Johannesburg [in June 1934 when Monica and Malinowksi were hosted by the Hoernlés during the New Education Fellowship conference] that I should let him know if the Institute were unable to publish ... It seems very doubtful whether they will publish in full without outside help. Would there be any chance of getting help from the recent Carnegie Grant for Educational and Social Research in the Union? ... Many many thanks for your constant help. There would be precious little chance of getting anything done without it.[81]

Mrs Hoernlé persuaded the Research Board in South Africa to offer financial support from the Carnegie Grant, which was explicitly acknowledged on the title page.[82] She later wrote a laudatory review of *Reaction to Conquest* which was published in *Africa* in 1937. It was the first in her series of reviews, prefaces and other writings in which she promoted the publications of her intellectual 'daughters'. In later chapters, I will discuss her reviews of Ellen Hellmann's two monographs, her preface to Hilda Kuper's *African Aristocracy* and her review of Eileen Krige's co-authored *Realm of the Rain-Queen*.

She began by highlighting the former Prime Minister Jan Smuts' prefatory comment that Hunter's study was 'worthy to be placed by the side of Junod's *Life of a South African Tribe*',[83] but claimed: 'I myself would go further and say that it is a more valuable book for the anthropologist and the sociologist than Junod's study ... ' She commended Hunter for her 'remarkably clear picture of the moulding forces at work in the *imizi* [homesteads]. For anyone who wishes to understand the tendencies at work making for a strong patrilineal organization, for a strongly emphasized patrilineal ancestor cult, for the peculiarly restricted and restrained lives of married women, this book is indispensable.' She praised Hunter for her incisive analysis of sexuality and gender relations in Pondo society, something that has also drawn laudatory comment from contemporary scholars. It is partly on these grounds

---

[80] WC, D11, Correspondence with the International Institute of African Languages and Culture, 1935–1939, Monica Hunter to J.H. Oldham, 16 April 1935, Isumba, Tanganyika.

[81] *Ibid.*, Monica Hunter to Hoernlé, Isumba, Rungwe District, South-West Tanganyika, 9 May 1935.

[82] *Ibid.*, J.H. Oldham to 'Mrs G.B. Wilson', 31 May 1935.

[83] J.C. Smuts, 'Foreword' in Hunter, *Reaction to Conquest*, viii.

88   Pioneers of the Field

that Jonny Steinberg has described the book as 'one of the finest ethnographic monographs ever penned in South Africa'.[84]

With regard to the sections of the book dealing with social change, she criticized Smuts for confining his praise to Hunter's analysis of tradition. Indeed, Monica privately doubted whether Smuts had read the latter part of the book on social change and contemporary politics, but was 'much relieved' that he did not. She feared that Smuts might allow the kind of segregationist sympathies that he expressed in his Oxford lectures in 1929 to colour his commentary on her empathetic concluding analysis of African nationalist organizations including the African National Congress. 'The book is introduced by him as a non-political study of objective facts which is just what I wanted.'[85] The review highlighted the particular value of Monica's analysis of African life in East London and Grahamstown, as well as her sensitive portrayal of the plight of African farm labourers. 'The position of Africans on European farms, as described by her [Hunter], is tragic and the gravity of this verdict is enhanced by the reminder that there are many other types of farming community where the lives of Africans are still more alarming.' Monica presented a summary of her case study of African labourers on twenty-nine Eastern Cape farms in Isaac Schapera's edited collection, *The Bantu-Speaking Tribes of South Africa: An Ethnological Survey* which was published in the same year as Hoernlé's review. As she explained in her opening line: 'Of the social life of the Bantu living on farms (approximately 35 per cent of the Native population of the Union) very little is known.'[86] Hoernlé concluded by commending Hunter for the lucid overview of the recent rise of African political organizations and religious movements,[87] the theme of her book which, as noted above, drew the most praise in a host of laudatory reviews.[88]

---

[84] Jonny Steinberg, *Three-Letter Plague: A Young Man's Journey through a Great Epidemic* (Johannesburg and Cape Town: Jonathan Ball Publishers, 2008), 242. See also Peter Delius and Clive Glaser, 'Sexual Socialisation in South Africa: A Historical Perspective' in Peter Delius and Liz Walker, *African Studies Special Issue: AIDS in Context*, 61, 1 (2002), 27–54; Peter Delius and Clive Glaser, 'The Myths of Polygamy: A History of Extra-Marital and Multi-Partnership Sex in South Africa', *South African Historical Journal*, 50 (2004), 84–114.

[85] WC, D5.1 Letters MW to her father, Monica Hunter to David Hunter, 28 May 1936, London.

[86] Monica Hunter, 'The Bantu on European-Owned Farms' in Isaac Schapera, ed., *The Bantu-Speaking Tribes of South Africa: An Ethnological Survey* (London: George Routledge and Sons, 1937), 389.

[87] Winifred Hoernlé, 'Review of *Reaction to Conquest*', *Africa*, 10, 1 (1937), 121–6.

[88] WC, H1.3 Reviews; for a summary, see Bank, 'The "Intimate Politics" of Fieldwork', 571.

An adopted daughter 89

There were many private admirers. Godfrey felt the book was 'rather good'. Malinowski was 'full of genuine enthusiasm', rightly regarding it as 'by far the best book on [culture] contact on the scientific market, and ... an excellent piece of really scientific anthro' – sociology.'[89]

Studying Christian communities in Bunyakyusa, 1935–1938

Monica's fieldwork in south-west Tanganyika would be even more thoroughly collaborative than her fieldwork in Pondoland had been. Here her primary partner in knowledge production was her husband, Godfrey. He too was brought up in a deeply religious Christian family. His father was the famous Shakespearian scholar John Dover Wilson (1881–1969), and his mother was the daughter of the vicar of Harston. Godfrey grew up in his grandfather's vicarage. He too was a socially committed Christian and active member of the Student Christian Movement, in his case at Oxford in the late 1920s.

They were both just twenty when they met at the conference in Geneva in September 1928. It was under her influence that Godfrey chose to take up social anthropology after graduating with a first. In 1932 he began studying under Malinowski at the London School of Economics. He proposed to her during her final three terms of doctoral study at Cambridge in 1933 when she attended the famous Malinowski seminar series, although she was never as loyal and closely bound to 'the master' as Godfrey, whom Malinowski came to regard as his favourite disciple.[90] After a difficult engagement on account of Godfrey's periodic depressions,[91] they got married at the Hogsback in the Amatola Mountains of the Eastern Cape in February 1935. This was where her family had established a holiday home and retreat, to which Monica herself would ultimately retire.

After a brief honeymoon in the Drakensberg, they travelled together to Tanganyika in late March 1935. They stayed in an old disused hospital building at Isumba, some 20 kilometres into the highlands of the Rungwe district of south-west Tanganyika with magnificent views of Lake Malawi and the Livingstone Mountains. Godfrey was a highly gifted

---

[89] WC, B4.4 Correspondence between Godfrey Wilson and Bronislaw Malinowski, Malinowski to Wilson, 1 December 1936.

[90] This much is evident from his reference for Godfrey in 1935. See WC, B4.4 Correspondence between Godfrey Wilson and Bronislaw Malinowski, Malinowski to Wilson, 15 August 1935 with enclosed reference labelled 'Bloody private'.

[91] S. Morrow, '"This is from the Firm": The Anthropological Partnership of Monica and Godfrey Wilson' (unpublished paper presented at the Monica Wilson Centenary Conference, Hogsback, 24–6 June 2008).

90   Pioneers of the Field

linguist and was relatively fluent in ki-Nyakyusa, based on the six months that he had spent in the field between August 1934 and January 1935. He and their young, educated, well-travelled Christian 'clerk' Leonard Mwaisumo had created an English–kiNyakyusa dictionary for her use. During her early months in the field she was deeply dependent on Leonard for his knowledge of the language. Her first unofficial 'field report', written as ever to Mrs Hoernlé, gives a vivid sense of their highly sociable daily lives in the field and her initial focus on working with women, as she had done in Pondoland.

> You said you would like to hear sometime how we are getting on. The weeks go by so quickly it seems as if I had just arrived ... I have been concentrating on the language, and can read texts, and understand quite a lot now; conversation is just beginning to come. Many roots are similar to Xhosa roots and that makes it easier to understand, but when apparently similar verb forms turn up with different meanings, speech is difficult. Godfrey has found over seventy tenses and a new one appears every two or three days ... Constantly people are dropping in to chat with us – chiefs, councillors, rainmakers, doctors, young men, women, all come to chat and share tea if it is going ... If Malinowski saw us at work I do not think he would be perturbed about our doing separate jobs. The subjects I have been investigating so far are marriage from the women's point of view, girls' initiation, 'ukuhlonipha' (here called okotila onkamwana) [African women's language of deference] and women's work. While Godfrey was talking to a man this morning, I was with his wives reaping a millet field![92]

If one pieces together her field-notes from these early weeks, here again recorded on separate slips of loose sheets rather than in well-ordered numbered notebooks as was Godfrey's habit, she was most interested in economics: the seasonal crops in April and May, the systems of planting, crop management and land tenure. She would reflect in later years how struck she had been by the beauty and bounty of Bunyakyusa, a landscape where the rich soils and warm climate provided sufficient food for subsistence. This was a marked contrast with her experience of African poverty in the dry areas of Pondoland in a time of economic depression. It may be that this regional contrast was one of the reasons why she underestimated the extent of prior colonial disruption in Bunyakyusa during the Great War and its aftermath, and was inclined to present too cohesive a portrait of traditional Nyakyusa culture in her later books.[93]

---

[92] WC, D11 Correspondence with the International Institute of African Languages and Culture, 1935–1939, Hunter to Hoernlé, Isumba, Rungwe District, South-West Tanganyika, 9 May 1935.

[93] James G. Ellison, 'Transforming Obligations, Performing Identity: Making the Nyakyusa in a Colonial Context' (unpublished D.Phil. thesis, University of Florida, 1999).

An adopted daughter   91

It is also difficult to disentangle her later reconstructions of Nyakyusa age-villages, kinship rituals and communal rituals from her memories of these years of passionate and productive work with Godfrey, on whose seventy-eight notebooks these three studies were heavily reliant. Rebecca Marsland has documented a divergence in their respective 'fieldwork styles'. She contrasts the field presence of Godfrey Wilson, the gregarious, immersed participant, with that of Monica, the more reserved and relatively remote observer. Marsland demonstrates that his notebooks reveal a degree of engagement with Nyakyusa culture which Monica was not able to achieve, for a complex of reasons that include her late start, her greater difficulty with the language, her taking primary responsibility for their domestic arrangements, her preference for conducting fieldwork close to missions, a serious bout of malaria which forced her to be 'invalided out' of the field for six crucial months during the most productive phase of the fieldwork, and especially to her inability to establish any equivalent to the masculine world of sociability that Godfrey was able to inhabit.[94]

Her field-notes reveal a deep reliance, even dependence, on their interpreter, Leonard.[95] He and his family were her initial source of information about Nyakyusa Christians. 'We have a very efficient clerk who writes texts, and is teaching me [the language]. He and his wife and mother are Christians, the rest of the family is pagan. Through getting to know them all I am learning about mission contact.' She began her participant observation of the Bunyakyusa Christian communities who she now decided would be the focus of her fieldwork at a Christian village three miles from their home base at Isumba. She explained to Mrs Hoernlé,

Besides a fairly large Christian community living on the mission land [at the Berlin Mission Station of Itete], there are Christian families scattered through the district. I visit them as I do pagans, attend services, and visit schools . . . Here we are keeping very fit and have had no fever so far, but the heat makes it difficult to get through as much work as was possible in Pondoland. It's annoying, but presumably inevitable in the tropics.[96]

---

[94] Rebecca Marsland, 'Pondo Pins and Nyakyusa Hammers: Monica and Godfrey in Bunyakyusa' in Bank and Bank, eds., *Inside African Anthropology*, 129–61.

[95] For a full account of the multiple roles performed by Leonard Mwaisumo in working with Godfrey and then with Monica, as well as of his life history, see Sekibakiba P. Lekgoathi, Timothy Mwakasekele and Andrew Bank, 'Working with the Wilsons: The Brief Career of a "Nyakyusa Clerk" (1910–1938)' in Bank and Bank, eds., *Inside African Anthropology*, 162–92.

[96] WC, D11 Correspondence with the International Institute of African Languages and Culture, 1935–1939, Hunter to Hoernlé, Isumba, 9 May 1935.

92   Pioneers of the Field

In October 1935 she moved with Godfrey and Leonard to the Moravian Mission Station of Rungwe in the highlands some 30 kilometres north of the small town of Tukuyu. They set up tent in a Christian village on the fringe of the mission station. With Leonard's assistance, she documented some thirty-five sermons delivered by the German missionaries and their African converts.[97]

The Wilsons took a break from the field in December 1935. They spent six months in London. Here they digested and wrote up some of their findings. Godfrey presented a paper at Malinowski's seminar. Monica negotiated final details about her Pondoland book, persuading the International African Institute to include forty photographs across twenty-eight plates. Monica now wrote her first essay based on her Nyakyusa fieldwork. Entitled 'An African Christian Morality' it was, significantly, the last time that she published under her maiden name. It offers, along with the opening pages of a draft introduction produced the following year, some indication of the approach that her intended book on Nyakyusa Christians might have taken had her intensely collaborative publications and Godfrey's tragic early death not intervened, encouraging her to write up 'his materials' rather than her own as 'a sacred trust and labour of love'.[98]

Her intended book was likely to have been titled *Cultural Conversion: A Study of Nyakyusa Christians*. She had drawn up a detailed scheme for it by November 1938.[99] Her draft introduction explained that 'the method adopted is to describe the life of the Christian section of the community, to compare it with that of the pagan section, and to analyse the cause of the differences between them'.[100] Christians were a far more significant minority in Bunyakyusa than in Pondoland. Where they comprised some 5 per cent of the population in the Pondoland reserve, they represented 16 per cent of the population of Bunyakyusa in 1937: that is, some 30,000 people spread in communities across the Rungwe District.[101] Monica's article set out by arguing that Christians formed a distinct 'community', or set of communities. They lived for the most part in their own villages adjoining mission stations or 'bush schools', or in separate sections of traditional villages. These African converts had

---

[97] WC, D4 Monica Wilson's field-notes in folder labelled 'Missions/Christian Influences'.

[98] Hammond-Tooke, *Imperfect Interpreters*, 83. This interpretation is imaginatively developed by Rebecca Marsland, 'Pondo Pins and Nyakyusa Hammers'.

[99] WC, B5.1, Monica Hunter to David Hunter, Livingstonia, 20 March 1939 where she refers to revising her earlier outline.

[100] WC, D4.7 Nyakyusa Christians, MW's notes, MS and TS, typed document headed 'Introduction', 1.

[101] Monica Wilson, *Rituals of Kinship among the Nyakyusa* (Oxford: Oxford University Press in association with the IAI, 1957), 197.

developed what she demonstrates to have been a clearly distinctive set of beliefs, albeit with considerable variation between the Moravian and Lutheran communities and between individuals. Indeed, her article is striking for its accommodation of diversity and her ability to convey a range of African Christian voices, from the liberal Christian theology of her research assistant Leonard, who was loth to accept the missionary messages about hell and damnation for his benighted pagan neighbours, to the hellfire theology of her closest friend at Rungwe mission station, a woman elder named Maria, who invited Monica on her lively evangelizing tours through the surrounding countryside.[102]

The organizing concept of 'An African Christian morality' was 'religious sanction'. Monica explored the way in which the religious ideas of the Christians constrained (or sanctioned) their behaviour, which tended to 'enforce social conformity'. This emphasis on social cohesion was very much in keeping with the functionalist model that she and Godfrey had inherited from Malinowski. The first set of beliefs encouraging conformity was 'fear of punishment in the present life'. She outlined the role played by newly constituted Christian 'courts', presided over by missionaries, elders and deacons, in establishing a new moral code. These courts were empowered to reprimand, and even expel and excommunicate, congregants found guilty of transgressing this moral code. Punishable offences included 'theft, adultery [given the Christian insistence on monogamy], fornication, quarrelling between husband and wife, attending pagan dances, consulting diviners, and whispering witchcraft'. The primary form of religious sanction was the belief in 'rewards and punishments in a future life'. 'Pagans believe in survival after death, but their afterworld is traditionally a land of shades, to which no one looks forward.' Christians, by contrast, almost uniformly held out great hope for eternal life, although many were also motivated by fears of damnation, which they had first heard about from the German missionaries. The majority of Christians, she observed, believed 'wrongdoers are in danger of hell fire'. The missionaries had taught that 'If you do not follow the difficult way, you will be burnt.'[103]

The most fascinating section of the article is its extended description of the dream narratives of heaven and hell presented by African Christians.[104] Collectively they demonstrated that, for some believers

---

[102] WC, Uncatalogued CD, Monica Wilson interviewed by Francis and Lindy Wilson, Hogsback, Eastern Cape, 'Bunyakyusa', 4 Jan. 1982.

[103] Monica Hunter, 'An African Christian Morality', *Africa*, 10, 3 (1937), 280–1.

[104] *Ibid.*, Subsection 'The Evidence of Dreams', 281–6.

94 Pioneers of the Field

at least, Christian dogma had become psychologically internalized. 'The evidence of dreams', as her subsection was entitled, was used to show that African Christians had absorbed the biblical message about 'rewards and punishment in the future life' not only in a rational, cognitive sense, in repetitions of fire-and-brimstone missionary sermons or recitations of biblical verses referring to heaven and hell, but at a deeply subconscious level. Her dream narratives of Nyakyusa Christians – and as in the case of her East London fieldwork, they feature much more prominently in the field-notes than in this later published work[105] – illustrate that she was as curious about the inner life and image-world of individual Christian converts as she was about the religious rituals which provided more obvious evidence of what she saw as a powerful sense of group identity among the Lutheran and Moravian congregations. This was to be part of her exploration of Christianity as 'an inner state', as she explicitly highlighted on the opening page of her draft introduction.[106]

Monica never completed her study of the Nyakyusa Christian communities, although parts of it did feature interspersed in chapters across her four monographs on the Nyakyusa as we will see. Godfrey spent a further eighteen months in the field in Bunyakyusa, and Monica close to a year on account of her illness. This time they worked most closely with a quieter, but equally industrious, Christian 'clerk' named John Brown Mwaikambo. He recorded some 2000 notebook pages of information in kiNyakyusa, which Monica used in the documents appended to her later monographs.

Monica and Godfrey began looking around for employment, initially as Mrs Hoernlé's successor at Wits, but then Godfrey was offered the unique opportunity of taking up a newly created post as the first director of the Rhodes-Livingstone Institute in Northern Rhodesia.

'The Co-Production of Scientific Knowledge': Monica and Godfrey in Livingstone, Broken Hill and Lovedale, 1939–1944

The Wilsons relocated to Livingstone in Northern Rhodesia. Godfrey began his urban fieldwork at Broken Hill in May 1939, the month that

---

[105] For an evocative rereading of her (mainly) unpublished dream narratives in the East London field-notes as indicative of deep social stress, as say in recurrent dreams of being chased by police, see Leslie J. Bank, 'City Dreams, Country Magic' in Bank and Bank, eds., *Inside African Anthropology*, 117–24.

[106] WC, D4.7 Nyakyusa Christians, MW's notes, MS and TS, typed document headed 'Introduction', 1.

An adopted daughter 95

Francis was born. Monica reported to her father that Mrs Hoernlé and her 23-year-old son Alwyn attended the christening that August.

They were paying a flying visit to the Falls while Professor Hoernlé was lecturing in Bulawayo ... Mrs Hoernlé is a dear. I maintain that she looked at Francis just as if he was a manuscript submitted for criticism, but anyway he met with approval.[107]

Monica spent most of her time looking after Francis, maintaining their household and writing with Godfrey, often by correspondence when he was away in the field. Their co-authored essay, *The Study of African Society*, was published as the second volume in the series of Rhodes-Livingstone Institute Papers that Godfrey founded. Written for missionaries and colonial officials in Africa, it presented social anthropology as an empathetic discipline based on sound scientific principles.[108] Monica only occasionally had time to join Godfrey in the field, reporting in one letter that she was 'snorting like a war-horse' at the prospect.[109] Sometimes her fieldwork involved making notes about African dress at dancing competitions in Broken Hill.

She later gave a full account of their three years in Northern Rhodesia, highlighting Godfrey's considerable achievements as the first RLI director, including sole or co-authorship of five of the first six papers in the RLI series, most notably his two-part *An Essay on the Economics of Detribalization* (1940 and 1941). As has been widely acknowledged, it broke new ground in recasting anthropology as a sociological discipline which could address themes of global economic development. He documented the emergence of a permanent African labour force in urban areas in Northern Rhodesia, which ran counter to government policy that Africans were but visitors in town.[110]

While his evidence of African urban permanence riled the government, his Christian pacifism and reluctance to enlist riled the settler

---

[107] WC, B5.1, Monica Hunter to David Hunter, Livingstone, 9 July 1939. For her evocative memoir of their three years at the RLI and Godfrey's substantial achievement during these years, see Monica Wilson, 'The First Three Years, 1938–1941', *African Social Research*, 24 (1977) 279–83. The concept in the section subheading is from Schumaker, *Africanizing Anthropology*, 1–22; 227–59.

[108] Godfrey Wilson and Monica Wilson, *The Study of African Society* (Livingstone: Rhodes-Livingstone Institute Papers, No. 2, 1939).

[109] Cited in Morrow, '"This is from the Firm"', 11.

[110] For detailed analysis of his methods of fieldwork in Broken Hill based on field-notes and correspondence, see Karen Tranberg Hansen, 'Urban Research in a Hostile Setting: Godfrey Wilson in Broken Hill, 1938–1940' in Bank and Jacobs, eds., *Kronos: Southern African Histories, Special Issue: The Micro-Politics of Knowledge Production in Southern Africa*, 166–92.

96   Pioneers of the Field

community, as did his 'fraternizing with Africans'. While Godfrey may have been following the precedent he established in rural Tanzania of warm, open and relatively egalitarian relationships across the racial and culture divide, his easy relations and political openness with African friends was seen as politically seditious by settlers, officials and mine managers. He was barred access to his field-site a few months after the Copperbelt Riots and was ultimately pressured into taking the drastic step of tendering his resignation as RLI director, which came 'as a bomb-shell' to their dear friends like Audrey Richards.[111]

Monica and Godfrey now returned to Lovedale along with Francis and their younger son Tim, born in 1941. Godfrey eventually decided that he would enlist in a South African Army ambulance unit, but was sent into the thick of battle in the Western Desert of North Africa. He and Monica were forced to complete by correspondence their theoretically ambitious and often undervalued study, *The Analysis of Social Change Based on Observations in Central Africa*. The first anthropological book to feature the concept of 'social change' in its title, it was press-ready by mid-1943 having been produced 'in the midst of professional disaster [Godfrey's dismissal from the RLI], unemployment, pregnancy, childbirth and wartime service'.[112] While generally read as an extension and deeper theorization of Godfrey's economic analysis of relations between the global and the local, between town and country, it also provides a case study of the intensification of settler racism in Northern Rhodesia and southern Africa more widely.[113] I read into it the dark sense of foreboding of a work crafted under the shadow of Nazism and the holocaust.

After a year in the army's education corps in South Africa, Godfrey's mental health deteriorated rapidly from December 1943, prompting a more serious recurrence of the mental illness from which he had suffered during his years working under Malinowski a decade earlier. He continued to write to Monica up to the day on which he committed suicide in May 1944.[114] 'For Monica his death was caused

[111] WC, B4.7 [GW] To and from Audrey Richards, MSS & TSS, Audrey Richards to Godfrey Wilson, 31 October 1940.

[112] Morrow, '"This is from the Firm"', 18.

[113] Godfrey Wilson and Monica Wilson, *The Study of African Society* (Livingstone: Rhodes-Livingstone Institute Papers, No. 2, 1939); Godfrey Wilson and Monica Wilson, *The Analysis of Social Change: Based on Observations in Central Africa* (Cambridge: Cambridge University Press, 1945).

[114] Seán Morrow, Personal Communication, 10 February 2012 based on his reading of the closed access letters between Monica Wilson and Godfrey Wilson contained in WC, B1 and B2.

An adopted daughter 97

as surely by the war as if he had been blown up by an enemy tank. She was devastated.'[115]

Anthropology and Christianity against apartheid, 1944–1973

Space constraints do not allow for a full account of the complex and courageous story of Monica Wilson's fight against apartheid with her mutually informing passions, anthropology and Christianity, as twin pillars across her three-decade career as a university lecturer and professor. Such an account would need to develop the following themes in detail.

First, one would need to track the continued importance of Christianity as a subtheme in her anthropological scholarship across these decades, for which she developed a growing international reputation. This theme was most explicitly developed in her six Scott-Holland lectures delivered at Cambridge University in 1969. Published in 1971 under the title *Religion and the Transformation of Society*, her lectures were an ambitious attempt at the end of her university career to combine her anthropological interest in social scale, social change and religious ritual with her personal practice and commitment as a Christian.[116] While some of her anthropological peers were critical of her admission of the centrality of personal belief and attitudes in the shaping of anthropological knowledge and her insistence on a universal impulse towards religion and ritual that went beyond scientific models of knowledge, most of her Christian friends and many theologians were moved by her self-reflective philosophical text.

Christian organizations, communities and intermediaries remained a significant subtheme in her scholarship across these decades, starting with the volume that she co-ordinated for the Keiskammahoek Rural Survey. This interdisciplinary rural study served as the model for her later co-authored study of social groups in Langa township.[117] She wrote on the role played by African converts as cultural intermediaries on the Eastern Cape frontier, most notably in a 1972 public lecture entitled *The Interpreters*.[118] This coincided with her late career 'turn to

---

[115] Francis Wilson, 'Monica Hunter Wilson: An Appreciation', 11.

[116] Monica Wilson, *Religion and the Transformation of Society: A Study of Social Change in Africa* (The Scott Holland Lectures, Cambridge: Cambridge University Press, 1971).

[117] Compare the chapter sequence and headings in Monica Wilson et al., *Keiskammahoek Rural Survey, Vol. 3 Social Structure* (Pietermaritzburg: Shuter and Shooter, 1952) with Monica Wilson and Archie Mafeje, *Langa: A Study of Social Groups in an African Township* (Cape Town, London and New York: Oxford University Press, 1963).

[118] Monica Wilson, *The Interpreters* (The Third Dugmore Memorial Lecture. Grahamstown: 1820 Settlers National Monument Foundation, 1972).

Figure 2.6: Members of the African Studies Department and senior students, Fort Hare Native College, 1946. Monica is in the centre of the middle row. Her friend and colleague Z.K. Matthews is seated on her left. Her talented graduate student Livingstone Mqotsi is seated at the end of the middle row, far left.[119]

history', or return to history, as Morrow and Saunders suggest in their reappraisal of her contribution to the landmark two-volume *Oxford History of South Africa* (1969, 1971). They show that Monica played the senior editorial role as well as the most prominent role as author in chapters which combined anthropological approaches to precolonial cultural groups, the Nguni and Sotho, with historical essays on missionaries and peasants on the changing Eastern Cape frontier of the nineteenth century.[120] The two-volume collection explicitly set itself up as a history against apartheid, identifying in its introductory pages the political mythologies on which the apartheid government based its policies. By contrast with apartheid's programme of racial separation, the *Oxford*

---

[119] WC, N2 Photographs of Monica Wilson in groups. For a poignant account of Mqotsi's frustrated career as a social anthropologist in South Africa during the 1940s and 1950s, see Leslie J. Bank, 'Witchcraft and the Academy: Livingstone Mqotsi, Monica Wilson and the Middledrift Healers, 1945–1957' in Bank and Bank, eds., *Inside African Anthropology*, 224–52.

[120] Seán Morrow and Christopher Saunders, '"Part of One Whole": Anthropology and History in the Work of Monica Wilson' in Bank and Bank, eds., *Inside African Anthropology*, 283–307.

An adopted daughter 99

History identified interaction across cultures and between so-called races as its organizing theme.[121]

Christianity also featured prominently in her last publication, the autobiography of her long-time friend and former Fort Hare colleague, Z.K. Matthews, entitled *Freedom for My People*. Her image of Z.K., already developed in article form, was of 'a man of reconciliation', a man of peace and Christian conscience whose political achievements were always deeply informed by his spirituality. She celebrated his Christian leadership, particularly during his years of exile when he served as African advisor at the World Council of Churches in Geneva.[122]

Second, one would need to document Monica's emergence as a prominent woman leader in public life, both in South African universities – at Fort Hare, Rhodes and UCT – and beyond. At UCT she played an active role in the defence of academic freedom from the mid- to late 1950s. She was a leading activist in the national campaign against the Extension of Universities Act of 1958, which prevented universities from having the right to appoint teachers and enrol students from all racial groups. She was the only woman professor in UCT Senate meetings from 1953 until 1966.[123] She courageously spoke out on the issue of academic freedom in Council at the time of the notorious Mafeje Affair of 1968, a sad chapter in the history of this historically liberal university. Contrary to a distorted recent account which implies that she was less than candid in private communications with Mafeje about the uncomfortable and shifting institutional politics at UCT, and thus somehow complicit with the authorities,[124] Monica was uncompromising in her promotion of Archie Mafeje. She regarded him as the best candidate for the advertised post as lecturer in social anthropology and was perfectly open in communications with him about the changing stance of the university towards his appointment.[125] She was fiercely vocal in university structures on the need for the University of Cape Town to defend in the strongest possible terms their academic freedom, including in this case, their right to appoint a black lecturer in the face of threats from the

---

[121] Monica Wilson and Leonard Thompson, 'Preface' in Wilson and Thompson, eds., *The Oxford History of South Africa, Vol. 1* (Oxford: Oxford University Press, 1969), i–vi.

[122] Monica Wilson, ed., *Freedom for My People: The Autobiography of Z.K. Matthews: Southern Africa 1901 to 1968* (London: Rex Collings; Cape Town: David Philip, 1981).

[123] *UCT Calendar, 1953–1967* (Cape Town: University of Cape Town). Thanks to Lesley Hart for drawing my attention to this.

[124] Fred Hendricks, 'The Mafeje Affair: UCT, Apartheid and the Question of Academic Freedom', *African Studies*, 67, 3 (2008), 432–52.

[125] WC, Uncatalogued correspondence 'M': letters between Monica Wilson and Archie Mafeje, 1960–1973.

100   Pioneers of the Field

National Party government. She wrote a letter to UCT Senate, which was officially adopted in its minutes, likening this political interference to that in the authoritarian dictatorships of Nazi Germany and Fascist Italy.[126] Former students and colleagues vividly recall her powerful address at a mass meeting of staff and students in May 1965, in which she made a personal and principled protest against the banning, and thus the ending of the long UCT career, of her friend Jack Simons on the grounds of his committed political opposition to apartheid.[127]

Her most active organizational affiliations were, however, with Christian church structures. Based in Geneva, Z.K. Matthews invited her to serve as an Africa representative at international annual meetings of the World Council of Churches. The boundaries between her identity as an anthropologist, as an anti-apartheid activist and as a Christian were typically blurred. At the local level she was appointed in 1964 to serve on the Archbishop of Cape Town's Committee on Social Responsibility. Part of their work was a wider educational drive to keep members of the Anglican Church better informed about, say, 'The Effects of Migrant Labour' on Africans, as one of their brochures sought to do.[128] She was also affiliated with, and at times actively involved in, the South African Council of Churches and other anti-apartheid organizations like the Black Sash. She also played an active role in the foundation of the South African Association of Anthropologists, in spite of what must have been her deep misgivings about the ideological disposition of the Afrikaans-university *volkekundiges* that dominated the organization.[129]

Third, one would have to acknowledge that it was in the field of teaching that she probably made her greatest contribution as an anti-apartheid intellectual. Shortly after Monica's retirement from UCT in 1973, Audrey Richards wrote that her friend had felt that 'continuous teaching of liberal ideas in South African universities was her special contribution to the African cause'.[130] Her teaching and her writing were of course inextricably linked, just as her anthropology was constantly energized and reshaped by her developing beliefs and practice as a Christian. In the most general of terms, I think it is fair to read her teaching career in the light of her teenage aspiration to contribute to

---

[126] UCT Libraries, Manuscripts and Archives Department, BC1072 Richard Luyt Collection, B2.2 Mafeje Affair 1968, see Monica Wilson's letter to Senate.

[127] On this speech and on her involvement in the campaign for academic freedom more generally, see Francis Wilson, 'Monica Hunter Wilson: An Appreciation', 20.

[128] WC, Uncatalogued materials, Box labelled 'Affiliations', Folder 'Archbishop's Committee'.

[129] *Ibid.*, Folder 'South African Association of Anthropologists'.

[130] Audrey Richards, 'Monica Wilson: An Appreciation', 1.

educational development and social service in South Africa. Certainly the collective records of her exhausting efforts on behalf of generations of anthropology students across three institutions suggest that she was driven by a deep underlying sense of social service beyond professional competence: something I read as a commitment that was at once spiritual and political.

If the roll-call of her students is anything to go by, we can certainly say that she was enormously successful in ensuring that the legacy of her socially and politically committed vision of anthropology remained alive. To begin with we should note that she *chose* to remain and teach in South Africa, preferring not to pursue interest from Cambridge and Oxford when distinguished male colleagues like Schapera and Gluckman were settling abroad. Leslie Bank and Seán Morrow have documented the hitherto hidden story of her dedicated mentorship of a talented core of African anthropologists at Fort Hare, most notably Livingstone Mqotsi, Nimrod Mkhele and Godfrey Pitje.[131]

It is during her twenty-one years as an undergraduate teacher and graduate supervisor at UCT that her legacy was most successfully established. Her mentorship is associated especially with her extended period as chair of the social anthropology department and head of the school of African studies at the University of Cape Town between 1952 and 1973. The talented students whom she trained during these decades included, in roughly chronological order, Berthold Pauw, Max Marwick, Peter Carstens, Peter Rigby, Archie Mafeje, Jean Comaroff, John Comaroff and Martin West, who was her successor as head of department. Jean Comaroff, who carried forward her interest in religion and ritual, has said: 'What we inherited ... was an epistemic commitment to a certain kind of questioning, and, more generally, to anthropology as an act, at once, of empathy and estrangement.'[132]

Her impact went beyond social anthropology, as her son Francis, a well published economist, has recently noted: 'There were also archaeologists, including Glynn Isaac and Carmel Schrire; lawyers such as Godfrey Pitje and Fikile Bam; theologians such as Axel-Ivar Berglund; and many others including, informally, Victor Turner and Rhys Isaacs.'[133] It also

---

[131] Leslie J. Bank, 'Witchcraft in the Academy' in Bank and Bank, eds., *Inside African Anthropology* 224–52; Seán Morrow, '"Your Intellectual Son": Monica Wilson at Fort Hare, 1944–1946' in Bank and Bank, eds., *Inside African Anthropology*, 201–2.

[132] Jean Comaroff, 'Monica Wilson and the Practice of "Deep Ethnography": Roundtable on South African Women Anthropologists and Ethnography' (unpublished paper presented at the Anthropology Southern Africa Conference, University of the Western Cape, September 2008).

[133] Francis Wilson, 'Monica Hunter Wilson: An Appreciation', 19.

Figure 2.7: Monica Wilson on a hike during her retirement, with the Hogsback Mountain in the background.

extended beyond her retirement. One of her informal students of the late 1970s, the late Colin Murray, movingly recalled 'a generosity of spirit and optimism of the will which deeply touched the lives of others'.[134] Another, Pamela Reynolds, has recounted her interactions with Monica at her fieldsite in Crossroads and at Monica Wilson's retirement home in the Hogsback. She reflected that 'Monica is famous for the emphasis she placed on the minute details and the search for the pattern of things.' More than any specific lessons, she seems to suggest that there was something akin to a spirit of transmission from teacher to student, a sense of her having taken forward something that went beyond the insistence on rigour in the field, on precision when writing, on integrity in social relations, something that is better conceived in affective or less tangible terms as an attitude towards engagement.[135] More recently, Reynolds commented that Monica 'had a very radical position in many ways'.[136]

---

[134] Colin Murray, '"So Truth be in the Field": Short Appreciation of Monica Wilson', *Journal of Southern African Studies*, 10, 1 (1983), 129–30.
[135] Pamela Reynolds, 'Gleanings and Leavings: Encounters in Hindsight' in Bank and Bank, eds., *Inside African Anthropology*, 315–19.
[136] Interview with Pamela Reynolds, 15 March 2013, Cape Town.

An adopted daughter 103

Afterword

Monica Wilson died peacefully after a long battle with cancer on 26 October 1982. Her funeral was attended, amongst others, by Archbishop Desmond Tutu and Muriel Bradbrook, a spiritual friend and college mate from Girton. She is buried alongside Aylmer and Godfrey in the family graveyard at Hunterstoun. She was busy, at the time of her death, with a Nyakyusa–English dictionary, an environmental history of the Hogsback and Amathole Mountains, and a memoir of her 1930s fieldwork commissioned by the historian of anthropology George W. Stocking.[137]

---

[137] WC, Uncatalogued materials, Correspondence 'S': Stocking, 1982.

3 Anthropology and Jewish identity: the urban fieldwork and ethnographies of Ellen Hellmann (1908–1982)

> I suppose Mrs Hoernlé has been the most potent influence on my life and our relationship developed from that of teacher to student to that of friends over more than thirty years and there was that quality of love – on both sides.
>
> Ellen Hellmann to her daughter, Ruth, Johannesburg, 20 March 1960, following the death of her beloved friend.[1]

Ellen Hellmann was the first Wits social anthropology student to engage in sustained and systematic ethnographic research following the modern professional method of long-term participant observation. If we think of Monica Hunter as the youngest member of the first cohort of professionally trained ethnographic researchers in southern Africa, along with Isaac Schapera and Audrey Richards, then Ellen was the first of the second cohort who began their fieldwork in the years between 1933 and 1936, and who included Winifred Hoernlé's other star students. Her thirteen months of intensive research based on daily visits to Rooiyard from March 1933 to April 1934, and the ethnography completed in May 1935 as a Wits M.A. thesis, predated the intensive fieldwork of her classmates and friends, Hilda Beemer and Max Gluckman in Swaziland and Zululand respectively, as well as the extended period of fieldwork by Eileen and Jack Krige in the Lovedu Reserve. Even though it was only published thirteen years later, at the prompting of Gluckman, then the outgoing director of the Rhodes-Livingstone Institute, it is still widely regarded as a classic in that it pioneered urban anthropology in the region, documenting in rich detail an urban working class subculture associated with women beer-brewers.

---

[1] E-mail letter, 15 January 2014, Dame Ruth Runciman to Andrew Bank. I am particularly grateful to Ruth Runciman for her enthusiasm about my engagement with her mother's life and work, and for generous sharing of memories and materials. Special thanks to Patrick Harries and the late Henrika Kuklick for commentaries on an earlier draft which has significantly reshaped my arguments. Thanks also to Jill Weintroub for research assistance in the Jewish Board of Deputies Library in Johannesburg, Andre Landman for valuable materials from the Colin Legum Collection at UCT, as well as to Clive Glaser, Nancy Jacobs, Adam Kuper and Milton Shain for comments and criticisms.

Anthropology and Jewish identity

Her substantive body of research over subsequent decades has, however, gone largely unacknowledged. This is partly because in the middle and later stages of her career she followed her role model and mentor, Winifred Hoernlé, in making a shift from being a university-based social anthropologist to being a public intellectual, welfare activist and, in her case, energetic political campaigner. She had worked for the Zionist Socialist Party in the 1930s and 1940s, and was a founding executive member of the Progressive Party from 1959 to 1971. It was, however, with the South African Institute of Race Relations (SAIRR), which she served in many capacities, including as committee member, Vice-President, President (1955–6) and research director that her name and legacy would most indelibly be associated, for better or worse, and in radical scholarship of the 1980s, invariably the latter. The standard overview of the discipline by Hammond-Tooke makes passing mention of her two major urban ethnographies, concluding that: 'Ellen Hellmann never became a professional anthropologist ... A warm and generous person ... [h]er main contribution to South African public life was in fact her work for the Institute.'[2]

This chapter makes the case that her contribution across four decades of politically engaged scholarship in the fields of urban anthropology and urban sociology was rather more significant than Hammond-Tooke admits. I revisit *Rooiyard*, making a case for its pioneering contribution to urban ethnographic methodology at a time when there were no blueprints for urban research work in Africa. I then highlight the significance of her other major urban monograph, that on African schools and youth culture in Johannesburg of the late 1930s, her series of incisive essays on South African Jewish history and cultural identity published from the late 1940s, in which she turned the ethnographic gaze from Other to Self, and her sociologically oriented writings of the apartheid era, when, as a well-recognized and outspoken South African liberal, she exposed what she like others termed 'the evil' of the apartheid government and the human tragedy of its repressive laws and brutal forced removals. I propose that they may be read, along with her slum-yard and township ethnography of the interwar years, as foundational texts in what would later be dubbed 'exposé anthropology'.[3]

Narrating the story of her life, which is arguably more intimately linked to her anthropological work than in the other cases documented in this

---

[2] Hammond-Tooke, *Imperfect Interpreters*, 144.
[3] This genre is usually associated with much later studies of the rural poverty in South African 'homelands' during the apartheid period. For an account of the 'exposé anthropology' of Marxist-influenced male anthropologists at UCT during the 1980s, see Hammond-Tooke, *Imperfect Interpreters*, 176–80.

106   Pioneers of the Field

study, has been challenging. Unlike the collections of papers left by her anthropological peers, the Ellen Hellmann Collection at Wits contains no personal papers at all. There is not a single letter nor portrait photograph, let alone a field-note or field diary. Ellen, it is clear, chose to preserve an archive that reflected only her public life. I have therefore relied on information derived from interviews and correspondence with her only child, her daughter Ruth Runciman, born in 1936, passing details she gave in late life interviews, the odd biographical sketch, occasional letters and diary entries from other archival collections and (as an exciting late discovery) a taped interview in which she spoke just months before her death about her German Jewish background and identity.

Jewish anthropologists in Southern Africa

The importance of Jewish identity in the history of social anthropology in southern Africa has been well acknowledged, especially in recent literature. As early as 1975 Archie Mafeje associated the empathy which Philip Mayer expressed towards the conservative 'Reds' of East London in the classic urban ethnography, *Townsmen or Tribesmen*, published in 1961, with the shared sense of marginality felt by an author with a Jewish background.[4] William Beinart's late life interviews with Philip Mayer have provided empirical substance to support this claim. The German-born Mayer learnt history from his father who was a professor at Berlin University and an acclaimed historian of the German labour movement. He had a deeply traumatic personal experience of Nazi violence when Nazi youth dragged him out of his university exam in Heidelberg in 1933. Beinart suggests that 'his early battle for survival and social identity had a significant impact on his work', particularly on his writings on inward-looking cultural identities and youth violence.[5]

In more general terms, Hugh Macmillan has made a persuasive case for the influence of the Jewish backgrounds of the leading scholars of the Rhodes-Livingstone Institute of the mid-twentieth century, especially Max Gluckman and A.L. ('Bill') Epstein, on their development of the

---

[4] He contrasted this with the background influence of Christianity in the approach of his former mentor Monica Wilson, who was more sympathetic to the 'School' than to the 'Red' migrants when they worked together on *Langa: A Study in Social Groups* (1963). See Archie Mafeje, 'Religion, Class and Ideology in South Africa' in Michael Whisson and Martin West, eds., *Religion and Social Change in Southern Africa* (Cape Town: David Philip, 1975), 164–84.

[5] William Beinart, 'Speaking for Themselves' in Andrew D. Spiegel and Patrick A. McAllister, eds., *Tradition and Transition in Southern Africa: Festschrift for Philip and Iona Mayer* (Johannesburg: Witwatersrand University Press, 1991), 32, 11–15.

Anthropology and Jewish identity

revolutionary new theory of 'ethnic identities' as situational, fluid and mobile rather than as 'fixed' in older functionalist constructions of 'tribal' identity. Unlike Philip Mayer, Gluckman and his Jewish colleagues, including Abner Cohen, wrote explicitly on the subjects of Zionism, Israel and Jewish cultural identity with Gluckman leading a major team research project in Israel during the 1960s.[6]

Isak Niehaus argues that Adam Kuper's formative experiences of anti-Semitism in South Africa of the 1940s and 1950s encouraged an orientation in his anthropological work away from narrow cultural analysis towards explorations of the universal, the cosmopolitan and the cross-cultural. Jewish intellectual networks are shown to have played a significant role in his career. His aunt Hilda used him as a driver on a fieldtrip to Swaziland in the early 1960s, which planted the seeds for his future interest. She later used her connections to allow him easier access to ethnographic field-sites during his research in Botswana in 1964. The main influence was his doctoral supervisor, Isaac Schapera, his mentor and close friend for over four decades.[7]

What about Jewish women anthropologists? After all, the roll-call of Jewish women anthropologists working in South Africa is as lengthy as that of their male counterparts. It includes Ellen Hellmann, Hilda Beemer, Selma Kaplan, Ruth Levin-Sacks,[8] Iona Mayer, Jean Comaroff, Sally Frankental and many others. How did the Jewish

---

[6] Hugh Macmillan, 'From Race to Ethnic Identity: South Central Africa, Social Anthropology and the Shadow of the Holocaust' in Patrick Harries and Megan Vaughan, eds., *Social Dynamics Special Issue: Essays in Commemoration of Leroy Vail*, 26, 2 (2000), 87–115. The importance of Gluckman's Jewish background had first been highlighted by Richard Brown in 'Passages in the Life of an White Anthropologist: Max Gluckman in Northern Rhodesia', *Journal of African History*, 20, 4 (1979), 227–42 and is taken up in James Ferguson, *Expectations of Modernity: Myths and Meanings of Urban Life on the Zambian Copperbelt* (Berkeley: University of California Press, 1999), 28–9.

[7] Isak Niehaus, 'Adam Kuper: An Anthropologist's Account' in Deborah James, Evie Plaice and Christina Toren, eds., *Culture Wars. Context, Models and Anthropologists' Accounts* (New York: Berghahn Books, 2010), 170–87.

[8] The anthropological research work of Ruth Levin-Sacks is less well known than it should be. She wrote a rigorous Master's thesis on marriage and gender relations in Langa, providing a remarkable contrast in political context to that of Wilson and Mafeje's later study. See Ruth Levin, *Marriage in Langa Native Location* (Cape Town: UCT School of African Studies, 1947). She taught as Monica Wilson's colleague in the anthropology department at UCT in the 1960s and early 1970s, but died quite suddenly of a brain tumour in 1971. The stiflingly conservative, almost all-male Senate refused to accept her 500-page doctoral thesis on the religious ritual and social structure of Muslim communities in Cape Town, despite letters from her supervisor Monica Wilson testifying to its excellence and completeness. This was simply on the technical grounds that there was 'no precedent' for posthumous doctoral awards. See the correspondence of Monica Wilson and her increasingly enraged husband with the UCT authorities in WC, Uncatalogued Materials, Correspondence 'S', Sacks.

108   Pioneers of the Field

backgrounds, identities and political affiliations of these women impact on their anthropological work?

The only essay-length sounding into the subject is again Beinart's festschrift chapter on Iona Mayer, in relation to Philip who was the senior researcher in their decades-long anthropological partnership. He indicates that Iona had a more Jewish-rooted upbringing than Philip as her father, Leon Simon, was a leading writer on cultural Zionism. She often wrote letters home in Hebrew and, as in the case of Philip, there is a strong case that her later empathy for marginalized Africans was implicitly associated with her Jewish identity. This relates to her work on kinsmen and kinswomen in the stateless Kisii society of Kenya of the late 1940s, which she documented most fully in her 1965 doctoral thesis, the 'encapsulated Reds', whose lives she assisted Philip in researching and documenting in the late 1950s and early 1960s, and the marginalized women migrants whom she interviewed in sensitive depth during the mid- to late 1970s in Grahamstown while affiliated to the Black Sash and radical feminist intellectuals like Marian Lacey and Jacklyn Cock.[9] In her case, a fuller analysis is warranted of the contribution of her series of 'hidden ethnographies', from her doctoral thesis through to her life histories of women migrants, one which pays close attention to the changing relationship between her family and professional life at the different stages of a three-decade long career in African anthropology.

In the case of Ellen Hellmann, however, the connection between her anthropology and Jewish identity was pronounced, given her activist involvement in Zionist Socialist politics during the time of her fieldwork, her writings about South African Jewish history and her liberal anti-apartheid Jewish networks in later years. Indeed, Ellen would be among the first scholars to highlight that Jews were prominent in liberal and radical anti-apartheid activism. As Milton Shain and Richard Mendelsohn have noted, 'Jews were conspicuously present – and overrepresented – in the struggle for democracy and human rights'. They go on to indicate that the reasons have been, and remain, hotly debated in a rich scholarly literature. Where scholars like James Campbell

---

[9] Beinart, 'Speaking for Themselves', 18–38. Her contribution is partly obscured by the fact that the festschrift volume compiled in her and Philip's honour in which the Beinart article appears is confined to southern Africa with little commentary or analysis of her two articles, short book and doctoral thesis on the Gusii. See Iona Mayer, 'From Kinship to Common Descent: Four Generation Genealogies among the Gusii', *Africa*, 35, 4 (1965), 366–84; *The Nature of Kinship Relations: The Significance of the Use of Kinship Terms among the Gusii* (Lusaka: Rhodes-Livingstone Institute Papers, No. 37, 1966); 'Studies in Gusii Kinship' (unpublished Ph.D. thesis, Rhodes University, 1966); 'The Patriarchal Image: Routine Dissociation in Gusii Families', *African Studies*, 34, 4 (1975), 259–91.

Anthropology and Jewish identity 109

highlight the impact of migration and its legacy of disruption and alienation in encouraging an affinity with the marginalized, Gideon Shimoni emphasizes the significance of Jewish 'cultural values' in South Africa, the role of the national Zionist movements in drawing many anti-apartheid activists into oppositional politics, and the need for historical sensitivity to the complex factors involved in individual cases. These include 'personality traits, chance exposures to inspiring role models, and the warm embrace of supportive groups'.[10] Shimoni provides a template which applies, point by point, to the case of Ellen Hellmann. We need to begin, however, with the intense marginalization she experienced as a German Jew in pro-British South Africa, something she shared with thousands of Jewish immigrants from Nazi Germany.

A German Jewish childhood, Johannesburg, 1908–1929

Ellen grew up in comfortable material circumstances in a German Jewish family in Johannesburg. Yet material comfort should never be mistaken for psychological security, as her deeply moving retrospective account of her painful childhood makes abundantly clear. One can scarcely exaggerate the significance of her traumatic childhood experiences which translated into what was evidently a deeply internalized sense of discrimination: initially as a German and as a girl, later as a Jew. Without wanting to anticipate my arguments later in the chapter, her childhood experience explained for me her choice, even compulsion, to associate her career with the most marginalized members of urban society, initially as an empathetic researcher and later as a social welfare activist and political campaigner. It also suggests to me why a supportive, stable, generous and engaged senior woman scholar like Winifred Hoernlé could have played such an important influence in her life, as the epigraph to the chapter reveals.

This is the story she told when interviewed about her Jewish background just a few months before she died. She was born in the Johannesburg suburb of Berea on 25 August 1908 to parents of German origin. Her

---

[10] Milton Shain and Richard Mendelsohn, 'Introduction' in Shain and Mendelsohn, eds., *Memories, Realities and Dreams: Aspects of Jewish Experience* (Johannesburg and Cape Town: Jonathan Ball, 2000), 11–12. For some, but still limited, engagement with the experiences of Jewish women, including Ellen Hellmann in a double page-spread on 'Bold Women: Challenging the Status Quo', see Mendelsohn and Shain, *The Jews in South Africa: An Illustrated History* (Johannesburg: Jonathan Ball, 2008), 140–1. For a collective biography of Jewish women that offers a partial corrective, see Veronica-Sue Belling, 'Recovering the Lives of South African Jewish Women during the Migration Years, c 1880–1939' (unpublished D.Phil. thesis, University of Cape Town, 2013).

110   Pioneers of the Field

father, Bernard Kaumheimer, had come to South Africa in 1894 at the age of sixteen. He was an orphan from a small town near Nunberg. 'He was really very poor' and so seized the opportunity of lowly employment offered by relatives who ran a retail business in Johannesburg. 'He always told us he got five pounds per month and saved one pound.' Having started out as a messenger, he had worked his way into a position of financial security by 1906 when he returned to Germany 'to look for a bride' as 'was the custom'.

He met this really lovely woman. My mom [Chlothilde] was really exceptionally beautiful. She had lots of suitors. My grandparents were terribly opposed [to her 'marrying down']. She even had a small dowry. They worried about her going to a wild place, Africa.

They only agreed on condition that he would promise to bring her home every two years, along with any children.

I had a childhood that was pretty difficult, both externally ... and in my own home. During the war years, the First World War, there was a terrible lot of anti-German feeling. I went to Barnato Park [junior school] and the children were really very patriotic, pro-Allies. I have never forgotten a terrible incident when they opened two buttons of my gym dress and had me standing in the playground in my bloomers, which in 1914 was a very terrible thing to happen to one ... [Pause] This was a very improper thing and it was meant to be demeaning.

Then they made a ring [around me] and shouted: 'Look at the Hun! Look at the Hun!' That was during playtime. Well, a little girl takes this badly. I was very aware that I was different and wrong because I was German. Actually I had relatives fighting on both sides.

At home I had difficulties because my parents brought me up on Victorian lines. It was late Victorian days when children should be seen and not heard. We had a lot of difficulties because I was always supposed to be saying sorry. When I didn't sound sorry, they put me in a corner. And I stood there for hours. I was a very, very stubborn little girl and they were disciplinarians. We did a lot of infighting. We just had different points of view. My mother was so anxious to iron out this constant fight between my father and me, which was somewhat ameliorated [by the birth of my younger sister, Inez].

Inez brought some joy into what was evidently a severe Victorian upbringing, one in which 'no extravagance was encouraged'. It is also clear that her father favoured his younger daughter.

I was simply known as the ugly duckling in this family. My father used to say: 'I don't know how you come into this family of beautiful women.' All of which I suppose was not very good psychologically speaking, I don't know.

While she retrospectively associated her memories of anti-Semitism with 'the rise of Hitler', there is no doubt that her Jewish identity was

Figure 3.1: 'The Family, 1922': Bernard and Chlothilde Kaumheimer with their daughters, Ellen (left, aged 14) and Inez (right, aged 10) at a public swimming pool in Johannesburg.[11]

central from her early years. 'I never wanted to deny that I was Jewish. Never! I was Jewish. I knew I was Jewish, but we were not in the least bit religious.' Her family's break from religion was associated with another painful incident of anti-German discrimination during the War. This time it was from within the Jewish community.

My parents had an unpleasant experience during the First World War when Jews on the Allied side were prayed for, and others were expressly excluded. And they resigned their membership of the Wolmaranstad synagogue. Religion was out from that moment.

She recalled that their family friends were almost exclusively German Jews and that 'the German Jewish community here was very close-knit'. There was still a stark divide between German Jews and Eastern European Jews, who they looked down upon. This would only change in her early teens when her father befriended a community leader called Wulf Uhlmann, who was an Eastern European immigrant. Uhlmann

---

[11] Wits University, William Cullen Library, A1419 Ellen Hellmann Collection [henceforth EHC], Family Photograph Album, 31.3.

112   Pioneers of the Field

persuaded him to use his business acumen to save the Jewish orphanage from financial ruin.[12]

The Jewish community of Johannesburg had grown from around 25,000 at the time of Ellen's birth to around 35,000 by the time she matriculated in 1928.[13] Almost half of the Jewish men in Johannesburg worked in commerce, finance or insurance, which was more than double the proportion in the case of the white population of Johannesburg. By contrast, around 60 per cent of Jewish women were housewives, again a substantially higher proportion than that among the white population of Johannesburg more generally. A mere 2.5 per cent of Jewish women worked in professions, which was half the proportion of women professionals in the white population as a whole.[14] There was a clear divide, then, between the public world of Jewish men and the private world of Jewish women, but times could change, as a self-made man like Bernard Kaumheimer, was well aware. He sent his elder daughter to Wits University after she had matriculated from Commercial Girls' High School in 1928. Her subject choice hints that she, like many other white women students of her generation, envisaged a career as a schoolteacher.

A woman anthropologist's apprenticeship, 1929–1932

Ellen's sense of identity with the Jewish community sharpened during her years at Wits. When she enrolled for her Arts Degree in 1929, Jewish students comprised about a third of the total student population: some 500 out of 1,609. This explains why the Stellenbosch University professor (and later apartheid Prime Minister), H.F. Verwoerd, famously dubbed Wits of the 1930s as 'a Jewish university with an appendage of Indian and native students'.[15]

---

[12] The extracts above are all taken from the University of Cape Town, Kaplan Centre Archive, BC949 Tape-recorded interviews by Riva Krut, Interview with Ellen Hellmann, Johannesburg, 3 June 1982.

[13] The number of Jews in Johannesburg consistently numbered around half the total number of Jews in South Africa. The total population figures are taken from Allie Dubb, *Jewish South Africans: A Sociological View of the Johannesburg Community* (Rhodes University, ISER, 1977, Occasional Paper No. 21).

[14] Henry Sonnabend, 'Statistical Survey of Johannesburg's Jewish Population, 1935' as cited in Mendelsohn and Shain, *The Jews in South Africa* and T. Adler, 'Lithuanian Diaspora: The Johannesburg Jewish Workers' Club, 1928–1948', *Journal of Southern African Studies*, 6, 1 (1979), 70–92, Table 2.

[15] Cited in Bruce K. Murray, *Wits: The 'Open' Years, 1939–1959* (Johannesburg: Wits University Press, 1997), 3. The student population grew to 2,549 by 1939. Murray, *Wits: The Early Years*, 317.

Anthropology and Jewish identity 113

Ellen's direct personal experience of anti-Semitism dated from her student years at Wits.[16] An associate and family friend commented retrospectively that her 'full' coming-to-consciousness as a Jew coincided with Hitler's rise to power.[17] She recalled that the turning-point was 'the accession of Hitler [in 1933], when Hitler took over in Germany, when Hitler came to light.' In her scholarly writings about the history of the Jewish community, she pinpointed the rise of the Nazis as *the* decisive moment in the history of anti-Semitism in South Africa. Within South Africa of the 1930s, she wrote, there began to emerge a deepening 'anti-Semitism, a wild anti-communism and all-out segregation'.[18] The liberal community on campus also came to influence her thinking. In a touching obituary to Alfred Hoernlé, she recalled his 1934 public address on 'Plato's *Republic* and Hitler's Germany' as 'a far-sighted and courageous analysis of the nature of the Nazi system and the evil which would inevitably spring from it.'[19] Milton Shain confirms her periodization, indicating that there was indeed 'a sea change in the nature and character of anti-Semitism' in this decade, a marked shift from private anti-Semitism to what he terms 'public or programmatic anti-Semitism'.[20]

There was a third reason for Ellen's closer identity with the wider Jewish community in Johannesburg. In March 1932, at the age of just twenty-three, she married a Jewish lawyer from a large Lithuanian immigrant family, Joseph Hellmann. This was a time when marriages between German Jews and East European Jews were rare and she recalls that there was much debate within the respective families about the wisdom of her 'mixed marriage'.[21] Her deep knowledge of East European Jewish history and cultural politics, articulated in her later articles,[22] is surely associated in part with her marriage to a man who was part of this branch of the South African Jewish diaspora. She would also later claim that her marital

---

[16] Her exposure to anti-Semitism may have predated this: she recalled having become intensely aware of inequality and discrimination after a personal incident in the early 1920s. See EHP, Box: Newspaper Cuttings, Pat Schwartz, 'A View from Both Sides of the Fence', 1981.

[17] Bernard Sachs, 'Dr Ellen Hellmann: Social Engineer' in Sachs, *South African Personalities and Places* (Johannesburg: Kayor Publishers, 1959), 188.

[18] Ellen Hellmann, 'Labour Zionism in South Africa', *The Pioneer Woman* (December 1944), 5.

[19] Ellen Hellmann, '"Heartbreak House": A Liberal Look at South African Native Policy', *Jewish Affairs* (April 1946), 9.

[20] Milton Shain, '"If It Was So Good, Why Was It So Bad?" The Memories and Realities of Antisemitism in South Africa Past and Present' in Shain and Mendelsohn, eds., *Memories, Realities and Dreams*, 79–88.

[21] Telephone interview with Ruth Runciman, 3 September 2011, London.

[22] See, for example, Ellen Hellmann, 'Plea against Jewish "Isolationism"', *Jewish Affairs*, 5, 10 (1950), 4–6.

114   Pioneers of the Field

status encouraged her to choose a nearby urban rather than a distant rural field-site.[23]

Before turning to the innovative and pioneering research that she did in Rooiyard, we need to set her study within the context of her undergraduate training under Winifred Hoernlé. She had stumbled into what was a completely unknown field of study on the day of her registration in February 1929.

> I wanted to major, as all good girls did in those days, in English and Psychology and to do Fine Arts as an extra subject. I wandered around and saw a thing called social anthropology. I had no idea what it meant, but it didn't clash. It fitted. I took it and was hooked for life – it was one of those extraordinarily lucky breaks.[24]

Coming from a family headed by an ambitious, self-made man who held what, one might assume, were conservative attitudes towards black South Africans, Ellen recalls being struck 'from the outset' by her teacher's insistence that 'the common humanity that all humans share is greater than the differences between them'. It was something that she would take on as the motto for her own life and work.[25]

She soon became close friends with her Jewish class-mates, Hilda Kuper and Max Gluckman. Hilda recalled that they began their studies 'in a time of optimism, in which we expected that "evolution" would bring "progress". Several of us were non-orthodox Jews struggling to achieve a non-ethnocentric ethical perspective.' The ways in which their lecturer fostered a sense of open-mindedness towards the different anthropological theories and approaches is well captured in Hilda's retrospective essay. 'Her lectures began with evolutionism, and she made us read selected pages in the original languages [English, French and German], and set them in broader historical context.' Given her background, Ellen read the German texts of Bachofen and Leo Frobenius, and would have taken a particular interest in the close attention their teacher paid to the German diffusionist school of anthropology.

> After the evolutionists we were grounded in the German *Kulturkreis* school ... There was a certain magnificence in looking at the world in terms of great cultural circles, speculating on how cultural 'things' that had come together in one part of the earth would reappear in another.

Then they were taught 'the theory of African sociology' that Hoernlé had co-founded with Brown just a few years earlier and the method of functionalism.

---

[23] Schwartz, 'A View from Both Sides of the Fence'.   [24] *Ibid.*
[25] See Ellen Hellmann and Quinton Whyte, 'Introduction', 1–5.

Anthropology and Jewish identity

Social anthropologists [we were taught] do not look at 'things' in isolation, but at relationships that are sometimes mediated by things – i.e. the social values that people have attached to things in relation to other people. These social relationships are not haphazard, but are integral parts of a system. Radcliffe-Brown derived his ideas largely from Durkheim, and with her usual thoroughness, Mrs Hoernlé introduced us to the great French school of sociology.[26]

Ellen and her Jewish classmates were given a taste of fieldwork in the university vacation in September 1930. They spent ten days working with Isaac Schapera at his new field-site of Mochudi in the Bechuanaland Protectorate. As we have learnt, he was standing in for Mrs Hoernlé who was visiting Malinowski in London and touring archaeological sites on the Continent.

Hilda's recollections about her subsequent induction into urban fieldwork as a graduate student are also relevant, here for understanding Ellen's decision to choose women beer-brewers as her primary subjects of study. There was a growing preoccupation among South African politicians and social scientists with poverty as 'a social and economic problem' that required research.[27] In 1931 the South African Institute of Race Relations launched a project on 'the social effects of the liquor laws'. Mrs Hoernlé got the Institute's director, Rheinallt-Jones, to send the twenty-one year old Hilda into prisons to interview African women beer-brewers.[28] Ellen took over this project when Hilda left to continue her anthropological studies under Malinowski in London, again at Mrs Hoernlé's prompting. She was tasked with tracking the social networks of the women brewers from the prisons back to their homes in the slum-yards of Johannesburg. The opening sentences of the original draft manuscript of her study, which were later deleted, reveal that it was Mrs Hoernlé who persuaded her to choose a slum-yard as her field-site.

In February 1933 I first became fully conscious of the existence of the 'yards'. Mrs Hoernlé, feeling that a survey of a yard would yield some useful information, arranged a 'conducted tour' of some yards in Doornfontein, Bertrams and the City. Miss Cowles, of the American Board Mission, took us on this tour and, amongst many other yards, to Rooiyard.

She and Mrs Hoernlé settled on Rooiyard because of its greater 'accessibility' from the city centre and its relative size. At about a thousand square

---

[26] Kuper, 'Function, History and Biography', 195–6.
[27] See Marijke du Toit, '*Binnelandse Reise* (Journeys into the Interior): Photographs from The Carnegie Commission of Investigation into the Poor White Problem, 1929/1932', *Kronos*, 32 (Nov. 2006), 49–76.
[28] Kuper, 'Function, History and Biography', 195–6.

116   Pioneers of the Field

metres it 'gave promise of providing contacts with a larger number of families' than did any of the other yards.[29]

'Rooiyard is a difficult place for a woman fieldworker', 1933–1934

In an overview of women's contributions to the development of social anthropology during the twentieth century, Lyn Schumaker suggests that the contribution of women as ethnographers has sometimes been acknowledged as, for example, in the case of Margaret Mead's studies of childhood and socialization in the Pacific and Audrey Richard's work on food and nutrition in Central Africa. However, the contributions of women in developing new forms of fieldwork practice are less often recognized.[30] This section attempts to present a sounding into this hidden history by making a case for the achievements of Ellen Hellmann as fieldworker.

Ellen spent thirteen months in Rooiyard. She began in March 1933 and continued through to April 1934 when the yard was closed down by the government and its residents forcibly removed to the township of Orlando. She conducted her research every day of the week, mornings and afternoons. As the men were at work and the children at school, it was the women of Rooiyard – most of whom were mothers and 95 per cent of whom were beer-brewers – who provided her with the information on which her study was based. Such a project, it is fair to assume, would simply not have been possible for a male anthropologist working in this period.

She recalled the relatively naïve spirit with which she began her fieldwork, though this was edited out of the published manuscript. 'In March 1933 I descended on Rooiyard, armed with a large box of penny-line chocolates and a notebook.'[31] She soon learnt that the police raided Rooiyard every few days. In fact, during her thirteen months in Rooiyard, the police made no fewer than 109 arrests. This was from among a population of 365 residents. There were sixty-five arrests for illegal brewing, fifteen for assault, one for assault with intent to harm, one for culpable homicide and one for murder, a case endlessly discussed in the yard. Many of the 'stabbing affrays'

---

[29] EHP, Box 35, 'Rooiyard, Original manuscript with photographs' (237 pp.), 1.
[30] Lyn Schumaker, 'Women in the Field in the Twentieth Century: Revolution, Involution, Devolution' in Henrika Kuklick, ed., *A New History of Anthropology* (Oxford: Blackwell, 2008), 277–8.
[31] EHP, Box 35, 'Rooiyard, Original manuscript with photographs', 1.

Anthropology and Jewish identity

went unreported.[32] In such a context she was inevitably viewed with suspicion and hostility.

It took more than a month before she 'could openly take notes in the yard'.[33] Unfortunately, her field-notes have not survived, making it impossible to chart in the kind of detail that Leslie Bank has done in relation to Monica Hunter's East London work, the ways in which her modes of writing in the field differed, how they built up into modes of ethnographic writing, and what kinds of themes featured in notes that were later muted in the scientific study.[34] Uniquely though, we have a vivid first-hand account of how she was viewed by her women informants. It comes from a Manyika healer named John Chafimbira, who lived in the yard and would soon be employed as her research assistant-cum-bodyguard.

Soon the white woman was the constant topic of conversation. The residents agreed that she treated them kindly. But why did she question them? ... Why did she write down everything they said? 'Surely her hand must be sore with all the writing,' they remarked. Who was she? Why did she come every day to such a place [Rooiyard], a place which white people avoided like the plague? It was most extraordinary. What was her business? Was she married? Had she children?[35]

Ellen introduced John to her Jewish friend, the psychoanalyst Wulf Sachs, who conducted what would become a famous study of John, whom he called 'Black Hamlet'. It was Sachs who recorded John's impressions cited above, and who later described a dramatic incident when John came to Ellen's rescue at the end of what would be her only night visit to the yard.

Whilst I [Sachs] was visiting the rooms, the anthropologist walked slowly through the narrow alleyways, concentrating upon her work of observation. For some time she was unnoticed. Then someone saw the tall, well-dressed European woman, noticed first with astonishment, and then with hostile resentment, the intrusion of a foreigner, and a white woman at that. The news of her presence spread like wildfire through the excited, hysterical mob. Muttered remarks grew to outspoken comments, became shouted threats ...

An ugly hostile atmosphere grew with alarming rapidity. She tried to reach the exit, but the narrow passage was thronged with people ... A crowd of roughs, inflamed with *skokiaan* [an intoxicating township brew], came very close to her,

---

[32] Ellen Hellmann, 'The Importance of Beer-Brewing in an Urban Native Yard', *Bantu Studies*, 8, 1 (1934), 57.

[33] EHP, Box 35, 'Rooiyard, Original manuscript with photographs', 1. This was also edited out of the published text.

[34] Leslie J. Bank, 'City Dreams, Country Magic', 95–126.

[35] *Black Hamlet* by Wulf Sachs with a new introduction by Saul Dubow and Jacqueline Rose (Baltimore: The Johns Hopkins University Press, 1996, originally published 1937), 193.

Figure 3.2: 'No. 4 Alleyway'. This was one of nineteen photographs that featured in the appendix to the belatedly published *Rooiyard* (1948). The large barrels were used for beer-brewing.[36]

touched her, swore at her in vile language, made sinister suggestions. Some of the women in the yard, now frightened for her safety and the terrible consequences to all of them should anything happen to the white woman, tried to form a protecting ring around her, but they were not strong enough. The roughs pulled them away. At this critical juncture John appeared ... he was able to guide her to the exit – not without sarcastic and obscene remarks from the crowd – to put her in the car, and see her safely away.[37]

Little wonder that she began her thesis by noting that 'I felt compelled to agree [with the police and the health inspector who had warned] that Rooiyard is a difficult place for a woman fieldworker.'[38] This was clearly an understatement. This wording was, unfortunately, altered in later published versions in ways that neutralize the sense she wished to convey of her feelings of vulnerability as a *woman* in such a dangerous place. She was, after all, just twenty-five years of age. When the sentence was republished in an

---

[36] EHP, Box 35, Rooiyard Album 35.4. [37] *Black Hamlet* by Wulf Sachs, 210.
[38] EHP, Box 35, 'Rooiyard, Original manuscript with photographs', 2.

Anthropology and Jewish identity

Figure 3.3: 'No. 17 John Chafimbira'. Ellen's research assistant and bodyguard in Rooiyard, 1933.[39]

article in *Africa*, the journal editor, Dietrich Westermann, changed it to 'Rooiyard was no place for the fieldworker',[40] while Max Gluckman, in his role as editor of the first full published version of the text in 1948, reinstated her reference to 'a difficult place', but retained the misleadingly gender-neutral reference, here to 'a fieldworker'.[41] While these editorial interventions were intended to convey a sense of scientific neutrality, what Clifford refers to as 'ethnographic authority',[42] they wrote out the deep underlying emotion associated with the original formulation.

One should also not underestimate the methodological challenge that Ellen faced in framing her study. We should bear in mind that there were

---

[39] *Ibid.*, 35.16.
[40] See Ellen Hellmann, 'Native Life in a Johannesburg Slum Yard', *Africa*, 8, 1 (1935), 34–62; Ellen Hellmann, *Rooiyard: A Sociological Survey of an Urban Native Slum Yard* (Livingstone: Rhodes-Livingstone Institute, RLI Papers No. 13, 1948), 125 pp. + 18 photographs.
[41] Hellmann, *Rooiyard*, 1.
[42] James Clifford, 'On Ethnographic Authority' in Clifford, *The Predicament of Culture: Twentieth Century Ethnography, Literature, and Art* (Cambridge, MA: Harvard University Press, 1988).

120   Pioneers of the Field

no models that could serve as a methodological guideline. Monica Hunter's account of her urban fieldwork was published the year after Ellen had submitted her ethnography in May 1935. She admitted to having 'commenced without a definite method of work'.[43] Her difficulties were lucidly set out in the first article that she published based on her fieldwork, a reflection on method that featured in a special issue of *Bantu Studies* dedicated to Winifred Hoernlé. Ellen began by asking whether 'the functionalist method elaborated by Malinowski and his followers' was 'sufficient equipment for the study of culture contact'. She explained how 'other students of culture contact' had attempted to grapple with this problem. Isaac Schapera, for example, compared present and past based on his interviews with old men. 'What if you do not have "ancients" to rely on for a picture of the old order?' What if you are studying in a place where African society 'does not form an integrated whole', but consists of a bewilderingly 'heterogeneous conglomeration' of migrants?[44] The problem was well-illustrated in the diagram with which her ethnography began. It revealed that there were members of no fewer than twenty-one different ethnic groups living in Rooiyard as neighbours and often as co-residents.

She went on to explain the research methods that she was forced to develop on site. She began with a household questionnaire, but then encouraged some of her informants to record their own budgets which provided information about occupation, kinship, material culture and diet.[45] The budgets were also a much needed device for 'building trust', the central problem at her field-site. '[T]he anthropologist, by immersing himself [herself] in the economic difficulties against which every household contends, eventually wins the confidence of his [her] informant – an undertaking more difficult in urban than in rural areas … The budget enquiry usually introduces the investigator to the most intimate affairs of the family.' This allowed her to identify a small group which provided the more 'qualitative' information on which she built her ethnography.[46]

The limitations which her study shared with other social scientific works of the period[47] should not be allowed to obscure her achievement

---

[43] EHP, Box 35, 'Rooiyard, Original manuscript with photographs', 4.

[44] Ellen Hellmann, 'Methods of Urban Field Work', *Bantu Studies: Special Issue Dedicated to Winifred Hoernlé*, 9, 3 (1935), 185–90.

[45] She used this information as the basis for an article on 'Urban Native Food in Johannesburg' published in *Africa*, 9, 2 (1936), 277–90.

[46] Ellen Hellmann, 'Methods of Urban Field Work', 190–5.

[47] They are relatively well known. There are passages in which European culture is explicitly described as being superior to African culture, in which the social and cultural organization of the 'parent cultures' in rural areas is presented too easily in functionalist terms as harmonious and integrated wholes to be contrasted with the dislocated nature of social

Anthropology and Jewish identity

in producing what was the first anthropological monograph in the region to focus specifically on women. A number of her women peers worked more closely with women than with men during their fieldwork. This was usually the case with wives who worked in wife-and-husband teams like Monica and Godfrey Wilson in Bunyakyusa in 1934–8, and Eileen and Jack Krige in Balovedu in 1936–8.[48] The aim of these collaborations, however, was always to combine the independently gathered information about the lives of men and women in order to present a picture of the 'whole'. Ellen's focus was on women as ethnographic subjects in their own right. This was unusual in the British functionalist tradition at the time.[49]

Africa's first urban ethnography (1935)

It is not only her field research that was innovative, but also her ethnography. It was written in lively and evocative terms. The daily experience of engagement and participant observation allowed for a rich, vivid reconstruction of the social and economic world of this confined urban space. Her study is notable for the 'thick description' generally associated with the ethnographies of the interwar period, in particular with those of students who studied under Malinowski. We know all too little about Ellen's brief period of work under Malinowski in London. She first met Malinowski at the New Education Fellowship Conference in Johannesburg in July 1934. One of the books in her private library, his *Sexual Life of Savages*, contains an inscription dated to 27 July: 'Inscribed for Ellen Hellman (sic) with words of friendship and admiration.'[50] In a letter to Eileen Krige written on 7 September, she refers to her preparations for a major journey. We know that she and a host of fellow South Africans were working in London with Malinowski by the end of October from his letter to Alfred Hoernlé. We can therefore assume

---

and familial relations in the urban context. The author also at one point endorses Wulf Sachs' theory that the socialization of young children in African cultures was 'overweaning' and encouraged a more dependent personality type. Her tone in relation to African sexual attitudes and practices does, at times, feature moral judgements in discussions about the extent of adultery, illegitimacy and prostitution.

[48] See Eileen Jensen Krige and Jack D. Krige, *The Realm of a Rain-Queen: A Study of the Pattern of Lovedu Society* (London, New York and Toronto: Published for the International African Institute by the Oxford University Press, 1943), xiv.

[49] Male informants, usually the 'old men of the tribe', were the privileged source of information in the texts of the 'founding fathers', which Hellmann had studied as an undergraduate, notably in Malinowski's founding texts on the Trobriand Islanders (1922, 1929 and then later 1935) and Radcliffe-Brown's work on the Andaman Islanders (1922).

[50] Ruth Runciman, E-mail communication, 2 February 2012, London.

122   Pioneers of the Field

that she spent the late months of 1934 in London, the very time when she was writing up her research findings. Her daughter Ruth recalls her fondness for telling a story about how she and Malinowski danced in London.[51] Her letter to Eileen also reveals the extent of Ellen's modesty about her research, in the deference she shows towards her fellow anthropologist and peer, but also the importance that female role models continued to play in her life.

> I doubt whether our stay in Zululand [on a recent joint fieldtrip] convinced you of the sincerity of my work. But one day, I hope to turn into a more serious and painstaking anthropologist. You may laugh at me – but honestly, I have always taken you as my model.[52]

In the opening chapter Ellen took her readers into Rooiyard as a lived space, paying close attention to the interiors as well as the exteriors of houses, to the layout of furniture in each of the rooms and the different family sleeping arrangements. Her success in allowing her audience to visualize the spaces of Rooiyard was greatly assisted by the publication of eighteen photographs that feature by way of appendix in the thesis and then in the published monograph. As the historian Marijke du Toit suggests, there is an unusual sense of movement and a swirling energy in her photographic record, a perspective that takes one inside the lived space as figures on the margins move in and out of the frames. The sense of flow, the lack of staging and the prominence of skewed views were more likely the product of the constraints of production rather than attempts to experiment with perspective, as Du Toit rather generously proposes.[53] Most of her Rooiyard photographs are 'stolen shots', images taken while the subjects were unaware that they were being photographed. I also find it instructive that while she recorded eight life histories of trusted women informants, she was only able to capture one of these women on camera ('Angela, photo 16').[54]

Her text made more prominent cross-reference to visual materials than was common in ethnographies of this period. She used the photographs to illustrate all of her main arguments: the limited social amenities in the

---

[51] Telephone interview with Ruth Runciman, 3 September 2011, London.

[52] Krige Collection, Killie Campbell Library, Ellen Hellmann to Eileen Krige, 7 September 1934, Johannesburg.

[53] Marijke du Toit, 'The General View and Beyond: From Slumyard to Township in Ellen Hellmann's Photographs of Women and the African Familial in the 1930s', *Gender and History*, 17, 3 (November 2005), 593–626.

[54] This is in marked contrast with the prominence of portraits in her much larger body of photographic work on the townships of Johannesburg in 1937–8 which I will discuss in more detail. I assume that this was because of the reluctance to be photographed among even her most trusted informants.

Anthropology and Jewish identity   123

yard (photo 1); the variation in housing structures, in particular the difference between brick and the more 'rickety' corrugated iron structures (photo 2); the poverty and dirt of the slum-yard (almost all the images); the technology and material culture associated with this beer-brewing industry, in particular 'the motley tins, ranging from one-gallon oil tins to large petrol drums, which are used in the preparation and storage of beer' (photos 3–10) with only occasional 'oases of cleanliness and order in the midst of the general litter' (photo 11).

Her best chapter documented the working activities of the women brewers.[55] Here she anticipated the work of social historians in South Africa in documenting an urban working class 'subculture of resistance'. Indeed, it is striking that her work would be partially rediscovered, not by South African anthropologists but by social historians of the 1980s who were seeking to document working class culture in South African cities. Their recognition was, however, confined to mining her work for empirical detail rather than appreciating its methodological innovation.[56]

Her tone was empathetic. The emphasis was certainly not on the evils of drink and associated forms of moral deviance, as some critics have suggested,[57] but rather on the innovations and industry of the women brewers, whom she evidently admired for their will to survive under the most arduous of circumstances. She explained the mechanics of their brewing process in meticulous detail, including their system of storage in 'subterranean passages'.

The chief labour is involved in cleaning the tin, which is buried several feet below the level of the ground, in digging up the opening every time beer is put in or taken out, and in firmly plastering down the earth again, so that the police may not notice the unevenness in the ground. This work demands rapidity and alertness, having to be performed in the intervals between police inspections. Yet it is not uncommon for a pregnant woman to continue her beer-brewing until the day before her confinement.[58]

Their predominantly male clientele could choose from a wide range of potions: *sekonvani* (Sotho) or *skokiaan* (Zulu) (made from yeast, sugar and warm water), *mqombothi*, *babaton*, *shimeya* or *shimeyani*, *isiqataviki*

---

[55] It was published as a journal article in 1934. See Ellen Hellmann, 'The Importance of Beer-Brewing in an Urban Native Yard', *Bantu Studies*, 8 (1934), 39–60.

[56] See, for example, Paul la Hausse, *Brewers, Beerhalls and Boycotts: A History of Liquor in South Africa* (Johannesburg: History Workshop Topic Series No. 2, 1984), 43.

[57] Chuck Ambler and Jonathan Crush, 'Alcohol in Southern African Labour History' in Crush and Ambler, eds., *Liquor and Labor in Southern Africa* (Athens, Ohio and Pietermaritzburg: Natal University Press, 1992), 8–9.

[58] Hellmann, 'The Importance of Beer-Brewing' 44.

124   Pioneers of the Field

('kill-me-quick') (made out of sour porridge, bread, syrup, brown sugar and yeast), and *ishishimeyane* which 'was first concocted by workers in sugar-cane fields. Its name is popularly conceived to be onomatopoeic, suggesting the swaying gait of an intoxicated man.'[59] Home-grown ingredients were common, ranging from pineapple-skins to carbide.[60] Her criticism was directed not at the women brewers whose industry was a matter of survival, but at the government for its criminalization of beverages that had long been an essential part of traditional life in African cultures across the region.[61]

Despite the individualism that came with intense economic competition in a time of depression, something that could spill over into conflict and violence, she presented strong evidence for a sense of what we might term 'community' among the women brewers. This was apparent in the sharing of space and brewing equipment, in alerting neighbours to the presence of police, in new urban 'voluntary associations' to use the language of later urban anthropologists.[62] She gave a detailed account of women's *stokvels* (which she rendered 'stockfairs' suggesting perhaps a limited knowledge of Afrikaans). She was also the first to describe, albeit in brief, the popular urban culture of leisure that included organized dances and concerts on weekends and 'marabi' dances striking for their degree of sexual display.[63]

She then followed 'the life stages' of African women through an analysis of ritual – from birth through childhood and puberty to marriage, adulthood and death. The sections on birth and marriage included intimate details about sex, contraception, abortion and virginity testing. Her evidence pointed to the continued importance of traditional rituals in the urban context, but again in ways that led her to highlight adaptation and innovation. In her concluding discussion of 'magic and witchcraft', she presented a richly detailed account of the practice of urban traditional healers, deeply influenced by the fact that

---

[59] *Ibid.*, 45.   [60] *Ibid.*, 55.

[61] Here she cited Eileen Jensen Krige, 'The Social Significance of Beer among the Balobedu', *Bantu Studies*, 6 (1932), 343–57.

[62] See Hilda Kuper and Selma Kaplan, 'Voluntary Associations in an Urban Township', *African Studies*, 3 (1944), 178–86; Wilson and Mafeje, *Langa*, 113–36.

[63] This popular culture of leisure was much more fully documented by Eddie Koch across six Doornfontein yards (of which Rooiyard was just one). Koch's account is well historicized and rich in detail based on extensive oral interviews especially about the musical forms of working-class culture. See Eddie Koch, 'Doornfontein and Its African Working Class, 1914–1935' (unpublished M.A. thesis, Witwatersrand University, 1983); Koch, '"Without Visible Means of Subsistence": Slumyard Culture in Johannesburg, 1918–1940' in Belinda Bozzoli, ed., *Town and Countryside in the Transvaal* (Johannesburg: Ravan Press, 1983), 152–75.

Anthropology and Jewish identity

her research assistant was a highly successful healer and provided her with a wealth of information about his craft.[64]

Saul Dubow has suggested that Wulf Sachs felt a particular affinity with John Chafambira on account of his Jewish identity. Was the 'mutual curiosity' between Ellen and John, here in relation to healing practices and the wider social life of Rooiyard, not also rooted in part in 'common underlying feelings of alienation from, or marginality to, their respective worlds',[65] despite the marked differences in their material circumstances? More generally, was Ellen's ability to empathize with the women of Rooiyard not in part, or even primarily, the product of her own painful experiences of discrimination: as a German, as a Jew and as a young girl and woman?

In concluding this section on what is rightly regarded as her best ethnography, it is interesting to reflect on the differences between Ellen's approach in *Rooiyard* and that of Monica Hunter in her excellent eighty-page analysis of African cultural life in East London, published the following year as Part III of *Reaction to Conquest*. Monica wanted to document urban African attitudes and beliefs rather than economic activities or cultural ritual. Monica's text is rich in conversation and conveys a sense of indigenous voice in a way that Ellen could not do given the multi-cultural field-site and her lack of knowledge of African languages, as well as her lack of comparable insider social networks. While Ellen's preoccupation with space, economics and ritual rather than women's perceptions of their world was a matter of necessity rather than choice, her ethnography is no less important for that.

The main difference lay in distribution and impact. Monica achieved an almost overnight reputation as an internationally respected social anthropologist following the publication of her study in 1936 in the highly prestigious Oxford University Press-IAI series. Ellen had to rely on her Jewish friends to belatedly publish and promote her study. Her full monograph would remain buried for thirteen years until her loyal former class-mate and life-long friend, Max Gluckman, used his influence as the second director of the Rhodes-Livingstone Institute to publish the ethnography in 1948 as the thirteenth volume in the RLI series. He generously promoted the book in a short introduction, describing it as 'comprehensive', 'precise' and 'the most valuable material to have been written to date about Africans in urban South Africa'. He insisted that the book remained intensely relevant despite the delay in publication, given the continued importance of its

---

[64] Hellmann, *Rooiyard*, 105.
[65] Saul Dubow, 'Introduction' in *Black Hamlet* by Wulf Sachs, 3.

126 Pioneers of the Field

sociological arguments about urban African poverty, the ethnic diversity of African urban communities and the strains on African family life associated with urbanization and industrial change.[66] Journal reviewers complimented the study for its 'painstaking observation of daily activities', identifying it as 'one of the earliest systematic sociological investigations among urban Africans'.[67] Meyer Fortes, another life-long Jewish friend and fellow anthropologist, would later write that '*Rooiyard* may be described, without exaggeration, as *the work* that inaugurated what has now become the established sub-discipline of social anthropology, Urban Anthropology'. He indicated that it continued to exert an 'intellectual and moral impact' in African studies into the 1970s, referring to its ongoing impact on urban studies in Ghana and the United States.[68]

Ellen did achieve some recognition for the five essays that she published on Rooiyard and on African urban life in South Africa between 1934 and 1937. The best known of these was her overview on 'The Native in Towns' in Isaac Schapera's edited collection, *The Bantu-Speaking Tribes of South Africa*. This essay drew attention to the new literature on urban Africans in South Africa authored by her women peers like Monica and Eileen. She then provided the first sociological overview of aspects of the African experience in South Africa: the mass movement of Africans to cities, the new material culture of townships and slum-yards, changes and adaptations in African family life. As in the case of her monograph, the central themes were forms of cultural adaptation under strained new circumstances and an appreciation of the resilience of African traditional cultural practices in a radically different setting. In keeping with her celebration of the subculture of resistance of the women of Rooiyard, her essay was unusual in drawing attention to the dynamism of urban African popular culture of the 1930s with its 'kaleidoscopic succession of concerts, meetings and dances'.[69]

---

[66] Max Gluckman, 'Introductory Note' in Hellmann, *Rooiyard*, i–ii. Earlier influential volumes in the series included the Nyakyusa and Ngonde work of Godfrey Wilson, Gluckman's predecessor and the founding director of the RLI, a short book on anthropological method by Godfrey and Monica Wilson, a study of the Bemba by Audrey Richards and a study on the Lozi by Gluckman himself.

[67] Cyril Sofer, 'Review of *Rooiyard*', *Africa*, 19, 1 (1949), 77.

[68] Cited in Wits University Archive, Hellmann Papers, E. Hellmann, Proposal for Award of D.Litt. Honoris Causa, 29 August 1977 compiled by David Hammond-Tooke and Allie Dubb.

[69] Ellen Hellmann, 'The Native in Towns' in Isaac Schapera, ed., *The Bantu-Speaking Tribes of South Africa*, 405–34. See the other four essays cited above, two published in *Africa*, two in *Bantu Studies*.

Anthropology and Jewish identity

Figure 3.4: Ellen and Ruth, aged two, 1938.[70]

African social welfare and applied anthropology, 1936–1940

Ellen's second major ethnographic monograph was a study of African education and youth culture in the townships of Johannesburg. The links between activism and anthropological research were more explicit in this second study. Indeed, it had been commissioned by the SAIRR to explore the reasons for African school-leaving and lack of employment opportunity.

Following the birth of her only child, Ruth, in January 1936, Ellen had thrown herself into welfare activism on a broad front. Her activities in these and subsequent years included, in addition to the Jewish political activism which I discuss below, lecturing in sociology at the Jan Hofmeyr School of Social Work, which trained African social workers, serving on the Johannesburg Joint Council of Europeans and Africans, as treasurer of the Alexandra township African Welfare Centre, and as a founder member of the Society for Jews and Christians in 1937. She also played an active role in the 'Urban Native Juvenile Delinquency Conference' held in Johannesburg in October 1938.

Deborah Posel identifies this conference as a 'formative event' in consolidating left-liberal social welfare ideology in this period. Partly under

---

[70] Ruth Runciman, Family Album, Private Collection.

128   Pioneers of the Field

Ellen's influence, the Conference made recommendations regarding African social welfare that were, in Posel's view, 'radical' for their time, even though they needed to be articulated within the existing legal framework of racially differential services.[71] Ellen reported to the delegates on her recent findings about the inadequate state of township schools in Orlando, Pimville, North-West Township and Sophiatown, where she had been conducting research for over a year. She estimated that only 40 per cent of African youth of school-going age actually attended school. For these 7,000 learners classroom facilities were woefully inadequate. Teachers were underqualified and underpaid. Classes were overcrowded. There were on average sixty-four pupils per class in the sub-standards where most township learners were concentrated. It was this learning environment, she argued, that explained why so many African pupils left school early. Economic circumstances were also important.

I found that one-fifth of children left school because of a poverty which made it impossible for the parents to pay fees and buy books. But I found that one-quarter of children left school because the school simply had no holding power; there was nothing to keep them interested; nothing to keep them at school.

The issue of improved schooling was inextricably linked to that of employment opportunity, the second theme of her study. 'It is extraordinarily difficult, and I have spent much time in investigating this problem, for a Native juvenile to find work ... Unless there is a Native Juvenile Affairs Board [established] on the same lines as the [existing] European Juvenile Affairs Board, I fear we will be faced with this problem of the Native juvenile who is not working and not attending school.'[72]

The two core sections of her study were followed by a list of practical recommendations. In relation to African schooling she advocated for compulsory and free education, increased provision for adult education and an urgent improvement in teaching conditions in township schools. In order to improve employment opportunities for African school-leavers, she called for the establishment of a Native Juvenile Affairs Board, the modification of pass laws, substantial wage increases, the creation of opportunities for more skilled work, as well as full legal recognition of African trade unions.[73] She also promoted the idea of developing sports

---

[71] Deborah Posel, 'The Case for a Welfare State: Poverty and the Politics of the Urban African Family in the 1930s and 1940s' in Saul Dubow and Alan Jeeves, eds., *South Africa's 1940s: A World of Possibilities* (Cape Town: Double Storey, 2005), 64–86.

[72] Wits University, William Cullen Library, AD843/RJ/ND4.1, Minutes of a Conference on Juvenile Native Delinquency, Johannesburg, 11–13 October 1938, 1–10. Thanks to Gabriel Mohalale for making scans of the Conference Minutes available to me.

[73] Ellen Hellmann, 'Report on the Problems of Urban Bantu Youth' (D.Phil. thesis, Wits University, 1939), 139–47, 207–13.

Anthropology and Jewish identity 129

clubs, gyms and other organizations to prompt township youth to get involved in 'healthy' forms of leisure. In a 1941 essay Ellen would insist on the need for 'a radical change in policy' in relation to wages, social services, employment, education, housing and health services for urban Africans, calling for the national government to take full responsibility for providing such funds. She located her proposals within the wider global movement towards a social welfare state.[74]

There is more to *Problems of Urban Bantu Youth* than schools, work opportunity and associated policy recommendations. This ethnographical richness of her study is again more apparent from the original text, here the SAIRR report and doctoral thesis submitted in 1939, than from the abridged and edited text in which 'scientific' findings were highlighted at the expense of some of the on-site texture of her cross-cultural encounters. For example, she made extensive use of visual documentation in her analysis of popular cultural forms in the townships of interwar Johannesburg. These photographs, including the selection reproduced in Figure 3.5 below, are a rare and rich record of township life in Johannesburg in the late 1930s, but very few feature in the published book of 1940.

Her thesis also includes an extended discussion of method, which was reduced to just two pages in the published version edited by Isaac Schapera. As in the case of 'Rooiyard', this presumably related to the editor's attempts (here Schapera rather than Gluckman) to enhance 'ethnographic authority' and downplay introductory subjective reflections about relationships in the field.[75] Her thesis reveals that she drew on her experience of working in Rooiyard: an initial questionnaire-based method, administered here in schools rather than households, laid the foundation for more intensive interviews with select informants who, again, were women. 'With some women I built a relationship of friendship after meeting them at a family investigation. For three months I visited some of these homes very frequently – at periods even daily. The relationship established has continued to date [1940] with five of these families.'

The next phase of the study involved acquiring information more directly from township youths. She did this through informal discussions during field-visits and, most innovatively, by means of student essays commissioned at five township schools on set themes: '(1) Why children

---

[74] Ellen Hellmann, 'Social Services for Urban Africans', *Race Relations*, 8, 4 (1941), 1–14.
[75] Ellen Hellmann, *Problems of Urban Bantu Youth* (Johannesburg: South African Institute of Race Relations, 1940).

130   Pioneers of the Field

leave school; (2) Why I go to school; (3) My home; (4) My parents; (5) What I intend to do when I leave school; (6) How I spend my days.'[76]

The section of her study on 'recreation' is particularly worth revisiting. While her work predates that of social historians by half a century, there is in this ethnography a similarly empathetic, even celebratory, quality. In the case of the very young boys, she wrote of their creating games in the absence of toys which their parents were unable to afford: games played with stones or marbles, or games of 'make believe'.[77] For the older boys, she described the multiple means used to earn petty cash in a way that suggests a richly detailed knowledge of township life and youth culture.

Some have regular part-time occupations, such as newspaper-selling or week-end caddying. Some, with rough hand-carts they construct themselves, carry bundles of washing for the women. Some buy a sack of oranges, a box of tomatoes, or such fruit and vegetable as is in season and sell it on the trains, at the station or street corners, or peddle from home to home. Some get odd jobs at the shops, weighing out sugar or mealie meal or sweeping out the shop. Some spend part of their time, especially over weekends, acting as guards to beer-sellers to give warning when the police approach. Some are regular *izimbamgothi* [hole-diggers], burying and unearthing the brew. Some, but only among the elder boys, are *fah-fee* or *pa-ka-pu* runners.[78]

In the case of teenage boys, she documented their subculture of gambling and gangs in terms that were unusually accepting. At the 1938 Conference, for example, she was discussant for a paper presented by Margaret Ballinger. She tactfully indicated that she had a different view of the street culture of African youth from that of Mrs Ballinger. 'There is more adventure in the locations themselves [than most whites realize], and the parents cannot stop children from indulging in gambling and so forth. I do not share Mrs [Margaret] Ballinger's view that gambling is a very undesirable thing.'[79]

She was surely the first social scientist in South Africa to write about township gangs. 'Gangs represent the most spontaneous effort of boys to create a society for themselves where none adequate to their needs

[76] Hellmann, 'Report on the Problems of Urban Bantu Youth', 1–18.

[77] Hellmann, *Urban Bantu Youth*, 47.

[78] Hellmann, *Urban Bantu Youth*, 46; Hellmann 'Report on Urban Bantu Youth', 86. The page references here are from the published version given that this section of the text was published unchanged. For reference to the popularity of *fah-fee* in Pretoria's Marabastad, see Eileen Jensen Krige, 'Social and Economic Facts Revealed in Native Family Budgets', *Race Relations*, 1, 6 (1934), 96.

[79] Address by Mrs E. Hellmann as discussant for the paper by Mrs Ballinger, Conference on Native Juvenile Delinquency, 10 October 1938.

Anthropology and Jewish identity 131

exists.'[80] She referenced the recent American literature on the rise of gang subcultures, especially in interwar Chicago. 'They [the Johannesburg gangs] have a leader whose decisions are said to be binding on every member of the gang; some bear a name – "The Squash Boys" and the "Spockies Range" are two common gang names found in Pimville, Orlando and Sophiatown; some wear an external distinguishing mark such as a black shirt with white buttons or distinctive stripes.'[81]

Her textual descriptions of a masculine culture of leisure and informal employment among township youth are best read alongside the forty photographs that feature in a ten-page appendix to her report. They were edited out of her published monograph, which featured just seven photographs on two back-to-back plates. As in the case of *Rooiyard*, there is a close relationship between image and text. Each set of photographs provided visual evidence for a general argument as the captions explained. Five images illustrated the vibrancy of popular street culture: 'A group of non-school-goers. Pimville', 'Pimville Play' (Page 2), and 'Waiting for a fare', 'Gambling' and 'Pimville' (Page 5). Four photographs illustrated the overcrowded state of schools and their inadequate facilities: 'Classes at Alexandra' (Page 7), (Page 9). Healthy forms of leisure were documented in a series of unusual images captioned 'The Day Club – Orlando'. Another series of photographs was taken inside an Orlando crèche.[82]

The second section of her study was more quantitative in orientation, anticipating her later 'sociological' case study of workers at a large Johannesburg business.[83] Here again her ethnographic fieldwork was impressive for its novelty, range and rigour. She visited more than fifty industrial and commercial firms. In each case she interviewed juvenile workers, trade union leaders, members of industrial councils and white employers; she also spoke to government and municipal officials. On this basis she gave an overview of the extent and nature of juvenile employment in Johannesburg. Her findings were sociologically significant. She revealed that 'Native Juveniles' (employees under the age of 21) made up as much as one-fifth of the urban work force, but that they were hidden from public record because companies were reluctant to admit to employing them and usually paid them very poorly. Most juvenile employees preferred to work in the informal sector as shop assistants, messengers, newspaper sellers or domestic servants. She concluded with

---

[80] Hellmann, *Urban Bantu Youth*, 49.   [81] *Ibid.*, 48.

[82] Marijke du Toit analyses these photographs in relation to the theme of the African family and Hellmann's concern with forced removals. See Du Toit, 'The General View and Beyond'.

[83] See the discussion of Hellmann, *Sellgoods* (1953) in this chapter.

Figure 3.5: Photographs from the appendix to Ellen Hellmann's doctoral thesis (1939).[84]

---

[84] EHC, Box 31, Photographic Album, 31.11.

Anthropology and Jewish identity 133

a fascinating ethnography of caddying based on extensive fieldwork at fourteen Johannesburg golf clubs. She demonstrated that this was one of the most important forms of juvenile employment for Africans with 646 young caddies being employed by these clubs by 1938. In fact, eight of these golf courses had established living quarters on site known as 'caddy compounds'. The caddies were bused in from different rural areas and, for the most part, indentured for a period of six months. Township youths were much more reluctant to get 'trapped into contracts' as she found from personal experience when trying to find jobs for a number of interviewees at one of the golf clubs. They were willing only to work as casual caddies on a part-time basis.[85] This interest in workers and their welfare overlapped with her involvement in socialist politics.

Zionist socialism and essays on South African Jewish culture, c 1938–1950

While Ellen's commitment to liberal politics and the Race Relations Institute has been well-recognized, her involvement in socialist politics has gone unnoticed. It was, in fact, in the Zionist Socialist Party that she cut her political teeth from the late 1930s.

In her own account of the Party's history, Ellen explained that it had been founded by Jewish immigrants from Poland and the Baltic in the early 1920s. It took on its name in 1931. While the early membership had been almost exclusively Yiddish-speaking, 'there was a growing realization' among a new generation 'that the future of Zionist Socialism could only be secured and its maximum effectiveness in terms of meeting the needs of young people for a political home be developed, by drawing into its ranks young, predominantly English-speaking Jewish youth'. The Zionist Socialist Party flourished in the 1930s. It had opened nine branches by the early 1940s. It sought to encourage the use of Hebrew in homes and schools, and strongly supported the establishment of a state of Israel. In its socialist aspect it saw itself in sympathy with working class interests and as part of a United Front of 'progressive forces and . . . pro-democratic and anti-fascist agencies'.[86] In 1944 she reflected on what had drawn young intellectuals like herself to Zionist Socialism.

The enormous inequalities between the different racial groups in our race-caste society and within the white group itself, and the very real and threatening menace of the Fascist opposition party [the Nationalist Party] have had the effect of

[85] Hellmann, 'Report', 173–8, 220–1.
[86] Hellmann, 'Labour Zionism in South Africa'; on the Party in wider context and Hellmann's involvement in it, see Gideon Shimoni, *Jews and Zionism: The South African Experience, 1910–1967* (Cape Town: Oxford University Press, 1980), 187–9.

134   Pioneers of the Field

arousing in young people a spirit of turmoil and ferment and revolt which seeks release in leftist activity. A number turned to the Communist Party and others sought an outlet for their drive towards change in other organizations. General Zionism with its emphasis on emotion could not hold them. Consequently Zionist Socialism with its clear-cut ideology, its synthesis of Zionism and Socialism ... has been able to provide a Jewish political home to many who were restless and frustrated or entirely remote and aloof from the Jewish scene.[87]

She was the treasurer of the organization and recalls being referred to by her comrades as 'Yekke' (German Jew).[88] She tried to canvas support, even on a trip to far-flung Umtata in 1943, as a letter to her close friend and fellow activist Colin Legum reveals.

I was a good girl today. I met my first Jew down here (I believe there are 7 or 8) – a prosperous trader. So I asked him to arrange a meeting for me with the Jewish community. I shall try and canvas ... Greetings to all chaverim, and especially Louis [Pincus, the Party leader].

In a talk given to the Labour Zionist Movement in later years, she remembered 'with nostalgia' her days as a Zionist Socialist Party activist and her gratitude for 'a friendship which has been one of the most precious in my life – ... [that] with Louis Pincus ... one of the kindest and most loyal hearts.'[89] Such friendships would have been particularly precious in the painful years following the suicide of her husband, Joe, in 1941 while serving with the South African forces in North Africa.[90]

Ellen was elected onto the Executive Council of the Jewish Board of Deputies in 1940. Her continued commitment to Zionist socialism is evident from her correspondence with Legum. In November 1944 she was en route to a World Jewish Conference in New York, and wrote to him from the West Indies. 'I have just been having a long talk with Mr Rens (I can never, as you know, cope with titles, but I am sure you know him – he was, I think, Secretary of the General Confederation of Belgian Workers), and have been utterly delighted – on this clipperful of important anti-Roosevelt businessmen – to meet a socialist and to hear sentiments expressed that I can accept! ... I have been trying to explain the complexities of our trade union and labour position in South Africa.' She also recorded her impressions about the systems of rule in the African countries they had passed through, 'a succession of screen shots [rather] than any sort of coherent script'. She was shocked by 'the unbelievable

---

[87] Hellmann, 'Labour Zionism in South Africa', 5.
[88] Kaplan Centre Archive, BC949, Tape-recorded Interview with Ellen Hellmann by Riva Krut, 3 June 1982, Johannesburg.
[89] EHP, Box 45, Talks.
[90] Telephone interview with Ruth Runciman, 3 September 2011, Cape Town-London.

DR. ELLEN HELLMAN

Figure 3.6: Ellen Hellmann, 1945.[91]

slums and poverty and plague of Dakar'.[92] She was taken aback by the narrow, male-dominated version of Zionism that she encountered in New York. The conference, she reported on her return, 'was composed almost exclusively of men who had achieved fame and leadership in Eastern Europe. I listened, but as I listened I revolted more and more against what these men, despite their knowledge, were saying.' She felt

[91] Taken from Ellen Hellmann, 'The Jewish American Scene', *Jewish Affairs* (August 1945), 4.
[92] UCT Libraries, Manuscripts and Archives Department, BC1329 Colin Legum Collection, Correspondence B11.48, Ellen Hellmann to Colin Legum, 11 November 1943, West Indies. Thanks to Andre Landman for alerting me to this and subsequent references to Ellen in the Legum Papers.

136   Pioneers of the Field

that they were unable or unwilling to see the connections between the cultural and political struggle of Jews and those of other oppressed social groups, notably members of the working class. This was something she took up in debates with the male-dominated South African Jewish community on her return.[93]

Ellen was now elected onto the Board's Public Relations Committee, which led the campaign against anti-Semitism in South Africa. They worked against organizations fronting for the Greyshirt Movement, an anti-Semitic group sympathetic to the Nazis that remained active in South Africa through the Second World War and beyond.[94] They engaged with political parties and the press on issues of Jewish interest. They promoted a positive message about Jewish identity through the journal *Common Sense*, aimed at fostering understanding between Jews and Christians. They proposed publishing a new Jewish cultural magazine in Afrikaans and oversaw the production of pamphlets which explained the Jewish religion to the South African public. One of their greatest successes was the publication in 1950 of a book on the Jewish contribution to the war effort.[95]

Between 1945 and 1951 Ellen wrote a series of essays on South African Jewish history in which she sought to apply anthropological concepts to Jewish culture. There are clear continuities between her studies of Africans and of Jews: both were centrally concerned with 'culture contact' and notions of citizenship informed by a case for 'assimilation' rather than segregation or 'isolation' (in the Jewish case). While these writings were directly related to her Zionist socialism, there was also an important personal dimension. Ruth recalls the deep impact of anti-Semitism on her mother (and herself) during the War years when she was a young girl. 'There were terrible stories of experiences of Nazi atrocities on my mother's side, stories of the loss of family members who were killed at Auschwitz.'[96] The scars of the holocaust came into their family home in an even more immediate sense after Ellen developed an intimate relationship in 1946 with a man who had deeply traumatic personal

---

[93] Ellen Hellmann, 'The Jewish American Scene'. For discussion of her debate with Simon Kuper, an influential figure on the Jewish Board of Deputies (and father of the anthropologist Adam Kuper), see Shimoni, *Jews and Zionism*, 192.

[94] For a full account, see Patrick J. Furlong, *Between Crown and Swastika: The Impact of the Radical Right on the Afrikaner Nationalist Movement in the Fascist Era* (Johannesburg: Wits University Press, 1991).

[95] The information in this paragraph is taken from Johannesburg Public, Library of the Jewish Board of Deputies, ARCH 809, Relations Committee Minutes 1944–1950, File on Ellen Hellmann. Thanks to Jill Weintroub for this information from the Jewish Board Library.

[96] Interview with Ruth Runciman, 5 September 2011, Cape Town-London.

Anthropology and Jewish identity

experience of death and torture at the hands of the Nazis. Bodo Koch, whom she married in 1948, was a wartime German Jewish refugee who practised as a surgeon. He had witnessed his mother being shot by the Nazis before his family fled from Germany in the late 1930s.[97] He had himself been tortured by the Nazis, as Colin Legum recorded in his private diary in November 1946.

> [9 Nov.] Ellen came up with Dr Bodo Koch this evening ... Bodo is a pleasant-mannered German refugee doctor. Has fairly deferential manner. Heavily-built, dark glasses, wears his hair long ...
> [10 Nov.] Talked to Ellen about Bodo Koch. [He was] Born in Germany of German father and Jewish mother. Unhappy childhood. ... Expensive and thorough surgical training. Advent of Hitlerism caused his imprisonment and torture – scar on forehead. Father returned all his medals to Hitler and when Bodo was released, escaped to Austria ... Ellen says his doctoring is a passion, surgery is his deep love.[98]

Ellen's sister, Inez, was now a leading figure in Zionist politics serving as the President of the Women's Zionist Organization of South Africa. She immigrated to Israel in the mid-1950s as apartheid repression made life in South Africa increasing difficult. Ellen for her part chose the painful path of opposition from within the system, largely through public writing in the form of newspapers, reports and essays. In *Jewish Affairs* of May 1951, she warned South African Jews that there was no room for complacency in the fight against anti-Semitism.

> For it is disquieting that today, in 1951, there is still a ban on Jewish member-ship of the Transvaal National Party. It is clearly a repudiation of democratic practice. It is disquieting that the Ossewa Brandwag ... has consistently adopted an overtly anti-Semitic tone in its recent publication, *Die Brandwag*. The recent re-emergence of the 'Hoggenheimer' caricature in its various associations is a further symptom that anti-Semitism in its political aspect is not far below the surface.[99]

Her 'assimilationist' argument about Jewish cultural identity had been most forcefully articulated in an article published in 1950 in response to another South African Jewish writer's call for the proactive

---

[97] Interview with Ruth Runciman, 3 September 2011, Cape Town-London.
[98] UCT Libraries, Manuscripts and Archives Department, BC 1329 Colin Legum Papers, F1.1.1 Diaries.
[99] Ellen Hellmann, 'The Jews Problems Cannot Be Isolated', *Jewish Affairs*, 6, 5 (May 1951), 8–9. On the history of the 'Hoggenheimer' stereotype, see Milton Shain, *The Roots of Antisemitism in South Africa* (Johannesburg: Wits University Press, 1994), 90–4, 106–8.

138   Pioneers of the Field

fostering of a separate South African Jewish culture. He had claimed that separation was necessary given South Africa's climate of 'racial rivalry'.[100]

Ellen began by quoting the Victorian anthropologist E.B. Tylor's definition of culture as 'that complex whole which includes knowledge, belief, art, morals, law, custom and any other capabilities acquired by man as a member of society'. She proceeded to extol the value of the functionalist theory of culture that she had learnt during her years at Wits, in which cultures are viewed as a composite of inter-related elements: economic, legal and religious institutions, beliefs and kinship structures. She suggested that this theory could be applied to the South African Jewish community who, despite the historic differences in their backgrounds, had come to forge a 'distinctive value system' and were developing shared 'attitudes regarding the past, present and future of Jewish people'. The South African Jewish community, as she described it, shared 'a rich symbolism of the past which expresses itself in everyday speech; by the extent and permanence of kinship ties and the acceptance of obligations and duties arising from them'. Despite the increasingly secular orientation of this Jewish community, religious rituals remained important in most South African Jewish homes, notably 'rituals surrounding the crises of life – birth, puberty, marriage and death'.[101] Yet like the urban Africans she had studied in the mid- to late 1930s, the strongly urbanized South African Jewish community of 1950 had to face the challenge that came with 'culture contact', which in this context involved exposure to an increasingly cosmopolitan world, a world of which she had direct experience from her recent trip to New York. '[S]port, cinema-going ..., and the whole system of "dating"', were a few among many examples of a new global youth culture to which South African Jews would need to adapt. 'Surely the enigma of Jewish history', she continued, again with echoes of her studies highlighting the resilience of urban Africans, 'lies in Jewish cultural adaptiveness'.

The age-long struggle of the Jewish people – a struggle which continues today – for complete equality of treatment has rested on this basis: that the Jew, while retaining his group identity, becomes merged, both in regard to major areas of behaviour and identity of civic and social interests, with the people among whom he lives. Any other approach appears to me as isolationist, hampering the

---

[100] E. Tannebaum, 'The Jew in South Africa's Fragmented Society', *Jewish Affairs*, 5, 9 (September 1950), 4–7.

[101] Ellen Hellmann, 'Plea against Jewish "Isolationism"', *Jewish Affairs*, 5, 10 (October 1950), 4–9.

Anthropology and Jewish identity

integration of the Jew, which remains, despite obstacles to its fulfilment, the overall aim of a free society.[102]

In short, I propose that we read her 1950 essay as an extension to South African Jews of the arguments about culture contact and social change that she had made in her ethnographies of urban African women and youth. These studies had sought to demonstrate the necessity for cultural adaptation in the context of rapid urban socio-economic change, simply because there was no alternative. Despite the serious 'problems' associated with this process, notably its disruption of African family life, to a much greater degree than latter-day critics have acknowledged, her two major ethnographies celebrated the ways in which African women brewers and especially male township youth invented new recreational and occupational forms on the streets and sidewalks, in spaza shops and even as caddies on the golf courses in white suburbs. South African Jews were likewise now called to let go of outdated 'tradition', especially in an increasingly secular world. The way forward was to embrace the realities of cultural change and continually adapt rather than retreat into the kind of isolationist laager that the Afrikaner nationalists were building around themselves.[103]

Anti-apartheid activism and sociological essays, 1948–1977

Ellen, Bodo and Ruth would move from West Dunkeld to Houghton in 1953, following the death of Ellen's father Bernard Kaumheimer. This was where she would live for the rest of her life.

She retired from active participation in Jewish cultural politics, resigning from the Board of Deputies in 1950, but remained a life-long supporter of the state of Israel, making regular visits to her sister and family into the 1970s. Like so many South African liberals, Ellen was deeply shocked by the National Party victory of 1948, disturbed by the barrage of laws that the apartheid state introduced and outraged by the human cost of this state engineering. Her courageous challenge to apartheid in the 1950s and early 1960s in particular has been blurred by retrospective accounts which tend to associate her with the conservative liberal views of an older generation, with the qualified liberalism of the Progressive Federal Party, of which she was a founder executive member in 1959, or even with her affluent living circumstances.

---

[102] *Ibid.*, 4–9.   [103] Hellmann, 'The Jews Problems Cannot Be Isolated', 9.

140   Pioneers of the Field

While Ellen remained a proponent of an educationally based, rather than a fully universal and democratic, franchise in South Africa, her opposition to apartheid was unambiguous. It was not only economically irrational in her view, given the irreversible pace of African urbanization and the necessity of racial integration in the economy, but was unjust and 'evil'. With the coming of apartheid, she became a political activist on a national level. The South African Institute of Race Relations served as the institutional base for many of her activities. Indeed, she became the leading figure of the organization during the apartheid years, serving as President in the mid-1950s, as an Executive Member across these decades and directing its research wing from the late 1940s into the 1970s. Indeed, the publication for which she is best remembered, and rightly so, is the compendious first edition, *Handbook on Race Relations in South Africa*, which was published to international acclaim by Oxford University Press in New York, London and Cape Town in 1949. Running into 778 pages, it featured essays from thirty-one authors, mostly liberals but also a few radicals like Jack Simons and Eddie Roux. It covered virtually every aspect of African life and race relations in South Africa, although it was weighted more towards policy and statistics rather than personal experience. The Institute's director acknowledged that: 'Without her [Ellen's] devotion to the task, it is very doubtful indeed if the volume would ever have reached the printer.' She was enlisted because 'the editorial work required the concentrated and detailed attention of a person expertly acquainted with the vast field of knowledge covered by the volume'.[104]

Her overview essay on the 'Urban Areas' was singled out by the ever-promotional Max Gluckman in a supportive review in *Africa*. He strongly recommended the volume to readers, despite some unevenness in quality and the lack of a sufficiently coherent methodological framework.[105] She combined extensive new archival work into official records, most notably government reports, commissions and enquiries, with a skilful synthesis of recent academic literature and a careful history of the complex array of legislative changes introduced by South African governments from Union to the present. She identified the Urban Areas Act of 1923 and the apartheid government laws that were being introduced at the very time of publication as dual landmarks in an emerging framework of repressive regulation of urban African life and movement. Like her earlier anthropological monographs, this

---

[104] J.D. Rheinallt-Jones, 'Foreword' in Ellen Hellmann, ed., *Handbook on Race Relations in South Africa* (Cape Town, London and New York: Oxford University Press, 1949), 3.

[105] Max Gluckman, 'Review of Hellmann, ed., *Handbook of Race Relations in South Africa*', *Africa*, 21 (1951), 72–3.

Figure 3.7: Ellen Hellmann addressing a public meeting during the 1950s, possibly at Entokozeni, a clinic in Alexandra with which she was actively involved.[106]

sociological overview highlighted the continued 'all-pervading poverty' among the urban working class and its 'widespread repercussions for African urban life'. But there were also signs of fresh developments. This is where her essay was most impressive: her ability to draw attention to the multiplicity and variation in post-War urban African life based on her first-hand ongoing experience of life in the townships of Johannesburg. She wrote of the recent rise of an African middle class, 'displaying the qualities of conservatism, orderliness, acquisitiveness that are characteristic of all middle-class groups', along with new organizational expressions of community solidarity from churches and *stokfels* to trade unions and political organizations. She was, in fact, among the very first to write empathetically about urban African family life, community spirit and not least protest politics. She concluded by warning of the consequences of a policy that failed to take account of 'the legitimate aspirations of urban Africans', most notably for land rights and political representation.[107]

---

[106] Ruth Runciman, Family Album, Private Collection.
[107] Ellen Hellmann, 'Urban Areas' in Hellmann, ed., *Handbook on Race Relations*, 229–74.

142   Pioneers of the Field

Her voice of protest became louder as the apartheid system took hold in a barrage of repressive racial laws introduced in the early 1950s, beginning with the Group Areas Act (1951) and the Bantu Education Act (1953). The National Party government was less open to criticism than its predecessors. Her daughter Ruth recalls that their house was often under police surveillance from the time she began her university studies at Wits in 1953. This was also because Ruth's new university friends, Bloke Modisane and Ismael Mohamed, were political activists who frequently visited their home.[108] Newspapers featured reports on Ellen's anti-apartheid campaigning, including, for example, this report in the *Daily Dispatch* in April 1954.

Hellmann is photographed by police when attending a meeting in Sophiatown where she felt it her duty to ascertain first the viewpoint of those directly affected by the relocation scheme. She accused police of intimidation and described their actions (of photographing them) as deplorable.[109]

In 1956 she got involved in the Defence and Aid Fund during the Treason Trials. Like fellow anthropologists Monica Wilson, Eileen Krige and Jack Krige, she testified against the proposed system of Bantustans at the Tomlinson Commission that year. She was now President of the Institute of Race Relations and her anti-apartheid addresses on *Racial Laws vs. Economic and Social Forces* (1955) and *In Defense of a Shared Society* (1956) were published and widely featured in the press.[110]

By this stage her career as a field-based ethnographer had ended. Her last field-site was a Johannesburg factory, symbolic of her opening up of new spaces for anthropological or sociological investigation. Based on six months of interviews, or rather data collection, from the 345 workers of a large Johannesburg retail firm (for which 'Sellgoods' was the fictitious pseudonym), she produced a quantitative study with dozens of tables synthesizing information about job description, wages, numbers of hours of work, length of service, union affiliations, places of birth, 'tribal' origins, educational backgrounds, marital status, present residences, religious affiliations and recreational activities. She concluded, in keeping with all of her other writings about Africans in the city, that the African presence was a permanent one. Most of the workers had long histories of service and increasingly powerful ties to the city. Her study was also interesting for more specific empirical data, as for example her finding that fully 45 per cent of the workforce of this 'respectable' Johannesburg

---

[108] Telephone interview with Ruth Runciman, 3 September 2011, Cape Town-London.
[109] *Daily Dispatch*, 8 April 1954. Thanks to Leslie Bank for this and the following reference.
[110] See, for example, 'Existing System of Apartheid', *Daily Dispatch*, 4 January 1956.

Anthropology and Jewish identity

business had been arrested at some point in their lives with obvious implications for attitudes towards law and policing.[111]

The most incisive of her anti-apartheid sociological essays was published in 1961 under the relatively unpromising title 'The Application of the Concept of Separate Development to Urban Areas in the Union of South Africa'. Drawing on a decade of anti-apartheid activism at the national level, it was an eloquent and incisive exposure of the rigid repression of the apartheid state against non-Europeans and especially Africans in urban areas. She wrote about the human costs of forced removals and the emergence of protest politics. Because the essay was published in London rather than in South Africa, she could present a damningly outspoken critique of apartheid racial laws and their tragic consequences in the lives of individuals. What was most impressive was the current state of her knowledge, both about the potentially bewildering array of legislative changes and of conditions in African locations. On numerous occasions she had to refer to legislation or conditions 'at the time of writing' (which was October 1959). Perhaps more than any of her other writings, this essay laid bare the dehumanizing, mechanistic treatment of 'non-Europeans' in what she termed 'the total machinery of "influx" and "efflux" control'. She provided extensive documentation of the changing culture of political protest of the 1950s and of women's protests, including the famous anti-pass march of August 1956. I read this essay as the culmination of her body of writing exposing the dark the underbelly of racial repression. In the interwar years this underbelly was revealed in the precarious lives of African women beer-brewers in inner-city slums. On the eve of war she uncovered the rootless lives of uneducated and unemployed African youth in the new townships. Here the narrative was a national one: a story of pass laws, forced removals and widespread police repression that impacted on every aspect of African urban life.

She continued to publish sociological essays on urban Africans and on the townships of Johannesburg across the following decade. In 1966 her essay on 'The Impact of City Life on Africans' focused squarely on the impact of forced removals. *Soweto: Johannesburg's African City* (1971) gave a short history of this vast new township, one that drew attention to the continued lack of adequate social services for Africans. She would later give evidence before the Cilliers Commission of Enquiry into the Soweto Riots of 1976. Her essay on 'Social Change among Urban Africans' (1971), published in

---

[111] Ellen Hellmann, *Sellgoods: A Sociological Survey of an African Commercial Labour Force* (Johannesburg: South African Institute of Race Relations, 1953).

144   Pioneers of the Field

a collection of anthropological and sociological essays about South
Africa edited by the sociologist Heribert Adam, gave a general history
of urbanization in twentieth-century South Africa, drawing attention
to the insights of a new literature on labour migration and identity.[112]
She promoted the new wave of urban anthropology through her unfai-
lingly generous reviews. Most were published in *African Studies*, given
her long-standing association with the journal and with Wits. Like so
many other anthropologists, she was particularly impressed by the
ethnographic richness of Philip and Iona Mayer's classic description
of the inward-looking subculture of the 'red' migrants of East Bank
Location in East London as described in *Townmen or Tribesmen*
(1961).[113] She warmly endorsed Monica Wilson and Archie Mafeje's
Langa: A Study of Social Groups (1963), Desmond Reader's *The Black
Man's Portion* (1961) and *Zulu Tribe in Transition* (1966), Mia Brandel-
Syrier's *Reeftown Elite* (1971) and *Coming Through* (1978), Martin West's
Bishops and Prophets in a Black City (1975) and Francis Wilson's *Labour
in the South African Goldmines, 1911–1969* (1972).[114]

Mention should also be made of newspaper articles for the wider
South African public. The titles of this small selection from the forty or
fifty articles she published in her mature years convey a clear sense of
her anti-apartheid politics. 'What it means to make the "black spots"'
(*The Star*, 2 October 1951), 'Family of five need 23 pounds a month
to survive' (*The Star*, 14 July 1958), 'Behind the global figures of
Bantu Education' (*The Star*, 3 March 1961), 'Verwoerd's plan for
great mass migration' (*Cape Times*, 2 March 1959), 'Non-Whites bear
brunt of Group Areas: Thousands more must move' (*Rand Daily
Mail*, 25 April 1962), 'Hint on how to strangle a township' (*The Star*,
11 April 1963), 'Take off your apron, Mr Botha' (*The Star*, 11 June 1963),
'Apartheid is built on race bias' (*Sunday Times*, 4 January 1970).[115]

Her last substantive article was, appropriately, a history of the South
African Institute of Race Relations. It was published on the occasion of
the organization's fiftieth anniversary. She was, again, an editor of the
volume.[116] In April 1978 she was awarded an honorary doctorate by

---

[112] Ellen Hellmann, 'Social Change among Urban Africans' in Heribert Adam, ed., *South
Africa: Sociological Perspectives* (London, New York, Toronto and Cape Town: Oxford
University Press, 1971), 158–76.
[113] Ellen Hellmann, 'Review of *The Black Man's Portion* and *Townsman or Tribesman*',
African Studies, 21, 1 (1962), 40–3.
[114] Reviews and draft reviews from A1419 Ellen Hellmann Papers.
[115] Newspaper cuttings from A1419 Ellen Hellmann Papers.
[116] Ellen Hellmann, 'The South African Institute of Race Relations, 1929 to 1979' in
Hellmann and Henry Lever, eds., *Conflict and Progress: Fifty Years of Race Relations in
South Africa* (Johannesburg: Macmillan, 1979).

Anthropology and Jewish identity

the University of the Witwatersrand. As in the case of her mentor and friend, Winifred Hoernlé, it was in the field of law.

A time of sadness, 1976–1982

Ellen suffered from crippling emphysema during the last years of life, which she met with characteristic determination. 'Dr Hellmann read proofs and manuscripts when she was barely able to move from one room to another.'[117] She died of a heart attack in 1982, by which time the emphysema was very advanced. She had been on oxygen cylinders for much of the time. Her funeral wishes were typically modest. 'She asked [her daughter] that there be no music, no words, at her funeral. There wasn't to be anything.'[118] What did survive was her passionate commitment to social welfare. In 1991 Ruth Runciman was awarded an O.B.E. for her work on drug policy and then a D.B.E. in 1998 for services to mental health, social welfare campaigns in which she remains actively involved.

I read a sense of sadness in the late life interviews with Ellen Hellmann, although one does need to bear in mind that she had been suffering for years with a crippling terminal illness. She lamented the deterioration in racial relations during the apartheid years. She certainly felt a sense of helplessness as a white liberal in the face of apartheid repression, a feeling that can be traced right back to private correspondence in the mid-1950s but which certainly intensified after the Soweto uprising of 1976. The signs of a turn to armed struggle flew in the face of Ellen's lifelong commitment to a reformist, parliamentary and peaceful solution to the racial conflict in the country. She had, after all, served for many years as an active member of Women for Peace. The changing politics associated with Israel and the growing crisis in the Middle East also played a role. When she was interviewed for a volume on notable South African personalities in 1959, she was said to 'speak with great candour on the Jewish question' and to be 'greatly impressed with the state of Israel'.[119] Her letters to Colin Legum reveal growing anxiety about the increasingly conflictual politics of Israel in the early 1970s. 'I have also spent quite a lot of time in Israel which continues to trouble me – among tens of millions of others of course. The handling of affairs of your old friend Nahim Goldmann was typically clumsy. It can only be explained by the real antipathy felt

---

[117] 'Ellen Hellmann' in P. Impson et al., eds., *A Tinge of Blue: 80 Years of Excellence* (Cape Town: South African Association of Woman Graduates, 2003), 71.

[118] Telephone interview with Ruth Runciman, 3 September 2011, Cape Town-London.

[119] Sachs, 'Dr Ellen Hellmann: Social Engineer', 185.

146   Pioneers of the Field

for him by Golda [Meir] and others.'[120] She also found it difficult to square opposition to the forced removal of Africans in South Africa with Jewish clearance of Arabs from their homes in former Palestine, along with the restrictions on Arab movement, education and citizenship.[121]

There was also a personal aspect, which she associated with the childhood difficulties of growing up as a German Jew and, in another interview, with a sense of loss in her teenage years. 'When I turned 17 [in 1925], I was profoundly sad because I knew I had reached a certain high in my life. Later on I discovered that this was the point at which I knew most. I certainly have never been as certain as I was then.' She expressed regret about decisions in her life, both private and public, 'mistakes in personal relationships, mistakes in the work I did, the beliefs I held ... ' This was, the interviewer wrote, 'one of many crises of confidence that beset her life'. The feelings of isolation were also born of family circumstance. Her only daughter left to study at Cambridge in 1956 and stayed on in England. 'My mother's whole generation was childless. My generation left South Africa because of the horrors of apartheid. She encouraged me to go. I used to feel it. It was a real loss for them.'[122] There is a contrast between her retrospective sense of contribution and self, and that, say, of the more self-assured Monica Wilson, although the religious convictions of Wilson and her firm belief in an afterlife must also have played a role.

Anthropology's amnesia

In the years after Ellen's death social historians associated with the Wits History Workshop began a process of rediscovering the value of her interwar ethnographies. They drew extensively on her work in their studies of Africans in Johannesburg in relation to themes of working class subcultures, beer-brewing, criminality and political violence.[123] More recently, Wits social historians have mined her work for

---

[120] See UCT Libraries, Archives and Manuscripts Department, Colin Legum Papers, B11.40 Hellmann (Koch) to Legum, 28 April 1970, 8 March 1971.

[121] Telephone interview with Ruth Runciman, 3 September 2011, Cape Town-London.

[122] Telephone interview with Ruth Runciman, 3 September 2011, Cape Town-London.

[123] See Koch, 'Doornfontein and its African Working Class, 1914–1935'; Koch, ' "Without Visible Means of Subsistence": Slumyard Culture in Johannesburg, 1918–1940'; John Iliffe, *The African Poor: A History* (Cambridge: Cambridge University Press, 1987), 128–9; Paul la Hausse, *Brewers, Beerhalls and Boycotts: A History of Liquor in South Africa* (Johannesburg: Ravan Press, History Workshop Topic Series No. 2, 1989), 39, 43, 44; Philip Bonner, 'Family, Crime and Political Consciousness on the East Rand, 1939–1955', *Journal of Southern African Studies*, 14, 3 (1988), 396, 402–3.

Anthropology and Jewish identity 147

information about African youth culture and changing African ideas about sexuality and family life.[124] Yet social anthropologists have lagged behind, and, in concluding, I would like to consider why Ellen Hellmann's pioneering urban fieldwork and ethnographies have effectively not made the cut in the standard history of anthropology in the region.[125]

First, her most important study was published only after considerable delay. As one of the reviewers commented, 'In reading this short documentary masterpiece, one does not know whether to admire the author or to lament the situation which prevented its complete publication for fifteen years'.[126] One might add that the Rhodes-Livingstone Institute's monographs, despite their excellent quality, did not enjoy the international distribution that applied in the case of the lengthier and more wide-ranging ethnographies of her anthropological peers like Monica Hunter, Eileen and Jack Krige, and Hilda Kuper whose books were published by Oxford University Press in association with the International African Institute.

Second, for reasons that seem to have related primarily to the triple discrimination she experienced in her childhood and youth (as a German, as a girl and as a Jew), she was modest to what truly does seem to have been a fault. She did not seem to have fully appreciated the value of her own scholarship, even in the case of her first and most intense ethnographic study. She wrote of *Rooiyard*: 'I felt it wasn't worth publishing and couldn't see the importance of it.'[127] Max Gluckman described in his introductory note quite how much persuasion it took to convince her to have her M.A. thesis published in what she regarded as an outdated form. She was not even sure about submitting it as a thesis for the M.A. degree at Wits! She did so only at Winifred Hoernlé's insistence. She was equally diffident about the merits of her second major study. Here too she only did so when her mentor insisted that she pay the 25 pounds necessary to have her extended report on school-leaving and

---

[124] Clive Glaser, *Bo-Tsotsi: The Youth Gangs of Soweto, 1935–1976* (Portsmouth, New Haven: Heinemann, 2000), 21, 23–4, 26, 27–31, 36, 61–2; Peter Delius and Clive Glaser, 'The Myths of Polygamy: A History of Extra-Marital and Multi-Partnership Sex in South Africa', *South African Historical Journal*, 50 (2004), 84–114 which draws on *Rooiyard* but also Hellmann, 'Social Change among Urban Africans' (1971).

[125] See Hammond-Tooke, *Imperfect Interpreters*, 143–4.

[126] K.V.L.S., *African Affairs*, 48, No. 190 (1949), 77. I have located only three other reviews: G. Gordon-Brown, *American Anthropologist*, 51 (1949), 303–4; Cyril Syfer, 'Review', *Africa*, 19, 1 (January 1949), 77; Winifred Hoernlé, 'Review', *African Studies* 7, 4 (1948), 191–2. Thanks to Isaac Ntabankulu of UCT Manuscripts and Archives Department for these references.

[127] Cited in Pat Schwartz, 'A View from Both Sides of the Fence', 10 February 1981.

148   Pioneers of the Field

employment among African township youth submitted for consideration as a doctoral degree.

Third, her choice of career path – becoming a political activist rather than a university-based anthropologist – meant that she had no students who could promote her ideas and legacy in the way in which she and her classmates, say, promoted the legacy of Winifred Hoernlé. Here we should note that it was Ellen who Winifred entrusted with her field diaries when she died in March 1960, although her inability to read all of her mentor's handwriting led her to pass it on to others who eventually did see them through to publication.[128] A study of the ways in which the classical scholar Jane Ellen Harrison, whose Cambridge lectures Mrs Hoernlé may well have attended, has been remembered highlights the crucial role played by intellectual disciples in the creation of a legacy. Part of this relates to the management of an archive, as Mary Beard demonstrates in accounting for how Harrison, the scholar of ancient Greece, has been 'invented' as the towering figure in classical archaeology, while the equally pioneering work of her talented colleague (and one-time friend) Eugenie Strong, a scholar of ancient Rome, has been all but forgotten.[129] Here we might reflect on the contrast between Ellen Hellmann and Monica Hunter Wilson, two women who were born and died in exactly the same years (1908–1982). Partly because of her much stronger historical orientation, Wilson carefully preserved a vast corpus of documentary material relating to her anthropological work and her personal life. The integrity of what is now called the Monica and Godfrey Wilson Collection was then carefully maintained after her death and passed down to her sons, Francis and Tim Wilson. The collection was then passed via her last student Pamela Reynolds to the University of Cape Town's Manuscripts and Archives Department where Lesley Hart would spend more than a year compiling a detailed inventory of contents in the mid-1990s.[130]

Ellen Hellmann bequeathed her papers to Wits University the year before she died with a further posthumous donation by her husband. She chose, presumably partly because of her self-effacing attitude, to

---

[128] Ellen produced a transcript, but was unable to decipher many sections of text. She passed them on to Peter Carstens in 1967, who made little further headway. It was left to Gerald Klinghardt to decipher the remaining sections of the text in 1985 and 1986, a considerable achievement as was his detailed annotation of the diaries. Klinghardt, personal communication, 3 November 2007.

[129] Mary Beard, *The Invention of Jane Harrison* (Cambridge, MA and London: Harvard University Press, 2000).

[130] For a biography of the Monica and Godfrey Wilson Collection, see Andrew Bank, 'Introduction' in Bank and Bank, eds., *Inside African Anthropology*, 26–34.

Anthropology and Jewish identity   149

preserve a documentary legacy that was almost entirely shorn of the personal. It contains no field-notes or field reports (of the kind found in the Wilson Collection) or field diaries (of the kind found in the Krige Collection at Killie Campbell Library in Durban). These are the kind of on-site records that would have allowed for a much richer, more personal and more closely historicized account of the processes of cultural knowledge production at her unusual field-sites, including the changing history of her social networks in the field. In addition, of course, Monica Wilson was a prolific ethnographer over half a century rather than an intense decade.

The main reason for the lengthy silence about Ellen Hellmann, however, is 'the liberal taint' if one might put it in those terms. For many scholars of the 1980s and 1990s her excellent research has been of less interest than her alleged commitment to what has all too often been cast in caricatured terms as an ambiguous and dithering liberal ideology. Take, for example, Paul Rich's ill-informed account in his Marxist critique of South African liberalism published in 1984. His arguments suggest a serious lack of acquaintance with her writings. He claimed that Hellmann's anthropological writings 'emphasized the separateness of African culture from Western civilization', despite the fact that her work was striking precisely for the degree to which it demonstrated the degree of 'culture contact' in interwar Johannesburg and the complexities associated with that process. He argued that her work 'paid little attention to the general social and cultural processes that underlay the conditions in South African towns and the formation of a black working class', a view expressly contradicted by the work of social historians of Johannesburg who have mined it for precisely these insights. And most seriously, he accused her of being in 'fundamental consensus' with 'the general trajectory of urban [segregationist] legis-lation' of the 1930s and with the apartheid government's policies of separate development,[131] despite her very substantial body of public and published writings directly to the contrary. These run across dozens of newspaper articles and scholarly essays from the early 1940s, when she first became vocal in public life, to the late 1970s when she remained an active and outspoken critic of apartheid.

In short, her late-life affiliations with liberal institutions, notably the Race Relations Institute but also the Progressive Party (which she was involved in founding in 1959 and for which she stood as a ward representative under her married name Ellen Koch in 1975) has

---

[131] See Paul B. Rich, *White Power and the Liberal Conscience: Racial Segregation and South African Liberalism, 1921–60* (Johannesburg: Ravan Press, 1984), 61, 71, 129.

150   Pioneers of the Field

tended to shape the way in which her anthropological work of the 1930s and 1940s was read. This work has been misread as an expression of a paternalist kind of liberalism, one that was detached and out of touch with the realities of African life. As examples, scholars have variously cited static functionalism, lack of interest in historical change, social reformist distance, and moralizing discourse about the need for progress-in-civilization. There has been little attempt in these assessments to provide what Pierre Bourdieu terms an 'adequate reading', one that is sensitive to the contexts and conventions of anthropological writing and reading during the period in which a given work is produced.[132]

An 'adequate reading' would need, in the first instance, to take account of her 'radical' political views during the 1930s and 1940s, which was the period when her ground-breaking urban ethnographies were in fact researched and written. Her politics in this earlier period was both more complex and much more closely associated with her Jewish background and identity than is generally acknowledged. Indeed, it is only in the context of her Zionist socialist politics of the late 1930s and early 1940s that we can properly understand her two pioneering monographs on marginalized Africans, the women of Rooiyard and the township youth, and her subsequent essays about the need for an engaged, 'assimilationist' form of Jewish identity in South Africa. Her left-wing politics also deeply informed her unusually empathetic accounts of African workers, whether migrant caddies living in 'caddy compounds' on Johannesburg golf courses or criminalized workers employed in a large and reputable Johannesburg firm. Her politics did become reformist rather than radical during the apartheid decades, but she remained unwavering in her opposition to racial segregation and her willingness to speak out against the 'evils' of apartheid as her prolific public and scholarly exposé articles and essays from the 1950s through to the 1970s so eloquently reveal.

---

[132] See Pamela Reynolds, 'Gleanings and Leavings' in Bank and Bank, eds., *Inside African Anthropology*, 309.

4 'A genius for friendship': Audrey Richards at Wits, 1938–1940

Mrs Hoernlé's academic reputation probably depends mainly on her unusual gifts as a teacher. Her lectures covered a wide field including archaeology, technology taught with the aid of the University Museum which she created, social anthropology and the ethnography of South Africa, which she considered to be part of the necessary training of a South African citizen. She spoke with clarity and vigour and with an enthusiasm and sense of purpose which attracted and held her students' interests. It was impossible not to become fond of such a warm-hearted, vigorous and direct personality.

> Audrey Richards, 'Obituary: Agnes Winifred Hoernlé: 1885–1960, With a Portrait', *Man*, 61 (1961), 53.

Audrey Isabel Richards (1899–1984) took over as senior lecturer and head of department of social anthropology at Wits University from January 1938, a position she held for what would be three highly productive years. In telling the story of her Wits years for the first time, I draw attention to two related themes: first, what her life-long friend Monica Wilson called 'a genius for friendship',[1] especially but by no means exclusively for female friendship, and, second, the role she played in consolidating the South African liberal school of social anthropology which her predecessor had co-founded. My central argument is that she was Winifred Hoernlé's heir in more than just the sense of being her successor. I will demonstrate through a close reading of her vibrant weekly letters from Johannesburg that she carried forward Mrs Hoernlé's

---

[1] WC, B6.14: Correspondence between Monica Wilson and Audrey Richards, Monica Wilson to Audrey Richards, 15 February 1982. This letter was written in the last year of Monica's life. In it she expressed appreciation for almost fifty years of friendship. Thanks to my research assistant Sue Ogterop for chasing down all manner of references on Audrey Richards; Sarah Walpole, archivist at the Royal Anthropological Institute Library in London for locating the photographs of Audrey Richards that feature in this chapter and providing information about the many other photographs she took in South Africa; fellow historian Christian Williams and Audrey's former anthropology student Suzette Heald for insightful comments on a final draft. Special thanks to Adam Kuper for sharing fond memories of his late friend and colleague at his London home on 8 May 2013. It is he who led me to foreground this theme of female friendship.

152   Pioneers of the Field

work as an excellent teacher and continued to develop the department's ethnographic museum. Most important, she developed close friendships during her years at Wits with the South African women anthropologists trained by Mrs Hoernlé. She also renewed her friendship with Monica Wilson, whom she had met in London some years earlier. It was especially after her departure from Wits in December 1940, as she took on an increasingly senior role in social anthropology in Britain, that she was able to promote, with unfailing generosity, the work of the younger women scholars who feature in these chapters. In concluding I highlight the range of contributions she made in carrying forward the work that Mrs Hoernlé had begun during the decades after her departure from Wits.

Before turning to the hidden story of her role as the surrogate mother of the South African liberal school, we need to locate this encounter in the context of Audrey's arrival at Wits, which was precipitated by Mrs Hoernlé's resignation at the height of her anthropological career. In the official letter Mrs Hoernlé wrote from Munich, where she and Alfred were watching the onward march of the Nazis with horror and arranging for the emigration of further relatives, she explained her decision as the regrettable result of domestic duties.

As you know, I have had the responsibility on my shoulders of having my old father [now 80] and an old aunt staying with me in the house, and their presence has inevitably meant conflicting duties, divided loyalties, and a constant strain which, especially in recent months, has made it increasingly impossible for me to do my University work with satisfaction, or to feel that I was doing full justice to it ... In these circumstances, I feel I have to choose between my family commitments and my University work and, to my great regret, I must give up the latter ... I have revelled in the work, especially during the years when I could still harmonize it with my family duties, and it is a severe wrench to give it up.[2]

Letters to colleagues confirm that she had been under strain in recent years with frequent references to periods of illness and being 'ordered [by doctors] to the coast'.[3] Clearly her deepening commitment to the field of social welfare, which goes unmentioned in the letter, was another major consideration. Audrey wrote shortly after her arrival: 'She [Mrs H.] runs half the social service in Johannesburg, natives, Indians and whites.'[4] Peter Carstens plausibly proposed a further reason: the stifling gender politics at Wits.

---

[2] WHP, Box 2: Personal Papers, Folder Biographical Records, Winifred Hoernlé to Clement Doke, Munich, 21 November 1936.

[3] UCT Libraries, Manuscripts and Archives Department, BC290 Goodwin Papers, Hoernlé to Goodwin, 10 December 1928.

[4] London, Archive of the London School of Economics, Audrey Richards Papers [henceforth ARP], Richards 18/3, File 1 Audrey Richards to Dame Isabel Richards, 8 February 1938, Johannesburg.

'A genius for friendship': Audrey Richards at Wits, 1938–1940   153

It is alleged that there was a certain faction within the University of the Witwatersrand that was hostile towards her husband, Professor R.F.A. Hoernlé. And within her own department, Mrs Hoernlé's superiority was resented by one or two men [like Clement Doke] who wanted to exercise full control. I believe she did become disillusioned with academic life, largely because of the factionalism and jealousy, the irritation of which was difficult to avoid, but also because these factors distracted from the important issues in social anthropology and the civic responsibilities in which she believed so firmly.[5]

It was, in the event, fortuitous as she could scarcely have wished for a more talented and generous successor, as the university was deeply aware when they scrambled to retain Audrey's services at the end of her three-year tenure. The rich posthumous biographical literature on the life, writings and teaching of Audrey Richards bypasses her South African years. If her time at Wits years is mentioned at all, it is merely in passing between the story of her pioneering decade of fieldwork and writing about the Bemba in the 1930s and that of her career as an applied anthropologist working closely with colonial governments in Africa, first from within the British Colonial Office from 1941 to 1945, and then, after a few years at London University, during her founding six-year directorship of the East African Institute of Social Research at Makerere in Uganda (1950–5).[6] (Her Wits years also go unmentioned in histories of anthropology in South Africa.) The prequel and the sequel to these periods in her working life are the career stages of her LSE training in the late 1920s, when she truly did come 'under the spell' of Malinowski, and the culmination of her career at Cambridge University (1956–66), where she served for some years as Vice-President of her alma mater, Newnham College, and established the African Studies Centre. It is the Audrey Richards of this fourth and final career stage that has shaped the way in which she has been, and still is, remembered.

This is partly because it was during her Cambridge decade that she received belated and, her women students rightly argue, only partial recognition for her enormous contribution to the British school of social anthropology.[7] She served as the first woman President of the Royal Anthropological Institute from 1959 to 1961 and for a quarter of a century she was the only woman to have held that position. She was

---

[5] Peter Carstens, 'Introduction' in Carstens et al., eds., *Trails in the Thirstland*, 11.

[6] David Mills, '"How Not to Be a Government House Pet": Audrey Richards and the East Africa Institute for Social Research' in Mwenda Ntarangwi, David Mills and Muftafa Babiker, eds., *African Anthropologies: History, Critique and Practice* (London: Zed Books, 2006), 77–98.

[7] See Jean S. La Fontaine, 'Audrey Isabel Richards, 1899–1984', *Africa*, 55, 2 (1985), 202; Jo Gladstone cited in Marilyn Strathern, 'Audrey Isabel Richards 1899–1984', *Proceedings of the British Academy*, 82 (1985), 449.

154   Pioneers of the Field

the second woman to serve as President of the UK African Studies Association from 1963 to 1965. The year after her retirement from Cambridge she was one of very few women to have been elected as a Fellow of the British Academy.[8]

Among the many tributes to Audrey by women scholars and friends, the most evocative are those written by three famous former students from Cambridge of the 1960s: Jean La Fontaine, Marilyn Strathern and Jo Gladstone. La Fontaine edited a festschrift on ritual in her honour in 1972, wrote an extended obituary essay (1985)[9] and edited the memorial issue of *Cambridge Anthropology* (1985), which featured outline portraits of Audrey by a wide cast of women colleagues and friends across her career.[10] The feminist historian and family friend, Jo Gladstone, published three incisive essays on Audrey, drawing more attention than any other scholar to the gendered politics of her background and training, and to the degree of gender discrimination she experienced (but was loth to complain about) in her early and mid-career.[11] Gladstone recalls the presence of Audrey as her teacher in her final undergraduate year in 1960. 'In her prime, Audrey was of medium height, with graceful embonpoint. Her delightful freckles matched her beautifully red frizzy hair. A magisterial manner was offset by a smile ... '[12] Marilyn Strathern was a member of the first cohort of Cambridge anthropology undergraduates whom Richards enlisted as research trainees in the Elmdon Village study from 1962. Strathern's warm obituary best captures the spirit of her lively, larger-than-life former lecturer and long-time friend.[13] She writes that Audrey could be 'by turn delightful, maddening, generous, unkind, witty – but never, never boring'.[14]

---

[8] Richard Werbner, 'Audrey Isabel Richards' in Ute Gacs, Aisha Khan, Jerrie McIntyre and Ruth Weinberg, eds., *Women Anthropologists: A Biographical Dictionary* (New York, London, Westport, CT: Greenwood Press, 1988), 312.

[9] Jean S. La Fontaine, 'Audrey Isabel Richards, 1899–1984', 201–6.

[10] See Helena Wayne, 'Audrey Some Recollections', Tanya Luhrmann, 'Nearer to the End', Rosemary Firth, 'An Unusual Friendship' in Jean La Fontaine, ed., *Cambridge Anthropology: Audrey Richards: In Memoriam*, 10, 1 (1985), 12–17, 29–31.

[11] Jo Gladstone, 'Significant Sister: Autonomy and Obligation in Audrey Richards' Early Fieldwork', *American Ethnologist*, 13, 2 (1986), 338–56; 'Audrey I Richards (1899–1984)', *Bulletin of the Society for the Social History of Medicine*, 40 (1987), 115–37; 'Audrey I Richards (1899–1984): Africanist and Humanist' in Shirley Ardener, ed., *Persons and Powers of Women in Diverse Cultures* (New York and Oxford: Berg Press, 1992), 13–28.

[12] Gladstone, 'Audrey I Richards (1899–1984): Africanist and Humanist', 13.

[13] Strathern, 'Audrey Isabel Richards 1899–1984', 439–53.

[14] *Ibid.*, 450. There has also been much written about her two famous monographs on the Bemba of Northern Rhodesia. See Audrey Richards, *Land, Labour and Diet in Northern Rhodesia: An Economic Study of the Bemba Tribe* (London: Oxford University Press in association with the International African Institute, 1939); Audrey Richards, *Chisungu: A Girl's Initiation Ceremony among the Bemba of Northern Rhodesia* (London: Faber and Faber, 1956); Henrietta L. Moore and Megan Vaughan, *Cutting Down Trees: Gender,*

'A genius for friendship': Audrey Richards at Wits, 1938–1940   155

Yet there is relatively little in these writings about Audrey Richards of the 1930s and 1940s. What was her 'personal style' and 'fieldwork style' before she acquired the 'magisterial' air of one who was widely regarded as 'The Grand Dame of British Social Anthropology'?[15] Her three years in South Africa are particularly revealing in this regard, for they expose a much more vulnerable Audrey Richards. In the core section of the chapter I will show that she chose to take the job at Wits University in 1938 because of gender discrimination elsewhere, but frequently felt frustrated at having to work in a sexist university culture. She was deeply disturbed by the divided and increasingly racist politics of white South Africa on the eve of the Second World War, as well as by the pending threat of the Nazis to the security of her home country and family. Despite these constraints, I argue that she made an important and hitherto unacknowledged contribution to the development of social anthropology in South Africa in the ways suggested above, as well as in what was a richly productive period as an ethnographer and essayist.

A colonial childhood and gendered education, 1899–1922

Adam Kuper proposes that we think of Audrey as a member of what Noel Annan termed 'the intellectual aristocracy', that 'very English intelligentsia wedded to gradual reform', and indicates that she remained true to these origins throughout her life.[16] Audrey's father was the son of a Welsh lawyer who served as a member of the Indian Vice-Regal Council between 1904 and 1909. Her mother, Isabel Butler, came from a well-to-do family of barristers and public servants with colonial connections: two of her maternal uncles were Governors in India, one of Burma and the other of the Central Provinces. Her mother's family also had strong university connections in England.

Born in Calcutta on 8 July 1899, she grew up in a family of daughters with her mother as the dominant parental influence. 'She [Isabel] had all the family's quick sense of the ridiculous, a dry humour and that piercing sense of judgement on which so much English fun depends.'[17] From her father she inherited the ability to tell stories. Jo Gladstone documents

---

Nutrition, and Agricultural Change in the Northern Province of Zambia, 1890–1990 (Portsmouth, New Haven, London and Lusaka: Heinemann, James Currey and University of Zambia Press, 1994).

[15] This is the term used by her friend and colleague, Raymond Apthorpe to describe Audrey in the late 1950s. Andrew Bank interview with Raymond Apthorpe, 15 May 2013, London.

[16] Adam Kuper, 'Audrey Richards: A Career in Anthropology' in Kuper, *Among the Anthropologists*, 115.

[17] Richards cited in Kuper, 'Audrey Richards', 116.

156   Pioneers of the Field

numerous examples of gender discrimination in Audrey's class-privileged colonial background.[18] Sensing from a young age that colonial India was a man's world, Audrey and her three 'prettier' sisters would play-act as heroic army officers in British India,[19] a tradition of masculine adventure on which she drew during her later fieldwork in Bembaland.[20]

Her secondary and tertiary education was equally gendered. The family returned to Oxford in 1911 when her father took up a post as Professor of International Law at All Souls College. Audrey was sent as a boarder to Downe House Girls' High School in Surrey and would champion the idea of separate schooling for boys and girls throughout her life. Although her parents were opposed to their daughters going to university, Audrey 'went up' to study Natural Sciences at Newnham College in 1919, the year in which British women were given the vote. She recalled a strong sense of sisterhood bred in part by an atmosphere of male hostility.

After the war, when the University was crowded with returning soldiers, women were of course resented. As they walked down the steps of the big lecture theatres to their places in the front row, every man behind them clumped and stamped in time with their steps.[21]

On her return to Newnham as Vice-Principal in much later years she was struck by how much 'livelier' their 'isolated community' of women college-mates had been.[22] It was a time when 'many of us had the sense that we were a special dedicated group'.[23]

She graduated with a degree in biology in 1922 and spent a year teaching at her old school before doing eighteen months of relief work with the Quakers in Frankfurt. This involved keeping meticulous daily records about hunger and nutrition, the very activities on which she concentrated during her ground-breaking fieldwork in Northern Rhodesia. On returning to London in 1924 she lived with her elder sister Gwynneth, who worked among poor communities in the London docklands area. Her social work orientation was reinforced by three years of work for the League of Nations Labour Department in the mid-1920s.[24]

---

[18] Jo Gladstone, 'Audrey I. Richards (1899–1911); Africanist and Humanist', 14.

[19] Richard Faber, 'Origins' in La Fontaine, ed., *Cambridge Anthropology*, 6.   [20] *Ibid.*, 6.

[21] Richards cited in Nancy Lutkehaus, '"She Was Very Cambridge": Camilla Wedgwood and the History of Women in British Social Anthropology', *American Ethnologist*, 13, 4 (1986), 780.

[22] Richards cited in Gladstone, 'Significant Sister', 340.

[23] Richards cited in Lutkehaus, '"She Was Very Cambridge"', 781.

[24] On her social work career, see especially Gladstone, 'Audrey I. Richards (1899–1984): Africanist and Humanist', 14–15.

'A genius for friendship': Audrey Richards at Wits, 1938–1940   157

Malinowski's favourite disciple, 1928–1932

It was, appropriately, the father of one of Audrey's Newnham 'sisters', the socialist political scientist Graham Wallace, who suggested that she enrol for a doctorate in Social Anthropology at the London School of Economics in 1928. 'Still somewhat marginal, not entirely respectable, it [the LSE] offered an ideal environment for an ambitious and creative outsider, and was more hospitable than the ancient universities to the aspirations of women.'[25] Although her three-year doctoral study was formally supervised by Malinowski's more genial colleague, Charles Seligman, she learnt her theoretical approach and method from Malinowski, who imbued her with a passion for their new discipline. This much is obvious from her touching obituary, where she wrote that it was 'his intensity' that most impressed his gifted cohort of students. In what reads as an autobiographical reflection, she commented that 'they learned to discuss their theses on bus-tops or dodging the market-barrows down Holborn side-streets' in the vicinity of the LSE. Like so many of his other famous students, she remembers his seminars as 'brilliant performances'. Sometimes he was 'provocative and prejudiced', at others 'profound, penetrating and constructive'. Yet he was always witty, direct and had 'a rare power of evoking ideas in others'.[26]

Audrey became very close to, indeed intimate with, Malinowski during her years of working with him as his doctoral student.[27] His later correspondence with his ailing wife, Elsie Masson, reveals just how central Audrey was to the life of his family. She provided temporary accommodation for them when they needed it, took regular care of his three daughters, made major decisions regarding their education and supported Elsie in the late stages of her neuralgia during his frequent periods abroad, right through to her death in 1935. She was even tasked with telling the daughters about their mother's death.[28] Indeed, they became so fond of her that they dearly wished that she would marry their father, but in the view of one of his daughters Helena, Audrey shared too many of their father's character traits:[29] which I read as wilfulness, willingness

---

[25] Kuper, 'Audrey Richards: A Career in Anthropology', 118.

[26] Audrey Richards, 'Obituary: Bronislaw Malinowski (1884–1943)', *Man*, 63 (1943), 1–4. For later essays in appreciation of Malinowski, including one by Richards on his concept of culture, see Raymond Firth, ed., *Man and Culture: An Evaluation of the Work of Bronislaw Malinowski* (London: Routledge and Kegan Paul, 1957), 15–28.

[27] E-mail correspondence, Michael W. Young, 15 November 2013, Canberra-Cape Town.

[28] See Helena Wayne (Malinowska), ed., *The Story of a Marriage, Volume II: The Letters of Bronislaw Malinowski and Elsie Masson* (London and New York: Routledge, 1995), 161, 193, 217, 236–9; also Helena Wayne, 'Audrey Some Recollections', 30–1.

[29] Helena Wayne (Malinowska), 'Bronislaw Malinowski: The Influence of Various Women on his Life and Works', *American Ethnologist*, 12, 3 (1985), 538.

158   Pioneers of the Field

to speak her mind, directness and a confidence, even flamboyance, associated with a relatively privileged upbringing. The memoirs of her Cambridge students and her letters reveal that she adopted a comparably direct and inquiry-based teaching method to that of Malinowski, albeit one that was less fiercely provocative than that of her much loved mentor and friend.

In his preface to *Hunger and Work in a Savage Tribe*, her reworked doctoral thesis of 1930, Malinowski lauded Richards' theoretical study of nutrition among the southern Bantu as 'scientific pioneering', 'the breaking of a new field', the 'work[ing] out of problems entirely untouched'.[30] This was not just enthusiastic exaggeration from a proud mentor. Despite her more modest description of the book as 'a pupil's exercise' which attempted to apply to eating what Malinowski had written about sex,[31] her study *was* the first systematic exploration of nutrition as a field of research. Famously opening with the claim that 'Nutrition as a biological process is more fundamental than sex',[32] her book made a powerful case for the centrality of eating and food in southern African cultures. She demonstrated the extent to which economic organization, kinship structures and rituals were organized around the production, consumption and distribution of food. Her book also explored ideas relating to food and eating in African cultures in the region, making a case for a complex and developed 'ideology of food' expressed in part through a rich symbolism.[33] Even the brief history of functionalism in her introduction was an important contribution.[34]

Audrey set off for the African field in May 1930. She initially intended to conduct a study of the impact of migrant labour on rural women and family life in Northern Rhodesia, where the copper mines had opened up less than a decade earlier. She recalled having been 'sent [by Malinowski] to study a matrilineal society [the Bemba] because it was thought particularly appropriate for a woman to study women'. In what Gladstone describes as 'a very rare, commemorative mood', Audrey told of 'the flustering send-off' Malinowski gave her when she left London by train to board the Union-Castle line in Portsmouth in early May 1930. 'He was a little late, and ran alongside her carriage with a parting gift of coloured pencils to facilitate her fieldwork. "Remember what I said!" she recalled him calling out after

---

[30] Bronislaw Malinowski, 'Preface' to Audrey Richards, *Hunger and Work in a Savage Tribe: A Functional Study of Nutrition among the Southern Bantu* (London: Routledge, 1932), ix.

[31] Malinowski had already published four books with sex in the title, most famously *Sex and Repression in Savage Society* (London: Routledge, 1927).

[32] Richards, *Hunger and Work in a Savage Tribe*, xvii.

[33] *Ibid.*, 'Chapter 7 Food as Symbol'.   [34] *Ibid.*, 19–23.

'A genius for friendship': Audrey Richards at Wits, 1938–1940   159

her. "The brown chalk is best for economics and I always use red for political organization!"[35]

The most vivid and extended account of her first fieldwork expedition from May 1930 to July 1931 was addressed, significantly, to her Newnham sisters in her (hitherto uncited) first published essay after returning to London from Bembaland. Here she began by noting that 'anthropology seems rapidly to be becoming the fashionable profession of women nowadays'. She referred to Margaret Mead's celebrated study *Coming of Age in Samoa* and its exploration of the issues of sexuality and childhood in New Guinea. She described her long journey into the field: the boat trip followed by a four-day train trip from Cape Town to Broken Hill (Kabwe) and then a truck journey on 'the Great Northern Road' to Kasama. With three stores and twelve houses this trading outpost was the biggest white settlement in the area. She told her Newnham sisters of how she spent a month working intensely on the language under the tutelage of the White Fathers based at the nearby Chilumba mission station. At this point she was joined by her elder sister Gwynneth for ten weeks. They 'chose a village to settle down in to get to know the people ... and to watch the passage of daily life'.[36] Spinsters, let alone single white women travelling in pairs, were not a 'normal' feature of Bemba society. She commented elsewhere that she and her sister found it necessary to 'invent husbands'. They 'hastily ... produced pictures of officials of the University of Cape Town [who partly funded her trip] to prove their [husbands'] existence, and then were obliged to invent a "family". Pictures of smiling babies, quickly torn from the condensed milk tins in their stores, were pinned up on tent walls and much admired by Native women.'[37] After her sister's departure she travelled around by bicycle, spending 'three or four weeks in one village, attending local ceremonies, helping the women in household tasks and talking with village elders'.

---

[35] Gladstone, 'Significant Sisters', 355 note 7.

[36] Audrey Richards, 'An Anthropologist in Rhodesia', *Newnham College Letter* (Jan. 1932), 60–8. It does not feature on the extensive bibliographies of her writings drawn up in retrospect. See Peter Gulliver, 'Bibliography of the Principal Writings of Audrey Richards' in Jean S. La Fontaine, *The Interpretation of Ritual: Essays in Honour of Audrey Richards* (London: Tavistock, 1972), 285–9 and more extensively Tom Luhrmann, 'Audrey Richards: A Bibliography' in Shirley Ardener, ed., *Persons and Powers of Women in Diverse Cultures*, 51–7. I find it equally significant that Monica Hunter's first, and again perhaps most evocative and unguarded account of her field experiences likewise addressed itself to her college-mates: in her case Girtonians. See Monica Hunter, 'In Pondoland', *The Girton Review*, 92 (Easter Term 1933), 27–9.

[37] ARP, Richards 20/4 Press Cuttings, 'Woman Learns of Secrets of Natives', *Evening News*, 10 November 1931.

160   Pioneers of the Field

To a greater extent than any of her later, 'more scientific' journal articles or books, this first account captures the mood of her encounter with a complex cultural mix of the old and the new, of tradition and modernity. On the one hand, she watched traditional proceedings at chiefs' courts, saw the sacred relics of the Paramount Chief and spent three weeks attending a girls' initiation ceremony (Chisungu). On the other, she reported on the widespread adoption of umbrellas and long trousers, the noticeable impact of Christianity in villages near mission stations where she heard the converts singing 'Once in Royal David's City', and conversations with Bemba migrants working in the copper mines around Ndola where she 'was able to talk to women in their new conditions'. She concluded, in the first of what would be many rallying calls to women to enter the fledgling field: 'If I could convey a tenth of the excitement and freedom of this kind of work [fieldwork], I think every Newnham student would at once apply for a research grant.'[38]

Press clippings in the Audrey Richards Collection suggest that she achieved a degree of notoriety in England and South Africa that has gone unnoticed in subsequent years, even if she was not quite as famous a woman public intellectual as Margaret Mead after her first fieldtrip to Samoa.[39] The titles of the newspaper articles convey a sense of a brave woman adventurer in the African wilderness: 'A Woman in the Wilds' (Cape Times, 25 July 1931), 'White Girl's Kraal Life' (Daily Mirror, 10 November 1931), 'Year Spent Among Natives in the Heart of Africa' (Daily Mirror, 10 November 1931), 'Bicycle "Magic" in the Jungle' (Star, 10 November 1931), 'Woman Learns Secrets of Natives' (Evening News, 10 November 1931). Some featured photographs. Others quoted her impressions of remote African peoples. The journalists usually commented on her appearance, as for example a report which cast her as 'a slim active girl with curly, bobbed, auburn hair and a merry twinkle in the eye'. She went where white people had never been before. She was 'a mythical "white goddess"' not least because of her unusual mode of transport, the magic bicycle, but also because of her alleged ability to hunt. She was, above all, a fearless adventurer. 'Once she awoke to find a hyena outside, but was never troubled by lions and leopards.'[40]

[38] Audrey Richards, 'An Anthropologist in Rhodesia', 60–8.
[39] On the first post-fieldwork phase in Margaret Mead's long and remarkable career as an American celebrity, see Nancy C. Lutkehaus, Margaret Mead: The Making of an American Icon (Princeton, NJ: Princeton University Press, 2008), 25–57.
[40] ARP, Richards 20/4 Press Cuttings.

Female friendships in Northern Rhodesia and London, 1933–1937

Audrey developed particularly close friendships with women co-workers, beginning in the years before she came to Johannesburg. She stayed with her sister Gwynneth in London and worked as an assistant lecturer at the LSE before returning to the field in January 1933 for what would be a second eighteen-month long expedition to Bembaland. Here she worked particularly closely with Lorna Gore-Browne, the young wife of Colonel Gore-Browne, who was the only large estate owner in the Northern region and who hosted many British visitors at his lavish mansion on Shiwa Ngandu. He would remain a highly influential figure in Northern Rhodesian politics for many decades. While the middle-aged Colonel liked to be treated as a 'great white chief' or 'like God', Audrey later warned Godfrey Wilson,[41] Lorna was less formal. Robert Rotberg's biography of Lorna's husband reveals that she was snatched as a teenager from her native England by a Colonel in quest of a wife and had long been deeply unhappy in her marriage. She was 'enchantingly happy' doing anthropological fieldwork with Audrey, 'savouring her companionship, the experience of doing scientific work of a meaningful sort, and – presumably – freedom from the shackles of Shiva'. When Audrey 'took Lorna away from him for longer and longer periods, [the Colonel] began more openly voicing his disquiet'.[42] He began referring to Audrey in letters as 'that anthropologist woman with her clever talk and meddling ways'.[43] Lorna left Shiwa immediately after Audrey returned to London in order to take up the study of agriculture at Cambridge (at Audrey's suggestion). They remained in close contact in England while Audrey was working at the LSE as a lecturer. As is well known, it was Lorna to whom Audrey dedicated her celebrated 1939 study *Land, Labour and Diet in Northern Rhodesia*, indicating that her friend's 'knowledge of the Bemba language and system of cultivation was invaluable to me'.[44]

The second Significant Other with whom Audrey collaborated in the field was, of course, her mentor. Malinowski spent almost a month in the

---

[41] WC, B4.7 [GW] To and from Audrey Richards, Audrey Richards to Godfrey Wilson, 28 September 1937, London; Audrey Richards to Godfrey Wilson, 20 June 1938, Johannesburg.

[42] Robert I. Rotberg, *Black Heart: Gore-Browne and the Politics of Multi-Racial Zambia* (Berkeley, Los Angeles and London: University of California Press, 1977), 133, 165–7. She argued with him bitterly after her return to Shiwa in 1936 and saw him infrequently during the World War II year. She lived apart from him in Lusaka after the War and they got divorced in 1950 (Rotberg, *Black Heart*, 199–200, 210).

[43] Cited in Christina Lamb, *The Africa House: The True Story of an English Gentleman and His African Dream* (London: Penguin, 2000), 188.

[44] Audrey Richards, *Land, Labour and Diet in Northern Rhodesia* (London: Oxford University Press in association with the International African Institute, 1939), xvi.

162 Pioneers of the Field

Figure 4.1: '*Shilusako citimene*, Audrey!' ('Don't worry about *citimene* [tree-cutting], Audrey!') Audrey researching methods of agriculture in the field, Bembaland, c October 1933.[45]

[45] London, Royal Anthropological Institute, Photographic Collection, Audrey Richards, RAI 27731. Here and in the other captions in this chapter the quotation marks are for Audrey's descriptions, as recorded on the back of the print. Here she is quoting a Bemba informant, possibly the figure in the photograph. Thanks to Mary Mbewe for the translation.

Figure 4.2: 'The Hockey Team!' Audrey and Lorna after a hockey match at Shiwa Ngandu. Audrey is standing with her stick in her left hand. Lorna is kneeling in front of the trophy, c 1933.[46]

---

[46] London, Royal Anthropological Institute, Photographic Collection, Audrey Richards, RAI 35583.

164   Pioneers of the Field

field with Audrey in Bembaland in July 1934 as part of his Grand Tour of Africa, which had begun with him featuring as the star turn at the New Education Fellowship Conference at Wits. Together he and Audrey witnessed the Muchapi witch-finding movement at its height. Audrey drew in part on Malinowski's field-notes in piecing together her important article 'A Modern Movement of Witch-Finders' published in *Africa* in 1935. Her essay indicates that her work was much more attuned to social change and its complexities than is usually acknowledged. Despite her evident distrust of the Muchapi leaders (whom she described as 'charlatans'), her article seeks to explain their popular success, relating it to their skilful appropriation of modern cultural symbols and performative styles. As we will see, her writings in (and on) South Africa were likewise concerned with social change as well as tradition.[47] This challenges the sometimes overdrawn image of Audrey as a romantic functionalist who naïvely bought into the narratives of powerful Bemba chiefs and ended up 'canonising' their newly 'invented traditions' in the language of an ahistorical timeless present.[48] Her essays on functionalist method and cultural change suggest to me that she had a more critical and self-reflective attitude towards her informants' narratives than this critique allows.[49]

Rosemary Firth recalled that Audrey was at the centre of the female-dominated circle in London involved in developing the field of applied anthropology in British colonies in Africa.[50] This circle included Rosemary, Audrey's fellow Newnham alumni Lucy Mair, whose 1934 monograph Audrey generously reviewed in *Africa*,[51] the missionary anthropologist Margaret Read, and Margery Perham. Audrey wrote a biographical essay on the headman of a small Bemba village outside Kasama for Perham's popular collection of ten life histories of Africans published in 1936, to which Monica had contributed the story

---

[47] For an emphasis on social change in her work, see also Jean S. La Fontaine, 'Introduction' in La Fontaine, ed., *Cambridge Anthropology: Special Issue 'Audrey Richards: In Memoriam'*, 2–3.

[48] This applies to some formulations in Henrietta Moore and Megan Vaughan, *Cutting Down Trees: Gender, Nutrition and Agricultural Change in the Northern Province of Zambia, 1890–1990* (Portsmouth, New Haven: Heinemann, 1994), xi–xxiv, 1–19 although in general their representations of her are complex and richly nuanced. After all, they do dedicate their study to her and Ann Tweedie-Waggot.

[49] This is evident, for example, in her recognition in essays that African informants gave very different types of information to anthropologists, missionaries and government officials.

[50] Rosemary Firth, 'An Unusual Friendship', 29.

[51] Audrey Richards, 'Review of Lucy Mair, *An African People in the Twentieth Century*', *Africa*, 7, 4 (1934), 497–8.

'A genius for friendship': Audrey Richards at Wits, 1938–1940   165

of Nosente.[52] Audrey was particularly close to the Australian anthropologist Phyllis Kaberry, who worked as her research assistant at the LSE in 1936 and whom she also warmly acknowledged for her help in 'the preparation of the text' of *Land, Labour and Diet*.[53] Monica and Godfrey Wilson were also close friends during their time in London in 1936 between their two extended periods of fieldwork in Bunyakyusa. Audrey had met Godfrey at Malinowski's seminars in 1933, but only met Monica for the first time in December 1935.[54] In the late 1930s, her friendship with Godfrey blossomed given their shared interest in Bemba culture about which they engaged intensely by correspondence during his time doing research in Broken Hill from 1938 to 1940. She also collaborated closely with the women scholars who served on the African Institute's Nutrition Committee, notably the London University biochemist, Dr Elsie Widdowson, who calculated the chemical composition of the sample diets of Bemba families that Audrey and Lorna had collected in the field. Audrey and Elsie's co-authored article on Bemba diet and nutrition was published in 1936 in a Special Issue of *Africa* devoted to nutrition.[55]

Teaching anthropology at Wits, 1938–1940

This issue also featured essays by two South African anthropologists whom she would befriend during her three years in Johannesburg: Ellen Hellmann and Winifred Hoernlé. Another of her circle of new women friends in Johannesburg, Hilda Beemer, published a lengthy essay on African diet in a later issue of *Africa*.[56] As these publications confirm, the South African women anthropologists were committed to a vision of anthropology that was 'practical', applied and local as well as to the development of theory and ethnography among an international network of scholars. It is to Audrey's developing friendships with Hoernlé and

---

[52] Audrey Richards, 'Chapter 1: The Story of Bwembya of the Bemba Tribe, Northern Rhodesia' in Margery Perham, ed., *Ten Africans* (London: Faber and Faber, 1936), 17–40.

[53] Richards, *Land, Labour and Diet*, xvi.

[54] WC, B5.1 Correspondence between Monica Hunter and her father, Monica Hunter to David Hunter, London, December 1935.

[55] Audrey Richards and Elsie Widdowson, 'A Dietary Study in North-Eastern Rhodesia', *Africa*, 9, 2 (1936), 166–96.

[56] Ellen Hellmann, 'Urban Native Food in Johannesburg', *Africa*, 9, 2 (1936), 277–90; Winifred Hoernlé, 'Supplementary Note to A.J. Orenstein, The Dietetics of Natives Employed on the Witwatersrand Gold Mines', *Africa*, 9, 2 (1936), 224–6; Hilda Beemer, 'Notes on the Diet of the Swazi in the Protectorates', *Bantu Studies*, 13, 2 (1939), 199–236.

166   Pioneers of the Field

her 'daughters' (Monica Hunter, Ellen Hellmann, Hilda Beemer and Eileen Krige) that I now wish to turn.

Audrey was in two minds about taking up the appointment at Wits. Malinowski prompted her to do so. Jobs were difficult to access for a woman scholar, even one with a growing international reputation and publication record like Audrey. She had applied for a lectureship at the LSE 'on Bronio's instructions ... I was told by all that they particularly wanted a man and not a woman, and there were four good men [who had applied]'.[57] Even more disappointing was the news in August 1937 of her rejection for the new position as the first director of the Rhodes-Livingstone Institute in Northern Rhodesia. She was the obvious candidate, having extensive fieldwork experience in the country. She also had an active commitment to applied anthropology and interdisciplinary research and had an established reputation as an internationally respected scholar. She explained to the new incumbent, her friend Godfrey Wilson, the background politics that preceded his appointment. 'You know I wanted that job and had been promised it [by the then colonial governor Hubert Young], but at the last minute Hubert told me that his financial backers wouldn't stand for a woman ... '[58] Although Audrey retrospectively downplayed the role of gender bias in her career, there is no doubt that she was deeply hurt by this rejection at the time. In a letter to her mother from Johannesburg, she introduced Godfrey as 'an old pupil of Malinowski's who got my job as Government anthropologist in Northern Rhodesia'.[59] The Wilsons were upset on her behalf, even embarrassed in Godfrey's case. Monica wrote in her cryptic typed notes on the history of anthropology in southern Africa, the year before her retirement: 'A.I.R. [Audrey] obvious choice for Director. Done work in N. Rhodesia, right age, but a WOMAN' [her capitals].[60]

Audrey's letters home reveal that she immediately took to Winifred Hoernlé and greatly admired her ability to balance teaching, welfare activism and family commitment.

All is well and I have had the most peaceful week ever. Mrs H, who has been an angel to me, arranged for me to have the time off for my book [Audrey was still finishing *Land, Labour and Diet*] ... Mrs H is a marvel, about 52, serene, efficient, keen, and a 'mother' to all the students and most of the staff, quite amusing and

---

[57] ARP, Richards 18/3, File 1, Audrey Richards to Isabel Richards, May 1937, London.

[58] WC, B4.7 [GW] To and from Audrey Richards, Audrey Richards to Godfrey Wilson, 3 September 1937, London.

[59] ARP, Richards 18/3, File 1, Audrey Richards to Isabel Richards, 27 April 1938, Johannesburg.

[60] WC, A2.15 MW Personal Papers, Notes: Anthropology in South Africa, recorded for Jom [sic]Fox, Behavioural Sciences Centre [Stanford], April 1972, 3.

'A genius for friendship': Audrey Richards at Wits, 1938–1940   167

easy to deal with ... Did the teaching here for 18 years during which time she reared a son, looked after house, and an invalid father who is still with her. Go thou and do likewise I say to myself forlornly.[61]

This is very much in keeping with Jo Gladstone's characterization of Audrey as a 'maternal feminist' who liked 'good wives' and committed parents. She was consistently critical of friends (including Malinowski) who neglected their children in service of their careers.[62]

'Mrs H' acted as Audrey's intermediary in Johannesburg in the early months. She organized for Audrey to stay in a flat in the leafy white suburb of Parktown just five minutes from campus by bus. She took Audrey to see four of the five African townships around Johannesburg within her first six weeks. On one of these visits Ellen introduced Audrey to John Chafimbira whom Audrey had read about in Wulf Sachs' *Black Hamlet*. Audrey and Ellen became close friends. 'Another night I dined with Mrs Hellmann, the Jewish anthropologist here and was the only Christian in a party of eight! We went on to a bad film afterwards.'[63] Audrey would recall dinners with the Johannesburg anthropologists held in the Hoernlé home, 'a cheerful, welcoming and stimulating place and a centre of politics and liberal thought. Many visiting anthropologists from this country [England] will remember its hospitality and the long dining table full of guests.'[64] No fewer than eight LSE-trained South African anthropologists came to her welcoming party.[65] Most of them had, in fact, been taught by Audrey in London. Apart from Ellen, this impressive guest list included Hilda Beemer, Eileen Krige and Jack Krige (who had come down from Pretoria), Max Gluckman, Julius Lewin and Isaac Schapera. The eighth member was Mrs Hoernlé herself on the grounds of her term attending the London seminar in 1930.

Monica and Godfrey Wilson were the ninth and tenth LSE-trained dinner guests to be hosted by the Hoernlés in the early months of 1938. They spent a week in Johannesburg in April en route to Northern Rhodesia, where Godfrey was to take up his post as first director of the RLI. Monica's letter to her father is revealing of the bonds between members of this female-dominated circle of social anthropologists, the centrality of Mrs Hoernlé and emerging friendships with Audrey.

---

[61] ARP, Richards 18/3, File 1, Audrey Richards-Dame Isabel Richards, 8 February 1938, Johannesburg.

[62] Gladstone, 'Audrey I. Richards (1899–1984): Africanist and Humanist', 22–3.

[63] ARP, Richards 18/3, File 1, Audrey Richards-Dame Isabel Richards, 8 February 1938, Johannesburg.

[64] Audrey Richards, 'Obituary: Agnes Winifred Hoernlé: 1885–1960', 53.

[65] ARP, Richards 18/3, File 1, Audrey Richards-Dame Isabel Richards, 8 February 1938, Johannesburg.

168   Pioneers of the Field

Yesterday we met the various Johannesburg anthropologists and some students at Mrs Hoernlé's and had a very lively 'seminar'. Godfrey was talking about the proposed schemes of work for the Rhodes-Livingstone Institute and I about what I had been trying to do in Bunyakyusa. This morning we spent with Audrey Richards in the university, collecting a bibliography on Northern Rhodesia (she worked for three years among the Bemba) and looking for reviews of *Reaction to Conquest* in scientific journals. I unearthed a kind one in the *American Anthropologist*. We are lunching with the Hoernlés on Saturday and with Ellen Hellmann (a Jewish girl who has been working in the slums here) and her husband on Sunday and dining with Audrey Richards tomorrow night. It's great fun . . .[66]

'Mrs H.' also drew Audrey into her social welfare network. Audrey was called upon to give talks on subjects ranging from Bemba culture to the progress of women in Africa to the state of England at war after she had returned from a visit home in December 1939. She reported on her continued flurry of commitments with characteristic humour.

Monday [late March 1940] I drove along the reef to speak at a native club on 'England'! Tuesday the young people [at Wits University] had arranged for me to give a lecture on 'Sex education for the Bantu' at which I had to preside, though feeling that our own ideas on the subject were so shaky that it was a pity to offer to instruct others, and that until we provided natives with sufficient wages to support their wives on, it was rather useless to attempt to give them sex education in favour of happy home lives. However, no-one else was as sceptical as me and so that was alright.[67]

'Mrs H' was president of the South African University Women's Association in 1938 and 1939. Their Johannesburg circle included women lecturers at Wits (of whom there were only half a dozen in the late 1930s, almost all in junior positions), wives of university men and women activists associated with the Institute of Race Relations. Audrey was struck by the commitment and seriousness of intent of the 'women university people', as she called them, describing them as 'far more feminist' than their English counterparts.[68]

Audrey's contribution as a teacher, mentor and role model is well documented for her Cambridge years. As noted above, her star students of the early 1960s have provided vivid accounts of her as an inspiring, even 'magisterial', presence in the classroom, of her open and engaged way of relating to graduates, and of her continued friendships with her women students as they followed anthropological

---

[66] WC, B5.1 Letters MW to her father, Monica Wilson to David Hunter, Johannesburg, 21 April 1938.
[67] ARP, Richards 18/3, File 1, Audrey Richards-Dame Isabel Richards, 4 April 1940, Johannesburg.
[68] *Ibid.*, Audrey Richards-Dame Isabel Richards, 2 April 1938, Johannesburg.

'A genius for friendship': Audrey Richards at Wits, 1938–1940   169

careers. Unfortunately, we have no comparable memoirs by famous former students at Wits University. We do, however, have the benefit of her own extensive commentary on her experience of lecturing and working at Wits articulated in her weekly letters home. While her teaching method was very similar to that of her Cambridge years – lively, engaging, encouraging of critical thinking and impatient of docility or rote-learning – the period and context, and probably her relative youth, explain the differences in style.

The warmth of her relations with her young students, typically just eighteen or nineteen years of age as anthropology undergraduates, is evident from the terms in which she described them in her letters. She referred to them endearingly as 'my pets', 'my butterflies' and 'my lambs'.[69] She commented frequently on the openness and innocence of these teenagers. 'I find them much easier to talk to than the corresponding English girl.'[70] The South African students, however, had had a poorer schooling than the English students she was used to teaching at the LSE. This doubtless had an impact on the approach she took. The one striking constant, though, is the depth of her commitment to getting her students 'into the field': in this regard she went beyond what her gifted pedagogical predecessor had done in earlier years. Whereas she would send her Cambridge undergraduates knocking door-to-door in her home village, Elmdon,[71] the equally keen but more naïve and younger South African undergraduates were taken on fieldtrips every university vacation. They went to Johannesburg townships, mining compounds and 'native' reformatories, but later further afield to South African native reserves and the neighbouring kingdom of Swaziland.

Audrey had been taken aback when 'Mrs H' explained quite what was involved in taking over her teaching responsibilities.

Most of the teaching is a detailed study of African societies and not the more general study of the world which I am used to [from the LSE]. Then it seems necessary to know all the history of South Africa, native legislation etc. and . . . the dates of Native Acts and so on. [This is all] Besides giving a course on the pre-history [archaeology] of Africa and getting to know the museum specimens. I have got to the stage that the very sight of a map of South Africa throws me into nervous twitters!! Then I found that I have ten lectures a week instead of a maximum of

---

[69] WC, B4.7 [GW] To and from Audrey Richards, Audrey Richards to Godfrey Wilson, 14 December 1938, Oxford.

[70] ARP, Richards 18/3, File 1, Audrey Richards-Dame Isabel Richards, 2 April 1938, Johannesburg.

[71] What began as a student fieldwork training project in the early-mid 1960s developed into a detailed case study of changing village life in England. For a generous review, see Monica Wilson, 'Review of Audrey Richards and Jean Robin, *Some Elmdon Families* (1975)', *African Studies*, 35, 3–4 (1976), 297–9.

170   Pioneers of the Field

four at the LSE [where her workload had been heavier than that of her male colleagues Driberg and Evans-Pritchard]. At least three [of these lectures] are repeats for evening students which means that three evenings a week, you finish at 7 p.m.[72]

She also took over some of Mrs H's tried-and-tested teaching techniques, including the use of new technology, notably phonographs and lantern slides,[73] and getting students to engage with the department's ethnographic museum which she continued to rebuild. She spent months cataloguing collections, gathering new materials and organizing for her students to curate exhibitions for visiting school groups. One such exhibition focused on 'native diet', drawing in part on Audrey's Bemba artefacts. She also introduced ethnographic films into the classroom, including one on initiation ceremonies.[74] She was delighted when Monica sent her ethnographic films and photos from Northern Rhodesia that she could share with her students.[75]

Mid-term vacation fieldtrips represented her most distinctive contribution to the teaching of social anthropology in South Africa. As we have learnt, she herself had found 'freedom' in fieldwork. She now went to great lengths to enthuse her young students, most of whom were women, with her sense of the joys of the field. In the Easter vacation of 1938 she took them to mining compounds and 'native reformatories' in Johannesburg. They were not allowed to interview miners, but were allowed to take photographs. There is a substantial collection of her images of mine dances, the interiors of the rooms of miners and the offices of the mining officials, held in the Royal Anthropological Institute's Photographic Collection.[76] In the winter vacation of 1938 she took her students to the townships and then on a ten-day expedition to Swaziland, evidently a turning-point in her teaching year. While her students had earlier complained about her reading demands and her unwillingness to provide them with lecture notes, they were now passionately interested in establishing an Anthropology Society on campus. She explained her field-vacation teaching method to a journalist from the *Star*. 'Each student in the party was given a particular aspect of work on which to concentrate (i.e. food, agricultural methods, house-building etc.) and they carried out research in their particular branch among the inhabitants

---

[72] *Ibid.*, Audrey Richards-Dame Isabel Richards, 1 February 1938, Johannesburg.
[73] *Ibid.*, Audrey Richards-Dame Isabel Richards, 16 March 1940, Johannesburg.
[74] *Ibid.*, Audrey Richards-Dame Isabel Richards, 21 August 1940, Johannesburg.
[75] *Ibid.*, Audrey Richards-Dame Isabel Richards, 7 July 1940, Johannesburg.
[76] See the nineteen images in London, Royal Anthropological Institute Photographic Collection, Audrey Richards, Folder 26b, Urban Native Johannesburg, RA1008-RA1026.

'A genius for friendship': Audrey Richards at Wits, 1938–1940   171

of the villages.' The article quoted her more generally on the benefits of anthropological fieldtrips in a context where 'students of social anthropology in recent years have taken an increasing interest in the practical side of their work in view of the possibilities of social welfare work among non-Europeans'. She made mention of her plan to develop a nationwide, university-based training programme in 'applied anthropology' which could be taken by welfare workers and government officials as well as by students of anthropology.[77]

Even though she occasionally griped about the amount of 'childcare' involved, she found the trip to Swaziland hugely inspiring. This was 'the most wonderful country imaginable ... strangely remote and attractive'. Her description of her first meeting with King Sobhuza II is worth citing at length, as one of several humorous accounts of the strange juxtapositions of tradition and modernity that she encountered in southern Africa of the 1930s.

The young girls' regiments were assembled for a dance when we came – naked except for gorgeous bead-girdles and hanging tufts of wool and toy shields – carrying the bundles of reeds they had packed for the King's kraal roof. Then arrives the King's car and chauffeur. He appears – a magnificent man – tall, fine, refined features and aristocratic hands – dressed in Swazi dress (coloured cloth and leopard skin), but carrying a cine Kodak with which he filmed the dance while chatting amiably to us. I asked him for an explanation of something in the dance and he said, 'Oh, haven't you read X's [Hilda Beemer's] article on the Swazi in *Africa*, volume X. It is such a good description. You would enjoy it!' This from a man who has thirty-nine wives and walks naked in the first fruits ceremony but yet has an office with files and a typewriter, three cars, a secretary and a chauffeur. He has two regiments of warriors to guard him who go everywhere in skins with spears – even to Johannesburg on business.[78]

Here I am reminded of Raymond and Rosemary Firth's remark about Audrey's 'eye for incongruity'. Marilyn Strathern also commented about Audrey's ability 'to notice the oddness in unique moments'.[79] Audrey photographed rather than filmed this dance of the girls' regiments. With the King's approval, she took her students on a tour of a hospital, a farm, an asbestos mine and the Swazi National School in Lobamba, which had recently experimented with the re-introduction of the traditional

---

[77] ARP, Richards 20/4 Press Cuttings, *The Star*, 1940.

[78] *Ibid.*, Audrey Richards-Dame Isabel Richards, 20 July 1938, Mbabane. The article he referred to here was Hilda Beemer, 'The Development of the Military Organization in Swaziland', *Africa*, 10, 1&2 (January & April 1937), 55–74, 176–205 which gave a detailed account of Swazi age-groups including their dance rituals.

[79] Raymond and Rosemary Firth, 'An Eye for Incongruity: Audrey Richards in a Light Mood' in La Fontaine, ed., *Cambridge Anthropology*, 18–31; Strathern, 'Audrey Isabel Richards 1899–1984', *Proceedings of the British Academy*, 443.

Figure 4.3: 'In Swaziland. Rock climb (staged) with Biesheuvels (lecturer in psychology here [at Wits University]).' An outstretched Audrey with Dr Simon Biesheuvel (1908–1991) and two students on their vacation fieldtrip to Swaziland, July 1938.[80]

amabutho system of age-regiments in its curricula at the prompting of Sobhuza and with the support of Mrs Hoernlé, Schapera and Malinowski.[81]

Her second trip to Swaziland was undertaken on the spur of the moment just two months later in September 1938. She describes how she had settled down to doing final edits on *Land, Labour and Diet* when Hilda Beemer 'rushed in [to her flat] in a great state'. Hilda had evidently been wired by Sobhuza with the news that his mother had died. He felt anxious as there was no ritual precedent for a funeral of a Queen Mother who died before a Swazi King. 'She [Hilda] felt she ought to go and write up the funeral but didn't want to go alone.' Audrey's description of the event anticipates her later arguments regarding the 'revival of tradition among the Tswana' in its emphasis on lack of historical precedent and the

---

[80] London, Royal Anthropological Institute Photographic Collection, Audrey Richards, Folder 26a Personal (South Africa), RAI 005.
[81] Hilda Beemer had documented this (ultimately failed) experiment in re-Africanizing Swazi education in an essay published in *Africa* the previous year. See Chapter 5 for details.

Figure 4.4: 'With Biesheuvels and the prettiest student.' Further adventures on the Swaziland fieldtrip, July 1938. Audrey is on the right.[82]

[82] *Ibid.*, RAI 007.

degree of ad hoc invention involved in the staging of 'traditional rituals' in modern times. As she explained in her letter: 'Primitive peoples are supposed to be hidebound by custom, but I was interested to see here as in [Northern] Rhodesia the extraordinary amount of indecision and discussion over the [funeral] ceremony.' These 'endless discussions' meant that they only got the body into the grave at four o'clock the following afternoon, and then all of the rituals of purification needed to be negotiated.[83] In a later published account of the Queen Mother's funeral, Hilda explained that the delay had been due mainly to the insistence of the Queen Mother's sister that her cards of Zionist Church membership be retrieved from the distant royal enclosure and placed beside her cowhide-shrouded body.[84]

In her second year at Wits, Audrey took her students to native reserves and Bushman rock art sites where she encouraged experimentation

Figure 4.5: 'Descending ravine to a native village. (Ainslie trying to show that there is *no* need to be alarmed).' Audrey, a colleague and their students on yet another adventurous vacation fieldtrip, 1939.[85]

[83] ARP, Richards 18/3, File 1, Audrey Richards-Dame Isabel Richards, 17 September 1938, Johannesburg.
[84] Hilda Kuper, *The Swazi: A South African Kingdom* (New York: Holt, Rinehart and Winston, 1963), 67.
[85] London, Royal Anthropological Institute, Photographic Collection, Audrey Richards, Folder 26a Personal (South Africa), RAI 003. Her emphasis.

'A genius for friendship': Audrey Richards at Wits, 1938–1940   175

with methods of copying. They had now begun to develop a taste for adventure. 'Students asked me to take them up to Northern Rhodesia in July [1939], thinking I should speak fluent Bemba to them, show them the [Victoria] Falls, and a thing called Indirect Rule. I told them not to be *fipuba* [fools in chiBemba] . . . '[86]

Audrey took over from Winifred Hoernlé not just as a teacher and head of department, but as the leading woman scholar in the university. This brought her into contact with male professors and in general her attitude towards them was far less forgiving than that of her predecessor. She was forced to work under the linguist Clement Doke, head of the School of Bantu Studies. Whereas Mrs Hoernlé had written of him fondly, Audrey found him 'moody', 'nervous' and intensely annoying from the outset.[87] She described him as 'the Baptist' in all her letters and clearly found it difficult to consider him her senior. 'My "boss" is difficult, no imagination and like a schoolboy over points of etiquette.' Her view of other male colleagues in the Bantu Studies Department is best encapsulated in her dismissive report about their responses to Isaac Schapera's classic *Married Life in an African Tribe*, which was published in 1940. While Audrey wrote a glowing review of the book, her male colleagues either felt that the book was too long and thus did not read beyond the first 100 pages,[88] or (in the case of 'The Baptist') felt that 'if that is social anthropology', by which he meant the book's 'obscenity', then 'he is thankful he doesn't touch it'.[89] As is well known, the book evoked a strong reaction in conservative Christian circles for its unusually explicit treatment of the theme of African sexuality. The Archbishop of Cape Town called for its banning and the Principal of UCT called on him to answer the wave of protest.[90] Audrey's attitude towards male professors in other departments was equally dismissive, as can be gauged from this description of her first Senate meeting in April 1938.

I was one of only six humble lecturer representatives and seem to be the only woman [in Senate] at the moment. Everything [is] very formal and standing to speak. Not a smile at any time, and rows of stern Dutch [Afrikaner] faces and that particular shape and physiognomy that seems to come from Bristol and Newcastle-on-Tyne.[91]

---

[86] WC, B4.7 Correspondence, Audrey Richards to Godfrey Wilson, 14 December 1938.
[87] ARP, Richards 18/3, File 1, Audrey Richards-Dame Isabel Richards, 9 March 1938, Johannesburg.
[88] WC, B4.7 [GW] To and from Audrey Richards, Audrey Richards to Godfrey Wilson, 27 August 1939, Johannesburg.
[89] *Ibid.*, Audrey Richards to Godfrey Wilson, 24 July 1940, Johannesburg.
[90] Kuper, 'Isaac Schapera: His Life and Times', 34.
[91] ARP, Richards 18/3, File 1, Audrey Richards-Dame Isabel Richards, 16 March 1938, Johannesburg.

176   Pioneers of the Field

When she attempted to pass a reformist motion at a later gathering, this stuffy, stern and stifling old guard closed rank, which she again reported with refreshingly detached amusement rather than the slightest hint of resentment. She found 'the Dutch', as her letters referred to Afrikaners, an unsettling presence, even though she made an effort to learn Afrikaans by reading *Die Burger* for half an hour every morning over breakfast.[92] The ideological tension between Wits University and Pretoria University is a regular theme, especially in the months before the outbreak of the war.

[T]he rows between our students and Pretoria University students (Dutch and very Nazi) don't make things any happier. The staff members at Pretoria University are publishing a paper advertised as scientific, [but] reproducing all Hitler's race theories and anti-Semitism ...[93]

She claimed that 'The N.P. [National Party] here are already very affected by Nazi policy', something that more recent historical research has fully supported.[94] She added that '*Mein Kampf* is one of the set-books for the students of Pretoria and Stellenbosch Universities'.[95] On other occasions her anxiety was more personal. She wrote of her deep discomfort at being forced to share a train carriage with a mob of Afrikaner nationalist students from Pretoria.

The spread of Nazism and anti-Semitism in South Africa is the dominant motif in her letters. She was immediately aware of the depth of anti-Semitism in South Africa. Shortly after her arrival she delivered a lecture to a meeting of Europeans and Africans at the Bantu Social Centre in Orlando township 'on the origin of the term Aryan to show how absolutely without biological foundation the use of that word was, and that seemed to interest them, and [I] also put in digs at anti-Semitism which I hope may do good in time.'[96] Her fears about Nazism were obviously most directly related to the threat of the impact of war with Germany on her home country and her family in Oxford. The issue of European politics took up more and more space in her letters, and the acquisition of a new radio in mid-1939 kept her abreast of the latest developments. But her fears about Nazism must also surely be read in light of the fact that her closest friends in South Africa were Jews. Apart from Ellen and Hilda, she befriended the South African Jewish writer, Sarah Gertrude Millin, whose outspokenness she admired. Most of her male colleagues were Jewish, Schapera, Gluckman and Julius Lewin among them. Even her

---

[92] *Ibid.*, Audrey Richards-Dame Isabel Richards, 25 November 1939, Johannesburg.
[93] *Ibid.*, Audrey Richards-Dame Isabel Richards, 25 June 1939, Johannesburg.
[94] See Furlong, *Between Crown and Swastika*.
[95] *Ibid.*, Audrey Richards-Dame Isabel Richards, 16 March 1938, Johannesburg.
[96] *Ibid.*, Audrey Richards-Dame Isabel Richards, 16 March 1938, Johannesburg.

'A genius for friendship': Audrey Richards at Wits, 1938–1940   177

students were predominantly Jewish. In her third and final year, her politics shifted somewhat to the left. The spineless appeasement of Chamberlain was the immediate prompt for her comment: 'Personally the result is to drive me from a mild pink to a deep red, and a study for the first time of communist literature, and a determination that politics is one of the only things worth working for if democracies of any kind are to survive at all.'[97]

As is well known, she befriended the South African Prime Minister, Jan Smuts. Even here her first impression was far from favourable. She met him at a Wits University seminar organized by the Hoernlés in October 1938 and found him 'queerly unimpressive'.[98] Raymond Firth's recollection about her relationships with male authority figures seems apposite here. 'Perhaps partly because of her background, she found it easy to take responsibility without anxiety, and to cope with the power structure nonchalantly at almost every level.'[99] On the first of what would be numerous weekend visits to the Smuts home in Irene, she reported that 'he said he had read my book [*Hunger and Work*] and should call me Audrey'. Adam Kuper relates that:

Audrey would tell a story about Smuts shaking her awake one morning when she was sleeping on the cot of the verandah at Irene. 'Come Audrey, we're going for a swim in the dam.' He was *stark naked.*[100]

Be that as it may, her first peaceful weekend at Irene was shattered by political events.

We came back to the news of the horrible anti-Jewish agitation and attempt to blow up the synagogue here [in Johannesburg]. Nazi agents have been pouring into the country of course for the last few years, determined on getting German South-West [Africa]. The Afrikaner element is rather in favour of them ... The Englishman [in South Africa] continues in ostrich fashion as usual saying 'Nazism can't come here.'[101]

One of her most eye-opening experiences regarding the rise of racism and Afrikaner nationalism in South Africa was a visit to the Northern Transvaal town of Louis Trichardt in December 1938. The Voortrekker Centenary celebrations happened to be under way at the time of her trip.

---

[97] *Ibid.*, Audrey Richards-Dame Isabel Richards, 4 October 1938, Johannesburg.

[98] *Ibid.*, Audrey Richards-Dame Isabel Richards, 4 October 1938, Johannesburg.

[99] Raymond Firth, 'Audrey Richards 1899–1984', *Man*, 20, 2 (1985), 343. Firth worked with Audrey on the International African Institute's Nutrition Committee before her time at Wits and then again in the Colonial Office as part of the Welfare and Development Programme during the early to mid-1940s.

[100] Adam Kuper, E-mail correspondence, 14 September 2013, London-Cape Town.

[101] *Ibid.*, Audrey Richards-Dame Isabel Richards, 29 November 1938, Johannesburg.

178   Pioneers of the Field

She was most struck by the gendered way in which Afrikaner nationalism was performed 'with bearded men and women in Voortrekker dress, no white family so poor that it hasn't been able to make the women and girls long print frocks with fichu and poke bonnet'. She 'got the drift' of the impassioned speeches: 'heat terrific and one dozed off to sounds of shouting, praying and beards wagging around – couples were married at the boom of a waggon as in the old days, three babies christened "Louis Trichardt" in the same way'. 'Not a happy augury for the future', she rightly concluded.[102] Whether observing the King of Swaziland filming Swazi women's dances, the grim faces of the Afrikaner and English male professors that sat in Wits University Senate, or the fervent speeches of bearded Afrikaner nationalists in a remote town in the Northern Transvaal, her commentary is typified by a combination of the dry humour of the English outsider and the razor-sharp sociological insight of a highly trained and experienced participant observer. In general, these letters provide an unusually in-depth ethnography of white South African society.

Racism and anti-Semitism were of course not confined to the Afrikaner nationalists. In fact the university authorities at Wits encouraged Audrey to stay on beyond December 1940 partly because she was not Jewish. She wrote home in August 1940, genuinely in two minds about whether to 'A) Return home and hope to do constructive work on colonial redistribution etc. with possible trips to Africa ... [or] B) Return here with a bigger department and running a social science training [programme] and anthropology ... [P]eople here want me to stay on the grounds of not being a Jew and having some ideas I think ... '[103] They were evidently more comfortable with having a colonial-born English woman as head of social anthropology than a left-wing Jewish woman like Hilda Kuper. Audrey made sure that the university authorities chose Hilda as her successor in 1941 after Leo Kuper had left Johannesburg to fight in North Africa.

Four essays and a book

In addition to the demands of teaching, there were the demands of writing. Audrey was rather more productive during her three years in South Africa than has been acknowledged. She was of course at the backend of a decade of prolific writing on the Bemba. She spent much of the second half of 1938 making alterations to *Land, Labour and Diet* in

---

[102] *Ibid.*, Audrey Richards-Dame Isabel Richards, 8 December 1938, Louis Trichardt.
[103] *Ibid.*, Audrey Richards-Dame Isabel Richards, 20 August 1940, Johannesburg.

'A genius for friendship': Audrey Richards at Wits, 1938–1940   179

energetic correspondence with the Wilsons in Northern Rhodesia and particularly with Godfrey, who generously tracked down all manner of Bemba-related queries, linguistic and otherwise, for a scholar whose work he had long admired.[104] During the summer vacation of 1938 she was still 'haunted by proofs'. She compiled the index to her book in the early months of 1939 while incorporating last-minute changes from readers, notably Godfrey and Lorna.[105] Her book was recognized as a significant ethnography from the time of its publication, given its systematic and meticulous documentation of one aspect of Bemba culture – nutrition – and her ability to include the material and the symbolic within a wide cultural framework. Godfrey described it as 'an obvious classic' and, on second reading, as 'extraordinarily impressive'. He had 'very little but admiration [for it]' and urged her 'to publish it more or less as it stands'.[106] He would later describe it as 'the Bible'.[107] Henrietta Moore and Megan Vaughan presented a powerful case for its value and continued relevance fifty years after its publication.

Her attention to gender relations, to the burden of women's workload in a rural economy, and her attempt to measure well-being in terms of diet, all found echoes in more recent literature [of the 1980s] on the problems of 'development' in rural Africa in general, and in the Northern Province of Zambia in particular. Her painstakingly detailed descriptions of what African rural producers actually do, and what they know about soils and vegetation, trees and bees, and mushrooms and caterpillars also found echoes in the academic and 'development' worlds, in the literature on 'indigenous knowledge' and in the literature on the ecology of Africa.[108]

Audrey was racked with self-doubt in the final stages of its production. Before submission of her final manuscript, she anticipated that it would be 'a failure', confiding to her mother that it 'has taken much more of my life than it should have and much more of my energy! Next time I shall write a novel or a learned work.'[109] She was equally deflated when she saw the finished product in October 1939. 'I think the pictures are disappointing and I am afraid that the whole is too. There are some good and interesting chapters but the whole is too long

---

[104] WC, B4.7 [GW] Letters to and from Audrey Richards, Audrey Richards to Godfrey Wilson, 20 June 1938, 27 August 1939, Johannesburg.

[105] ARP, Audrey Richards to Dame Isabel Richards, 8 December 1938, Louis Trichardt; Audrey Richards to Dame Isabel Richards, 23 March 1939, Johannesburg.

[106] WC, B4.7 [GW] Letters to and from Audrey Richards, Godfrey Wilson to Audrey Richards, [n.d. early September 1938] and 17 October 1938, Kasama.

[107] *Ibid.*, Godfrey Wilson to Audrey Richards, 26 March 1940, Broken Hill.

[108] Moore and Vaughan, *Cutting Down Trees*, xii.

[109] ARP, Audrey Richards-Dame Isabel Richards, 1 February 1838, Johannesburg.

180   Pioneers of the Field

and written with too many audiences in mind – the "practical" man, the anthropologist, the general public etc. ... '[110]

Her self-criticism was not confined to her famous book. The best-known of four significant essays that she wrote during her three years in Johannesburg was an extended analysis of 'The Political System of the Bemba of North-Eastern Rhodesia'. It was published in 1940 in the landmark volume *African Political Systems*, edited by the Oxford-based anthropologists Meyer Fortes and Edward E. Evans-Pritchard.[111] This essay on Bemba chieftainship can be seen as a turning-point in her scholarship. During the 1930s her primary focus had been on nutrition and economics. From 1940 onwards her scholarship would focus on chieftainship and political systems in Africa, and especially in Uganda, where she did fieldwork on Buganda politics during the 1950s and then published two books on traditional political systems and social change.[112] By contrast with colleagues like Godfrey Wilson, she found the new edited collection uninspiring and described her own essay and Evans-Pritchard's as 'boring'. Her lukewarm attitude towards the new volume needs to be read in the light of her deep distaste for 'the structuralist turn' in British social anthropology from the early 1940s led by Evans-Pritchard and Radcliffe-Brown at Oxford. This much is clear from her letters to Monica and Godfrey after her two-month visit to England, during which she sat in on some of Radcliffe-Brown's Oxford seminars. With Malinowski having left the LSE for the United States in 1938, she clearly felt that there was no gifted leader to take over his mantle and that the most dynamic work in African anthropology was now being produced by applied anthropologists who were based in Africa.

Anthropology in England is in a deplorable state. A.R.B. [Radcliffe-Brown] is doing nothing at Oxford – no attempt at anything constructive on the colonial problem side – no adaptation to the world situation ... Have been to seminars and he doesn't seem to have moved since 1922! Fortes is desperate for a job and it makes him bitter and defeatist ... E.P. [Evans-Pritchard] is working away. Nuer book in proof ... Oxford anthropology is doing nothing and no students.[113]

---

[110] *Ibid.*, Audrey Richards-Dame Isabel Richards, 4 October 1939, Johannesburg.

[111] Audrey Richards, 'The Political System of the Bemba of North-eastern Rhodesia' in Meyer Fortes and Edward E. Evans-Pritchard, eds., *African Political Systems* (London: Oxford University Press, 1940), 83–120.

[112] See esp. Audrey Richards, *East African Chiefs: A Study of Political Development in Some Uganda and Tanganyika Tribes* (London: Faber and Faber, 1960); *The Changing Structure of a Ganda Village: Kisozi 1892–1952* (Nairobi: East Africa Publishing House, 1966).

[113] WC, B4.7 [GW] Correspondence between Godfrey Wilson and Audrey Richards, Audrey Richards to Godfrey Wilson, 10 February 1940, 18 March 1940, Johannesburg.

'A genius for friendship': Audrey Richards at Wits, 1938–1940   181

Her review essay on the 'Nuer book' in *Bantu Studies* early in 1941 does not feature in the standard bibliographies of her published work, but it should do. Along with a twin review of Schapera's *Married Life of an African Tribe* published in the previous issue of the journal, it provides one of the most lucid statements of the reasons for her continued commitment to an empirical model of functionalist scholarship based on years of immersed participant observation and her scepticism regarding abstract theory based on inadequate data. We ought to begin by noting that these essays were but the most prominent among her numerous contributions to *Bantu Studies*. She had taken over from Winifred Hoernlé as the only woman member on the Editorial Board from 1938 to 1940. (It would be more than half a century before the renamed *African Studies* appointed another woman member on their Board.) She wrote half a dozen reviews of works in French as well as English,[114] numerous reports on manuscript articles, and negotiated between authors and two out-of-touch male editors: 'the Baptist' and J.D. Rheinallt-Jones. In the case of Godfrey Wilson's acclaimed article on 'Nyakyusa Burials', for example, she needed to convince 'the Baptist' that it was even worth publishing. 'He [Doke] says it [Godfrey's article] is longer than is easy for him and that he doesn't understand the first few pages. Now this wouldn't prevent them from being the best pages in the [Godfrey's prospective] book . . . ' She had to persuade a reluctant Godfrey to cut back on his theory.[115]

Her review essay on *The Nuer* (1940) began by acknowledging the difficulty of the conditions under which Evans-Pritchard had collected his field data. His book is famous for its introductory account of what he dubbed 'nuer-osis': the aloof, touchy and intensely hostile attitude of his informants. However, she went on to criticise the book for its complete lack of interest in social change: it 'gives practically the impression of having been written before the arrival of the White man'. She was especially dissatisfied, in fact 'irritated', by the 'rigid' exclusion of descriptive data at the expense of grand theories about 'social structure'. There is, she lamented, 'no account of "social situation", few Native texts or comments, no concrete case studies . . ., no

---

[114] Audrey Richards, 'Review of *Le Sorcellerie dans les pays de mission* (Paris, 1937)', *Bantu Studies*, 17, 2 (1938), 145–6; 'Review of Margaret Read, *Native Standards of Living and African Culture Change* (1937)', *Bantu Studies*, 17, 3 (1938), 346–8; 'Review of Wilfred D. Hambly, *Source Book for African Anthropology*', *Bantu Studies*, 17, 3 (1938), 348–50; 'Review of *Le Bulletin des Missions*', *Bantu Studies*, 18, 1 (1938), 327; 'Review of C.G. Seligman, *The Races of Africa* (2nd edition, 1938)', *Bantu Studies*, 18, 1 (1938), 327–8.
[115] WC, B4.7 [GW] To and from Audrey Richards, Audrey Richards to Godfrey Wilson, 4 November 1938, Johannesburg; Godfrey Wilson to Audrey Richards, 13 November 1938, Livingstone.

182   Pioneers of the Field

individual or group case-histories, no mention of Native personalities, and not a statistic in the book.' She asked her readers to reflect: 'Can social groups really be studied in abstract without a rather detailed knowledge of the activities in which they are engaged and the network of sentiments and laws that bind them?'[116]

Contrast this with the tone and content of her review essay on Isaac Schapera's *Married Life of An African Tribe* published in the same year as Evans-Pritchard's study. She began by highlighting the author's credentials as a fieldworker. Schapera's study was based on a full decade of intermittent fieldwork among the Bakgatla of the Bechuanaland Protectorate for which he had been awarded the Rivers Medal for Fieldwork in 1939. She described his book as 'the first full study of Bantu marriage institutions planned on the comprehensive scheme which Malinowski made famous some years ago in a similar monograph on the sex and procreational institutions of the Trobriand Islanders'. Schapera's task was more difficult given the greater extent of contact with White culture and his book documented in the greatest of detail how marriage functioned in traditional Tswana culture as well as the transformation of the institution in the modern era. Successive chapters analysed the reasons for the choice of mate in Kgatla society, customary methods of courtship, methods of courtship adopted from European culture, traditional and modern wedding rituals, the marital relationships, the erotic, legal and economic aspects of marriage, traditional attitudes towards procreation and parenthood, traditional and modern educational practices, as well as the degree of marital stability before and after colonial contact. The dominant impression is 'the sheer magnitude of the social changes' based on a 'wealth of concrete data'. 'In fact, to those South Africans who still cherish romantic notions about distant reserves where Natives live simple tribal lives, this account of the new African family will probably come as something of a shock.' She was moved by Schapera's documentation of African poverty in the Native reserves. 'There is probably no more convincing picture of present-day poverty in the Native reserves than in the section Schapera has headed "Making end meet", with its pitiful letters of anxious saving husbands in the urban areas and its revelations of the stark necessity in some of the deserted households in the countryside.' Finally, she praised the author for his methodological rigour and innovation, from 'the careful use of statistical sampling' to the effective use of letters written to the author by informants or obtained from them, 'a new technique in the South African

---

[116] Audrey Richards, 'A Problem of Anthropological Approach. Review of E.E. Evans-Pritchard, *The Nuer*', *Bantu Studies*, 15, 1 (1941), 45–52.

'A genius for friendship': Audrey Richards at Wits, 1938–1940   183

area'. She concluded by advertising it as 'undoubtedly the best work on Bantu marriage that exists'.[117]

She was in the process of completing her own (much more frustrating) fieldwork among the Bakgatla, in her case in a Native reserve 70 kilometres north of Pretoria.[118] Her enthusiasm about Schapera's study must also be seen in relation to her recent publication of a short (and again undervalued) book on Bemba marriage, where the themes of tradition and social change were central. Her voluminous correspondence with Godfrey Wilson, with occasional letters from Monica, reveals quite the amount of collaborative effort that she and the Wilsons put into the production of her 123-page book, *Bemba Marriage and Present Economic Conditions*. It was written from start to finish in Johannesburg and published in September 1940 in the series of Papers of the Rhodes-Livingstone Institute, which Godfrey had launched.[119] Her powerful central argument, in keeping with her emphasis on complexity and social change, was that the impact of colonialism on African social institutions (here, Bemba marriage) needed to be dealt with on a case-by-case basis, and in a way that took close account of the strengths or fault-lines in the ability of traditional cultures to adapt to rapid change. She presented a persuasive case that the matrilineal Bemba system of marriage was particularly vulnerable to the disruption brought by colonial rule and drew, often explicitly, on her South African experiences in contrasting this with the greater resilience of the patrilineal cultures that she encountered there in her teaching and fieldwork.[120] The judges of the Wellcome Medal Committee of 1940 were unanimous in awarding it to Richards for this book ahead of Godfrey Wilson for his well-known study on *The Economics of Detribalization* and Max Gluckman for his famous two-part essay *The Bridge*.[121] Yet for the reasons set out in my introduction, their studies have been lauded and hers largely forgotten.

To label her condensed two-page note in *Man* on 'Some Causes of a Revival of Tribalism in South African Native Reserves' as a fourth Johannesburg 'essay' may seem overly generous, given its length and

---

[117] Audrey Richards, 'Review of Isaac Schapera, *Married Life in an African Tribe*' (London: Faber and Faber, 1940)', *Bantu Studies*, 14, 3 (1940), 456–60.

[118] See her field diary for a wonderfully entertaining account of the daily frustrations of her fieldwork in Makapanstad on two separate expeditions in July and August 1939 and then September and October of 1940, see ARP, Richards 5/2 Makapanstad.

[119] Audrey Richards, *Bemba Marriage and Present Economic Conditions* (Livingstone: Rhodes-Livingstone Institute Papers, No. 4, 1940).

[120] *Ibid.*, 29, 92, 91, 95, 115.

[121] Robert Gordon, 'Max Gluckman in Zululand' (unpublished seminar paper, Anthropology Southern Africa Conference, Wits University, September 2013).

184   Pioneers of the Field

the fact that it was published after her return to London. However, it was the product of four months of fieldwork which she had initially intended as the basis for three full articles.[122] Moreover, its argument was incisive and unusual in its anticipation of much later writing about 'the invention of tradition', a perspective that is equally evident in her reports on fieldtrips in the letters cited above. In short, I fully endorse Adam Kuper's assessment:

> Intermittent fieldwork among a Tswana group in the Northern Transvaal yielded only one paper, but it is a brilliant piece, analysing the revival of 'tribalism' in an area in which traditional cultures had been destroyed a decade earlier. She argued that the movement had nothing to do with nostalgia for a golden age, or with traditionalism, but was rather to be explained as a manoeuvre in the competition for land rights.[123]

Hoernlé's heir, 1940–1984

My main argument concerns Audrey Richards' unheralded contribution – albeit as an outsider – to the consolidation of social anthropology in South Africa. Despite the striking differences between Winifred Hoernlé and Audrey Richards, in terms of depth and extent of their fieldwork, the quality and range of their published writing and their degree of recognition within the discipline, they shared a common goal: that of promoting the work of young women anthropologists. We have seen how Audrey had championed the initiation of women into fieldwork from the time of her very first essay on her Bemba fieldwork, published in the Newnham Newsletter in 1932, with a rallying-call for her college-mates to apply for research grants for fieldwork. Her role as a champion of younger women scholars would be life-long, most fully realized during her period of headship of Newnham College in the late 1950s and her supervision of the above-mentioned women anthropologists at Cambridge in the early to mid-1960s.

In relation to the South African women featured in these chapters, Audrey's intellectual friendship and support can be tracked across four

---

[122] In her report to the South African National Research Council, she listed the titles of these prospective papers as 'Some causes of a revival of tribalism in a present-day native reserve in the Transvaal' (see note below), 'Some effects of the decay of polygamy on the political balance of a South African native tribe' and 'A comparison between the tribal organization of the Kgatla peoples within and without the Union'. ARP, Richards 5/4, Makapanstad 1940–1942: 1. Report on Second Expedition to Makapanstad in September 1940.

[123] Kuper, 'Audrey Richards: A Career in Anthropology', 125. See Audrey Richards, 'Some Causes of a Revival of Tribalism in South African Native Reserves', *Man*, 41 (1942), 89–90.

'A genius for friendship': Audrey Richards at Wits, 1938–1940   185

decades. She was closest to Monica Wilson, as the volume of correspondence between them would suggest: 110 letters between 1940 and 1982, the year of Monica's death.[124] Audrey's promotional work on Monica's behalf began less than a year after they had first met at the London seminar. She trumpeted the merits of *Reaction to Conquest* in an essay published in the *London Spectator* in September 1936.[125] She highlighted the methodological innovation of a book which studied Africans in town and on farms, as well as those in the more traditional setting of the 'native reserve'. She was a confidante and loyal friend to Monica in the sad and lonely years following Godfrey's death. Monica would have been deeply touched by the moving obituary to Godfrey that Audrey published in *Man* in 1944.[126]

Audrey wrote laudatory references in support of Monica, including one for her successful application for a job as the first woman professor at Rhodes University in 1946. She characterized Monica as 'a person of unusual distinction' and 'shrewd common-sense', one with 'a balanced judgement of people and affairs', 'an indefatigable worker' with 'charm, humour and clarity of mind'.[127] She published another laudatory review of Monica's work, this time of *Rituals of Kinship among the Nyakyusa* (1957), a time when they were both intensively involved in the study of African ritual. (Audrey's *Chisungu* had come out the previous year.) They communicated frequently during the 1960s, initially about Monica's co-authored book *Langa: A Study of Social Groups*, which Audrey endorsed in a reader's report to Oxford University Press; then, at great length, about the fluctuating Cambridge career of Monica's star UCT anthropology student and co-author, Archie Mafeje, whom she had sent to do doctoral research with Audrey. Theirs was a deeply emotional bond and one gets the sense that, for Monica, this friendship was a lifeline to sanity in an increasingly insane society. Audrey came over to present a series of lectures to Monica's undergraduate classes in 1963, while Monica visited Audrey in Cambridge in 1969 when she delivered the Scott Holland lectures. Their contributions in the respective festschrifts of 1972 (Monica on Audrey) and 1975 (Audrey at much more length on Monica) bear testimony to the enormous mutual respect they held for

---

[124] WC, B6.14, Correspondence between Monica Wilson and Audrey Richards, 28 August 1940 to 15 February 1982: 110 letters.

[125] Audrey Richards, 'Review of *Reaction to Conquest*', *London Spectator*, 9 October 1936.

[126] Audrey Richards, 'Obituary: Godfrey Wilson', *Man*, 44 (1944), 125–6.

[127] BC880, B6.14 Correspondence between Monica Wilson and Audrey Richards, Audrey Richards to Rhodes University Appointments Committee, 'Reference for Monica Wilson', 15 June 1946, Draft version.

186   Pioneers of the Field

one another as human beings as well as scholars, but also – especially in the case of Audrey's thirteen-page appreciation – of the depth of engaged knowledge and insight they had about each other's work.[128] This was partly the result of their shared interest in the central themes in social anthropology over the decades from culture contact and social change in the 1930s to ritual in the 1950s to more localized studies of village life in the late 1970s, with Monica taking her chance to boost her friend's scholarship by publishing a warm and perceptive review of Audrey's co-authored study of *Some Elmdon Families* in *African Studies* in 1976.[129]

Audrey's other close friend was Hilda Kuper. The surviving correspondence is not quite as voluminous as that with Monica, but it does reveal that they had a friendship of comparable warmth and depth. This friendship began at Wits. Audrey ensured that Hilda got appointed as her successor. As we will see in the next chapter, she continued to promote Hilda's career in subsequent decades. She published a typically engaged and perceptive review in *Man* of the first, and still the best known, of Hilda's many books, *An African Aristocracy* (1947).[130] Audrey was staying with Hilda and Leo in North Carolina when their daughter Jenny was born in August 1948. She had come over to give guest lectures.[131] Jenny recalls: 'Audrey was always called my "godmother" by Hilda because she was around when I was a baby – though years later Audrey explained to me that "godmother" was a title that comes with a certain (Christian) formality, which did not really apply to our situation! Nonetheless, she assumed a rather special role in my life.'[132] Audrey corresponded more actively with Hilda from the mid- to late 1950s, mostly about their joint studies of ritual. Hilda had embarked on a challenging study of Indian religious rituals in Durban, for which, at Audrey's recommendation as the first woman President of the British Royal Anthropological Institute, she was awarded a Rivers Medal for Fieldwork in 1961. 'I realise that if you hadn't been President, I'd not have been receiving the medal.'[133]

---

[128] Audrey Richards, 'Monica Wilson: An Appreciation' in Whisson and West, eds., *Religion and Social Change in Southern Africa*, 1–13; Monica Wilson, 'The Wedding Cakes: A Study of Ritual Change' in Jean S. La Fontaine, ed., *The Interpretation of Ritual*, 187.

[129] Monica Wilson, 'Review of Audrey Richards and Jean Robin, *Some Elmdon Families*', 297–9.

[130] Audrey Richards, 'Review of Hilda Kuper, *An African Aristocracy*', *Man*, 48 (1948), 142–3.

[131] WC, Uncatalogued correspondence 'K', Hilda Kuper to Monica Wilson, North Carolina, 28 April 1949.

[132] Jenny Kuper, E-mail correspondence, 5 October 2014, London-Cape Town.

[133] ARP, Richards 16/36, Hilda Kuper to Audrey Richards, Durban, n.d. [1961].

'A genius for friendship': Audrey Richards at Wits, 1938–1940   187

As was the case with Monica, Audrey acted for Hilda as a calm and steadying influence in times of severe stress. In Hilda's case, as Chapter 5 relates, the stress was that of seeing her husband arrested and banned in 1956, the apartheid state closing round the University of Natal in subsequent years, leading to the painful decision to emigrate to the United States in 1961 and then, perhaps most traumatic of all, feeling that she had made the wrong decision by relocating to the United States rather than England. There is a depth of emotion in these letters which has no counterpart in any of Hilda's other correspondence, even that of the remarkably warm and mutually supportive letters between her and Monica across the eight years when she served as Monica's external examiner at UCT, often staying in the Wilson house during her visits.[134] Jenny frequently stayed with Audrey during visits to England and the lives of Jenny and Mary, Hilda's younger daughter born in South Africa in 1949, were the subject of many letters across thirty-five years of correspondence, right through to Audrey's last letter to Hilda, written just a few months before she died.[135]

Audrey's friendship with Eileen Krige was also warm and supportive. Perhaps the most significant of Audrey's many hidden contributions to South African anthropology was taking responsibility for seeing Eileen and Jack's *The Realm of a Rain-Queen* through to publication by Oxford University Press. As I document in Chapter 6, this proved to be no easy task. The Kriges, rightly, felt that without Audrey's energetic interventions their much delayed book might never have seen the light of day. Here, yet again, she followed up her support in the production process with a generous review in a prominent anthropological journal. Published in *Man* in 1944, her review provided a much more balanced and, frankly, well-informed account than the hostile review that had been published earlier the same year by Max Gluckman, whose private correspondence showed that he did not feel particularly warm towards the Kriges.[136] Eileen visited Audrey whenever she travelled to England, including on a vacation in 1964, as did Ellen on her more frequent trips abroad. In their cases, unfortunately, there are no comparable paper trails that allow for fuller reconstruction of these lifelong friendships,

---

[134] WC, Uncatalogued correspondence 'K': Correspondence between Monica Wilson and Hilda Kuper, 1953–1960.

[135] ARP, Richards 16/36, Audrey Richards to Hilda Kuper, 20 February 1984, Cambridge.

[136] Audrey Richards, 'Review of *The Realm of a Rain-Queen*', *Man*, 44 (November–December 1944), 148–50; Max Gluckman, 'Review of *The Realm of a Rain-Queen*', *African Studies*, 3, 2 (1944), 146–7. See for example WC, B4.11 Correspondence regarding the Rhodes-Livingstone Institute, Max Gluckman to Godfrey Wilson, 4 November 1941.

confirming the role that Audrey came to play as 'the surrogate mother of South African anthropology'.

One might imagine that Winifred Hoernlé loomed large in their recollections during their reunions. Audrey's obituary in *Man*, as the extract quoted in my epigraph confirms, testified to her deep admiration for the woman whose role she inherited, not only as head of the Wits department and senior woman intellectual in that university, but as mentor of this gifted generation of women anthropologists.

5 Historical ethnography and ethnographic fiction: the South African writings of Hilda Beemer Kuper (1911–1992)

> Dr Winifred Hoernlé, my first teacher in Social Anthropology, introduced me to the complexities of Indian culture in South Africa, and by her knowledge, insight, and sympathy awoke in me, as in so many of her students, both an interest in research and a respect for humanity.
>
> Hilda Kuper, 'Changes of Caste of the South African Indians', *Race Relations Journal: Special Issue: Homage to Winifred Hoernlé*, 22, 4 (1955), 18.[1]

Unlike those women anthropologists whose contributions are discussed elsewhere in this book, Hilda Beemer Kuper (1911–1992) had no festschrift written in her honour when she retired in 1977, after fifteen years as Professor and Chair of Social Anthropology at UCLA. This was, in large part because of the difficulty a team of prospective editors had in getting authors to reflect on her body of experimental writings, which was well ahead of its time in anticipating the 'literary turn' in social anthropology.[2] While Hilda had been trained in the most rigorous of terms in this discipline, her work is notable for its diversity and creative experimentation. Her anthropological monographs (or at least sections of them) read like histories with close attention to chronology, detail and divergence, as well as their intense interest in individuals, variation and contingency rather than the general laws sought by many of her peers. Her body of ethnographic fiction is substantial and sophisticated. It includes sixteen short stories, one novel and two plays, one of which (*A Witch in*

---

[1] I am deeply indebted to Hilda's two daughters, Jenny and Mary, for their generosity in sharing memories and family photographs, and patiently reading and correcting numerous drafts. Thanks to Robert Gordon for scans of Hilda's political essays and the correspondence regarding 'the Schoeman affair', as well as Bob Edgar and Sondra Hale for information about Hilda as a teacher and supervisor at UCLA.

[2] Sondra Hale explains that a festschrift had been planned for Hilda. It was to be edited by three of her UCLA doctoral students (Beth Rosen Prinz, Dawn Chatty and Hale), but that they realized that 'they could not find enough contributors within anthropology who could adequately assess her literary work ... Had we tried to do the Festschrift even five years later, we would have found a plethora of anthropologists who could have written about Hilda from a literary point of view.' Sondra Hale, E-mail communication, 8 October 2014, Los Angeles-Cape Town.

189

190   Pioneers of the Field

My Heart) she understandably regarded as her finest achievement as a writer.[3] She was also a talented poet and passionate political essayist.

This range of creative writing is far from apparent in the standard overview of social anthropology in South Africa, where the analysis of her contribution is confined to little more than a single page, which discusses just one of her four major monographs: *An African Aristocracy: Rank among the Swazi.*[4] Even this widely acknowledged classic is grossly caricatured as a static, functionalist 'tribal' monograph, with no proper reference made to its sequel, *The Uniform of Colour: A Study of Black-White Relationships in Swaziland.*[5] She is alleged to have made 'no lasting contribution to anthropological theory' since 'Societies conceived of as wholes are not suitable subjects of study. They are idealized (almost mystical) concepts.'[6]

Fortunately, there have been better informed assessments of her extensive body of anthropological work in biographical dictionaries and obituary articles, although none of these exceeds a few pages in length.[7] In fact, this chapter is the first (and long overdue) essay-length appraisal of her life and work, apart from her reminiscences presented to a seminar at UCLA in May 1981 that were taped, transcribed and published.[8] In general, I attribute much greater significance to her four-and-a-half decades in South Africa (1917–1961) and to the southern African focus of all of her anthropological work than she was inclined to do after twenty years of immersion in American scholarly circles. More specifically, I accord more weight to the importance of the Jewish background which

---

[3] Hilda Kuper, *A Witch in My Heart: A Play Set in Swaziland in the 1930s* (Oxford University Press published for the International African Institute, 1970). It was written in the 1950s in English, translated in isiZulu in 1962 and into siSwati in 1978.

[4] Hilda Kuper, *An African Aristocracy: Rank among the Swazi* (London, New York and Toronto: Oxford University Press in association with the International African Institute, 1947; 2nd edn. 1965; 3rd edn. 1981).

[5] Hilda Kuper, *The Uniform of Colour: A Study of Black-White Relationships in Swaziland* (Johannesburg: Wits University Press, 1947, 2nd edn., New York: Negro University Press, 1969).

[6] Hammond-Tooke, *Imperfect Interpreters*, 90–1.

[7] Katy Moran, 'Hilda Beemer Kuper (1911-)' in Ute Gacs et al., *Woman Anthropologists: A Biographical Dictionary* (New York: Greenwood Press, 1988), 194–201; M.G. Smith, 'In Search of Swaziland: An Obituary to Hilda Kuper', *The Guardian*, 4 May 1992; Margo Russell, 'Hilda Kuper, 1911–1992', *African Studies*, 88 (1993), 145–9; Hugh Macmillan, 'Hilda Beemer Kuper (1911–1992)', *Oxford Dictionary of National Biography* (Oxford: Oxford University Press, 2010); Robert Gordon, 'Hilda Kuper (1911–1992)' in R.J. McGee et al., eds., *Theory in Social and Cultural Anthropology* (Thousand Hills: Sage, 2013).

[8] Hilda Kuper, 'Function, History, Biography: Reflections on Fifty Years in the British Anthropological Tradition' in George W. Stocking, ed., *Functionalism Historicized: Essays on British Social Anthropology* (Madison, Wisconsin: University of Wisconsin Press, 1984), 192–213.

Historical ethnography and ethnographic fiction   191

she shared with her classmates, Max Gluckman and Ellen Hellmann, than she was inclined to give in late life retrospect. In keeping with the other chapters in this collection, I highlight the importance she accorded to the influence and methods of her mentor Mrs Hoernlé. Based on a close reading of her truly voluminous published writings, I pay fuller attention to her contribution to the study of history and social change in southern Africa that can be tracked across her four major monographs: *An African Aristocracy* (1947), *The Uniform of Colour* (1947), *Indian People of Natal* (1960) and *Sobhuza II* (1978).[9]

My central concern, however, is to highlight the significance of her body of creative writing in the genre usually described as 'ethnographic fiction'.[10] While her creative writing has productively been read as contributing to a rich but often disavowed subgenre within British and American anthropology, and to an emerging anti-segregationist 'protest literature' in South Africa, I seek to add a further layer by closely historicizing her creative writing. In particular, I explore the links between her experimental fiction and her more formal anthropological scholarship. To begin with, I locate her turn to fiction within the context of her historically sensitive anthropological method and richly descriptive ethnographic style as developed in her pioneering Swaziland ethnography of 1942, published five years later in two separate books but initially written as a 692-page doctoral thesis at London University.[11] During what I demarcate as her first phase of creative writing, dating to the early to mid-1940s, I indicate that her work was experimental with character and plot still relatively underdeveloped, but also strongly biographical with a female researcher as the central protagonist in most of the short stories that she set in Swaziland and South Africa. During her second phase of creative writing, after she and her husband Leo had returned to South Africa in 1952 with two young daughters, she developed the theme of social change, of the confrontations between tradition and modernity, in a much more sophisticated way. I read her mature ethnographic fiction of the mid- to late 1950s, most fully articulated in her two plays, *A Witch in My Heart* and *The Decision*, and her novel, *A Bite of Hunger*, in the context of her more intense investigation of inner life that is the hallmark of her truly remarkable but unheralded study of the history and practices of the

---

[9] Hilda Kuper, *Indian People in Natal* (Pietermaritzburg: Natal University Press, 1960; 2nd edn. New York: Greenwood Press, 1974); Hilda Kuper, *Sobhuza II Ngwenyama and King of Swaziland: The Story of an Hereditary Ruler and his Country* (London: Gerald Duckworth & Co. Ltd., 1978).

[10] Nancy J. Schmidt, 'Ethnographic Fiction: Anthropology's Hidden Literary Style', *Anthropology and Humanism Quarterly*, 9, 4 (1984), 11–14.

[11] Hilda Beemer, 'Rank among the Swazi of the Protectorate' (Ph.D. thesis, London School of Economics, August 1942), 692 pp.

192   Pioneers of the Field

Hindu religious communities in Durban. As she herself so eloquently put it: 'The drama, the novel, the poem, and the [ethnographic] monograph complement each other, each presenting a different facet of the whirling worlds within and around the self.'[12]

In short, Hilda Kuper was a creative writer who straddled the disciplines of anthropology, history and literature, one who experimented with narrative in different ways at different stages of what was a highly productive and dynamic South African anthropological career. It is only by paying attention to the importance she accorded to experimental writing and her great talents across different forms of this art that one can develop a full appreciation of the extent of her significance as a social anthropologist in southern Africa and indeed beyond.

Growing up in a Jewish family, 1911–1928

Ever alert to contingency, diversity and the mark of the individual in history, Hilda began her memoir with the reflection that 'despite all the common experiences that we' – that is, she and her internationally famous South African peers (Meyer Fortes, Isaac Schapera, Max Gluckman, Monica Wilson, Eileen Krige, Ellen Hellmann and Jack Simons) – 'recall when we talk to each other, each of us came to anthropology as the result of particular personal experiences'. In relation to her background, she reflected,

No doubt it was partly fortuitous events over which I had no personal control: the fact that I was born in the little town of Bulawayo, in the then British colony of Rhodesia (Zimbabwe), where the white settler population held very privileged positions. My parents, however, were first generation immigrants from continental Europe – my father from Eastern Europe and my mother from Vienna – and very early in life I was made aware of certain political conflicts.[13]

Her parents were Jewish. Hilda's father, Josef Beemer, was a Lithuanian-born Jewish trader who had set up shop on the outskirts of Bulawayo around the turn of the century. Her mother, Antoinette Renner, was an attractive Jewish woman from an upper-middle-class Viennese family who had come to this remote town to attend her sister's wedding. Here she met Josef, whom she married despite her parents' disapproval. Born on 23 August 1911, Hilda was a much indulged youngest child. During the First World War her father was sent to fight in East Africa, but died of influenza in 1917.[14] The best glimpse into her early childhood is her

[12] Hilda Kuper, 'Introduction' to *A Witch in My Heart*, xi.
[13] Hilda Kuper, 'Function, History and Biography', 192.
[14] Interview with Jenny Kuper, London, 13 May 2013.

Historical ethnography and ethnographic fiction 193

deeply moving short story entitled 'The Photograph'. It tells of the pain experienced by a sensitive young girl who sees her mother being torn by conflicting allegiances: on the one hand, to a husband fighting for the British; on the other, to a beloved brother fighting for the Germans. The photograph of the title is of the Austrian brother, Uncle Franz, and the central moment in the story occurs when her mother is forced to remove the picture from their lounge wall, as it has become an image of the enemy. From this moment onwards, her mother no longer spoke to her and her siblings in German, no longer regaled them with heroic stories from her Austrian past, nor sang romantic *lieder*. The account ends with the young girl returning from school to find her mother bereft, a letter in her hand announcing the death of Uncle Franz not long before the signing of the Armistice. She could not bring herself to accompany her children to the railway station where the crowd was celebrating the return of the victorious British soldiers, including her own long-absent husband.[15]

Hilda also vividly remembered a visit to her aunt's farm when she witnessed her uncle beating his black farm-workers. It was her first intense experience of the brutality of whites towards Africans. After the death of her husband, Antoinette took her family to Johannesburg. They stayed with Josef's brother, Uncle Yoshie, who ran a department store.[16] Hilda became aware of anti-Semitism for the first time and of being regarded as a 'stranger'. The family's social network was almost exclusively Jewish, although her upbringing was not orthodox. She and her sister Ellie, to whom she was very close, were sent to boarding school at Parktown Girls. They were independent, free-spirited and attractive young girls. Hilda was apparently pursued by a string of Jewish boys, including Max Gluckman, whom she befriended at the age of fifteen and dated for a time.[17] (Ellie would later be immortalized as 'The Blue Princess' of her one-time admirer Herman Charles Bosman's poems.) Hilda's teenage ambitions fluctuated between wanting to study to be an actress in England and following a career as a criminal lawyer in South Africa on account of (what she would retrospectively identify as) 'her increasing awareness of discrimination and the plight of innocent victims [in South Africa]: servants living in the backyard, the brutal treatment of blacks by whites, and her own Jewish heritage'.[18]

---

[15] See Hilda Kuper, 'The Photograph' in Kuper, *A Witch in My Heart, Short Stories and Poems* (Wisconsin: African Studies Program, University of Madison-Wisconsin, 1992), 99–100. This final scene is presumably a fictive twist given that her father died a year before the Allied victory.

[16] London School of Economics, Malinowski Papers [henceforth MP], Malinowski 7/3 Students 1932–1934, Winifred Hoernlé to Bronislaw Malinowski, Johannesburg, 7 September 1932.

[17] Interview with Jenny Kuper, London, 13 May 2013.

[18] Hilda Kuper cited by Moran, 'Hilda Beemer Kuper (1911-)', 194.

194   Pioneers of the Field

In the end she chose to do a BA degree at Wits University, beginning in February 1928, at the age of sixteen.

Reading anthropology with Hoernlé and Malinowski, 1929–1934

As is customary with South African undergraduate degrees, Hilda took a wide range of subjects. She began by intending to major in French and English literature, with history as an additional subject, but stumbled upon anthropology in her second year. 'I had a spare course, and while I was talking to a friend about possible subjects, she suggested an interesting course she had taken, taught by a very interesting woman.'[19] She later took other subjects in the Bantu (African) Studies undergraduate programme, including Native Law and Administration and isiZulu. But it was anthropology for which she developed a passion, owing to the gifts of her lecturer. Hilda's unusually vivid recall of the central themes of the undergraduate lectures that she attended with Ellen and Max were cited in an earlier chapter, as well as the way in which their teacher set them to work on language texts associated with their different backgrounds or skills. Hilda was put to work on 'the great French school of sociology' with particular attention to the writings of Durkheim.

> It opened up a new world. She [Mrs Hoernlé] had insisted that anthropology was a factual discipline based on observable behaviour, and we had read such ethnographies as Boas' Eskimo, Lowie's Crow and Junod's *Life of a South African Tribe*. I had also read Spencer and Gillen, and when I read Durkheim's interpretation of Arunta rituals in the *Elementary Forms of the Religious Life*, a thousand ideas, connections, meanings and new insights flooded my mind. I had a particularly heavy dose of Durkheim because in our allotted reading, Mrs Hoernlé gave me specific responsibility for Durkheim.[20]

She got Hilda to translate the entire text of Durkheim's *The Rules of Sociological Method* from French to English,[21] which suggests an unusually advanced degree of fluency and conceptual ability for a nineteen-year-old. She remarked that this early 'saturation' in Durkheim 'made an indelible impression on me ... His conceptualisation of society, social facts, equilibrium, types of solidarity dominated my thinking for many years.'[22] The emphasis on the ritual affirmation of social cohesion in her famous first monograph was one mark of his influence.

Isaac Schapera's lectures, by stark contrast, were dry and 'droning'. 'Schapera was not an inspiring lecturer ... [Y]ou had to tell yourself,

[19] Kuper, 'Function, History and Biography', 194.   [20] *Ibid.*, 196–7.   [21] *Ibid.*, 196.
[22] *Ibid.*, 196.

Historical ethnography and ethnographic fiction

"Don't go to sleep ... "' Like Ellen and Max, however, she did find her first experience of fieldwork on their vacation trip to Mochudi in September of her final year instructive. She related an amusing anecdote about their shared Jewish backgrounds.

Gluckman and Schapera stayed with the trader, and all the women [Ellen, Hilda and a visiting Cambridge-trained anthropologist Camilla Wedgwood] at a Dutch Reformed mission station, which created problems because the fieldwork trip coincided with the Jewish Day of Atonement. My mother did not want me to go, but the Chief Rabbi [Dr Landau] – a great friend of ours – said that it would be all right if I fasted. So I fasted while my Jewish colleagues ate; they thought it funny, but the missionary concluded that I was the only one worth 'saving'.[23]

There was more to Mrs Hoernlé's influence than lessons about reading distant European schools of anthropology in their own languages, their own terms and with an open mind. As we have seen, she encouraged in her students a tolerant attitude towards inter-racial relations grounded in a universal moral politics which emphasized common human values and virtues, against the background of a South African political culture obsessed by racial and cultural difference. She persuaded Hilda to become actively involved in the Indian Joint Council during her Honours year in 1931. Mrs Hoernlé was chair and Hilda served as the secretary. She organized a research project for her, funded by the South African Institute of Race Relations. Hilda was confronted, for the first time, by the dark underbelly of her society.

My research involved finding out what happened to the children of [beer-brewing African] mothers rushed off to prison. There were hours spent in jail with these women, getting information so that I could go back to their homes, find out how their children were, and come back and report – partly as researcher, partly as someone who could help them. The prison was so soul-destroying and dehumanizing, but what astonished me was the courage of the women, their resilience, [and] their willingness to start brewing again as soon as they returned home.[24]

She did the research partly out of financial necessity. For the second time in her life, she and her family had lost their male patron in sudden and tragic circumstances when Uncle Yoshie fell down a lift shaft.[25]

---

[23] *Ibid.*, 196–7. Following this fieldtrip Wedgwood and Schapera co-authored a short article on string figures, otherwise known as 'Cat's Cradle's', a topic popularized by her former and Winifred Hoernlé's former Cambridge supervisor A.C. Haddon and his daughter, Kathleen Haddon who published a book on the subject in 1911 entitled *Cat's Cradles from Many Lands*. On Wedgwood as a pioneer women scholar in the Pacific, see Nancy Lutkehaus, '"She was very Cambridge"'; on their article including figures and photographs, see Wedgwood and Schapera, 'String Figures in the Bechuanaland Protectorate', *Bantu Studies*, 4, 3 (1930), 251–68.

[24] *Ibid.*, 197.   [25] Interview with Jenny Kuper, London, 13 May 2013.

196   Pioneers of the Field

Mrs Hoernlé explained the implications of 'the catastrophe' in 'a card of introduction' to Malinowski, penned in September 1932, the month before she sent Hilda to further her graduate studies under the great master in London. She introduced Miss Beemer, in the first instance, as 'a Jewess' from a non-orthodox background. Hilda was a 'very bright girl' who 'has shown very fine grit and determination. Her father died many years ago but she had been brought up ... by a bachelor uncle who suddenly died when his affairs were very involved so that she and her mother were left very badly off indeed.' Mrs Hoernlé also noted that Hilda was already set on Swaziland as her future field-site. She intended to do a doctoral thesis on 'The nature and function of Magic among the Swazi'. She had settled on social anthropology as her chosen career. 'She is young, of course, and at present thinks her whole life is to be devoted to Anthropology ...'[26] Her SAIRR research director and former lecturer in Native Law and Administration, R.D. Rheinallt-Jones, was said to have warned her that: 'You [will] face two disadvantages: first, that you are a woman, and second, that you are Jewish.'[27]

Neither was a deterrent in the view of Malinowski, whose London seminars were notable for the diverse origins of his students. He would write tongue-in-cheek in one of his first letters to Hilda in the field: 'It is with some distress that a pure Nordic like myself finds that among the best pupils I have to register one Bantu [ZK Matthews], one pure-bred West African, three Jews [Gluckman, Fortes and herself] and a half-caste Chinaman.'[28] He was also known for his active encouragement of women scholars. Hilda's classmates included Margaret Read, Lucy Mair and Susan Fortes. They were joined in her second year by Monica Hunter, fresh from Pondoland. Where there had been four students in her class at Wits, there were now twenty-three graduates attending the weekly seminars.[29] Their seminars were dedicated to a page-by-page proof-reading of his third and final Trobriand monograph, *Coral Gardens and Their Magic* (1935).[30] It is easy to imagine that a literary-minded scholar-in-the-making like Hilda would have been profoundly influenced by this intimate exposure to Malinowski's richly descriptive narrative style.

Given her long-standing interest in theatre, she greatly admired the weekly one-man performances of the self-appointed 'Conrad of anthropology'. He

---

[26] MP, Malinowski 7/3 Students 1932–1934, Mrs Hoernlé to Professor Malinowski, Johannesburg, 7 September 1932.
[27] Kuper cited by Katy Moran, 'Hilda Beemer Kuper (1911-)', 199.
[28] MP, Malinowski 7/3 Students 1932–1934, Malinowski to Beemer, 15 December 1934.
[29] MP, Malinowski 7/3 Students 1932–1934.
[30] Meyer Fortes, 'An Anthropologist's Apprenticeship', *Annual Review of Anthropology*, 7, 1 (1978), 5.

Historical ethnography and ethnographic fiction

taught by what he, with typical lack of modesty, liked to describe as his 'Socratic method'. In her memoir Hilda told of the intellectual roasting to which he subjected 'the Mandarins', those interlopers who had come to anthropology from other disciplines (like her friend Meyer Fortes who had been trained in psychology). She would write more frankly in private to Audrey.

> It was excruciatingly embarrassing to watch him use his razor wit! ... [H]is mind was as quick as lightning. One couldn't relax in his seminars; he himself was almost frighteningly tense and watching his audience like a lynx ... He gave an impression of arrogance and sensitivity, of cruelty and kindness; he was a complex mix of snob, connoisseur and humanist.[31]

Hilda and Malinowski were well suited temperamentally. She was described at the time as 'rather romantic' and 'idealistic',[32] characteristics that Malinowski shared. She was also not afraid to speak her mind, something that he liked in his students.

The main lesson that she learnt from Malinowski was 'an awareness of the care and skill that were involved in doing fieldwork'.[33] He encouraged a very particular regimen of field-writing, which she would follow to the letter during her two years of doctoral field research in Swaziland. I am tempted to interpret her later experiments with genre, at least in part, as an outgrowth of her induction into diverse modes and styles of field-writing. For everyday purposes there were field-notes, recorded on site, ideally without any help from a research assistant. These should include extensive records of texts and terms in vernacular languages. In the evenings the field scientist – and all of his students emphasized Malinowski's rigorously scientific conception of their craft – could record their private feelings and thoughts in a diary. As Malinowski's own journal would so scandalously reveal, the diary could serve as a psychological release for the culturally alienated (and sexually frustrated) anthropologist. He succeeded in persuading almost all his students to keep diaries, although sadly Hilda burnt hers.[34] Then there was the field report, an altogether more energetic endeavour. Malinowski expected his field-researchers, of whom he supervised more than a dozen in the years after 1932, to send him detailed descriptions of their progress and findings on a monthly

---

[31] MP, 37/32 M3182, Hilda Kuper to Audrey Richards, 4 April [n.d., c. 1970]
[32] MP, Malinowski 7/3 Students 1932–1934, Hilda Beemer: Copies of testimonials: Isaac Schapera to Joseph Oldham, 11 May 1933; R.S. Jacobs in extract of a telegram from Professor Seligman, 15 June 1933.
[33] Kuper, 'Function, History and Biography', 199.
[34] UCLA, Special Collections, C1343 Hilda Kuper Papers [henceforth HKP], Box 40, Folder 22 Correspondence with Raymond Firth, Hilda Kuper to Raymond Firth, 25 October 1974.

198   Pioneers of the Field

basis. Hilda's and Godfrey Wilson's dense and extended field reports say as much about the unusually high levels of expectation of their supervisor as they do about the gifts of these two as writers and fieldworkers. In both cases he wrote to request their permission to read their reports to his seminar students. He also gave them constant advice. In Hilda's case, for example, he warned her to keep her own observations clearly distinct from those of her informants. Finally, there were the famous 'charts' that he expected fieldworkers to record in a separate, more visually-oriented, notebook, which would also feature village maps and genealogical diagrams. His functionalist chart was an abstract grid of information arranged by 'institution' (law, kinship, economics, land tenure and religion), in which specific data was plotted onto the general template in order to assist researchers in conceptualizing each aspect of culture as part of an interrelated system. Like Audrey, Hilda recalled being able to visualize Malinowski's chart before she entered her field-sites.[35]

The lessons in London went beyond the seminar and its magic circle. Hilda was psychoanalysed during her first six months. She attended lectures on psychoanalysis and Marxism. She also attended Zulu language classes and lectures on economic anthropology by Raymond Firth. Her interest in left-wing politics gave rise to concern on Malinowski's part. He sternly warned her against associating with the ideas of Harold Laski[36] and ordered her to 'Keep off that Jewish nihilistic communism which is the undoing of the best minds of your race.'[37] A lesson of a more personal kind came in the mid-year break between her two academic years in London. Hilda returned to South Africa in June 1933 and got engaged to Isaac Schapera.[38] We know very little about their romance. The International African Institute's records reveal their concern about the impact that the proposed marriage might have on the fieldwork of a young woman scholar whom Malinowski and Firth had come to consider as 'among the two or three ablest students who have been studying at the LSE'.[39]

---

[35] The information in this paragraph is based mainly on my reading of Hilda's and Godfrey's correspondence with Malinowski from the field. For Hilda's correspondence, see MP, Malinowski 7/3 Students 1932–1934, Hilda Beemer; for Godfrey's correspondence, see WC, B4.4 [GW] To and from Bronislaw Malinowski, MSS and TSS, 22 November 1934 to 11 November 1938. See also Hilda Kuper, *Sobhuza II*, 'Chapter 1: An Essential Introduction' where she describes her first two weeks of fieldwork with Malinowski in Swaziland.

[36] MP, Malinowski 7/3 Students 1932–1934: Malinowski to Beemer, London, 26 April 1934.

[37] MP, Malinowski 7/3 Students 1932–1934: Malinowski to Beemer, London, 22 November 1934.

[38] Their engagement was brief. See Kuper, 'Isaac Schapera: His Life and Times', 36.

[39] Wits University, William Cullen Library, Rheinallt Jones Papers, AD843/RJ/K6.18.1, File for the Inter-University Committee for African Studies, Oldham to Rheinallt-Jones, 5 July 1933 on the IAI Council Meeting in Belgium.

Historical ethnography and ethnographic fiction 199

Whatever the circumstances, the break-up is said to have shaken Hilda deeply and left her emotionally fragile for some time. However, soon after these events she began to date Leo Kuper, a criminal lawyer who was three years her senior and who came from an orthodox Jewish family.[40] She had met him during her graduate years at Wits. They got engaged less than a year after she had returned to Johannesburg from London in May 1934. They would marry in January 1935 and form a deep intellectual and emotional partnership across almost six decades.[41] The IAI 'had a policy that married women refund any money they had received, on the assumption that they would end their fieldwork and careers'. Hilda assured them that she did not mean to shelve her career in anthropology merely on account of marriage.[42]

A historical anthropology of the conquering aristocracies of Swaziland, 1934–1942

In later life, Hilda reflected: 'To some it [fieldwork] is a confrontation and an ordeal; to others a series of encounters; and to others a transforming and humanizing experience.' Hilda's fieldwork in Swaziland clearly fell in the last category. It began on 28 July 1934, when she and Malinowski set off by bus from Johannesburg to Mbabane after her mentor's recent performance at the New Education Fellowship Conference at Wits.[43] It was at this conference that Hilda first encountered the Swazi Paramount Chief Sobhuza II (1899–1981). She vividly recalled seeing him in the audience of the lecture-hall. 'I observed [leaning slightly forward as if to catch each word] a man in the mid-thirties, of medium weight and build, with a strong face, deep brown in complexion, a wide forehead, broad flared nose, high cheek bones, bright deep-set penetrating eyes, a short, natural untrimmed beard and smiling mouth. But it was not the build or general features that set him apart as much as a general impression of animated intensity and personal dignity.'[44]

---

[40] Interview with Jenny Kuper, London, 13 May 2013.

[41] Skype interview with Mary Kuper, Cape Town-London, 13 August 2011; Interview with Jenny Kuper, London, 13 May 2013. In his contribution to Leo's festschrift, their close friend Pierre van den Berghe would describe it as an 'exceptionally harmonious intellectual companionship'. Pierre van den Berghe, 'Biographical Sketch and Bibliography of Leo Kuper' in Van den Berghe, ed., *The Liberal Dilemma in South Africa: Essays in Honour of Leo Kuper* (New York: St Martin's Press, 1979), 153.

[42] Hilda Kuper cited in Katy Moran, 'Hilda Beemer Kuper (1911-)', 198.

[43] For a full account of his African tour, see Michael W. Young, *Malinowski, Vol. 2* (New Haven and London: Yale University Press, forthcoming).

[44] Hilda Kuper, *Sobhuza II*, 1.

Figure 5.1: 'Princess Topi and Hilda Beemer outside her house at Lobamba.' This photograph was probably taken by Malinowski during his fortnight in the field with Hilda in late July and early August 1934.[45]

Much has been written about the relationship between Sobhuza II and 'his' anthropologists. This literature does show, in a refreshing reversal of the usual charges against anthropologists as agents of colonialism, that Sobhuza II 'used' social anthropologists to promote his, rather than their, agendas. Hugh Macmillan has demonstrated that Hilda and Malinowski entered Swaziland at a time when the Paramount Chief was actively promoting the reinvention of Swazi tradition. This involved energetic attempts to resurrect declining traditional cultural institutions and rituals, most notably the rituals of kingship of which the annual *incwala* ceremony was the most important national event.[46] In the year that she entered the field, he skilfully enlisted the support of all the most influential

---

[45] HKP, Box 62, Folder 4, Photo album of Swaziland. Quoted caption taken from the album.

[46] Hugh Macmillan, 'Swaziland: Decolonisation and the Triumph of "Tradition"', *Journal of Modern African Studies*, 23, 4 (1985), 643–66; High Macmillan, 'A Nation Divided? The Swazi in Swaziland and the Transvaal, 1865–1986' in Leroy Vail, ed., *The Creation of Tribalism in Southern Africa* (Los Angeles and London: University of California Press and James Currey, 1989), 289–323.

Historical ethnography and ethnographic fiction 201

Figure 5.2: 'Photo of Hilda Kuper in the field.' This photograph was probably taken by Leo Kuper when he visited her field-site on the eve of her departure for her three-month tour of Swaziland, beginning in September 1934. From left to right: Sobhuza II, Hilda Beemer and her guide-cum-research assistant, standing alongside her car with its TJ (Transvaal, Johannesburg) registration number.[47]

anthropologists of the day – Schapera, Hoernlé and Malinowski, as well as Hilda herself – to support his plan to have the system of education of the traditional Swazi male military regiment (the *libutvo* system) introduced as part of the curriculum in Swazi schools.[48]

Hilda's fieldwork would simply not have been possible without Sobhuza's support, as she generously acknowledged throughout her career. The need for royal endorsement would be brought home when her friend Max Gluckman was summarily expelled from his field-site in Zululand in 1938 after he had offended the Zulu regent and was never allowed to return.[49] Sobhuza, by contrast, called a general meeting

[47] HKP, Box 60, Folder 2, Loose black and white photographs – Swaziland, Quoted caption taken from the album.
[48] Hugh Macmillan, 'Administrators, Anthropologists and "Traditionalists" in Colonial Swaziland: The Case of the "Amabhaca" Fines', *Africa*, 65, 4 (1995), 545–61. See also Paul Cocks, 'The King and I: Bronislaw Malinowski, King Sobhuza II of Swaziland and the Vision of Culture Change in Africa', *History of the Human Sciences*, 13, 4 (2000), 25–47.
[49] See Robert Gordon, 'Max Gluckman in Zululand' (unpublished paper presented at Anthropology Southern Africa, September 2013).

202   Pioneers of the Field

to reassure people of the motives of the 23-year-old '*umlungu*' (white person); allowed Hilda to stay in the queen's royal enclosure at Lobamba; ordered one of his two senior wives to 'adopt' her; and selected a man from his royal regiment to protect, guide and translate for her in the early months, including on a three-month motoring tour of Swaziland in late 1934, for which he planned the route and provided the necessary royal references.[50] He also generously shared information on all aspects of Swazi culture, from 'secret' and 'sacred' rituals to an in-depth knowledge of Swazi pre-colonial and colonial history, something which would influence her to develop what she termed a 'historical functionalist approach'.[51] Finally, he acted as a reader and censor of her early published articles. His unusual scholarly interest would, in fact, result in a drama around the politics of representation of Swazi culture in which Hilda played a leading role.

The drama began when the Afrikaans short story writer Pieter Johannes Schoeman, who had done some months of intermittent fieldwork in Swaziland and been awarded a doctorate in *volkekunde* from the University of Stellenbosch, published a short article in the June 1935 edition of *Bantu Studies* entitled 'The Swazi Rain Ceremony'.[52] Schoeman had spent a term attending Malinowski's seminars in London and had been advised by Malinowski to publish chapters from his thesis before Hilda's research bore fruit. Malinowski had encouraged Hilda to leave the male side of Swazi culture to Schoeman. 'Remember that you work mainly from the "women's point of view".'[53] Given Malinowski's intervention, the journal editors (Doke and Rheinallt-Jones) put aside Mrs Hoernlé's concerns that 'the English was bad and the article poorly constructed'. She then sent her critical summary version 'down to Miss Beemer [in Swaziland] for her information'.[54] On reading the notes, Hilda immediately recognized that there were glaring inaccuracies, quite apart from the static and shallow representations of Swazi ritual. She showed the summary to Sobhuza, who was outraged. 'How are we to know whom we can trust? Is there no check which can be held over so-called anthropologists?'[55] Hilda agreed to his request that she publish an immediate rebuttal in *Bantu Studies*. Mrs Hoernlé insisted that this critique

---

[50] Hilda Kuper, *Sobhuza II*, 1–16.

[51] Hilda Kuper, 'Social Anthropology as a Study of Culture Contacts', *South African Journal of Science*, 41, 1 (1945), 88–101.

[52] Pieter Johannes Schoeman, 'The Swazi Rain Ceremony', *Bantu Studies*, 9, 2 (1935), 169–76.

[53] LSE, Malinowski Papers, Malinowski 7/3 Students 1932–1934, Malinowski to Schoeman, Tirol, 30 August 1935; Malinowski to Beemer, London, 22 November 1934.

[54] Thor and Dulcie Krige Collection, Mrs Hoernlé to Jack Krige, 11 July 1935, Johannesburg.

[55] LSE, Malinowski Papers, Malinowski 7/3 Students 1932–1934, Beemer to Malinowski, 8 July 1935, Lobamba.

Historical ethnography and ethnographic fiction 203

be published in the September issue, a volume dedicated in her honour. In what was her first published article, Hilda questioned the authority of Schoeman's oral sources, indicating that his interviews were with marginal figures in the ritual; upbraided him for failing to corroborate the accuracy of his account with the Paramount Chief or Queen Mother; pointed out many inaccuracies, most notably his failure to recognize the central importance of the Queen Mother in the ritual; and insisted on the need to locate the ritual in an economic and political context instead of exotic beliefs in 'magical powers'. She also took the unprecedented step of featuring a signed preface by Sobhuza 'corroborating the corrections'.[56] Incidentally, Hilda's field-notes reveal that her own extended two-part essay on the history of the male regimental (*libutvo*) system in Swaziland was proofread, or perhaps one should say censored, by Sobhuza before Hilda got the go-ahead to have it published in *Africa* in 1937. In fact, she explicitly proposed, as a matter of method, that anthropologists obtain an endorsement by indigenous leaders of their accounts before going to print.

While the Schoeman case is revealing of what it says about the degree of intellectual dependence of anthropologists, including Hilda, on Sobhuza, it is also a fascinating moment in the fragile politics of South African social anthropology. It reveals the already growing divide between left-liberal English-speaking social anthropologists like Hilda and Afrikaner *volkekundiges* like Schoeman.[57] While Mrs Hoernlé was supportive and Malinowski diplomatic, advising Hilda to be generous to a man who had preceded her in the field,[58] most South African anthropologists were angered by her intervention: none more so than Schoeman's doctoral supervisor, Werner Eiselen. As the head of the *volkekunde* department at Stellenbosch University, a member of the board of *Bantu Studies* and a leading voice in the South African Inter-University African Studies Committee, Eiselen was among the most powerful anthropologists in interwar South Africa.[59] He later became a leading ideologue of apartheid.[60] In an interview late in

---

[56] Hilda Kuper, 'The Swazi Rain Ceremony, critical comment by P.J. Schoeman', *Bantu Studies: Special Issue: Homage to Winifred Hoernlé*, 9, 3 (September 1935), 273–80.

[57] Robert Gordon has uncovered political essays by Schoeman, published just a few years later, in which he openly champions the role of the anthropologist as the handmaiden of separate development. See Robert Gordon, '"Tracks which cannot be covered": P.J. Schoeman and Public Intellectuals in Southern Africa', *Historia*, 2007, 98–125.

[58] MP, Malinowski 7/3 Students 1932–1934, Malinowski to Beemer, London, 22 November 1934.

[59] On Eiselen's role in founding *volkekunde* as a distinct Afrikaner ethnological tradition in South Africa, with German missionary and linguistic roots and an overtly segregationist politics, see Andrew Bank, 'Fathering *Volkekunde*: Race and Culture in the Ethnological Writings of Werner Eiselen, Stellenbosch University, 1926–1936', 163–79.

[60] On his anthropology and its relationship to his apartheid ideology, see Cynthia Kros, *The Seeds of Separate Development: Origins of Bantu Education* (Pretoria: UNISA Press, 2010).

204   Pioneers of the Field

her life, Hilda confirmed that her attack on Schoeman 'cost me many friends and deeply antagonized Schapera'.[61]

Two other incidents of conflict during Hilda's time of fieldwork confirm the depth of her loyalty to her Swazi patron and, in one case, her willingness to intervene outspokenly in public on his behalf. Hilda reported to Malinowski on her intervention at a meeting between the Swazi National Council and the Resident Commissioner, A.G. Marwick, in December 1934 in defence of the tradition of Swazi regimental youths beating to death a bull during their famous annual *incwala* ceremony.

> I listened in a dazed condition until one after another of the old *indunas* [headmen] got up and explained how the killing of the bull was an integral part, was 'chained to' the many other acts of the great national ceremony. Marwick then got up and said of course he realised etc. but other Europeans didn't etc. etc. . . . Well, all my Jewish reverence for old tradition and respect for the laws of another race forced me, despite that cautiousness which is also an integral part of my heritage, to contradict. So I pointed out that this custom was [well] known to the Europeans . . . [and] that the 'sports' of 'civilised' people, foxhunting and bullfighting were still allowed.[62]

The Council resolved that the killing of the bull would continue, although Sobhuza did later forbid excessive 'pummelling'.[63]

The second incident dates to March 1935. Missionaries had laid an official complaint with the Resident Commissioner about Hilda's involvement in the promotion of Swazi tradition after her participation in the women's *umcwasho* ceremonies. They requested that the practice be outlawed and that Hilda be deported from Swaziland, one assumes because they felt that the ritual and her presence undermined their efforts to promote Christianity. The Resident Commissioner, a long-time friend of Sobhuza's and an enthusiast of anthropological writing about 'tradition', denied their request.

The main challenge, however, was not winning over white missionaries, but securing the trust of Swazi informants. She recalled in later memoirs that the patronage of Sobhuza made her as many enemies as friends. To jealousy about her relationship with the Paramount Chief was added the deep suspicions of a conservative peasant society towards someone they regarded as another in a long line of 'strangers'. The recent history of black–white relations in Swaziland added further layers of suspicion. Her insightful discussion of Swazi stereotypes of Europeans in *The Uniform of*

---

[61] Interview notes, Robert Gordon interview with Hilda Kuper, Los Angeles, 16 April 1987.
[62] MP, Malinowski 7/3, Students 1932–1934, Hilda Kuper to Malinowski, 20 December 1934, Lobamba.
[63] Kuper, *An African Aristocracy*, 213.

Colour (1947) drew in part on personal experience. She related how children in remote areas of the country cried at the sight of her, having long been told that whites kidnapped Swazi children. In more general terms, she indicated that the Swazi combined a respect for the magical technology of whites with a lack of respect for their morality: white cruelty being typically contrasted with the generosity and kindness of fellow Swazi.[64] It was only through the work of language learning and patient communication with her informants that she was able to extend her social network beyond the world of royal wives and princesses. She long recalled the 'incredible night that I [first] dreamt in siSwati'.[65]

The joys of fieldwork were followed by a frustratingly extended period of writing up. Her doctoral thesis was only finally submitted in August 1942 three months after Malinowski's death. The delay was partly because of the massively ambitious scale of her project, which produced in effect two books rather than one. She was also delayed by recurring bouts of malaria, which she had contracted in the field and, above all, by the devastating news that Brian Marwick, a relative of the Resident Commissioner who had conducted intermittent fieldwork during his seven years as a colonial official in Swaziland, was to get in ahead of her and publish a general ethnography of Swaziland through Cambridge University Press. Audrey wrote to Godfrey of the dispiriting impact this had on her new friend. 'Marwick's Swazi book is bad and I am sorry he cut across Hilda like that. She had three-quarters written of a general monograph and then changed to a special study of rank when she heard his book was coming out.'[66] The publication of the thesis took a further five years, being severely affected by paper shortages during the Second World War. She was pushed into agreeing, to her life-long regret, that her study be published in two volumes by two different presses.

Her contribution to political anthropology would surely have been more fully acknowledged had her study come out around 1940, the year of publication of *African Political Systems*, edited by Meyer Fortes and E.P. Evans-Pritchard, which is usually regarded as the book that introduced political anthropology as a new subfield within the discipline. All the same, *An African Aristocracy* met with rave reviews in a dozen journals. Even Evans-Pritchard, who felt that her study was thin on theory, praised the book as 'clear, concise, and relevant to its theme' with 'descriptions that could scarcely be bettered'.[67] Audrey drew attention to the

---

[64] Kuper, *The Uniform of Colour*, 32–6.
[65] Kuper, 'Functionalism, History and Biography', 202.
[66] ARP, Audrey Richards to Godfrey Wilson, 7 July 1940, Johannesburg.
[67] Edward E. Evans-Pritchard, 'Review of *An African Aristocracy*', *The Geographical Journal*, 109, 4 (1947), 248.

206   Pioneers of the Field

underlying empathy that informed the book. 'Dr Kuper writes with affection for the people amongst whom she lived and worked for so long and with continual flashes of imaginative insight', rightly predicting that 'her description of the famous *incwala* is likely to become a classic for its richness of detail and interpretation'.[68] Max proclaimed it as 'the most interesting and vivid, and in many ways the most illuminating, account yet published of any southern Bantu tribe',[69] a view endorsed by Monica in later references for Hilda.[70]

Indeed, her dense description of the *incwala* ritual would serve as the inspiration and empirical basis for his famous re-analysis of the ritual in terms of class conflict in his 1952 Frazer Lecture, later published as *Rituals of Rebellion in South-East Africa* (1954) and dedicated to Mrs Hoernlé.[71] The seeds of his reinterpretation were clearly spelt out in his review. While other scholars might have felt aggrieved to see their rich descriptive narrative being appropriated in the service of their peer's theories, Hilda was pleased with the use to which Max was able to put her account.[72]

None of the reviewers fully appreciated the historical importance of her book. We should recall that when Hilda's first two monographs were published, African history had not been established as a scholarly discipline, and the methodologies of oral history and pre-colonial history had not been developed in any self-reflective way. This makes the opening section of her study all the more remarkable. To a much greater extent than any of her peers, including even the historically oriented Monica, Hilda's ethnography was grounded in a deep understanding of the pre-colonial history of the Swazi, based on more than a hundred oral interviews.[73] It would only be in the 1980s through the research and

---

[68] Audrey Richards, 'Review of *An African Aristocracy*', *Man*, 48 (December 1948), 142–3.
[69] Max Gluckman, 'Review of *An African Aristocracy*', *Africa*, 18, 1 (1948), 63–4.
[70] Wilson Collection, Uncatalogued Correspondence: Folder K, File Kuper. Monica Wilson, Academic reference for Hilda Kuper, 26 September 1960.
[71] Max Gluckman, *Rituals of Rebellion in South-East Africa* (Frazer Lecture 1952, Manchester: Manchester University Press, 1954). For a close analysis of reinterpretations of the *incwala* ritual by Gluckman, Thomas Beidelman and other scholars, giving a clear sense of the long-term significance of Hilda's account, see Andrew Apter, 'In Dispraise of the King: Rituals "Against" Rebellion in South-East Africa', *Man*, 18 (1983), 521–34.
[72] Kuper, 'Acknowledgements and Preface', *An African Aristocracy* (London, New York and Toronto: Oxford University Press with the International African Institute, 1961 edition), vii.
[73] This estimate is based on my reading of my microfilm copy of Hilda Kuper, 'Fieldnotes of Anthropological Research in Swaziland and South Africa, 1931–1985, Reel 1: Notebooks 2–9 (1934–5), Reel 2: Notebooks 13–19 (1935–6), Reel 3: Notebooks 20–8 (1936–1941), Selected for filming by the author by UCLA Special Collections, 1991.'

Historical ethnography and ethnographic fiction 207

writing of Philip Bonner that Hilda's historical groundwork was properly recognized.[74]

Hilda resumed her historical narrative in *The Uniform of Colour*. While this sequel rightly met with a more mixed response from reviewers, again her study must be judged in relation to the existing literature. *The Uniform of Colour* was the first systematic and coherent history of Swaziland in the colonial era and certainly the first to be told from a Swazi perspective. While her pre-colonial history had been constructed on the basis of Swazi oral tradition, her colonial history was crafted from the empirical details gleaned from documentary sources, including the Blue Books on Swaziland, Union Year Books and local tax registers, along with her interviews with Sobhuza, who had quite recently been involved in efforts to challenge the conquest in the British courts. Though conventional in its empiricism and chronological arrangement, it was highly unusual in tone. This was a strident critique of the 'oppressive' and 'underhand' paper conquest of Swaziland by the British during the 1880s and 1890s, an exposure of the deeply coercive nature of British colonial rule in the early 1900s driven by the imperatives of land acquisition, enforced taxation and migrant labour recruitment for the mining industry, as well as a lucid dissection of the complex of racist stereotypes and myths that underpinned these processes.[75]

Short stories, poems and political essays written in Johannesburg, 1942–1947

The years immediately following the submission of her thesis were enormously productive for Hilda, arguably her most prolific period as a writer. In addressing this first phase of her creative writing, I highlight the wide range of genres and themes with which she experimented during the 1940s, from private poetic expressions of longing for Leo, who was away at war, through partly autobiographical, partly fictional short stories to cultural and political essays penned for wide public consumption, as well as her scholarly writings.

Her best-known publications of these years were the twin monographs discussed above. They presented a 'historical functionalist approach' as she termed it in an address delivered during her year-long presidency of the Anthropological Section of the South African Association for the Advancement of Science (1944). In later years she was increasingly

---

[74] Philip Bonner, *Kings, Commoners and Concessionaries: The Evolution and Dissolution of the Nineteenth-Century Swazi State* (Cambridge: Cambridge University Press, 1983), esp. 1–3.
[75] Kuper, *The Uniform of Colour*.

208   Pioneers of the Field

assertive about the distinctiveness of her historical orientation and its departure from the ahistorical functionalist model of the founding fathers of the British school of social anthropology, Malinowski and Radcliffe-Brown.[76] Following her address she published a richly detailed stage-by-stage account of the ritual events involved in the marriage of a Swazi princess, Princess Bahushule, based on close participant observation (1945), using the same narrative technique she had developed in her documentation of the *incwala* ceremony. This was the first of three thickly descriptive accounts of traditional weddings.[77] She also published an essay on 'The Swazi reaction to missions' (1946), which featured as a chapter in *The Uniform of Colour*. Last but not least, she contributed to the field of African urban anthropology with an article on 'voluntary associations' at her new field-site, the townships in Johannesburg, paying particular attention to African women's organizations known as *stokvels*, which offered financial security to desperately impoverished African families. It was co-authored with Selma Kaplan,[78] one of Hilda's talented women graduates at Wits (where she lectured from 1941 to 1946), of whom Ruth First would be the most famous.

Her impetus towards writing for a wider market is evident in her essays written as accompaniments to published collections of ethnographic photographs. The first was her considered introduction to A.M. Duggan-Cronin's photographs of the Swazi as featured in his series on *The Bantu Tribes of South Africa*.[79] She also provided paragraph-length captions to each of the thirty-two photographs in the volume. The second was a popular essay, featuring alongside a selection of her fieldwork photographs of the *incwala* ceremony, published in 1947 in *Libertas*, a government-sponsored magazine known for its extensive use of visual materials.[80] Hilda's primary motivation here was to generate wider interest in Swazi culture among white South African readers. For the visual historian of today, however, the contrast between the two sets of photographs is

---

[76] Compare Kuper, 'Social Anthropology as a Study of Culture Contacts', *South African Journal of Science*, 41 (1945), 88–101 with Kuper, 'Functionalism, History and Biography', 203–5.

[77] The 'sequels' published in *Bantu Studies* in 1955 and 1956 documented and analysed, in the same case study format, a Tamil-Hindu marriage in Durban and a Hindustani marriage in Durban through successive ritual events, again with an emphasis on a single climactic moment.

[78] Kuper and Kaplan, 'Voluntary Associations in an Urban Township', 178–86.

[79] Hilda Beemer, 'The Swazi' in Alfred M. Duggan-Cronin, *The Bantu Tribes of South Africa: Reproductions of Photographic Studies, Vol III, Section IV: The Swazi* (Cambridge and Kimberley: Deighton, Bull & Co. and the Alexander McGregor Memorial Museum, 1941), 9–32.

[80] Hilda Kuper, 'Swazi Feast of the First Fruits', *Libertas*, 71 (1947), 38–41.

striking. Duggan-Cronin created a series of highly aestheticized, romantic portraits of individuals in traditional costume, with particular attention to royals like the Queen Mother. Hilda's account, which featured more fully in the sixty-one photographs published in her two monographs, presented Swazi society in collective terms, most dramatically of course in the ritual scenes of the *incwala* and the *umcwasho*, but also in many scenes of everyday activities, from women working in the fields to women mending reed mats within the royal enclosure.[81] Representations of social change were equally prominent in her published visual record: they included photographs of the migrant labourers' buses, mine compounds in Swaziland, Christian weddings and political meetings of the Swazi National Association in Sophiatown.[82]

Hilda also penned dozens of poems in these years in three genres: love poems to Leo, war poems decrying the brutality of the Second World War and occasional 'ethnographic poems' written for publication with titles

Figure 5.3: 'Recruits for the gold mines of the Rand lined up with their papers and bundles, ready to get on the bus for the first stage of their long journey out of Swaziland.' Photographer Hilda Beemer, c 1935.[83]

[81] Kuper, *An African Aristocracy* (1947), 'List of Illustrations', xi–xii.
[82] Kuper, *The Uniform of Colour*, 'List of Illustrations'.
[83] HKP, Box 60, Folder 2, Loose black and white photographs – Swaziland. Caption from Hilda Beemer, *The Uniform of Colour* (1947), Plate 32.

210 Pioneers of the Field

Figure 5.4: A photojournalistic sequence capturing an incident in the Johannesburg city centre in the mid-1940s. It involved a young milkman

Historical ethnography and ethnographic fiction 211

like 'Native Bus at Night' and 'The Black Man's Pass'.[84] In general, though, her poetry was intensely private, a form of catharsis during her painful five-year separation from Leo following his enlistment in the South African army in 1941. Theirs was, in many ways, a conventional marriage. Leo had been the breadwinner from the outset, with some of the expectations that went along with that role. Hilda took the job as a lecturer at Wits primarily because she needed the money. If her poems are anything to judge by, she was bereft. She visited Leo whenever possible, whether in military camps in the Eastern Transvaal, where she completed her first full draft of her thesis, or in Kenya, where he was posted for a time, or in Italy where Leo was sent after two years of service in North Africa. I read her war-time love poems as a catalyst in her career as a creative writer, an exploratory foray into writing about human emotions and inner psychology. While her first surviving poem, entitled 'Marriage', dates to January 1935, most of her love poems were written during the war years. Among her many beautiful love poems is this, entitled 'To Leo: Letter from Italy, June 1944'.

> He wrote of poppies, yellow daisies, and an almond tree.
> He wrote a lovely song to me, the lover's song of Italy.
> He wandered through the villages defeated by despair.
> He wept beside the weeping child whose parents were not there.
> He heard the guns come near, and watched the bombers soar,
> And with his friends went marching through the wheat to war.
> He spoke to lonely peasant lads who did not know to fight.
> I felt the anguish that he felt from what he did not write.[85]

Hilda's daughter Jenny remembers that her mother was given to reciting snatches of poems and that poetry evoked intense emotion in her; she wept when reading to Jenny the war poems of Rupert Brooke.[86] War-time

---

Caption for Figure 5.4: (cont.)

falling off a bicycle followed by animated pavement discussion about the incident between a young white teenager and a group of stylishly dressed township youth. It is her eye for the unusual incident, for the personal and the particular that made her such a gifted story-writer.[87]

---

[84] HKP, Box 44, Folders 4–5 'Poetry by Hilda Kuper', Handwritten list headed 'Verse already published' [n.d.].
[85] HKP, Box 44, Folders 4–5 'Poetry by Hilda Kuper'.
[86] Interview with Jenny Kuper, London, 13 May 2013.
[87] HKP, Box 60, Folder 4: Photographs of Johannesburg.

212   Pioneers of the Field

anguish, separation and loss were, as we have seen, central features of her life history.

Her political essays, by contrast, were written expressly for a general readership. She published half a dozen of these in South African literary and cultural magazines between 1943 and 1945. Most were fierce left-liberal critiques of white racism and segregation in South Africa. 'How Black Sees White (A Reply)', published in February 1944 in *Trek* challenged the stereotype of docile Africans presented in the shallow, psychologically based analysis of a previous writer. Black South African attitudes towards whites were, she insisted, complex and varied, profoundly shaped by African groups' different experiences of white domination and the different status positions of African individuals in South African society. 'What Is a Native?' (*Trek*, June 1945) presented a theoretically informed critique of white racist mythology. Drawing on the recent anthropological literature on race and racism that had emerged in reaction to the rise of Nazism, by authors like A.C. Haddon and Ruth Benedict, Hilda emphasized the lack of scientific validity of the biological concept of racial type that was coming to dominate white South African politics.[88]

She later recalled that this was the central emphasis of her social anthropology lectures at Wits. This kind of thinking was a revelation for white undergraduate students like Prudence Smith, later a prominent BBC radio presenter on Africa, who remembers having 'stumbled through my childhood, close to and yet far distant from the black people and children of my home' in a 'swept and trim' white suburb of Johannesburg. 'Hilda, her lectures and the warmth and care of her friendship, began to make sense of the world I lived in. She helped me to look into the fearful face of poverty and cultural dislocation as well as, on the other side, prejudice and self-interest.'[89]

The most interesting of her Johannesburg essays were those on the cultural politics associated with new media. In the only essay she ever published in Afrikaans, 'Die Oorlogsrolprent in Suid-Afrika' ['The War Film in South Africa'], Hilda drew attention to the crudely propagandistic nature of war films, with the death and brutal mutilation of human beings being celebrated in simplistic stories about the achievements of

---

[88] Hilda Kuper, 'What Is a Native?', *Trek* (1 June 1945), 14.

[89] Prudence Smith, *The Morning Light: A South African Childhood Revalued* (Cape Town: David Philip, 2000), 191–2. In her later career Smith broadcast a recording of Hilda talking about her research on the Indians of Natal which was aired on BBC radio in 1956 and published in transcript form as Kuper, 'The Indians of Natal' in Smith, ed., *African in Transition: BBC Talks on Changing Conditions in the Union and the Rhodesias* (London: Max Reinhart, 1958), 115–24.

Historical ethnography and ethnographic fiction   213

'our heroes'. While she would certainly have supported the necessity to fight 'a just war' against the evils of Nazism, her war poetry and this essay provide evidence of the depth of her aversion to violence. As we will see later, her fascinating study of the Hindu religion practised in Durban during the mid-1950s would reinforce her commitment to the politics of non-violence. In a lighter vein discussing with readers of the *African Radio Announcer* 'What I Expect from My Radio', Hilda made a case for the didactic value of this relatively new channel of mass communication, for more informed political debate, more prominent airing of African music and more sophisticated entertainment for what she clearly imagined as an intellectual middle class listenership. 'I want to hear ideas well expressed, good music well played, drama finely produced, news hot from scenes of action, comedy rich with humour.'[90] She had already written about working-class responses to radio in the years after the introduction in 1940 of a war-time service to the Johannesburg townships.[91] Here too she found that the didactic potential of the new technology was not being properly realized, as too many of the programmes were culturally insensitive, if not blandly propagandistic. These 'ethnographies of radio reception' are brief but intriguing soundings into social change in a modernizing South Africa.

The most experimental of her writings were short stories. Hilda was a more prolific and better published short-story writer than has been acknowledged, even by the two scholars who have written about her ethnographic fiction.[92] Most of her stories were published in cultural and literary magazines in South Africa, notably *Trek*, which featured 'Work Missus' (1943), 'Boy without a Job (Not Such a Bad Boy)' (1944), and 'The Orgy' (1948), its successor, *South African Opinion* ('The Polygamist', 1947), *The Forum* ('Wine of Destiny', 1946) and *Africa South* ('The Amazement of Namahasha', 1956). *Trek* was a bilingual fortnightly left-liberal magazine which also published essays by other protest writers like Nadine Gordimer, Doris Lessing and Lionel Abrahams. A number of Hilda's stories were published abroad: 'Saturday

---

[90] These texts were located in HKP, Box 44, Folder 2, Writings, articles and clippings by Hilda Kuper, c 1945-'.

[91] *Ibid.*: Hilda Kuper, Benedict Vilakazi and Ernst Westphal, 'SAIRR Report on Radio Reception in Western Native Township', 1943. Township radio services were aired for a brief moment in the early 1940s as a medium of wartime propaganda. The service was discontinued in 1945 and then re-introduced as a weapon of Afrikaner nationalist and apartheid propaganda in 1949.

[92] For example, Kerry Vincent bases his analysis of her short stories on just three of her sixteen stories. Vincent, 'Literature as Laboratory: Hilda Kuper's Factional Representations of Swaziland', *African Studies*, 70, 1 (2011), 89–102. Nancy Schmidt did wonderful work in compiling the texts of her stories, but was able to track the original source of publication for only a few.

214   Pioneers of the Field

at the Location' (1944) in *Common Sense*, an English literary journal edited by George Orwell, 'He Smelt White' was translated and published as 'Demone kam aus Johannesburg' ['Demone comes from Johannesburg'] in *Der Tag* in 1958, while another essay was translated and published in a French literary magazine.[93]

There are different ways of understanding her turn to ethnographic fiction. Nancy J. Schmidt, the first scholar to draw attention to the importance of Hilda's body of ethnographic fiction, locates her work in the most general of terms, as a hidden literary subgenre within social or cultural anthropology, one that the mainstream discipline had tended to disown. Writing at a time of heightened interest in the literary aspect of anthropology in the late 1970s and early 1980s, Schmidt remarked on the depth and breadth of Hilda's ethnographic fiction.[94] On the other hand, Kerry Vincent proposes that we read her stories as a contribution to an emerging tradition of 'South African protest literature'. The centrality of her critique of the migrant labour system and racially discriminatory laws, expressed in tragic stories of broken African lives, supports his case for the underlying political nature of her fiction. He also highlights the extent to which the image of Africans in her short stories, play and novel challenged the static and overly romanticized representation of the Swazi in British imperial literature, such as Rider Haggard's *She*.[95]

I would add that we need to locate her early ethnographic fiction in relation to her fieldwork, given the expressly autobiographical resonance of many, if not most, of the stories, in which the leading protagonist or even the first-person narrator is a young white woman researcher. While Hilda herself would retrospectively draw a sharp line between the genres of literature and social anthropology, and associate her literary experimentation with disillusion with the abstract new structuralist school of anthropology,[96] her attitude to the discipline was still optimistic in the early to mid-1940s. She certainly remained active in new fields, despite the demands of teaching and writing. Apart from return trips to Swaziland in 1938 and 1941, her fieldwork was now conducted in the mines, prisons and townships of Johannesburg. It involved, in successive phases, conducting interviews with, and administering questionnaires

---

[93] I tracked down the publications dates and details in the UCLA, Special Collection, Coll. 1343 Hilda Kuper Papers, Box 44, Folder 2, Writings, articles and clippings by Hilda Kuper, c 1945-. The full texts of all sixteen of her short stories are republished in Hilda Kuper, *A Witch in My Heart, Short Stories and Poems*, 65–126.

[94] Nancy J. Schmidt, 'Ethnographic Fiction', 11–14; Schmidt, 'Introduction' to Hilda Kuper, *A Witch in My Heart, Short Stories and Poems*, 1–3.

[95] Kerry Vincent, 'Literature as Laboratory', 89–102.

[96] Kuper, 'Introduction' to *A Witch in My Heart*, 3–4.

Historical ethnography and ethnographic fiction

to, Swazi mineworkers (1937 onwards), interviewing African women prisoners as part of a research project into penal reform (1938–9), interviewing Africans in townships about their reactions to radio broadcasting (1942) and leading a team of graduate women researchers, including Ruth First, to produce a study of African life in Western Native Township, Johannesburg. Provisionally titled 'Life in Poverty' (1945), this ambitious questionnaire-based study across 204 households was planned as a book, with chapters on household composition, standard of living, education, race, kinship and marriage, where they argued that African marriages in the township were stable and enduring, contrary to the standard image in the anthropological literature. The manuscript remained unpublished, probably because the research was cut short by Hilda and Leo's move abroad in 1947.[97]

I see Hilda's short stories as creative experiments arising out of her fieldwork encounters. While plot summaries can convey only a partial sense of the power of her creative imagination, they do indicate the kind of themes that she sought to explore in her experimental writing. Three of the stories are set in the townships of Johannesburg; another on a migrant labourer bus returning from Johannesburg to a 'native reserve'. 'Work Missus' is her most powerful piece. The only one of her stories with a male protagonist, it tells of the progressive disillusionment of a male migrant labourer from Swaziland when confronted with the harsh realities of unemployment and white racism in the big city.

Most of the stories are set in Swaziland. Here, too, the central theme is the clash between tradition and modernity. The most evocative of these, 'The Tooth' (*Modern Reading*, 1945), tells how a middle-aged Swazi woman implores a young white woman researcher to take her ailing child to the hospital in Mbabane. They are prevented from doing so by the patriarch of the homestead, who insists that the child's rotten tooth and hideously infected mouth be treated by a traditional healer. It is only when the girl is on the point of death that the young woman is given permission to take her to the hospital. Even though her life is saved by the doctor, in what is a typically bleak ending the story concludes with the young woman hearing the tragic news that her young baby has died of neglect back home. Most of the other Swazi short stories are tales of the young woman researcher's encounters with distasteful characters: a corpulent and lustful Swazi polygamist, an old missionary whose isolation made him turn to alchemy, a frenzied prophet of a new

---

[97] HKP, Box 41, Folder 6: Unpublished study of Western Native Township, 1945 HK. The title page of the manuscript indicates that it was co-authored by Hilda and four of her women graduate students: Ruth First, Myrtle Canon, Selma Kaplan and Kay Theron.

216   Pioneers of the Field

Christian sect, and a racist and anti-Semitic English guest-house owner (here set in the Transkei).[98]

In general, I am struck by the pessimistic tone and outcomes of these stories. Hilda sought to reveal the dark side of South African and Swazi society at a time of social and economic dislocation, one that is only partially exposed in her scholarship. She retrospectively characterized her short stories and poems as 'a safety valve', a form of psychological release in a time of personal and societal stress.[99] They were attempts to channel this anxiety into creative forms that pushed the boundaries of her established mode of writing. I see them as literary experiments, the attempts of a scholar whose descriptive abilities were well recognized to find a new and different voice and medium by straddling the boundaries between the personal and the political, between the individual and the collective, between fact and fiction. It was only in her mature ethnographic fiction of the mid- to late 1950s that Hilda was able to make a more complete break with her identity as a fieldworker.

A liberal family abroad, 1947–1952

Hilda's five-year interlude abroad was an unsettled time. It began with the delight of her falling pregnant shortly after their arrival in Chapel Hill, North Carolina, where she had followed Leo, after his major mid-career decision to shift from law to sociology. A serious car accident in Johannesburg some years earlier had raised doubts as to whether Hilda would be able to bear children. Mary was born eighteen months after Jenny in Johannesburg, when the serious illness of Leo's sister forced Hilda and Leo to return for some months to South Africa.[100]

Hilda's outrage at the new apartheid government's policies is recorded in a political essay she penned after her return in which she compared the extent of democratic freedom and civil rights in the U.S. Constitution and as practised in the US North at least, with the complete absence of civil rights for black South Africans under apartheid.[101] The Kupers were unwilling to stay in apartheid South Africa and set off for Coventry in England, where Leo was completing his doctoral thesis. Hilda felt isolated in this 'parochial' town. It had been badly bombed during the war and

---

[98] See, respectively, 'The Polygamist' (n.d., *South African Opinion*), 'The Old Missionary (Wine of Destiny)' (*Forum*, 16 February 1946), 'Meal at a South African Guest Farm' in Kuper, *A Witch in My Heart, Short Stories and Poems*, 101–4, 119–21 and 87–90.

[99] Kuper, 'Function, History and Biography', 206.

[100] Interview with Jenny Kuper, London, 13 May 2013.

[101] Hilda Kuper, 'Civil Rights: U.S. and South Africa Comparisons', *Trek* (May 1949), 8–9.

Historical ethnography and ethnographic fiction   217

Leo's first field research focused on the process of urban reconstruction.[102] Things were little better when he took up a lectureship at Birmingham. Here she suffered the trauma of having a stillborn child,[103] and the disappointment of having to turn down a job as a Reader at the London School of Economics because of ill health.[104]

She published just one article during these five years, albeit arguably her best scholarly essay. This was her finely incisive analysis of the structure of kinship in Swazi society published in the seminal collection on kinship edited by Radcliffe-Brown and Daryll Forde (first edition 1950).[105] She also produced a short overview of Swazi culture in a survey series designed for university students, dedicating it to Jenny and Mary in this and the numerous subsequent editions.[106]

A monograph, two plays and a novel written in Durban, 1952–1961

It can only have been with relief that Hilda heard the news of Leo's appointment as head of the Department of Sociology at the University of Natal, although she would surely have felt apprehension about the changing political climate in the country. They returned to South Africa in the early stages of the 1952 Defiance Campaign and threw themselves into anti-apartheid political activism from the outset. Indeed, their decade in Durban was the high point of their careers as left-liberal political activists, and their intellectual work was more deeply infused with their protest politics than has sometimes been acknowledged.

Leo's role in South African liberal politics of this period has been more fully documented than that of Hilda. He began his first monograph, *Passive Resistance in South Africa* (1955), with an extended and vivid description of his participation in a joint ANC-Indian Congress political rally in 'Red Square' in Durban on 9 November 1952. His study situated the meeting in the passive resistance tradition of Mahatma Gandhi and

---

[102] Kuper, 'Function, History and Biography', 206–7.
[103] Interview with Jenny Kuper, London, 13 May 2013.
[104] Kuper, 'Function, History and Biography', 206–7.
[105] Hilda Kuper, 'Kinship among the Swazi' in A.R. Radcliffe-Brown and Daryll Forde, eds., *African Systems of Kinship and Marriage* (London, New York and Toronto: Oxford University Press with the International African Institute, 1950), 86–110. This collection had gone into a ninth impression by 1967.
[106] Hilda Kuper, *Ethnographic Survey of Africa, South Africa, Part I: The Swazi* (London: International African Institute, 1952: series editor Daryll Forde), which was slightly reworked in Kuper, *The Swazi: A South African Kingdom* (New York, Chicago, San Francisco, Toronto and London: Holt, Rinehart and Winston, 1963) and then again in *Ibid.*, 1985. She published a shorter essay on 'The Shona' (1954) in Forde's African Institute Series.

218   Pioneers of the Field

provided a close reconstruction of the events of the 1952 Defiance Campaign. He does not mention whether Hilda was present with him at the meeting, although I think it is fair to assume that she would have been. They were among the founders in 1953 of the Liberal Party of South Africa, which remained their political home for a decade. The recollections of their colleagues, students and friends indicate that the Kuper home became a significant space for anti-apartheid political solidarity across the colour line, although the official history of the Liberal Party makes no mention at all of Hilda's contribution.[107] Leo was more prominent in the public activities of the party. He was arrested in December 1956, along with Alan Paton and four Indian Congress members, for taking part in 'an assembly of Natives' in the Gandhi Library Hall in Durban, a meeting at which he and others launched a defence fund for the 156 Treason Trialists. This would later become the London-based International Defence and Aid Fund. Hilda had been arrested earlier in the year, along with Fatima Meer, when they marched with thousands of other women from Cato Manor in protest against new laws extending the pass system to 'non-European' women.[108] By the late 1950s the Kupers were subject to increasing harassment from the apartheid state, with spies attending their sociology and anthropology lectures, and the threat of banning hanging over Leo. They were eventually forced to go into exile, at Hilda's instigation.[109]

This context of left-liberal anti-apartheid political activism deeply informed Hilda's anthropological research during her productive decade in Durban. Contrary to a recent claim that Hilda's ethnographic study of Indians in Durban is 'remarkably depoliticized',[110] the politics of national belonging and racial discrimination in apartheid South Africa were at the very heart of her study. Her ethnography of the Hindu community of Durban, published in 1960 as *Indian People in Natal* and based on four years of fieldwork in three Indian suburbs between 1953 and 1957, was written as an explicit refutation of the National Party's view that South African Indians were 'strangers' who, it was often explicitly said, should

---

[107] Randolph Vigne, *Liberals against Apartheid: A History of the Liberal Party of South Africa, 1953–1968* (London: Macmillan, 1997), but for details of her involvement, see Pierre van den Berghe, *Stranger in their Midst* (Colorado: University of Colorado Press, 1989), 153–77; Margo Russell, 'Obituary: Hilda Kuper (1911–1992)', 145–9.

[108] Moran, 'Hilda Beemer Kuper (1911-)', 196.

[109] For a vivid account of the Kupers under siege in Durban, see Van den Berghe, *Stranger in Their Midst*, 157–60.

[110] Thomas Blom Hansen, *Melancholia of Freedom: Social Life in an Indian Township in South Africa* (Princeton: Princeton University Press, 2012), 60. For a more generous recognition of the context and value of her study, see Chris Fuller, 'Book Review: *Ambivalence about Apartheid. Anthropology of This Century*', *LSE Research Online*, October 2012.

Historical ethnography and ethnographic fiction 219

be deported back to India rather than encouraged to integrate into a society to which they did not belong. This was despite the fact that they outnumbered Africans and whites in Durban when Hilda began her study. The underlying political argument of the book is that the Indian communities of Durban had become distinctively South African through a century-long process of migration and adaptation to their new environment and that their Indian cultural heritage, notably the relatively rigid caste system, no longer played a fundamental role in their family and religious life. These two central themes were explored in rich detail in this under-appreciated ethnography. In fact, the conclusion to her study hints that her own Jewish background encouraged in her an underlying association with Indians as fellow 'strangers' pushed to the margins. 'Like Jews ..., the Indians in South Africa can be, and have been used as a scapegoat by other national groups. Sufficiently wealthy to serve as bait for greed, too few to be feared, and, in the main, ideologically opposed to counter aggression with physical violence, their ethnic difference and cultural diversity serve as excuses for discrimination and oppression.'[111]

While the Jewish community had remained Hilda's main point of reference during her Johannesburg years, her decade in Durban saw her becoming integrated into a more cross-cultural left-liberal community of whites and middle-class Indians. Her daughter Jenny remembers visits to the homes of Hilda's Indian friends.

JK: There was a family called the Singhs. He [Ashwin] was a doctor. And their daughter was a friend of mine. I adored her. And I remember going to their house and seeing them praying. They had little statues. It was all totally compelling ...

AB: Were your Indian friends well-to-do?

JK: Yes. The ones we visited were. They wore saris and sumptuous garments ... They were a very important part of our lives. When she [Hilda] was engaging with a particular community she really did connect.[112]

She and Mary sometimes accompanied Hilda on her fieldtrips.

We would go to these amazing festivals which I absolutely loved. They would take us as quite young children. And we would see people walking over coals with bare feet, people with things piercing their tongues, people pulling wagons with hooks in their backs ... and she would say, 'Don't worry. They are not feeling any pain.'[113]

---

[111] Hilda Kuper, *Indian People of Natal*, 271.
[112] Interview with Jenny Kuper, London, 13 May 2013. Mary Kuper also recalls their close friendships with Indian children. Skype interview with Mary Kuper, Cape Town-London, 13 August 2011.
[113] Interview with Jenny Kuper, London, 13 May 2013.

Figure 5.5: 'Dolly's wedding.' Hilda Kuper's photograph of her daughters, Mary (right) and Jenny (left), at a Hindu wedding celebration in Durban, 1954.[114]

Hilda's thick description of these *kavady* rituals, involving participants going into states of trance and performing seemingly impossible feats of physical endurance in their altered states of consciousness, was the most unusual chapter.[115] Jenny also vividly recalls visits to the Indian market in the city centre.

> We [the Kuper family] often used to go to the Indian market in Durban in the square, the big Indian market. We used to be the only white people there ... I loved that place, the colourfulness of the Indian saris. And it was all just so vibrant ... the colours and the smells.[116]

Hilda chose this as the scene with which to begin her ethnography, evoking an image of 'stalls crammed with oriental jewellery and trinketry, with

---

[114] Jenny Kuper, Private Family Photograph Album, London.
[115] Kuper, *Indian People of Natal*, 217–34; see also Hilda Kuper, 'An Ethnographic Description of Kavady, A Hindu Ceremony in South Africa', *African Studies*, 18, 3 (1959), 118–32.
[116] Interview with Jenny Kuper, London, 13 May 2013.

Historical ethnography and ethnographic fiction 221

a variety of lentils, rice, beans and oils, with betel leaf and areca nut, lime, camphor, and incense sticks, with curry powders, masala, all kinds of fruit and herbs, as well as with more familiar goods which themselves become unfamiliar in the excited atmosphere of oriental bargaining'.[117] If there is any lasting impression that the reader takes from the *Indian People of Natal*, it is surely of the richness, diversity and vibrancy of the Indian communities of Durban, with their complex and varied genealogies as third- or fourth-generation descendants of indentured and 'passenger' immigrants; their wide-ranging religious affiliations, predominantly Hindu, but also partly Muslim and partly Christian; their widely disparate socio-economic conditions; and, of course, their bewilderingly complex linguistic heritage (Tamil, Telegu, Gujarati, Hindustani and Urdu). As Hilda complained to Monica and Audrey in her letters, how could one possibly capture this enormous complexity in a single monograph?[118]

The acknowledgements are revealing of quite the extent of her reliance on Indian friends as intermediaries and testimony to the warmth of her relations with them. She thanked her two research assistants 'and close friends', Mrs Radhi Singh and Mrs Fatima Meer, then a Master's student of Leo's, with whom Hilda would co-author a short monograph entitled *Indian Elites* (1956);[119] seven Indian health educators, her colleagues at Sidney Kark's Institute of Family and Community Health, who accompanied her on visits to Indian homes and established a network of contacts for her; the Pandits and Swamis, who shared with her their religious knowledge and hosted her in their temples and houses; as well as half-a-dozen Indian intellectuals who had read and 'corrected' her manuscript,[120] following the precedent she had established in her work in Swaziland.

Hilda's connection with the community and culture she was studying had in some senses been closer in Swaziland. In Durban she neither lived in the Indian suburbs, which was illegal for a white researcher in apartheid South Africa, nor became fluent in Hindi. She discontinued lessons with her Brahmin teacher once she realized that 'his version of the language was "too high" for the man on the street'.[121] However, her ethnography demonstrates that she developed a deep understanding of Hindu religion and philosophy: its rich history, its literature, its changing rituals in the

---

[117] Kuper, *Indian People of Natal*, xiii.
[118] WC, Uncatalogued correspondence, Folder K, Kuper: Hilda Kuper to Monica Wilson, 10 March 1955, Durban; ARP, Richards 16/36, Hilda Kuper to Audrey Richards, 4 February 1957, Durban.
[119] Hilda Kuper and Fatima Meer, *Indian Elites* (Pietermaritzburg: University of Natal Press, 1956).
[120] Kuper, *Indians in Natal*, x–xi.   [121] *Ibid.*, xx.

222   Pioneers of the Field

South African context and especially its underlying ethos. She wrote to Monica that she had not intended to immerse herself in the sacred literature of Hinduism, but had been forced to do so as she became aware of its continued importance to religious practice among South African Hindus.[122] It is evident that her fieldwork experience had a profound impact on her own spiritual identity and philosophical outlook, which came to be marked by a universalism and inclusiveness, a breadth of vision, an appreciation of the core values of non-violence and compassion, which are at the heart of Eastern religions and which, in Mahatma Gandhi's *satyagraha* tradition, became associated with the politics of non-violent protest in South Africa. She wrote to Audrey: 'Strangely enough, I've decided that I am religious, [though] not in any orthodox way – which would make life much easier.'[123]

Hilda's book was reviewed in surprisingly few journals, probably because of its publication by a South African press. Again, Max was her most generous reader. He described it as 'a studious, though fascinating, analysis of the social relations of Indians and their culture', one which 'illuminates South Africa from an unusual angle' and 'deals penetratingly with the theme of adaptation'.[124] He did have a close knowledge of her study, as she did much of the writing up during an energized year at Manchester on a Simons Fellowship. In the literature on the history of anthropology in South Africa, Hilda's Indian study is seldom mentioned, if at all.[125]

What was its anthropological significance in the broader view? First, it was an important contribution to the emerging field of South African urban anthropology. Hilda's book was published before the famous 'Xhosa in Town' trilogy under the directorship of Philip Mayer and the analysis of social groups in Langa by Monica Wilson and Archie Mafeje.[126] Her study was based on lengthier and much more immersed fieldwork than these better-known urban studies: Mayer worked largely through questionnaires, given the political difficulties of working in East London townships during

---

[122] WC, Uncatalogued correspondence, Folder K, 'Kuper': Hilda Kuper to Monica Wilson, 10 March 1955, Durban.

[123] ARP, Hilda Kuper to Audrey Richards, 27 September 1960, Durban.

[124] Max Gluckman, 'Review of Hilda Kuper, *Indian People in Natal*'. For shorter and generally warm reviews, see D.F. Pocock, *Africa*, 31, 1 (January 1961); S.H. Morris, *The British Journal of Sociology*, 12, 1 (March 1961), 74; R.J. Davies, *The Geographical Journal*, 126, 4 (December 1960), 521.

[125] Hammond-Tooke, *Imperfect Interpreters*.

[126] Philip Mayer with Iona Mayer, *Townsmen or Tribesmen: Conservatism and the Process of Urbanization in a South African City* (Cape Town: Oxford University Press, Xhosa in Town Series, 1961, 2nd edn. 1973; Monica Wilson and Archie Mafeje, *Langa: A Study of Social Groups in an African Township* (Cape Town, London and New York: Oxford University Press, 1963).

Historical ethnography and ethnographic fiction 223

an intensely volatile period,[127] and the relatively inexperienced Mafeje's fieldwork was brief by comparison and done under time pressure.[128] Second, as I have argued in the case of *An African Aristocracy*, few scholars have recognized the historical importance of her work. Here again the opening section of her book provided a detailed and pioneering history, here of South African Indians based on a combination of oral and documentary sources: extensive family interviews about ancestors presented as case histories; shipping records to track patterns of migration; and reports of the Protector of Indian Immigration. Third, the body of the text advanced our understanding of the history of religion, especially of religious ritual, in South Africa. In both these senses, it furthered the study of social change in South Africa. While its publication by a relatively small press might have contributed to its neglect, it is difficult to avoid the impression that the book's limited appreciation related to its failure to conform to the binary categories within which works of South African anthropology have been evaluated: studies of traditional African culture and/or African culture in transition; and later studies of traditional African religious systems and African forms of Christianity.

It is against the background of this anthropological research that I propose to read her second, more mature phase in writing ethnographic fiction. To begin with, we should note that Hilda returned to fictional writing only in the mid- to late 1950s, producing at least one short story,[129] two plays and a novel within a few years. Given my focus here on depth rather than range, I will provide a close analysis of just one of these important works: her best-known and favourite offspring, *A Witch in My Heart*. She wrote the play in Durban between 1956 and 1958, when it was performed by African medical students from the University of Natal.

Explicitly subtitled 'A Play Set in Swaziland in the 1930s', it is a tragedy with Shakespearian overtones, a play that makes rich use of the techniques of dramatic irony, soliloquys and foreshadowing, and reveals a heightened sense of drama reflected in storms, lightning and a dark preoccupation with the workings of witchcraft. It is essentially a story of culturally inappropriate love, of the romantic love between a Swazi man (Sikova) and his favourite but barren co-wife (Bigwapi), of the

---

[127] Leslie J. Bank, *Home Spaces, Street Styles: Contesting Power and Identity in a South African City* (London: Pluto Press, 2011), 41–5.

[128] Andrew Bank with Vuyiswa Swana, '"Speaking from Inside": Archie Mafeje, Monica Wilson and the Co-Production of Langa: A Study of Social Groups in an African Township' in Bank and Bank, eds., *Inside African Anthropology*, 253–79.

[129] She described 'The Amazement of Namahasha', published in *Africa South* in 1956, as her best short story. (Schmidt, 'Introduction', 3.) Like her subsequent Swazi play and novel, it was centrally concerned with witchcraft.

consequent jealousy of her two co-wives (the sisters Big Lahlophe and Little Lahlophe), and the negative judgement of his wider family in this patriarchal society. It tells of the devastating consequences that result from all this: his humiliation when he goes to Johannesburg to find work in order to pay for traditional medical intervention, his falling in with bad company, his arrest and imprisonment, and finally his return home only to find that his beloved is on the point of being expelled from the homestead, having been found guilty of witchcraft after a traditional healer (*sangoma*) had confirmed his co-wives' suspicions that Bigwapi had caused one of them to bear a still-born baby. The play ends with the broken husband on the point of returning to the dark city, no longer feeling that he can remain in his rural home, and the barren co-wife about to be cast adrift from the homestead and, in her traumatized state, proclaiming that there is 'a witch in my heart'. The settings thus

Figure 5.6: The Kuper family on a visit to Chatsworth House in Derbyshire in 1958. Hilda was on a Simons Fellowship at Manchester University organized by Max Gluckman. Jenny is on the left alongside Leo, Mary on the right alongside Hilda and their cousin John Beemer is in the middle.[130]

---

[130] Jenny Kuper, Family Photo Album, London.

Historical ethnography and ethnographic fiction

shift from the Swazi homestead to Johannesburg before returning to a scene of physical, social and spiritual death back at the homestead. The central ethnographic themes are clear: kinship relations in traditional African societies, notably relationships between husbands and co-wives in polygamous societies; patriarchal male attitudes towards wives, in particular barren wives; the enormous power of the traditional belief in witchcraft and the devastating personal consequences that can result from beliefs in seemingly abstract, intangible dark forces; and the disruptive impact that migrant labour and city life can have on traditional African values and families.

The theme of tragic love is also at the heart of the other play and the novel she wrote at the time. While her novel was only published in New York in 1965 under the title *A Bite of Hunger*, she had written the first draft in Manchester in 1958. The novel is set in interwar Swaziland with a young woman (here a princess) as its central character. Here too the leading protagonist, Lamtana, is caught between tradition and modernity, and comes to be accused of witchcraft. 'The Hunger' in the title refers both to the play's setting in a time of drought and to Lamtana's deep desire for learning and books, and the magical powers she associates with them. Hilda based the character and experiences of Lamtana on one of the Swazi queens whom she had known intimately.[131]

The Decision is a play about the love of a young South African Indian woman for a political activist involved in the Indian Congress, about her parents' opposition to her choice, their attempts to force her into an arranged marriage with a man she did not love, and her tragic decision to commit suicide rather than face an awful future trapped in a loveless marriage. Hilda indicated in private correspondence that her work had emerged directly out of her fieldwork encounters among Indian communities in Durban in the mid-1950s.[132] We know that the play was performed by Indian medical students at the University of Natal in June 1958. Hilda indicated that an Indian couple came up to speak to her immediately afterwards and threatened to sue her as they thought that the play exposed their own family history. She vowed that she had never met them but, given the sensitivity around the subject, she put off revising the play and in fact was working on a final version when she died in April 1992.[133]

---

[131] Interview with Adam Kuper, London, 10 April 2013.

[132] Hilda Kuper to Nancy Schmidt, 19 July 1990, cited by Schmidt, 'Introduction', 1, Footnote 5.

[133] The play is given in outline form in Hilda Kuper, *A Witch in my Heart, Short Stories and Poems*, but there is a thirty-page text version hidden in the Hilda Kuper Papers, Box 44, Folder 2: Writings, articles and clippings by Hilda Kuper, c. 1945-. The *Anthropology*

226   Pioneers of the Field

What was Hilda's underlying motivation in crafting *A Witch in My Heart*? Drawing on postcolonial theory, Kerry Vincent has argued that the play sought to present a Western feminist critique of African patriarchy, polygamy and witchcraft. The first problem with this interpretation is that the play was written in the late 1950s in South Africa rather than the late 1960s in the United States when feminist theory came to the fore. Hilda was in fact critical of feminist anthropology. She bravely presented an outspoken defence of the polygamous family structure in traditional Swazi society in a keynote address at an international conference in 1975 on the changing status of women in the modern world. Ever independent of mind, she provocatively argued that co-wives in a traditional polygamous African society were more socially secure than the modern woman in their alienated, overly competitive American society.[134] The second problem is that her attitude towards Swazi traditional beliefs, including polygamy and witchcraft, was always more ambiguous than this analysis would suggest. Indeed, her daughter Mary recalls that:

Some concepts from her fieldwork – a belief in witchcraft for example, certainly came across to us as children as valid realities, and at one point in Durban she performed an exorcism in our house for someone, possibly one of the people who worked for us. Certainly when she talked about say, in Swaziland, a snake appearing and being addressed as an ancestral spirit, she presented this as reality, not as an alien or strange practice ... I also clearly remember the model of the polygamous family structure being presented in a favourable light.[135]

While it is fair to read her play as a critical commentary on patriarchy in traditional African society, her technique was not to adopt the voice of the Western feminist but to seek to reveal the painful inner journey of the woman who suffers from these attitudes, in particular Swazi attitudes to barren women. I see her fiction as being closely related to her scholarly work at the time. Her study of the Indian communities in Durban was about attempting to engage with and then convey a sense of an inner world, the world of belief and spirituality, of which the ritual public expressions were but the overt manifestation. Likewise, the play is primarily concerned with the inner rather than the outer, with emotion rather than behaviour. As she explicitly indicated in her introduction to the 1970 edition, the play

---

and Humanism Quarterly had wanted her cut this down to a twenty-page version in the early 1990s, but Hilda was not able to rework it in time.

[134] Hilda Kuper Papers, Box 48: Folder Women-Wisconsin, Talk on 'What We Have in Common', April 1975.

[135] Mary Kuper, E-mail communication, London-Cape Town, 21 April 2014.

Historical ethnography and ethnographic fiction 227

is 'less about witchcraft and more about the heart – a symbolic heart reflecting deep human emotions – love, hate, jealousy, hope, and despair'. She went on to explain that ethnographic fiction gave her the freedom to explore matters of the heart. She contrasted this with the constraint she had often felt as a scholarly writer working from within a policed, bounded 'discipline' with its more rigid conventions and style. Elsewhere she described ethnographic fiction as an alternative to the stiflingly abstract, depersonalized and lifeless language of structuralism that came to dominate mainstream social anthropology in the 1950s.[136]

> The writer of fiction, on the other hand, is allowed greater freedom of expression and imagination. She is expected to personalize general experiences, is permitted to develop her own style and eccentricities, and encouraged to avoid technical formulations and conventions in making her own commitments. She may deliberately use the ambiguity of words to extend the reader's perception. Her history may not be chronological nor social, nor her cosmology computable. She may take for granted that the mind sets its own pace as it wanders through an existential labyrinth.[137]

It is also possible to read the play autobiographically, in line with my reading of her short stories. As noted earlier, Hilda had at one stage feared that she herself was barren (and we also know that she bore a still-born child, as one of the co-wives does in the play), so it is fair to assume that her empathetic portrait of the conflicted female protagonist drew in part on personal experience. She is thoroughly persuasive in conveying the injustice of the hostile and judgemental attitudes of Swazi family members towards Bigwapi as well in analysing, in rich ethnographic detail, the sense in which an infertile woman was regarded in Swazi society as socially worthless.[138]

We know relatively little about the play in performance. Mary Kuper recalls that, at the age of nine, she and her elder sister watched the play from upstairs overlooking the stage, when it was first performed in a hall at the University of Durban Medical Campus. Most of its stage life was in the classrooms of Swaziland in the 1961 Zulu language translation, *Inhliziyo Ngumthakathi* by Hilda's University of Natal colleague, Trevor Cope. Long before Lucy Dlamini taught the 1978 siSwati translation to her students at the University of Swaziland as a Professor of African Literature, she encountered the Zulu language text in junior secondary school in Mbabane in 1966 and 1967. She and her classmates 'loved' the

---

[136] See esp. Hilda Kuper, 'Anthropology and Literature', Typescript of a public address [n.d., c 1970] in Hilda Kuper Papers, Box 22, Folder 8.
[137] Hilda Kuper, 'Introduction' to *A Witch in My Heart*, 4–5.
[138] Hilda Kuper, 'Introduction', 6–17.

228   Pioneers of the Field

play. 'I don't know of anyone who never loved it. The response has always been positive.' Perhaps because of Hilda's success in portraying Bigwapi's fate with such empathy, 'the girls were better readers than the boys', but boys and girls alike were highly entertained.

> We never even knew it was a translation … It was very powerful. It was very interesting. It was funny. It mirrored Swazi culture. The men going to the mines, buying gifts for the wife, and then usually in a polygamous situation, the husband will be more in love with one of the wives …[139]

The play was also performed at least once by undergraduate anthropology students at Manchester University. When Max mentioned her novel and plays to his colleague John Barnes in January 1965, 'he asked me why I did not have a play reading for my first-year students with your [witchcraft] play … This seems an excellent idea to me: one could have one of the students standing in front of a blackboard on which one could draw the genealogy [of Sikova's extended family that features on the opening page] so that who they are was made clear and get them to read the different parts.'[140] She thought it an excellent idea. 'I confess that I am more excited about it than any of my anthropological writing.'[141] On the basis of his experiment, Max persuaded the International African Institute to publish an English language edition in 1970. He prompted her to write what was an excellent introduction organized around the theme of women as wives and mothers in Swazi society. Max wrote a short preface. Kerry Vincent, based at the University of Swaziland in 2000, indicated that the 1978 siSwati translation of the play 'is still used extensively not only as an aid in teaching siSwati, but also as a point of departure for discussing traditional Swazi culture. It is perhaps not too great an exaggeration to suggest that the play has influenced the way in which many Swazi youth perceive themselves.'[142] Its life as a classic is far from over. Macmillan has published a fresh edition of the play for use in schools in Swaziland as part of a 'new series of plays and screenplays written by playwrights and screenwriters all over the world'.[143]

---

[139] Interview with Lucy Dlamini, Manzini, Swaziland, 14 July 2011.

[140] HKP, Box 40, Folder 20: Correspondence – Max Gluckman: Max Gluckman to Hilda Kuper, 25 January 1963, Manchester.

[141] HKP, Box 40, Folder 2, Hilda Kuper to Barbara Pym of the IAI, 25 September 1969, Los Angeles.

[142] Kerry Vincent, 'Translating Culture: Literature, Anthropology, and Hilda Kuper's *A Witch in My Heart*', *Current Writing*, 12, 2 (2000), 113–30.

[143] Andrew Bank, Correspondence with Stephanie Kitchen of the International African Institute and review of manuscript of Hilda Kuper, *A Witch in My Heart* (Johannesburg: Macmillan, 2015).

Historical ethnography and ethnographic fiction 229

Between two worlds, Los Angeles and Swaziland, 1961–1992

Hilda found her last years in Durban and the move to Los Angeles in October 1961 enormously stressful. The decision to leave South Africa was a very difficult one and was driven primarily by her: Leo was more ambivalent but also a little less anxious about the future. Hilda had taken a post as Senior Lecturer in the Social Anthropology Department at the University of Natal after Jack Krige's sudden death in 1959. She was a gifted teacher. Her most talented undergraduate, Eleanor Preston-Whyte, remembers her as 'an extraordinarily good lecturer'.[144] But the apartheid government was closing in on white liberal universities. The Extension of Universities Act of 1958 made it illegal for African and Indian students to attend white universities. The Medical School at Natal University, which trained African nurses and doctors, was put under the Native Affairs Department and the University of South Africa. Hilda had close contact with the nurses, as she was then researching a chapter on African nurses for Leo's *An African Bourgeoisie* (1965).[145]

By 1960 Hilda had come to the view that their lives were unsafe, given their political commitments, that their children's education and well-being would be hampered if they did not go abroad and that Leo's burgeoning career as a sociologist needed a wider stage.[146] But her private correspondence reveals that she felt an enormous sense of guilt about abandoning her fellow activists in the Liberal Party, her friends in the Indian community and her liberal colleagues at the University of Natal. Their departure would create an irreparable breach with many Liberal Party members, notably Alan Paton, who 'was very critical and hostile with us for having left South Africa and broke what was once a wonderful friendship'.[147] Their decision was so fraught that they chose not to inform their daughters about this radical change in their family life. While Hilda may have felt that their move to Los Angeles was a necessary evil done in the interests of their children, Jenny still feels a sense of pain at the memory of being 'kidnapped' from a South African city which she loved for colourfulness, vibrancy and dynamism, and where she felt politically connected.[148] Neither Jenny nor Mary felt at home

---

[144] Telephone interview with Eleanor Preston-Whyte,. Johannesburg-Cape Town, 5 February 2014.

[145] Hilda Kuper, 'Nursing' in Leo Kuper, *An African Bourgeoisie: Race, Class and Politics in South Africa* (New Haven and London: Yale University Press, 1965), 216–33.

[146] He had published three books during the 1950s with the field research for his fourth and most major forthcoming study, *An African Bourgeoisie* (1965), already completed.

[147] HKP, Box 40, Folder 2, Hilda Kuper to Pierre van den Berghe, Los Angeles, 3 September 1975.

[148] Interview with Jenny Kuper, London, 13 May 2013.

230   Pioneers of the Field

in the United States, and they both emigrated to England at a relatively young age. Hilda wrote to Audrey after a fortnight in Los Angeles:

I have died quietly inside for days and feel quite empty with bereavement. For what we did originally for the children – taking them from South Africa – has brought nothing. What can children get here in this harsh country? Anti-Russian propaganda in the schools, a narrow American nationalism, a hardness that none of us have, that we don't feel like . . . Oh Audrey, if only I could undo the past two weeks . . . I feel that I have betrayed all my own values by this decision . . .[149]

Mary recalls: 'I have a clear memory of finding her sitting at her desk in L.A. with tears in her eyes. She would say that she just had hay-fever.'[150]

Hilda's letters reveal a sense of restlessness through her first decade in the United States. In 1967, having effused about her seven-month return field-trip to Swaziland, she wrote of the pain of having to return to the United States. 'I left with great sadness, feeling that I could do something more meaningful than teaching anthropology to American students.'[151] She chose not to take an American passport, trading her South African passport for a Swazi one when she was offered citizenship in 1970. After retirement from her position as Chair of Anthropology at UCLA in 1977, she seriously considered relocating to Swaziland, but Leo's lack of fluency in siSwati and his reluctance at giving up his public position as an international scholar meant that they stayed in Los Angeles. When interviewed in 1981 about her recently published biography of Sobhuza II (1978), she told the journalist from the *Rand Daily Mail* that she felt more Swazi than American, proudly revealing that her children had been given Swazi names.[152] The history of her thirty years in Los Angeles may be con-sidered a time in which Hilda lived between two worlds: those of UCLA, where she found an intellectual home with stimulating colleagues and bright students, and Swaziland, which became her new spiritual home. She made more than a dozen return trips to Swaziland. Mary recalls her great surprise at her realization on the family's visit for the independence celebrations in 1968 that her mother was more than 'a scatty housewife', prone to losing keys and forgetting to pick the children up from school.

I think she was very, very happy there. She was valued. She was respected. We had a kind of status as her family. It was very odd to realize that she had this other life. It was pretty amazing that she managed to keep it going.[153]

---

[149] ARP, Hilda Kuper to Audrey Richards, Los Angeles, [n.d. but c November 1961].
[150] Skype Interview with Mary Kuper, Cape Town-London, 13 August 2011.
[151] HKP, Box 40, Folder 22: Fortes – Correspondence, Hilda Kuper to Meyer Fortes, July 1967, Los Angeles.
[152] 'It's A Fine Finale for Hilda' *Rand Daily Mail*, 6 August 1981.
[153] Skype interview with Mary Kuper, Cape Town-London, 13 August 2011.

Historical ethnography and ethnographic fiction   231

Sobhuza gave Hilda permission to have Jenny, then a film and media student at UCLA, make a film about the *incwala* ceremony. This rare, private twenty-minute footage again illustrates Hilda's interest in exploring other media. It introduced Jenny to 'her Swazi world, which until then had been a hidden part of her life. I saw her in a completely different light – so vibrant.'[154]

One of Leo's UCLA graduate students, Bob Edgar, witnessed 'how royally they [Hilda and Leo] were treated' at the 1973 celebrations of Sobhuza's 50th year on the throne.[155] Hilda was one of the three main speakers at the televised funeral of Sobhuza in 1982. On her last return trip of 1991 she was awarded an honorary doctorate by the University of Swaziland.

There is much more to be said about Hilda's years in Los Angeles than her feelings of dislocation. Her fifteen years as a teacher, writer and editor at UCLA were highly productive. A full account of her American years would have to examine the contribution of her two significant edited volumes of 1965, the second with Leo, which emerged out of the work she did as organizer of the UCLA African Studies Center's seminar series. They were significant collections on the themes of urbanization and law in Africa that straddled disciplines and featured a host of internationally acclaimed scholars including Jan Vansina, Immanuel Wallerstein, Michael Banton and Max Gluckman.[156] They pushed her in the direction of the more universal anthropological orientation of her late career: of her view of anthropology as a humanistic discipline with an emphasis on the importance of comparative and cross-cultural study. One would also have to examine in detail her cultural and symbolic turn of the early 1970s. She had gone back to Swaziland to re-examine ritual in the context of social change, and was struck by the degree of cultural continuity. She wrote a succession of articles which were published in the most prestigious anthropological journals between 1971 and 1973, which examined the themes of clothing, space and symbolism in ritual contexts,[157] the last prompted by the

---

[154] Jenny Kuper, E-mail communication, 5 November 2014, London-Cape Town.
[155] Bob Edgar, E-mail correspondence, 1 October 2014, Washington-Cape Town.
[156] Hilda Kuper, ed., *Urbanization and Migration in West Africa* (Berkeley: University of California Press, 1965); Hilda Kuper and Leo Kuper, eds., *African Law: Adaptation and Development* (Berkeley: University of California Press, 1965).
[157] Hilda Kuper, 'Color Categories and Colonialism: The Swazi Case' in Victor Turner, ed., *Colonialism in Africa, 1870–1960* (Cambridge: Cambridge University Press, 1971), 286–309; Kuper, 'The Language of Sites in the Politics of Space', *American Anthropologist*, 74, 3 (1972), 411–25 [repr. in Setha Low, ed., *The Anthropology of Space and Place* (Malden: Blackwell, 2003)]; Kuper, 'A Royal Ritual in a Changing Political Context', *Cahiers d'Études Africaines*, 12 (1972), 593–615; Kuper, 'Clothing and Identity', *Comparative Studies in Social History*, 16 (1973), 348–67; Kuper, 'Costume and Cosmology: Animal Symbolism in the Ncwala', *Man*, 8, 4 (1973), 613–30.

232   Pioneers of the Field

writings of Victor Turner, to whom she dedicated the poem 'To Vic Who Blazed the Trail'.[158]

Above all, one would have to provide a sensitive account of the difficulties and frustrations of writing the official biography of Sobhuza over six years, from 1972 to 1978. It was something she took on only after much deliberation, out of a sense of service and obligation to her former patron and with some prompting from Leo. It proved to be a massive endeavour and ultimately 'a burden'.[159] The strictures of the official committee appointed to oversee the project meant that she was not free to write exactly what she wished to, and her somewhat sanitized account of Sobhuza's anti-democratic politics in the years after independence can only be properly evaluated in this light. The main obstacle was that in 1974 she lost a tin trunk containing all her taped interviews of two years, masses of documentary material and numerous cherished gifts from Swazi friends. It was only with Leo's support that she could be persuaded to continue. One would also need to appreciate her achievement, in this richly illustrated 374-page work, in balancing insights into the private life of Sobhuza with those relating to his skilful statesmanship, which she so greatly admired, his resilience in keeping at bay the forces of British colonial authority and the South African state, and charting a course based on cultural nationalism, which ultimately saw Swaziland through to independence.[160] Most reviewers praised the work, although some questioned the degree to which her relationship with Sobhuza and the political authorities in Swaziland had compromised her ability to be objective.[161]

One would also need to take account of her contribution as a teacher and mentor of a new generation of women anthropologists. At one time she had sixty first-year students in her class and seven doctoral students under her supervision, four of whom were working on southern Africa. There was a constant flow of South African students from the University of Natal and visitors from Swaziland, including Ben Magubane and Anthony Ngcobo, Leo's research assistants in Durban who came over to further their graduate studies, and later Thoko Ginindza, Hilda's research assistant from Swaziland who took an M.A. in African Studies at UCLA and then worked on a Ph.D. under Hilda while registered at

---

[158] Kuper, *A Witch in My Heart, Short Stories and Poems*, 129.
[159] Hilda Kuper Papers, Box 52, Folder 7: Correspondence 1970s-1980s, Hilda Kuper to Bengt Sundkler, Los Angeles, 1977.
[160] Kuper, *Sobhuza II*.
[161] For the most generous review, see Hugh Macmillan, *English Historical Review*, 96, 380 (1981), 675; for the most critical, see Angela P. Cheater, *American Anthropologist*, 82, 1 (1980), 210–11.

Historical ethnography and ethnographic fiction 233

Figure 5.7: Hilda's research assistant and later UCLA graduate student, Thoko Ginindza, doing tape-recorded interviews in the field for Hilda's biography of Sobhuza II, c 1973. The project almost derailed when the tape and a mass of other field materials went missing in Johannesburg in 1974 before they could be posted to Los Angeles.[162]

another university. Hilda's former graduate student and research assistant, Sondra Hale, still vividly recalls Hilda's contribution as teacher, mentor and female role model.

Hilda had the posture of authority and an upper-class theatrical accent to go with it. In graduate seminars Hilda was brilliant as a facilitator. She talked just enough and set an atmosphere that was comfortable for people to contribute. She was particularly exacting when it came to writing. I must have revised my 550-page dissertation on Nubians in Sudan some six or seven times, and I felt she still was not happy with it in the end... Those of us who knew her work knew that she was a brilliant writer so her comments on our writing were taken seriously.[163]

Another former student Barbara Meyerhoff, who later produced famous documentary films of American Jewish culture, eloquently described

---

[162] HKP, Box 60, Folder 2, Loose black and white photographs – Swaziland. For a record of the warm decades-long relationship between Hilda and Thoko Ginindza, see Hilda Kuper Papers, Box 24, Folder 20: T. Ginindza – Correspondence.
[163] Sondra Hale, E-mail communication, 8 October 2014, Los Angeles-Cape Town.

234   Pioneers of the Field

Hilda's style of supervision as 'a forcing of patience, a reflectiveness, a kind of listening'. She claimed that working under Hilda was a 'transformative experience' that allowed her to develop a more humanist attitude towards others.[164]

Her writing and teaching needed to be balanced with her family commitments, ensuring that Leo was happy and affirmed. One would certainly also have to take account of her return late in life to fiction. She had taught courses on ethnographic fiction, anthropology and literature, and on anthropology and biography during the 1970s, attended conference panels on these themes in the late 1970s and early 1980s, and had written an incisive self-reflective essay on biographical writing in African history, which foregrounded the complexity of the relationship between the biographer and his or her subject.[165] She wrote to her students and friends of her desire to return to creative writing, but was never able to devote as much time as she would have liked to her fiction. Sadly, she died before being able to author the introduction to the volume of plays, poems and short stories published in the year of her death by the University of Madison-Wisconsin. Finally, one would also wish to record her qualities as a person. Her colleague M.G. Smith referred to her having retained a sense of youth and a bubbling sense of joy throughout her life. Her daughter Mary touchingly remembers her as 'very expansive'.

She talked to everybody. She had the ability to connect to people extraordinarily well. She was such a source of warmth. You were lucky to be in her sphere.[166]

Conclusion

Hilda Beemer Kuper's contribution to the South African school of social anthropology deserves a book-length biography rather than a single essay. She was, as this chapter has sought to demonstrate, among the most prolific and eloquent anthropological writers of her generation: certainly in South Africa and arguably beyond. She produced four major monographs in a career spanning over half a century, following her undergraduate and graduate training in the British functionalist tradition

---

[164] Barbara Meyerhoff cited in Lewis Langness and Gelya Frank, eds., *Lives: An Anthropological Approach to Biography* (Novato, California: Chandler and Sharp, 1981), 155. On Meyerhoff's distinctive contribution to American anthropology, see Gelya Frank, 'The Ethnographic Films of Barbara G. Meyerhoff: Anthropology, Feminism and the Politics of Jewish Identity' in Ruth Behar and Deborah A. Gordon, eds., *Women Writing Culture* (Berkeley, LA and London: University of California Press, 1995), 207–32.

[165] Hilda Kuper, *Biography as Interpretation* (Indiana University, African Studies Programme, 11th Hans Wolff Memorial Lecture, April 1980), 25–59.

[166] Skype interview with Mary Kuper, Cape Town-London, 13 August 2011.

Historical ethnography and ethnographic fiction 235

under Winifred Hoernlé and Bronislaw Malinowski between 1929 and 1934. I have drawn attention to the importance of her background as a 'stranger' in white South African society, largely on account of her Jewish identity; to her life-changing fieldwork experience in Swaziland, between July 1934 and February 1937, highlighting the importance of what would be her five decade friendship with Sobhuza II. I have paid more attention than she did in her late-life seminar presentation to the significance of her South African writings during the two productive decades following the submission of her voluminous London University thesis in 1942.

I am referring to the launch of her parallel career as a creative writer, prompted initially by the need for catharsis, both personal, during the painful five years of separation from Leo, and political, during that depressing decade when liberal welfare activists like herself watched South Africa become swamped by the politics of racism, segregation and Afrikaner nationalism. The most notable feature of her first prolific period of creative writing, that which I associate with her time in Johannesburg between 1942 and 1947, was its versatility. While reviewers of her scholarly monographs published in these years remarked on her gifts as a writer, she was turning her skills to the crafting of beautiful love poems, deeply moving war poems, passionate political essays, fascinating commentaries on the reception of film and radio in South African locations and suburbs, and experiments in the writing of short stories which were also deeply political in their explorations of the pains of African experiences of migrant labour, the pass system, imprisonment and cultural alienation.

It was during her second, equally prolific, period as an experimental writer, her decade in Durban between 1952 and 1961, that her ethnographic fiction emerged in full form with more deeply developed characters and plots, although the theme of exploring African (and now Indian) experiences of conflict between tradition and modernity remained the same. While others have productively read her ethnographic fiction as South African protest literature (Vincent) and as part of a creative hidden genre in anthropology (Schmidt), I have explored the relationship between her fiction and her fieldwork by highlighting the importance of the autobiographical framing of the first phase of writing, and then her central concern with exploring inner worlds during the time of her remarkable study of Hindu religion in Durban. This 'turn to the heart', to the world of individual emotions and inner psychic life, was associated with her increasing sense of disillusion with the abstract and depersonalized structuralism that had come to dominate the British anthropological tradition from the 1940s to the 1960s. Her study of South African Indians, like her last and

236   Pioneers of the Field

most difficult monograph, her official biography of Sobhuza II, showcased her skills as an historian with its careful attention to evidence, detail and sensitivity to individual experience.

Why, we might ask, has a gifted and versatile writer who produced such an impressive body of work been neglected to the extent that her writings are seldom taught in South African anthropology departments today? Many South African graduate students have no knowledge at all of her texts. Some of the reasons echo those that I proposed in relation to the amnesia associated with Ellen Hellmann. Hilda was, like all the women featured in this volume, modest about her substantial intellectual contributions (although she was confident rather than self-effacing). She was touched and surprised when Audrey nominated her for the Rivers Memorial Prize for Fieldwork in 1961, commenting that Max was more concerned to promote her anthropological career than she herself was. She also always seemed to put Leo's career above her own, from the time of their moves to North Carolina, Coventry and Birmingham, when he established his career, to her insistence in private communications with the editor of his festschrift, Pierre van den Berghe, that the celebration be about him rather than her.[167] She also might have been neglected in part because of her political association with liberal rather than radical politics, although authors often like to mention her attendance of classes on Marx during her London years and her arrest during the Women's March of 1956.

There are two other reasons. One is the relative silence in histories of anthropology about writings that lie outside of journal articles and scholarly monographs. Her most significant contribution was her experiments with genre, her bold and precocious willingness to take ethnography outside of the constraints of scholarly convention and to begin to explore new and more intimate ways of communicating about cultural experience, as she did in her short stories, plays and novel. I find it significant that the only two authors who have paid close attention to her ethnographic fiction are literary scholars rather than anthropologists by training. The other is what I would call 'the tribal taint', here perhaps 'the royal tribal taint'. The work of Hilda Kuper is too often reduced to those writings most strongly associated with her relationship with the Swazi king: *An African Aristocracy* and *Sobhuza II*. Even Adam Kuper, who has expressed great indebtedness to Hilda for introducing him to anthropology and fieldwork, and whose relationship with Hilda was

---

[167] HKP, Box 40, Folder 2, Hilda Kuper to Pierre van den Berghe, Los Angeles, 14 August 1975.

Historical ethnography and ethnographic fiction   237

always deeply affectionate,[168] echoes the caricatured view that Hilda was yet another romantic celebrator of royalty and tradition: here in contrast with a male scholar. 'Schapera's own ethnography is free of the kind of celebration of traditional leaders that characterized some contemporary South African studies, notably *The Realm of the Rain-Queen* (1943) by E. Jensen Krige and J.D. Krige, and Hilda Kuper's *An African Aristocracy* (1947).'[169]

In the following chapter, I will address the narrow association of Eileen Jensen Krige's diverse and complex body of work with a simplistic romantic view of royal tradition. To read Hilda's immediately recognized classic simply, or primarily, as a romantic account of traditional leadership denies the complexity of her arguments about Swazi kinship, her important case for the unrecognized significance of

Figure 5.8: Hilda Kuper and Sobhuza II at the Reed Dance in Lobamba in September 1981.[170]

---

[168] He accompanied her as a driver on a fieldtrip to Swaziland in his late teens and she drew in later years on her anthropological networks to assist his access to field-sites in the Kalahari for his Cambridge doctoral research. Interview with Adam Kuper, London, 13 May 2013. For letters documenting the warm relationship between Adam in the Kalahari and Hilda in Los Angeles, see HKP, Box 40, Folder 29.
[169] Adam Kuper, 'Isaac Schapera', 30.
[170] HKP, Box 60, Folder 4, Photographs – Swaziland.

238   Pioneers of the Field

women in Swazi society. It also obscures the narrative artistry that readers found in her description of the *incwala* and her incisive sociological interpretation of the ritual as 'a drama of kingship', a pageantry in which rank was re-affirmed but also challenged in the songs of abuse of the king that allowed for Max's famous class-based reinterpretation. More seriously though, it denies the unusual degree of interest Hilda displayed in history. This was pronounced in all four monographs: *An African Aristocracy*, the accompanying volume of which it was initially part (published as *The Uniform of Colour*), her remarkable study on Hindus in Durban published in 1960 and her sensitive and complex biography of Sobhuza II (1978). A sense of history was also at the very heart of that creative body of ethnographic fiction which I have showcased in the foregoing pages. Her short stories, plays and novel explored, through character, plot and narrative, the relationship between tradition and social change in Swazi and South African culture. It was, rather ironically, only because it was so far ahead of its time, predating by decades the worldwide 'literary turn' in social anthropology, that it was never showcased in the festschrift which Hilda so richly deserved.

6 Feminizing the discipline: the long career of Eileen Jensen Krige (1904–1995)

> If we ask ourselves what was the secret of this remarkable woman's [Winifred Hoernlé's] wide influence and valuable contribution to social anthropology and human welfare, the answer I think is to be found not in her intellectual brilliance, nor yet in her balanced outlook and wonderful efficiency, important though they were. It lay in her complete selflessness. In all her work there was never any thought of self or desire for personal recognition. She never sought the limelight; she worked for causes. She was candid and fearless in her opinions and criticisms but so obvious was her sincerity and all-pervading kindliness that people seldom took exceptions to her criticisms.
>
> Eileen Krige, 'Agnes Winifred Hoernlé: An Appreciation', *African Studies*, 19, 1960, 143.

Perhaps to an even greater extent than any of the other career histories featured in this volume, Eileen Jensen Krige's life-work[1] exposes the limitations of the retrospective criterion by which scholarly 'contribution' to South African anthropology has typically been assessed in the male-dominated canon.[2] The two conventional yardsticks, an exaggerated emphasis on a single type of 'theoretical innovation', adherence to the so-called one-society approach,[3] and on the sole-authored field-based

---

[1] I have had the great privilege of having Eileen Krige's granddaughter, Emily-Ann Krige, as a constant guide, informal research assistant and covert co-author in many cases. It is difficult to acknowledge adequately her contribution to this chapter. In addition to my relying on her 144-page index to her grandmother's papers, compiled over fifteen months between 2001 and 2002, I have drawn on her step-by-step introduction to the hidden treasures in the Eileen Jensen Krige Collection, her provision of the rich materials from her grandmother's private papers at her parents' family home and her generous engagements with earlier drafts of this chapter. Thanks to Emily-Ann's parents, Thor and Dulcie Krige, as well her former students Eleanor Preston-Whyte and Patricia Davison (informally), and her former colleague John Argyle, for their enthusiasm, memories and materials.

[2] See Hammond-Tooke, *Imperfect Interpreters* who, to be fair, is more generous to Eileen than the other women scholars featured in this volume (85–9), perhaps because, as was the case with Monica, he had a warm personal relationship with her.

[3] Associated with a lineage of male scholars from Radcliffe-Brown through Schapera to Gluckman, this tradition is seen to have challenged and replaced the older, politically suspect, 'tribal' model introduced by Malinowski and rightly insisted on the need for the study of colonizer and colonized within a single analytic framework. See Andrew Bank, 'Introduction' in Bank and Bank, eds., *Inside African Anthropology*, 10–12.

240   Pioneers of the Field

monograph as the expression of published scholarship offers precious little purchase in understanding the depth and complexity of Eileen Krige's anthropological legacy. This is because she only produced one monograph, *The Social System of the Zulus*, published in 1936 when she was still in her early thirties. This was primarily a synthesis of a century of existing research on the Zulu rather than a field-based ethnography. Her best-known book, *The Realm of a Rain-Queen: A Study of Pattern in Lovedu Society* (1943), was co-authored with her husband Jack, officially a more senior scholar in the South African university departments in which they worked.[4]

As for the 'one-society' approach, her methodology has typically been read as a doggedly outdated functionalism associated with a suspect, if not outright tainted, racial politics. She is said to have been regarded as 'a stooge of the Nationalists' by at least some radicals at Natal University around the time of her retirement.[5] From her early career association with that champion of trusteeship and separate development, Jan Smuts, the uncle of her husband Jack and author of the Foreword to their book, to her late career ties with Gatsha Buthelezi, who contributed a chapter to her 1978 festschrift volume,[6] she is seen to have symbolized a conservative, 'tribal' brand of racial politics, the very embodiment of what outspoken Marxist-influenced Africanist critics like Archie Mafeje and Bernard Magubane would dub 'colonial anthropology'.[7] Indeed, Magubane professed that what he himself identified as his 'intense "hatred" of anthropology' began in Eileen's social anthropology classroom at the University of Natal in the late 1950s,[8] while Mafeje derided 'Ma-Krige' and her 'merry' view of Africa in private correspondence from

---

[4] Eileen Jensen Krige, *The Social System of the Zulus* (London: Longmans, 1936; Pietermaritzburg: Shuter & Shooter, 2nd edn 1950, 3rd impression 1965); Eileen Jensen Krige and Jack Krige, *The Realm of a Rain-Queen: A Study of the Pattern of Lovedu Society* (London, New York and Toronto: Oxford University Press in association with the IAI: reprinted 1943, 1947, 1956 and 1965). For her only other book-length publication, see Eileen Jensen Krige and John L. Comaroff, eds., *Essays on African Marriage in Southern Africa* (Cape Town and Johannesburg: Juta and Co. Ltd., 1981).

[5] Telephone Interview with Gina Buijs, Cape Town-Bedford, Eastern Cape, 26 April 2014.

[6] Mangosuthu G. Buthelezi, 'Early History of the Buthelezi Clan' in John Argyle and Eleanor Preston-Whyte, eds., *Social System and Tradition in Southern Africa: Essays in Honour of Eileen Krige* (Cape Town: Oxford University Press, 1978), 19–35.

[7] Archie Mafeje, 'The Ideology of Tribalism', *Journal of Modern African Studies*, 9, 2 (1971), 253–61; Mafeje, 'A Commentary on [Sally Falk Moore's] *Anthropology and Africa*', *CODESRIA Bulletin*, 2 (1996), 6–13.

[8] Bernard M. Magubane with Mbulelo V. Mzamane, *Bernard Magubane: My Life and Times* (Scottsville: University of Kwazulu-Natal Press, 2010), 143.

Feminizing the discipline 241

the mid-1960s.[9] 'Colonial anthropologists' like Eileen were charged with and found guilty of clinging to an ideology that romanticized 'tribe' and 'tradition', and took little account of history and social change.

Eileen's personal style doubtless reinforced this caricatured image of an out-of-touch maternal figure from a bygone era. She typically chose a plain and understated manner of dress, always tidy but with little interest in the flash and flamboyance of the new generation. Like Ellen Hellmann, she was modest to a fault. Her family remember her as someone who never spoke, let alone boasted, of her many achievements.[10]

It is in John Argyle and Eleanor Preston-Whyte's twelve page introduction to her festschrift that we can locate the seeds of a different kind of image of Eileen.[11] I endorse and extend their case for the central role of Winifred Hoernlé in Eileen's career as a student, ethnographer and teacher. The leitmotif of my version of her life story follows theirs in narrating her life as a tale of determined and courageous engagement with (and sometimes triumph over) considerable obstacles at successive stages of a long career. In general, I pay closer attention to the private and the personal, facilitated by my access to the voluminous and beautifully indexed Eileen Jensen Krige Papers, which are housed in the Killie Campbell Library in Durban. I highlight the methodological innovations in her fieldwork, again because I have been able to draw on fresh archival materials in the form of field-notes, diaries, published talks and transcripts of late-life reminiscences. In the most general of terms, I have chosen to foreground a particular image of Eileen as 'the university woman'. This is because her long career in founding the discipline in South African universities seems to me her most distinctive contribution in comparative terms.

Telling the story of Eileen as a university woman involves tracing her career from the time of her enrolment as an undergraduate student at Wits in its founding year in 1922 through to her formative role in consolidating social anthropology as a university subject at the University of South Africa in the early 1930s, Rhodes University in the early to mid-1940s and especially at Natal University from 1948 to 1970, the date of her retirement as professor and chair of what had become a thriving women-centred department. Her involvement in ethnography and the South African university-based discipline continued in the form

---

[9] WC, Uncatalogued Correspondence: M, Archie Mafeje to Monica Wilson, 15 December 1966, Cambridge.

[10] Interview with Thor and Dulcie Krige, Durban, 19 January 2014.

[11] John Argyle and Eleanor Preston-Whyte, 'Eileen Jensen Krige: Her Career and Achievements, Together with a Bibliography' in Argyle and Preston-Whyte, eds., *Social System and Tradition in Southern Africa*, ix–xxi.

242   Pioneers of the Field

of seminar and conference presentations and a flourish of publications from 1970 through to 1981, or we should say 1985, the year in which she attended her last South African Anthropological Association Conference and undertook her final field-trip, now at the age of eighty. In particular I will highlight her contribution to 'feminizing the discipline' by fore-grounding African women as subjects of her own ethnographic research and that of her many African, Indian and white women students whose careers as fieldworkers and ethnographers she energetically promoted.

A tomboy from a lower middle class 'frontier' family, 1904–1921

Eileen Claire Berenice Jensen was born on 12 November 1904 in Pretoria. She was the fourth of the six children of an immigrant Danish book-keeper, Arnold Otto Valdemar Jensen, and his wife, an independent-minded woman of Cape Afrikaner descent, Magdalena Maria (Maggy) Marais.[12] From the limited information we have about Eileen's childhood, it seems that her mother was the dominant influence. Maggy was a woman with unusually liberal ideas about the education of girls. Eileen's early child-hood was spent in the town of Wolmaransstad in the Eastern Transvaal. The family then moved to the 'frontier town' of Pietersburg (Polokwane) in the far northern Transvaal where Eileen completed her primary and early high school studies. She and her two sisters were offered the same opportunities as their brothers, seemingly against the inclinations of their father. Maggy firmly believed that modern women needed to earn their own keep. Eileen's parents separated in the 1920s, something relatively rare among white South Africans at the time. They got divorced in the 1930s so that Maggy would have the financial independence to run her own business, a boarding house establishment in Pretoria.

It was with the world of her brothers that Eileen would most strongly identify. She was closer in age to them than to her sisters, and her youthful inclinations were towards sport and outdoor pursuits. She spent her last two years of school at Pretoria Girls' High. The school found her a home with a family whose elder daughter was one of Eileen's classmates. In her matric year she was a boarder. Here she befriended Cato Smuts, daughter of 'Oom Jan', who would enrol with her at Wits in 1922 and became a life-long friend.

---

[12] The following information about her childhood and family background derives from her granddaughter, Emily-Ann, who was very close to Eileen in her old age. E-mail corre-spondence, Emily-Ann Krige to Andrew Bank, Durban-Cape Town, 5 April 2014.

Feminizing the discipline 243

Figure 6.1: Eileen and her university friends, Johannesburg Training College Hostel, c 1922. From left to right: Louise Jongbloed, Maisie Eaton, Cato Smuts and Eileen Jensen.[13]

---

[13] Thor and Dulcie Krige Family Papers, Durban (henceforth TDKP), Eileen's Personal Photographs, Labelled by Emily-Ann Krige, identification by Eileen Krige, c 1989.

244   Pioneers of the Field

Mrs Hoernlé's first disciple, Wits University, 1922–1928

Eileen's parents could not afford to pay university fees. There was one other option available to her. This was the Transvaal Education Department's loan scheme for trainee teachers, who were permitted to study part-time for a B.A. over four years. She took the loan and enrolled at Wits along with a thousand other students in February 1922, the year of its inauguration as a fully-fledged university. She stayed in a student hostel along with eleven other women students.[14] She studied History and Economics as her majors, being taught by the liberal historian William Miller Macmillan, whose research on poverty would encourage her to study poor relief in Johannesburg in her early graduate years. She completed her B.A. in three years, choosing to take social anthropology as an extra subject in her third and final year in 1924. This was the first time the subject had been offered. Given that there were just two students in Eileen's part-time class,[15] she formed a close bond with the social anthropology lecturer, Mrs Hoernlé. She recalls that her mentor was deeply influenced by Durkheim and his emphasis on social structure,[16] something that Eileen would develop across her long career.

Her correspondence with university friends points to an inner conflict as she struggled to balance the limited career expectations of white women of the time with her own more competitive and ambitious desire to succeed in a man's world. The division between male and female students, in her accounts, suggests that there was a much starker gender divide in the early 1920s than would be the case even five years later. Her descriptions resonate with those of Audrey Richards in post-war Cambridge, contrasting with those of younger peers like Monica Wilson and Hilda Kuper, who took their undergraduate degrees in Cambridge and Wits in the late 1920s. Eileen confessed that 'I much prefer the conversation of men among themselves to those of ladies … ' and described herself as 'a boy in thought and ideas'. 'I find it difficult to act the girl.'[17] She wrote of another inner struggle, that of the need to develop a sense of purpose and discipline in her early years of study. This required control of what she variously referred to as the 'frivolous' or 'baser' side of her nature. Letters from former school friends hint that during her second year at Wits she had already taken on the more serious attitude of the young woman scholar-in-the-making.[18]

---

[14] Emily-Ann Krige, E-mail correspondence, Durban-Cape Town, 7 April 2014.
[15] Patricia Davison, Interview with Eileen Krige, Durban, 4 December 1990.
[16] Eileen Jensen Krige, 'Agnes Winifred Hoernlé: An Appreciation', 142.
[17] TDKP, Eileen Jensen, Loose Notes ('Private Diary'), 18 March 1923, 20 March 1923 and 26 January 1924, Johannesburg.
[18] TDKP, Elsa Boyd to Eileen Jensen, 27 October 1924, Pretoria.

Feminizing the discipline 245

The most interesting document dating from her undergraduate years is her diary of the 1922 General Strike. Recorded just a month after she began her university career, her fifteen-page handwritten account of the progress of the strike between 15 and 22 March 1922 reveals exactly why Bruce Murray describes this as 'the most turbulent year in Wits University's history'.[19] I read her diary as her first ethnography. She displays not just a fluency and ease of writing style in simple accessible prose, but the characteristic attention to different viewpoints that is the essential requirement of the skilled fieldworker. The diary describes the General Strike literally exploding around her and her fellow students. Above all, it is the sense of immediacy, participant observation if you like, but especially her openness to the conflicting perspectives of the various protagonists – white strikers and Africans, male students and female students, the government and the rebels – that stands out in this brief but remarkable record.[20]

Three years later she experienced her first real taste of an ethnographic encounter. The events she describes took place during the vacation in the midst of her Honours degree in Economics.

In 1925 Cato and Valda Inglis [another student girlfriend] and I spent the July vacation with Mr Lennox Impey of the Witwatersrand Native Labour Corporation at Zoekwater, Northern Transvaal. Mr. Impey knew Modjadji's Chief Councillor, Moneni, who promised to conduct us to the famous Rain-Queen whom we had heard about. At that time few white people had actually seen her and we set out with great anticipation. The road turned out to be shocking; there were little water furrows crossing it every fifty yards or so, and though the distance from Duiwelskloof to the Queen's capital is only 21 miles, it took us the whole afternoon to reach the bottom of the steep hill leading up to the Chief's kraal. At that stage we broke an axle or spring . . . and we realized that we should not get back that night. We climbed the steep, stony hill and arrived at the top after dark. On hearing of our arrival, the Queen ordered a hut, sometimes used by a missionary when visiting the Christian village near the Queen's kraal, to be cleaned and prepared for us. We were given sleeping mats and offered food, which we refused as we did not relish mealie meal porridge and blackjack leaves. Early the next morning a basket of oranges arrived for Cato as daughter of General Smuts from the Queen, together with an invitation to meet her in her private reception hut.[21]

Eileen was fascinated by the Queen and resolved to return. Her university friends arranged another fortuitous meeting, that with Jacob Daniel (Jack) Krige the following year. Still just twenty-one, Eileen was completing her Masters' degree in Economics part-time. Jack was a man

---

[19] Murray, *Wits: The Early Years*, 71.
[20] TDKP, Eileen Jensen, 'Diary of the General Strike, 9–15 March [1922]'.
[21] TDKP, Eileen Krige to William Keith Hancock, 1 June 1966, Durban.

Figure 6.2: Envelope labelled 'July 1926 [sic]: Holiday with Lennie Impey at W.N.L.A., Zoekmakaar [sic].' Left to right: Valda Inglis, Lennox Impey, Eileen Jensen, Cato Smuts.[22]

of the world. Close to his thirtieth birthday, he had travelled widely overseas and had already been engaged twice.[23] After obtaining a distinction for his undergraduate science degree at Stellenbosch University (or Victoria College as it was still called), having majored in zoology, he won a Rhodes Scholarship to study law at Oxford in 1921–22, spending a year working for the International Labour Organization in Geneva after completing his degree.[24] He was a year into his articles at the Johannesburg Bar when Eileen met him.

For Jack it was love at first sight. Within two months he had proposed. She accepted and from May 1926 onwards he addressed her as 'Darling' or 'My dearest Eileen' rather than as 'Miss Jensen'. The thirty-seven surviving letters from Jack to Eileen during their two-and-a-half year engagement[25] suggest that their relationship was highly intellectual from the outset. While he doubted that he himself would ever 'undertake

---

[22] TDKP, Eileen's Personal Photographs, Envelope caption recorded by Eileen in late life.
[23] Interview with Emily-Ann Krige, Durban, 24 January 2014.
[24] Max Marwick, 'Obituary: Professor J.D. Krige', *African Studies*, 18, 3 (1959), 146–8.
[25] The first of these letters dates to 10 March 1926 shortly after they had met and the last dates to 10 November 1928, a few days before they got married. TDKP, Eileen's Personal Correspondence.

Feminizing the discipline

Figure 6.3: Eileen and Jack at the time of their engagement, 1926.[26]

something as formidable as original work', he clearly regarded anthropology as a fascinating field with great future potential in South Africa. Jack was an eclectic thinker with wide interests. He admitted to having some ten books on his bedside table, indicating that he liked dipping into each in turn.[27] Although not as widely read, Eileen was more focused on her intellectual path. She persuaded Jack to join her in studying social anthropology with Mrs Hoernlé the following year, when she both completed the second and final year of the undergraduate course and her Masters in Economics with a thesis on poor relief.[28] She continued her day job as a high school teacher. She was one of sixteen Wits students to be awarded a Master's degree between 1922 and 1927.[29] Jack's letters indicate that Eileen was Mrs Hoernlé's pet disciple. He gave an amusing account of how Mrs Hoernlé uncharacteristically delayed giving them a lecture simply because Eileen was unable to make the class.

One cannot help feeling great warmth towards Jack on reading his love letters. The letters reveal him to have been a deeply sensitive man with an

[26] TDKP, Eileen's Personal Photographs.
[27] TDKP, Jack Krige to Eileen Jensen, 8 April 1926, Johannesburg.
[28] Killie Campbell Library, Durban, Eileen Jensen Krige Papers (henceforth EJKP), File 14 Theses, Eileen Jensen, 'Problems of Poverty with Special Reference to Johannesburg' (unpublished M.A. thesis, Economics, Wits University, 1927), 62 pp.
[29] Murray, *Wits: The Early Years*, 149. She was among the first cohort of graduates in 1924.

248 Pioneers of the Field

unusually liberal attitude towards the place of women in the modern world, doubtless one of the many reasons why Eileen had agreed to his marriage proposal. Eileen found high school teaching frustrating. Jack empathized. He rightly suggested that she would be better suited to teaching people of her own age. Jack found his own job frustrating. He was a man of high ideals who was not willing to do the social networking necessary to get ahead in his profession. He too was poorly paid. The recurring theme in his letters is financial difficulty. His letters suggest that during their first year of engagement, as he put it, 'we are both passing through a rather depressing period of our lives'.[30]

Their mood changed quite suddenly in July 1928. This was a direct result of Eileen's first month-long fieldtrip to Modjadji. She was also now in the middle of her first year of part-time Honours in social anthropology. The classes were one-on-one sessions at Mrs Hoernlé's home. Her mentor proposed that she embark on her first fieldtrip, set up contacts with the Berlin Society missionary's daughter at Medingen mission, Marie Krause, and offered some gentle advice about fieldwork over tea.

The only preparation I had for my fieldwork was at afternoon tea with Mrs Hoernlé for an hour or more in which she stressed the importance of keeping one's interpreter on hand, insisting he was to regard himself as my mouthpiece, a lesson I have never forgotten ... She described how [gifts] for children had acted as a powerful incitement for Khoi adults to come to her, given that she had arrived out of the blue in an ox-wagon ... My introduction to the Queen was much easier, introduced as I was into her presence by Marie Krause, a week or so after I had begun on the mission station.[31]

Jack's letters reveal that fieldwork had given her a new-found sense of mission, one which re-energized both of them and would have lasting consequences for their career paths. He wrote touchingly of his great pride in her 'pioneering work'. 'I don't expect many other women will follow your example, but the possibilities and avenues of women's interests are thereby greatly increased.'[32]

Four months later, on 13 November 1928, Jack and Eileen got married.

Becoming an anthropologist, 1928–1936

Argyle and Preston-Whyte characterize Eileen and Jack's first joint fieldtrip of July 1930 as the beginning of their thirty-year anthropological

---

[30] TDKP, Jack Krige to Eileen Jensen, 9 October 1927, 5 April 1928, Johannesburg.
[31] EJKP, File 418, 'Writings and Jottings about Early Fieldwork Experiences', August–September 1986.
[32] TDKP, Jack Krige to Eileen Jensen, 13 July 1928, Johannesburg.

Feminizing the discipline 249

partnership. This view probably derives from Eileen's own romantic retrospective reconstruction in the years after Jack's death when she began referring to this trip as their 'second honeymoon'.[33] On my reading, their anthropological partnership in the full sense only began in April 1936, at the beginning of their seventeen months of intensive joint fieldwork in the Lovedu Reserve.

Between 1928 and 1936 Eileen was far more active than Jack in fieldwork and writing. Jack's work commitments as director of the programme of university correspondence courses in Pretoria meant that he was able to do just a single month of joint fieldwork, on the basis of which he published an important article on Lovedu law and marriage-cattle.[34] Contrast this with Eileen's dynamic anthropological research on three fronts, culminating in the publication of five major articles in local and international journals and one 412-page book published in London.[35] Before their major joint fieldwork, their intention seems to have been to promote her academic advancement, qualifications and research profile in the field of social anthropology. After all, he was a Rhodes Scholar and had a law degree from Oxford. He generously took a backseat in an unusual role reversal that allowed him to support his wife's fast-track career.

The first area of Eileen's research was the continuation of her Lovedu research. At the end of 1930 she had resigned as a high-school teacher and began her long career of university teaching, in the University Correspondence Courses for which Jack was director from 1931. They lived near their work in a flat in Pretoria. Eileen took charge of the undergraduate curriculum for social anthropology and ethnic history, including for students at the University of South Africa. Her passion was fieldwork, but funds for graduate research were difficult to come by. As the government's Native Affairs Department no longer offered grants, Mrs Hoernlé prompted her to apply to the Bantu Studies Committee at Wits. Eileen's grant application indicated that she intended

---

[33] Patricia Davison interview with Eileen Krige, Durban, 4 December 1990 cited in Patricia Davison and George Mahashe, 'Visualizing the Realm of the Rain-Queen: The Production and Circulation of Eileen and Jack Krige's Lobedu Fieldwork Photographs from the 1930s' in Diana Wylie and Andrew Bank, eds., *Kronos: Southern African Histories, Special Issue: Documentary Photography in South Africa*, 38 (November 2012), 50.

[34] Jack Krige, 'Bridewealth in Balobedu Marriage Ceremonies', *Bantu Studies*, 8, 2 (1934), 135–50.

[35] Eileen Jensen Krige, *The Social System of the Zulus*; 'Agricultural Ceremonies and Practices of the Balobedu', *Bantu Studies*, 5, 2 (1931), 207–39; 'The Social Significance of Beer among the Balobedu', *Bantu Studies*, 6, 3 (1932), 343–57; 'Some Social and Economic Facts revealed in Native Family Budgets', *Race Relations*, 1 (1934), 94–108; (with G.W.K. Mahlobo), 'Transition from Childhood to Adulthood among the Zulu', *Bantu Studies*, 8, 2 (1934), 157–91; 'Changing Conditions in Marital Relations and Parental Duties among Urbanized Natives', *Africa*, 9, 1 (1936), 1–23.

250   Pioneers of the Field

'Camping in the reserve and with aid of interpreter [Andreas Matatanya] gain[ing] information especially into agricultural customs and customs concerning women'. Jack would do preliminary investigations into Lovedu law and politics. Their thirty pound budget was meant to cover 'rail-fare, motor-transport, subsistence, tent equipment', with additional money for 'interpreters, gifts etc.'.[36] We know that they took with them a Zeiss camera, of which Eileen made liberal use, capturing over a hundred photographs during her 1930 and 1932 fieldtrips. Most of these were 'visual field-notes', informal shots showing the micro-social world of the field and the research assistants and informants with whom they worked. In their second extended period of joint fieldwork, their photography would be more structured and oriented towards images that could be used to illustrate general themes in a functionalist monograph.[37]

Eileen had spent two years studying Southern Sotho at Wits, which gave her a further advantage over Jack, even though this was diminished by the fact that the Lovedu spoke a dialect of Northern Sotho inflected by tshiVenda for which there was no dictionary. Marie Krause was fluent in khiLovedu and served as their first translator.[38] They camped in an area of the Lovedu Reserve run by a woman headman.

[Our camp site] commanded a view over the whole of the Northern Transvaal Lowveld up to the borders of the Kruger National Park . . . Reaping was in full swing and I had the experience of watching the whole process of winnowing after loosening millet in the ear . . . The idea of my article on 'The Social Significance of Beer' was born when harvest beer was being carried by various files of women, usually to in-laws or in payment of a debt to a doctor . . . I [then] found [that] beer was & is also used as a food, even babies being fed on *kepeye*, a fermented porridge.[39]

Published in *Bantu Studies* in 1932, her article was the first in the field to make a compelling case for the complex cultural role played by beer in traditional African societies.[40] As such it may be read as opening up an entire subtheme in South African anthropology.[41]

---

[36] Wits University, William Cullen Library, Rheinallt-Jones Papers, AD843/RJ, Kb32.2.1.5, Box 182, SAIRR: Education: Wits Department of Bantu Affairs: Bantu Affairs Research Committee, 1930–1, E. Krige.

[37] This is the argument presented in detail in Patricia Davison and George Mahashe, 'Visualizing the Realm of the Rain-Queen', 47–64, which also gives a vivid sense of the spatial layout of their field-sites in 1930, 1932 and 1936–8.

[38] EJKP, File 418, 'Writings and Jottings about Early Fieldwork Experiences', August–September 1986.

[39] *Ibid.*

[40] Eileen Jensen Krige, 'The Social Significance of Beer among the Balobedu', *Bantu Studies*, 6 (1932), 343–57.

[41] For the most recent monographs, see Pat McAllister, *Building the Homestead: Agriculture, Labour and Beer in South Africa's Transkei* (Aldershot: Ashgate, 2001); *Xhosa Beer Drinking Rituals: Power, Practice and Performance in the South African Rural Periphery* (Durham, NC: Carolina: Academic Press, 2006).

Feminizing the discipline

251

The second subfield in which she produced research in these years was that of urban anthropology, albeit in a far less detailed and engaged way than her peers Monica Hunter and Ellen Hellmann. Eileen also went into South African townships in the early 1930s, a time when the field of urban anthropology in Africa had yet to be established. It is fair to assume that it was Mrs Hoernlé's welfare-oriented engagement with the new anthropological field of 'culture contact' that prompted Eileen to begin studying three African locations on the north-western outskirts of Pretoria in the early months of 1932, and then again from March to May 1934. Her interest was in the living conditions of Africans in what seemed to be relatively well-established urban settings, by contrast, say, with the thoroughly marginalized slum-dwelling beer-brewers that Ellen was studying in Rooiyard. Her main field-site, Marabastad, was almost as old as Pretoria itself, having been established in the 1890s. She found that even in this well-settled community, where there were third-generation urban-dwellers, the degree of poverty as gauged from wages, expenditure and African family budgets was absolutely dire. 'There are not many families', she concluded in the essay she published for a liberal audience in the *Race Relations Journal* in 1934, 'that can be said to be well fed and well clothed, and almost all saving that takes place, is at the expense of the daily necessities of life.' Eileen demonstrated the way in which community networks offered a support system for families living on the poverty line and the extent to which urban African families were forced to rely on women's work for their very survival.[42]

The essay she published in *Africa* in 1936 was a more ambitious attempt to gauge 'culture change' in relation to the theme of African marriage. Here she examined the complex new array of African marriage forms in these urban locations, highlighting African innovation in a context of dislocation. Rural values still operated, but were typically diluted, modified or adapted as in monetary payments for *lobola*.[43] This theme would be something to which she returned in more detail in her late-life research.

The most important research subfield in this formative phase of her career was her Zulu ethnography, culminating in the publication of *The Social System of the Zulus* in 1936. Her book has generally been read as a structural-functionalist overview of Zulu culture with kinship and the life-stage rituals foregrounded, but one which addressed the economic, political and cultural aspects of Zulu life, including song, dance and

---

[42] Eileen Jensen Krige, 'Some Social and Economic Facts revealed in Native Family Budgets', *Race Relations*, 1 (1934), 94–108.

[43] Eileen Jensen Krige, 'Changing Conditions in Marital Relations and Parental Duties among Urbanized Natives', *Africa*, 9, 1 (1936), 14–15.

252   Pioneers of the Field

folktales. While her rigour in synthesizing a century of scholarship on Zulu culture was the book's foremost achievement, I am, following John Argyle, also inclined to highlight the degree of methodological innovation, in particular the importance of her collaborative work with a Zulu court interpreter in the Port Shepstone district named George Washington Mahlobo. Eileen indicated to Argyle that her Zulu study had commenced in her years as an Honours student in the late 1920s, but it really took off when she established contact with Mahlobo, who was one of her correspondence students. She had already experimented in her earlier Lovedu research with combining teaching with the acquisition from her students of research data from the field.[44]

This methodology was a response to the difficulties of finding research funding for fieldtrips. She developed it on a large scale in her work with Mahlobo. He provided extensive information about Zulu culture himself, interviewed Zulu informants in his local area, wrote to old friends in Zululand where he had grown up, produced an ethnographic manuscript on Zulu marriage (which predated his work with Eileen) and then co-authored with her an article that was published in *Bantu Studies* in 1934. Working within the tight frameworks set out in Eileen's questionnaires, Mahlobo submitted the data in a succession of 'letters' from the field, as they were referenced, posted from Port Shepstone between 1932 and 1934.[45] These materials served as the effective data base for Eileen's analysis. Mahlobo thus effectively acted as an insider anthropologist at a time when the South African Inter-University African Studies Committee was reflecting on how anthropologists could make more effective use of African interlocutors on site in their field research.[46]

The Krige–Mahlobo article, which also featured as a chapter in her book, includes fascinating analyses of the succession of Zulu male life-stage rituals: some still being practised, others effectively obsolete.[47] Its importance as a rare example of relatively full 'co-production of scientific knowledge'[48] should not be underestimated. For four decades their article was the only fully jointly researched and co-authored publication by a

---

[44] Patricia Davison Private Papers, Andreas Matatanya to Eileen Krige, 20 September 1931, 9 January 1932, 5 February 1932, Balobedu School. Eileen sent Andreas materials and study notes for his matric, having filled in the forms and assisted in his choice of subjects. She also sent gifts to him and his wife, items of clothing that were evidently treasured and Andreas named his first child Daniel after Jack whose second name was Daniel.

[45] The Eileen Krige Papers, unfortunately, do not include any traces of these letters nor their initial correspondence regarding his anthropological studies nor indeed his earlier manuscript on Zulu marriage.

[46] See Isaac Schapera, 'The Present and Future State of Ethnographic Research in South Africa', *Bantu Studies*, 8 (1934), 272–3.

[47] Krige and Mahlobo, 'Transition for Childhood to Adulthood among the Zulu', *Bantu Studies*, 8, 1 (1934), 157–91.

[48] Schumaker, *Africanizing Anthropology*, 1–22.

Feminizing the discipline 253

white anthropologist and a black anthropologist to feature in *Bantu Studies*, or *African Studies* as it was known from 1942.

Eileen's study also made extensive use of the knowledge of government officials, again garnered by correspondence. She thanked the only African member of the teaching staff at Wits, the Zulu linguist Benedict W. Vilakazi, for proof-reading her manuscript. Her most effusive acknowledgement was reserved for her mentor.

> I have to express something more than indebtedness to Mrs. A.W. Hoernlé, Senior Lecturer in Social Anthropology, University of Witwatersrand, Johannesburg, to whom I owe all my anthropological training. Although I cannot hope to have done justice to her deep insight and understanding, I can still willingly and gratefully acknowledge that whatever is valuable in this work, the background of ideas into which I have classified my material and the enthusiasm that has enabled me to complete my study – all this and more I owe to her tuition, encouragement and assistance.[49]

Although the book was ready for publication before Eileen and Jack left for London in March 1935, where they would spend a year attending lectures at the LSE and Malinowski's famous seminars, having just scraped together enough funding, her study only came out just after they had entered the field a year later, for what would truly be 'joint fieldwork'. In April 1936 Mrs Hoernlé wrote to Modjadji to send Eileen a copy of a warm review of her book from the *Times Literary Supplement* in London. 'On Sunday I think there should be a long one by Mr Hoernlé in the *Sunday Times*. I shall send that along too. So far they have all been very favourable.'[50]

Her book was indeed favourably, albeit sparsely, reviewed in scholarly journals, most notably by Melville Herskovits in the *American Anthropologist*.[51] Eileen's Zulu ethnography has stood the test of time. In the 1970s Meyer Fortes wrote that it was regarded as a 'classic'. In his obituary essay, John Argyle comments that revisiting the text in 1995 confirmed his initial impressions regarding its rigour, comprehensiveness and overall sense of cohesion.[52]

---

[49] Eileen Jensen Krige, *The Social System of the Zulus* (London: Longman, 1936), ix–x.
[50] EJKP, Mrs Hoernlé to Eileen Krige, 27 April 1936, Johannesburg.
[51] Mellville Herskovits, 'Review of Eileen Jensen Krige, *The Social System of the Zulus*', *American Anthropology*, 39, 4 (October–December 1937), 690–2. See also Cullen Young, 'Review of *Social System of the Zulus*', *Man*, 37 (January 1937), 15.
[52] Meyer Fortes, 'Preface' in Harriet (Sibisi) Ngubane, *Body and Mind in Zulu Medicine: An Ethnography of Health and Disease in Nyuswa-Zulu Thought and Practice* (London: Academic Press, 1979), viii; John Argyle, 'Eileen Jensen Krige (1904–1995)', *African Studies*, 54, 2 (1995), 113.

254   Pioneers of the Field

Malinowski, Richards and *The Realm of a Rain-Queen*, 1936–1939

Writing in 1977 Monica Wilson reflected that 'Eileen Krige's most important book is still *The Realm of a Rain-Queen* (1943) which she wrote with J.D. Krige. The anthropologists' comment used to be that Eileen's chapters were the best! ... This book still stands as an excellent field study.'[53] *The Realm* remains the ethnography with which Eileen is most strongly associated, albeit usually rather too exclusively.

One of the marked features of her and Jack's study was the gendered division of labour. This can be traced back to Eileen's preliminary field-trips of 1928, 1930 and 1932, when she focused on women's work and women's ceremonies. According to a grant application,

(1) Mrs Krige would study the position of women in the social, political and religious activities, in an attempt to estimate their place and function in the relevant institutions and organisations; the position of the Queen of the tribe and the ritual of rain-making; the initiation of girls and the economic system of the people ...

(2) Mr Krige would investigate the system of law ..., the political system, boys' initiation and sib [clan] organisation ...[54]

Although their book, like Eileen's *Social System of the Zulus*, would identify Mrs Hoernlé as their primary inspiration, famously being dedicated to 'The Mother of Anthropology in South Africa', there is little doubt that their study was equally strongly influenced by Malinowski. Eileen recalls having found 'the mental atmosphere' at the LSE and the London seminars 'tremendously stimulating'.[55] More generally, Malinowski's influence can be seen in the depth of their commitment to an extended period of immersed participant observation, seventeen months in all, as well as in their explicitly stated commitment to the functionalist model of analysing a traditional culture as a composite of different 'elements' that they too interpreted as being relatively harmoniously integrated into a single whole. 'Our main object', they declared in their November 1939 Preface, had been 'the task of showing the nature of the parts and their relation to one another'.[56]

---

[53] WC, Uncatalogued correspondence re: Eileen Krige, Monica Wilson, Draft of reference to Prof. J.V.O. Reid, 14 February 1977.

[54] Wits University, William Cullen Library, Rheinallt-Jones Papers, AD843/RJ, Kb18.4 (file 3), Inter-University Committee for African Studies, 1934, J.D. Krige and Eileen Krige to Rheinallt-Jones, Pretoria, 20 July 1934.

[55] EJKP, File 417, Eileen Krige, Curriculum Vitae, 1959, 1.

[56] Eileen Jensen Krige and Jack D. Krige, 'Preface' to Krige and Krige, *The Realm* (London: Oxford University Press, 1943), written from Pretoria in November 1939 (xii).

Feminizing the discipline 255

Figure 6.4: Deputy South African Prime Minister Jan Smuts visiting Eileen and Jack at their field base, 1937. He later wrote the Foreword to their book. From left to right: Cato Clark (née Smuts), Jack Krige, Eileen Krige, Bancroft Clark, Jan Smuts, two local men and three children (unidentified).[57]

Most of the book's reviewers commented on their achievement in overcoming particular difficulties associated with their field-site. Their letters from the field in the early months confirm that their excitement about joint fieldwork had given way to disappointment when faced with realities on the ground. To begin with there was the matter of trust. Despite Eileen's history of contact, they were still regarded with suspicion, made all the more acute by the well-known reserve of the still isolated Lovedu and especially their secrecy regarding the royal matters which Eileen was investigating: the Queen's rain-making powers and other royal ceremonies and customs.[58] They were initially anxious about whether their funds would allow them to spend enough time to

[57] Jack and Eileen Krige Photographic Collection, Iziko South African Museum, Cape Town.
[58] EJKP, File 418, 'Writings and Jottings about Early Fieldwork Experiences', Aug.–Sept. 1986, 2.

256   Pioneers of the Field

do their study thoroughly. Worries about finance had of course been a constant theme of their frustrating attempts to plan for the future.

The language remained a more persistent hurdle. Eileen commented, after a further year in the field, that she was hoping to make 'one last effort to master the language [khiLovedu]'. Late-life reminiscences reveal that they were only able to develop a 'working knowledge' of, rather than the complete fluency in, khiLovedu.[59]

This meant a great dependence on research assistants. Her field diaries and notes reveal impatience and then growing frustration as she struggled to find an adequate replacement for Andreas Matatanya, who had now taken up a post as a government clerk. She and Jack each needed an interpreter, as they generally worked in different places on different themes. It was, in fact, only as late as November 1937, about a year into fieldwork, that Eileen found an effective replacement. This is how she recalls her early work with him.

I tried teaching one or two promising people to write [texts for us] ... by giving them the symbols used by the International African Institute [for recording Bantu languages], but only one, a man of about 22 who had just returned from migrant labour and who had reached Standard IV displayed any interest or facility. Simeon began writing children's stories such as those I was hearing at the herd-boys' fireplace at night ... [This] helped me a great deal because of the repetitive songs and episodes in the tales. Then I thought of asking him to write on a few ethnographic topics and much later to write a diary of events of interest to him and also to me, especially in the period after we had left [the field].[60]

As is well known, Eileen developed an unusually engaged long-term working relationship with Simeon Modjadji, who would become a close friend over half a century of collaborative fieldwork. He typically addressed her by her Lovedu name, *Malefokana*, which meant 'mother of the bushveld'.[61] The remarkable story of the subsequent half-century of cultural knowledge co-production between Eileen and Simeon has yet to be written. It would reveal that he produced an estimated 2,800 40-line pages of text for her in khiLovedu across his field-notes, diaries and letters,[62] the latter in reply to her ever-insistent and obsessively detailed questionnaires. In the 1960s he came to her house in Durban to work with her for a fortnight on the analysis of field materials, confirming my impression that he would much more appropriately be described as an insider anthropologist rather than as a research assistant.[63]

---

[59] *Ibid.*, 2.   [60] *Ibid.*, 2.

[61] EJKP, File 71: Letters from Simeon Modjadji to Eileen Krige. This differs from the definition given in Davison and Mahashe, 'Visualising the Realm of a Rain Queen', 50.

[62] Interview with Dulcie Krige, Durban, 22 January 2014.

[63] The analysis awaits the translation of this voluminous body of texts from khiLovedu to English.

Feminizing the discipline 257

She and Jack wrote up their findings swiftly, presumably mindful of their need to find proper employment. The preface to the book dates to November 1939, a year after a burst appendix had forced Jack to leave the field. He had earlier contracted malaria and had relapses which also meant absences from the field.[64] It was left to Eileen to make a series of short visits in the early months of 1939 to capture their last data. Their book was only published four years later, mainly because of substantial delays following the outbreak of war.

It was Audrey Richards who effectively saw the book through to publication. Private correspondence between Audrey and Jack, dating to 1941 and 1942, reveals quite how demanding this task proved to be.[65] Audrey had been one of their lecturers at the LSE and they had become close friends during her three years at Wits from January 1938. Ever generous to her intellectual friends, Audrey went further. She wrote what was, in my view, the only fully engaged review of their study. It ran across three pages of *Man*. She began by advertising the book as 'an important new monograph', 'a mine of information on a little known area'. She drew attention to their use of Malinowski's concept of 'reciprocity'. 'They show the part played by different systems of joint work and reciprocal services in agriculture and social life … I know of no more stimulating account of the contrast between the competitive individualistic economy of the European, known and despised as a *bisniz* transaction, and the Bantu system of reciprocal co-operation.' Audrey was taken with the 'detailed descriptive knowledge of their environment, its soil, flora and fauna, and general agricultural possibilities'.

She was the only reviewer to recognize the innovative quantitative approach that Eileen brought to the study of witchcraft.[66] This involved compiling a meticulous record of exactly who it was that made witchcraft accusations. Eileen did this by calculating the numbers of cases brought before courts by 'strangers' and 'relatives', respectively, with relatives subdivided into categories of co-wives, husbands and wives. She found that close family members dominated as accusers, allowing her then to explore the relationship between witchcraft and the underlying Lovedu kinship structures within which they were embedded.

---

[64] EJKP, File 363, Eileen Jensen Krige, Rough Notes for a Talk on her Early Fieldwork entitled 'Reminiscences of an Anthropologist in the Field', 9.

[65] See esp. TDKP, Audrey Richards to Jack Krige, Oxford, 20 June 1941.

[66] Audrey Richards, 'Review of *The Realm of a Rain-Queen*', *Man*, 44 (November–December 1944), 148–50. The book was also reviewed in prominent journals like *African Studies*, the *American Anthropologist*, as well as the popular press. The 1965 dustjacket cites extracts from *The Times Literary Supplement*, *The New Statesman* and the *Belfast Telegraph*.

258   Pioneers of the Field

Audrey might have made more of Eileen's enduring insights into the unusual prominence of women in Lovedu society, especially given her own experience of working in a matriarchal society. Eileen's chapters on kinship and ritual revealed women's prominence in positions of political and ceremonial authority, from the Queen and her 'wives' through to women headmen and women officiators in religious ritual. The overall argument of the study was for the distinctiveness of the Lovedu cultural complex, or 'pattern', in the book's subtitle, and the need to understand this complex, as far as possible, from the inside.

Eileen submitted her chapters on magic, ritual and witchcraft as a Wits doctoral thesis, presumably at Mrs Hoernlé's prompting, for which she was awarded a D.Litt. in June 1940.[67]

Applied anthropology and teaching with Jack at Rhodes and Natal, 1940–1959

In her last letter to Jack before their book's publication, Audrey wrote to congratulate Eileen on a 'triple birth'.

> I hope that by the time you get this you will be a proud father of a beautiful son (or daughter) and very pleased with life. For Eileen to take on a new leadership and produce a child seems to me a very gallant effort. Not to mention of course the book. It makes a kind of triple birth which is very impressive.[68]

Eileen was thirty-seven years old when Dan was born in Grahamstown in April 1942. She had consciously put off becoming a mother in order to pursue her passion for anthropology. Friends and relatives are said to have been 'startled' by the news that she had fallen pregnant.[69] But there is no doubt that she had always planned to have children and, as we shall see, she would be a loving and thoroughly committed mother to her two sons. Their second son, Thor, was also born in Grahamstown, in March 1946.

The third of Eileen's births was the launch of her career as a university lecturer. We should recall that, unlike any of the other women featured in this study, she had formally trained as a teacher. She had, in fact, been offered a full-time lectureship at Wits as a replacement for Audrey Richards, who was negotiating with the university to return to war-torn Europe. We do not know exactly why she turned down the offer in favour of following Jack to Rhodes, as she was undoubtedly his senior in terms of both teaching experience and research profile. She may have felt that her

---

[67] EJKP, File 15, Draft of Eileen Krige, 'Medicine, Magic and Religion of the Lovedu' (unpublished D.Litt, Social Anthropology, Wits University, 1940), 255 pp.
[68] TDKP, Audrey Richards to Jack Krige, London, 5 April 1942.
[69] Interview with Thor Krige, Durban, 19 January 2014.

Feminizing the discipline

Figure 6.5: Eileen and baby Thor, Durban, 1946.[70]

primary commitment was to his career, given that he was already in his mid-forties. She was probably also motivated by the prospect of their being able to establish a new African Studies Department and spread the discipline of social anthropology to another South African university. At this time there were just six anthropology departments across South Africa.

Jack's appointment at Rhodes was as a senior lecturer in social anthropology and head of the newly created Department of Bantu (African) Studies, which included a Department of African Languages and one of African and Comparative Law, in which he also lectured. Eileen initially

---

[70] TDKP, Eileen's Personal Photographs.

260   Pioneers of the Field

threw herself into research in Grahamstown location as we will see below. Then at an advanced stage of pregnancy, she was offered and agreed to take on a leadership role in creating a new School of Social Sciences. She was appointed as a lecturer in Sociology and put in charge of the general organization of the new department. When she resigned at the end of her third year due to the pressure of running a home and looking after a baby boy, the department was firmly established with over sixty registered students.[71]

Eileen's decade of work in social welfare projects may be traced back to August 1940 when, at the request of the Wage Board, she embarked upon a three-month study in Grahamstown location, which had a population of around 10,000 people. Ever meticulous, she filled twenty-seven notebooks with information about diet, family budgets and living conditions, with particular attention to her select sample of thirty families.[72] Her final report, presented in the form of a memorandum to the National Health Commission in 1942, reveals that she was shocked by the depth of poverty of Africans in the location, a poverty that went far beyond what she had experienced in the Pretoria location of Marabastad. The tone of her report is well captured in its concluding paragraph.

The figures speak clearly enough. But their full implications in terms of the actual misery, squalor and distress among people can only be realised when they are interpreted in the light of the evidence provided by personal observation. There were, for example, cases of old women and young children suffering hunger, going without food periodically, as they pathetically awaited the coming of the next pay day . . . It is literally impossible for the average location Native, with the means at his disposal, to obtain a sufficient quantity of food. The extent of malnutrition, judged by the scale referred to . . ., can only be described as so alarming that far-reaching measures and remedies are both indispensable and urgently needed.[73]

In keeping with her ethnographic writings both before and after, her sympathies lay mainly with African mothers and wives who always seem to have been her primary informants. It was the women, she emphasized, who bore the burden of rearing families.

The research drove her to undertake welfare projects, following the precedent of Mrs Hoernlé. She took the lead in establishing a TB clinic, a children's crèche and a soup kitchen in the location, which she could do in

---

[71] EJKP, File 417, 'Anthropological Investigations Applied to Social Welfare' in Eileen Krige, Curriculum Vitae, Prepared for application for Chair of Social Anthropology [at Natal University], c. May 1959, 4.

[72] EJKP, Files 1–6, Notebooks of Family Budgets from Grahamstown Locations.

[73] EJKP, File 7, 'Memorandum submitted to the National Health Commission by E. Jensen Krige, Social Science Department, Rhodes University College on "Nutrition among Natives of Grahamstown Locations"', 9.

Feminizing the discipline 261

part because of her position as President of the local branch of the National Council of Women (1942–3) and Executive Member of the District Council of Grahamstown (1942–6).[74]

Eileen's energetic commitment to African social welfare was carried over to Durban after she and Jack moved to the University of Natal in late 1946 to start another anthropology and African Studies Department. In her history of the Valley Trust and Health Care Centre in Botha's Hill, Natal, Diana Wylie reveals that Eileen and Jack became involved in this initiative as early as 1946–7, five years before the Centre was formally launched. Wylie goes on to demonstrate that Eileen and Jack were 'an influential force' in the Valley Trust throughout the 1950s, obtaining fellowships from Oxford's Nuffield Foundation to support fieldwork on social change by a talented new cohort of African students, most notably Absolom Vilakazi and Harriet Sibisi.[75]

Eileen's day job, from January 1948, was as a lecturer and, from 1953, a senior lecturer, in the Social Anthropology Department, working alongside Jack. Their younger son, Thor, recalls the deep affection which they continued to have for one another and the hands-on dedication of Eileen in her belated role as mother. She used to fetch and carry her boys to and from school every weekday lunch break to ensure that they had a proper home-cooked meal. Thor's boyhood memories are, however, dominated by the atmosphere of his parent's dedicated commitment to the university.

My father sat at his desk virtually the whole day and into the evenings. My mother always seemed to be working. I never saw her reading anything that wasn't work related. She would spend days and days just writing references ...[76]

This strict discipline and hard work need to be understood in the context of the demanding period in which they worked. Argyle and Preston-Whyte recall that there was an almost complete lack of administrative support in the formative years of their department's history. The apartheid laws meant that from the late 1950s Eileen and Jack were forced to teach their students in racially segregated classes. They also had part-time and full-time streams. This meant 'sometimes delivering the same lecture four times in a teaching week that had to be extended to Saturdays and even Sunday mornings!'[77] Little wonder that Eileen felt that her

---

[74] *Ibid.*, 3.
[75] Diana Wylie, *Starving on a Full Stomach: Hunger and the Triumphs of Cultural Racism in Modern South Africa* (Charlottesville and London: University Press of Virginia, 2001), 191–2.
[76] Interview with Thor Krige, Durban, 19 January 2014.
[77] Argyle and Preston-Whyte, 'Introduction', xix.

262   Pioneers of the Field

anthropological peers at Cambridge were 'in clover compared with Natal University staff'.[78]

They not only taught together, but continued to write articles together and jointly ran adult education courses.[79] They were both actively involved in university administration, for which Jack had a particular gift.[80] It seems appropriate to conclude this section on their teaching partnership with this endearing anecdote told on the occasion of the award of an honorary doctorate to Eileen.

It is impossible to think of either of these two professors of this University [as Eileen had also become from 1960] without immediately thinking of the other. They were a team, so wedded to each other and Social Anthropology that one scarcely ever asked the question 'Which Krige?' because the answer was inevitably 'Both'.[81]

A triple loss, 1959–1964

Eileen and her boys were devastated when Jack suffered a fatal heart attack while driving home from campus on 10 April 1959. They knew that he had suffered from a weak heart for many years. But none of this diminished the shock of his sudden death at the age of sixty-two.

Student demands meant that Eileen had little time to recuperate. She wrote in typically understated terms to Killie Campbell. 'I have found it somewhat of a strain to be back at the University where everything all the time reminds me of the one thing I must try to keep out of my mind at present.'[82] Thor recalls that his mother took sleeping pills for two years to cope with the loss.[83]

Hilda Kuper was employed as a substitute lecturer for Jack. But the responsibility of running a department with a growing cohort of graduates and over a hundred undergraduates now fell entirely on the shoulders of Eileen. In January 1960 she was formally appointed as the new head of department and promoted to a full professorship.

[78] EJKP, File 417, Copy of letter from Eileen Krige to Killie Campbell, 23 October 1964, Somerset, England.

[79] For example, they ran a course on African culture at the adult education section of Natal Technical College in Aug. 1953, giving lectures on alternate week-nights. See EJKP, File 206.

[80] Max Marwick, 'Obituary: Professor J.D. Krige', *African Studies*, 18, 3 (1959), 147–8.

[81] J.V.O. Reid, 'Citation for Honorary Doctorate, D. Soc. Sci. to Eileen Jensen Krige', 1977 in Reid, *Honoris Causa II: Laudations spoken in presenting Honorary Graduates in the University of Natal, 1968–1980* (Durban: Academic Ceremonials Committee, University of Natal Press, 1984), 57.

[82] EJKP, File 417, Copy of letter from Eileen Krige to Killie Campbell, 26 April 1959, Durban.

[83] Interview with Thor Krige, Durban, 19 January 2014.

Feminizing the discipline 263

The losses, like the births, came in clusters. On 17 March 1960 Mrs Hoernlé died at the age of seventy-five. While this was less of a shock, it also affected her deeply.

Eileen had returned to the Lovedu Reserve for the funeral ceremony of Modjadji II and inauguration of Modjadji III in 1959, and resumed her Lovedu fieldwork during the winter vacations of 1961 and 1962. She used her first semester sabbatical of 1964 to re-engage in earnest with her Lovedu research, planning to write a monograph on social change by means of a detailed comparison of the 1930s and the 1960s. The central theme was the changes in social structure, especially in family and wider kinship relationships. Her ultimate failure to carry through this ambitious vision was, as much as anything else, a loss of confidence in her ability to revisit the 1930s materials thoroughly because of the disappearance of many of her notebooks. In late-life reminiscences she cryptically recorded: 'Loss of my 1936–8 field-notes. Probably taken away by rubbish collectors on return from field before going to Russia.'[84] This was in late 1964. Eleanor Preston-Whyte, a newly-married graduate student of Eileen's, staying in the upper section of Eileen's house at the time, recalls:

That was a disaster of major proportion. Eileen came back from the field with boxes of notes. She took the boxes and put them on the rubbish bins at the top of the long driveway before parking her car. She forgot them there in the excitement of returning home. The rubbish collectors took the boxes the next morning. I was sent tearing off to try and retrieve these wretched boxes. She did have some of the genealogies, but had lost many of the old field notebooks. The loss was huge. I am not sure that she ever really recovered.[85]

'Undaunted she worked her way around the problem and probably few outside her circle knew of the loss.'[86]

Training women anthropologists, 1960–1970

The last two decades of Eileen's career as a teacher and ethnographer were arguably the most important in terms of her legacy. Now her focus turned to ethnographies of African women and social change. We need to consider her contributions to these fields both in relation to her own prolific late career research and writing, and in relation to the research and writing of her students, most of whom were directed by Eileen into the fields of women and gender studies during the 1960s.

[84] EJK Papers, File 363, EJK, 'Reminiscences of an Anthropologist', Notes for a Talk, c. 1986.
[85] Telephone Interview with Eleanor Preston-Whyte, Johannesburg-Cape Town, 4 Febuary 2014.
[86] Reid, 'Citation for Honorary Doctorate. D. Soc. Sci.: Eileen Jensen Krige', 57.

264 Pioneers of the Field

Four of her best-known women students, Angela P. Cheater, Eleanor Preston-Whyte, Harriet Sibisi and Sabitha Jithoo, contributed to the 1978 festschrift published in her honour. All four went on to complete doctoral theses in social anthropology; three published significant monographs in the field and three became heads of social anthropology departments, two in South Africa and one in the United States.

It is of course Eleanor Preston-Whyte who is remembered as Eileen's most dedicated disciple. She describes Eileen's style of supervision as direct and eminently practical with the dedicated commitment to fieldwork being her driving passion.

> She taught me all I know about how to do anthropology and writing up ethnography. She would pump me on what I had been doing, me telling her what had been going on in the field the previous week. Those meetings went on all afternoon. They made one an ethnographer. She believed profoundly in ethnography. For her social anthropology was effectively ethnography.[87]

The most important lesson was about the discipline and the meticulousness required in the recording of field-notes.

> She stressed that you must write your field-notes before you go to sleep at night. You must, must write down everything. Then read over very carefully and you will see what is actually relevant ... The first run through must record everything. I can remember keeping to this. In [later work in] rural areas I had to run off and write all this with a candle in someone's latrine in a bush. It was the best advice I ever had. It was something that I passed on to my own students.[88]

Eleanor also commented interestingly on Eileen's 'feminism'. Although Eileen, like all the other women anthropologists featured in this book, did not take to feminist theory in anthropology as it developed from the late 1960s, she was emphatically in Eleanor's view 'a practising feminist'.

> She believed firmly that women could make a contribution. Listen, her life ... she never did not do things [because of gender expectations]. She was an extraordinary woman in that respect. In the real sense of the word she was certainly a feminist.[89]

Eleanor accompanied Eileen on numerous field expeditions to Modjadji to give her a taste of rural fieldwork. 'It was very exciting. She arranged for one of the Lovedu women to take me around.' Following the model of Mrs Hoernlé, who had taken such a devoted personal interest in Eileen as

---

[87] Telephone Interview with Eleanor Preston-Whyte, Johannesburg-Cape Town, 4 February 2014.
[88] *Ibid.*   [89] *Ibid.*

Feminizing the discipline

one of her most talented students, Eileen became very much more to Eleanor than an undergraduate lecturer-turned-graduate mentor. 'She was someone whom you loved. I mean I loved her to bits . . . I was sort of her child.'[90]

The sociologist Fatima Meer was another of her undergraduate students, although, as noted in Chapter 5, she worked more closely with Hilda Kuper. Fatima and Eileen kept up a friendship. Eileen's daughter-in-law, Dulcie, recalls the powerful impact that Eileen's undergraduate lectures on race and culture had on the thinking of white students like herself, who had also grown up in racially conservative white families. Eileen challenged their comfortable assumptions that racial classification had a scientific basis and that race offered an adequate framework for the understanding of African cultures.

The whole lecture room [in the Social Anthropology I class of 1965] was full. She wore a gown and had a stick with which she would knock on the table. She spoke and she spoke passionately. She was never at a loss for words. She forced us to reconsider our inherited ideas about race.[91]

Her influence on women students extended beyond the University of Natal and well into her retirement.

There were also numerous male students influenced by Eileen who went on to follow academic careers. The most notable of these was Absolom Vilakazi, whose study of urban Zulu culture in Durban was entitled *Zulu Transformations: A Study of the Dynamics of Social Change* (1962). 'I can never thank her sufficiently for her quick and sympathetic understanding, her expert advice on Zulu ethnography, and her untiring efforts to get this book published.'[92] Eileen and Absolom kept up an active correspondence after his emigration to the United States in the late 1950s.[93] Mphiwa Mbatha was another male insider ethnographer who worked with Eileen in this period. She supervised his 1960 M.A. thesis on migrant labour and its effects on tribal and family life among the Nyuswa Zulu of Botha's Hill. Another in the lineage was Trevor Cope, the Zulu linguist, who translated *A Witch in My Heart* for Hilda Kuper in

---

[90] *Ibid.*

[91] After marrying Eileen's son Thor in 1970, Dulcie found that Eileen was not only an active grandmother to their children, but strongly supportive of her academic career in geography and development studies. See Dulcie Jean Krige, 'The Urban Informal Sector in South Africa: What Options for Development? A Case Study of KwaMashu, Natal' (unpublished M. Soc. Sci. thesis, Natal University, 1985), 251 pp.

[92] Absolom Vilakazi, 'Preface' to *Zulu Transformations: A Study of the Dynamics of Social Change* (Pietermaritzburg: Natal University Press, 1962), x. The book was dedicated to Jack who had been the supervisor of his thesis.

[93] EJKP, File 257, Absolom Vilakazi to Eileen Krige, 20 October 1972, Hartford, Connecticut.

266   Pioneers of the Field

1962. Cope spent many years working as Eileen's colleague in the Department of African Studies at Natal in the 1960s. Like Vilakazi and Mbatha, he had been one of Eileen and Jack's anthropology undergraduate students of the mid-1950s.[94]

Eleven essays and a hidden ethnography on women and social change, 1968–1981

One of Eileen's fellow anthropologists commented on her 'remarkable resurgence of research activity and publication' during the 1970s.[95] The pressures of parenting, teaching under demanding circumstances, running a department and taking on leadership in the university had meant that she was able to publish only two essays during her first two decades in the anthropology department at Natal.[96] Between 1968 and 1981, by contrast, she produced eleven essays, now at a rate of almost one a year rather than one a decade.

In general, this writing was directed much more squarely at an international scholarly community than her earlier work had been. This was related to the fact that she now had more contact with scholars outside of South Africa than had been the case in the interwar years. Aided by the new possibilities of air travel, she attended many international conferences before and after her retirement: in Cambridge in 1964 where she met again with Audrey and Meyer Fortes, Moscow in 1966 where she met with Margaret Mead, Tokyo in 1968, Boston, San Diego, Washington and Miami in 1970 and 1971 and then Kent in 1972, where she and a younger generation of southern Africanists including John Comaroff came up with the plan to publish an edited collection on African marriage. I see a clear difference in her methodological orientation in the late essays. The functionalist framework of her early writings, with her particular emphasis on economics and kinship within the overall system, was now combined with an interest in detailed reconstructions of cultural rituals, through description or close textual analysis in particular case studies, along with what she termed 'a historical approach'.[97]

---

[94] Trevor Cope, 'Towards an Appreciation of Zulu Folktales as Literary Art' in Argyle and Preston-Whyte, eds., *Social System and Tradition*, 183–205.

[95] Hammond-Tooke, *Imperfect Interpreters*, 89.

[96] Eileen Jensen Krige and Jack D. Krige, 'The Lovedu of the Transvaal' in Darryll Forde, eds., *African Worlds: Studies in the Cosmological Ideas and Social Values of African Peoples* (OUP with IAI, 1964), 55–83; 'Property, Cross-Cousin Marriage and the Family Cycle among the Lovedu' in R.F. Gray and P.H. Gulliver, eds., *The Family Estate in Africa* (London: Routledge and Kegan Paul), 155–96.

[97] Eileen Jensen Krige, *Social Structure and Political Arrangements of the Lovedu in the Setting of Historical Change* (Pretoria: Report Submitted to the H.S.R.C., 1975), xxiii.

Feminizing the discipline

While African women had been Eileen's primary informants and subjects of analysis in her early ethnography, as well as her applied anthropology, the ethnography of African women now took centre-stage. This is best illustrated in the two seminal essays that she published in *Africa*. The first of these, published in 1968, was an analysis of Zulu girls' puberty songs. She related the songs and their symbolism with a wider ritual complex, including 'rites associated with fertility, rain, and the prevention of seasonal disease in man and crops'. She concluded by identifying five significant points on which Max Gluckman's interpretation of Zulu women's agricultural rites as 'rituals of rebellion' was 'either erroneous or dubious'.[98] For an arch-empiricist like Eileen, Gluckman's reshaping of 'fact' to fit theory did not sit well.[99]

The second article she had published in *Africa* (1976) examined the institution of 'woman-marriage', which she defined as 'the institution by which it is possible for a woman to give bridewealth for, and marry, a woman, over whom and whose offspring she has full control, delegating to a male genitor the duties of procreation'. She went on to demonstrate that the institution of woman-marriage was unusual but regionally widespread in Africa with particular characteristics that varied across time and culture. Her essay located her case study of Lovedu woman-marriage squarely in the context of a rich comparative literature. She went on to show that the institution was also flexible historically and had continued to thrive in the modern context, where it had the effect of 'cushioning the disruptive influences of migrant labour on marriage and family life'. She concluded by suggesting that the institution of woman-marriage in Africa challenged the very concept of marriage as a sexual partnership between one man and one woman, as was sometimes assumed in the existing literature.[100]

Her article highlighted the rich, complex and variable history of the institution of marriage in Africa. This was the central theme of the excellent collection of essays on African marriage in southern Africa that she co-edited with John Comaroff.[101]

Social change was the central theme of what I regard as a rich hidden monograph that Eileen submitted to the Human Sciences Research

---

[98] Krige, 'Girls' Puberty Songs', 184–5.
[99] She went on to use this method of meticulously detailed textual analysis of ritual song in relation to a Lovedu prayer in an article that featured in a special edition on Black Religion in South Africa. See Eileen Jensen Krige, 'A Lovedu Prayer: The Light Thrown on the Ancestor Cult' in Allie Dubb and A.G. Schutte, eds., *African Studies: Special Issue on Black Religion in South Africa*, 33, 2 (1974), 91–8.
[100] Eileen Jensen Krige, 'Woman-Marriage, with Special Reference to the Lovedu', *Africa*, 44 (1974), 11–37.
[101] Eileen Jensen Krige and John L. Comaroff, eds., *Essays on African Marriage in Southern Africa* (Cape Town and Johannesburg: Juta and Co. Ltd., 1981).

268   Pioneers of the Field

Council as a report in 1975. Her study ran across 406 pages with 46 figures, 13 genealogical charts and 7 diagrams.[102] I am struck by the gap between her enormous investment of effort in data-gathering in the field, stretching across more than a decade and collectively representing some twenty-four months of fieldwork, and the lack of circulation of her research outside of the chapter discussed above that was adapted as an essay. The core section tackled the issue of social change between the 1930s and the 1960s. Its tone and analysis had resonance with other South African urban ethnographies of social change with attention to the impact of new media, in particular radios, new modes of transport notably weekend bus services and accelerated labour migration by men, but also now by women. She marked out the emergence of new social groups in what was now a more clearly 'differentiated society' which included 'a small elite of educated Christians – school principals, teachers and nurses ... with European-style houses, radios and radiograms', 'ordinary Christians including evangelists and descendants of 1930s mission converts' and 'those involved in [the structures of] tribal administration, largely members of the royal family'.[103] She ended with an examination of the changes in kinship structures between her two periods of intensive fieldwork.

Why has this absorbing monograph remained buried in a single archival collection in the Killie Campbell Library in Durban? According to Monica Wilson, who provided meticulous annotated critical commentary on the manuscript at Eileen's request, the problem was 'partly as some conclusions differed from those already published, partly because of difficulty in maintaining the confidences of people still alive and in precarious political positions [in what was now the homeland of Lebowa]'. Monica also mentioned, in more general terms, that Eileen was intensely self-critical and this doubtless also played a role.[104] She seems to have been unaware of the devastating loss of field materials in 1964 which, as hinted above, might have been the primary reason for Eileen lacking full confidence in the rigour of her new historical analysis. Monica's suggestions for revision were also so thorough, usually calling for more overview and less detail, that Eileen might have felt daunted, in her early seventies, to take up the challenge.

---

[102] Eileen Jensen Krige, *Social Structure and Political Arrangements of the Lovedu in the Setting of Historical Change* (Pretoria: HSRC Report, 1975).

[103] *Ibid.*, 75–6.

[104] WC, Uncatalogued Correspondence: K, Monica Wilson to Prof. Reid, 'Reference for Eileen Krige with respect to the award of an Honorary Doctorate', Hogsback, 21 February 1977.

Feminizing the discipline

Conclusion

Eileen presented her last conference paper at the South African Anthropological Association meeting at University of Cape Town in 1985. This was also the year of her last field-trip to the Lovedu reserve, although she would make the long journey one more time to attend the funeral of her long-time friend Simeon in 1993. She died two years later at the age of ninety. Her family scattered her ashes in the cycad forest at Modjadji.

In this chapter I have argued that Eileen Jensen Krige's true contribution to the history of anthropology in South Africa has been obscured by retrospective judgements about her racial politics and adherence to functionalist theory. In both cases her views were far more complex and flexible than her critics allow. In developing Argyle and Preston-Whyte's case for contribution, I have traced her dual legacies as a teacher and a researcher who feminized the discipline in South Africa over the course of a career that began as a student in the early 1920s and only effectively ended in the mid-1980s.

Figure 6.6: Eileen at Modjadji in the early 1980s. She is greeting the late Mantwa Modjadji who was one of the wives of Modjadji III.[105]

---

[105] Jack and Eileen Krige Photographic Collection, Iziko South African Museum, Cape Town. Thanks to Patricia Davison for drawing my attention to this image and identifying Mantwa Modjadji.

270   Pioneers of the Field

Eileen was formally trained as a teacher, partly because this was the only way she could afford to study at Wits University. It was initially as an economist that she trained at Wits with a dual major in history, being in the very first cohort of B.A. graduates of 1922–4 after the university was officially recognized and then relocated to its current Milner Road location. She was also among the first dozen Master's students when she graduated in Economics in 1927. But during the mid- to late 1920s, her life took a different direction. She came under the influence of another highly talented teacher Winifred Hoernlé, who initiated her into social anthropology: by introducing her to a new theory of society in undergraduate lectures from 1924, impressing on her the wider social importance of this field of study and then encouraging her to do original field-based research. She chose the Lovedu Reserve, largely because of a chance encounter in the winter vacation of 1925. Her month-long fieldtrip in July 1928 was the turning point in her shift from economics to social anthropology, one which gave her a new and intense sense of mission and, ultimately, influenced her then fiancée, Jack Krige, to shift from law to social anthropology. Between 1928 and 1936 Eileen's career as a social anthropologist flourished with a string of essays and a monograph on the Zulu social system that remains the most authoritative text on the subject eighty years after its publication.

Her career as a teacher of anthropology at South African universities also dates to these highly productive years. Following five years as a school teacher, she taught by correspondence in the early to mid-1930s, effectively establishing a department of social anthropology at UNISA. Her first experience of the lecture hall was, appropriately enough, at her alma mater, Wits, as her mentor's stand-in for the second semester of 1936 and she would, in fact, have begun her long teaching career at Wits had she not turned down the offer of a full-time post in 1940 in favour of following Jack to Rhodes University. Their celebrated Lovedu monograph, *The Realm of a Rain-Queen*, was published after war-time delays, in 1943. Eileen was the first author, but the strength of the work was the integrated overview of their combined work, as fieldworkers over seventeen months and then as co-authors. For two decades Eileen threw herself into teaching and, to an extent that has not been appreciated, welfare work in African townships, most actively in Grahamstown but also in Durban. She balanced this work with the demands of motherhood. She and Jack were a formidable teaching team and in a period when establishing and running university departments was particularly onerous, they set up the African Studies Department and discipline of social anthropology at both Rhodes and Natal.

Feminizing the discipline

In many ways it was only after Jack's tragic death from a heart attack in April 1959 that Eileen, determined and courageous in the face of loss, fully came into her own as a teacher. As head of department at Natal during the 1960s she mentored a new generation of South African anthropologists, especially women scholars, most notably Eleanor Preston-Whyte, Harriet Sibisi Ngubane, Angela P. Cheater, Sibitha Jithoo but also Susan Middleton, Patricia Davison and many others. She also trained, supervised and influenced several young African male scholars in the making, most notably Absolom Vilakazi. It is only through their direct testimony, written and oral, that we can get a true sense of the depth of her commitment and extent of her influence. It was in particular in promoting field-based ethnography on women and social change that this influence was most profound.

Equally impressive was her late life resurgence in research and publication. Between 1968 and 1981, she published eleven essays, primarily on the themes of women and social change with a much more strongly international engagement than had been the case in her earlier work. The full recognition of her contribution as a researcher has been limited partly because of her inability, for a complex of reasons including the loss of a mass of field data, to see through to publication her major monograph of these years, based on some two years of fieldwork in the Lovedu Reserve. To return to the issue I raised in opening this chapter: in the case of a rich, complex, extended and thoroughly collaborative career like that of Eileen Jensen Krige, do the standard yardsticks of the field-based monograph and theoretical innovation offer any real understanding of a life's work and its legacy?

Conclusion: a humanist legacy

> I met Mrs Hoernlé once in 1946 when she visited Cape Town where Max Gluckman had arranged for newly joined research officers of the Rhodes-Livingstone Institute to attend sessions which gave a short introduction to Africa, Bantu Languages and Urbanization. I have always thought that she was the mother of South African anthropology, and said so once in an informal talk that I gave to the Anthropology Department at Manchester when it celebrated its 50th Anniversary.
>
> Elizabeth Colson to Andrew Bank, E-mail Communication, Monze, Zambia-Cape Town, 23 January 2014.

Much more could be said about the reasons for the limited acknowledgement of the achievements of the six women scholars featured in preceding chapters. My introduction highlighted the way in which they have been written out of a male-dominated canon in the history of South African and British functionalist anthropology. Successive chapters foregrounded the extent to which their liberal rather than African nationalist politics led to a lack of appreciation – among Marxist-influenced radical scholars of the 1970s and 1980s – of the extent to which they and their liberal peers had actively challenged segregation and apartheid. The lack of 'an adequate reading' of their lives, works and anti-segregationist politics[1] was already strikingly apparent in the discussions among exiled radical scholars about the legacy of South African anthropology that were published in a Special Issue of the *Journal of Southern African Studies* on history and anthropology in 1981. Here anthropologists lamented the lack of radicalism, and the position of class privilege, of their intellectual ancestors. John Sharp (one of few contributors to that volume who was writing from within South Africa) concluded his essay on the roots and development of the Afrikaner nationalist *volkekunde* tradition by suggesting that scholars in the liberal functionalist tradition in South Africa, like those featured in this volume, were part of the same apartheid-complicit lineage. They too were members of the 'ruling class' who had studied

---

[1] For incisive application of this concept from Bourdieu to the work of Monica Wilson, see Pamela Reynolds, 'Gleanings and Leavings', 310–12.

Conclusion: a humanist legacy

dominated classes without questioning 'the structure of South African capitalism and their and their subjects' places within this system'.[2]

Marxist and Africanist critiques of the South African social anthropological traditions alleged a lack of radicalism, support for 'the ideology of tribalism', Eurocentrism and, most recently, blindness to African realities.[3] These criticisms continued pretty much unabated, with a heightened moment in the late 1990s when Archie Mafeje proposed that African anthropology was 'colonial anthropology' and ought to be consigned to the dustbin of history.[4] In general, this critique may be framed as a charge of anti-humanism. In this sense Marxist, Africanist and postcolonial critics have been at one in their characterization of South African and African social anthropology. They have presented it as an intellectual discipline in which members of a colonial, capitalist or 'ruling class' use a Eurocentric epistemology to invent a theory that African cultures are, in fact, simply static and bounded tribes. They saw this theoretical stance as lending support to the divisive racial politics of segregation and apartheid in South Africa, and that of indirect rule in Central and East Africa.

In concluding, I want to argue exactly the opposite: that the discipline of social anthropology in South Africa was a profoundly humanist endeavour. It certainly went far beyond any of its sibling disciplines in the humanities and social sciences in its degree of engagement with African cultures and languages. It provided a deeply historicized and nuanced understanding of African societies that was unusual, one might even say radical, during the interwar years especially, given the near consensus in white politics about racial difference and the need for racial segregation. What is most striking about the engagement of the women scholars whose work is showcased in the preceding chapters was their willingness to challenge conventional boundaries in South African society: those between races, cultures, sexes and, to some extent, classes.[5]

---

[2] John Sharp, 'The Roots and Development of *Volkekunde* in South Africa' in Terence Ranger and Colin Murray, eds., *Journal of Southern African Studies: Special Issue: Anthropology and History*, 8, 1 (1981), 35. Subsequent writings by South African anthropologists, Sharp and Hammond-Tooke, have reinforced this conflation of anti-segregationist left-liberal social anthropology with the pro-apartheid Afrikaner nationalist ethnological tradition. See Hammond-Tooke on Eiselen as the joint consolidator of South African social anthropology in *Imperfect Interpreters*, 56–69; Sharp, 'Serving the *Volk*: Afrikaner Anthropology Revisited' in James et al., *Culture Wars*, 32–44.

[3] Francis B. Nyamnjoh, 'Blinded by Sight: Divining the Future of Anthropology in Africa', *Africa Spectrum*, 47, 2–3 (2012), 63–92.

[4] Archie Mafeje, 'Anthropology and Independent Africans: Suicide or the End of an Era?', *African Sociological Review*, 2, 1 (1998), 1–43. On the influence of his critique, see Adebayo Olukoshi and Francis Nyamnjoh, eds., *CODESRIA Bulletin: A Giant Has Moved On: Archie Mafeje (1936–2007)*, 3–4 (2008).

[5] This was certainly also true of the work of their typically more highly esteemed male colleagues, Isaac Schapera and Max Gluckman.

274   Pioneers of the Field

Let us begin with the latter. While it is true that these six women scholars were, in the abstract sense, 'white' and 'middle class', can they really be regarded as members of 'the ruling class'? After all, until 1930 these women did not have the right to vote in South Africa. Their financial circumstances were precarious in at least two cases, those of Beemer and Jensen Krige, whom we might describe as having come from lower middle class rather than ruling class backgrounds. Financial stress was a marked feature of the graduate years of these two women and the early university career of Hunter (now Wilson).

What of their 'whiteness'? Again, the life histories reveal a more complex story than dualistic critiques of whites who study blacks might suggest. Their ethnic origins were strikingly eclectic, especially if we contrast them with the common history of the pro-segregationist, Afrikaner nationalist *volkekundiges*.[6] Hoernlé came from a family of English settlers, Hunter from immigrant Scottish missionaries, Hellmann from immigrant German Jews, the Indian-born Richards from English and Welsh intellectuals and colonial officials. The Bulawayo-born Beemer had a well-to-do Viennese Jewish mother and a poor Lithuanian Jewish father, Jensen had a Danish father and a Cape Afrikaner mother. Their religious backgrounds and affiliations were variously Christian (Hoernlé and Hunter), Jewish (Hellmann and Beemer) or agnostic (Richards and Jensen).

Yet there were important features common to their life histories. To begin with, the four intellectual daughters were born in southern Africa around the time of Union. The politics of European and South African nationalism was a defining feature of the childhood and youth of all of them. In all cases they rejected the racism of imperial and, later, Nazi Germany, and the racism of Afrikaner nationalism. For Hellmann and Beemer anti-racism was born of painful personal experience, both of growing up as Jews in a deeply anti-Semitic society, but also of the taint of German or Austrian nationalism in their backgrounds. Their interest in documenting the rich and diverse possibilities of cultural expression were, in all cases, based on a profound rejection of the racially based forms of nationalism that dominated in Europe and South Africa during the first half of the twentieth century.

---

[6] Take the founding generation: Werner Eiselen and his eight MA or doctoral graduates at Stellenbosch University from 1930–6. They were all men. They were all of a slighter older generation than the South African women scholars featured in this study, having been born around the time of the South African War (1899–1902), typically in rural areas in former Boer Republics. They shared a fervent commitment to a Dutch Reformed Church theology and an ideology of essential racial difference. For details on their shared backgrounds and ethnographies structured around African sexual deviance, see Andrew Bank, '"*Broederbande*" ["Brotherly Bonds"]: Afrikaner Nationalist Masculinity and African Sexuality in the Writings of Werner Eiselen's Students, Stellenbosch University, 1930–1936', *Anthropology Southern Africa*, 38, 3–4 (2015), 180–97.

Conclusion: a humanist legacy

They were all pacifists, although they supported a 'just war' against the Nazis. But I am equally struck by the fact that four of these six women (Hunter, Hellmann, Richards and Jensen Krige) chose not to express their deeply political and moral understanding of South African society through formal party political channels. This was because of their rejection of the racially exclusive nature of party politics in South Africa, their preference for working through welfare structures and through their teaching, or their underlying scholarly distrust of emotive mass politics, of which there was such abundant evidence in Afrikaner nationalism and German Nazi ideology.

In short, an inclusive South African nationalism was central to their identities and scholarly projects. (Here Richards was an exception in that she was clearly English by descent and affiliation.) Winifred Hoernlé nurtured this inclusive nationalism as well as a humanism that was universal. This was evident in her anthropological teaching. We can read of this in Beemer's account of her tolerant attitude towards different traditions, including the English, French and German schools of anthropology, which she encouraged her students to understand in their own terms and through their own languages. In this spirit she encouraged them to engage with African cultures in their own languages and through their own conceptual frameworks, even if she herself had experienced less success in this regard than they would. Beyond awakening a passion for anthropology as a discipline both scientific and fieldwork-driven, she conveyed to them a sense of the significance of their field in ways that had nothing to do with intellectual concepts or party politics. Max Gluckman eloquently expressed this as a sense of fellow citizenship with others in a multi-cultural and multi-racial society, something which related to the 'here-and-now' of their lives in a way that differed fundamentally from the more detached scholarly exercise of African anthropology as conducted from distant centres in Europe and America. Eileen Krige recalled it as an attitude to self as much as to society: a sense of selflessness, a generosity, a commitment to others, whether this was expressed through working for 'causes', or in care and attention to individuals (including her students). Whether through Hoernlé's influence or otherwise, we might say that modesty and generosity are characteristics that apply to all six women scholars right through their impressive careers.

They also shared a love of fieldwork and all entered the field at a young age.

Herein lay the most important explanation for the unusually prominent role played by women in the fledgling science of social anthropology in South Africa, apart from the obvious fact that their main mentor and role

276   Pioneers of the Field

model was a woman scholar (and that they were then ably supported by her female heir). Their identity as young women researchers allowed them to move beyond the initial suspicion and establish the kinds of relations of trust on which effective fieldwork is always based. They were able to establish friendships and productive working relationships with African interpreters which proved to be crucial to the success of their projects. As I suggested in my chapter on Ellen Hellmann, urban field research in a context of daily police raids would not have been possible for a white male. In the racially stratified environment of a country in which segregationist laws were becoming entrenched, police interventions in African townships or slum-yards were a reality of daily life and suspicion towards white outsiders was a feature of township life. The white woman researcher was a less threatening presence than her male counterpart. This explains why the women anthropologists featured in these chapters were able to pioneer the field of urban anthropology in South Africa during the 1930s. Even in the rural areas they had a great advantage. They may have been seen as freakish or ignorant by elderly African men, and as scary by little children, but (with patronage) they and their questions were tolerated. This was not the case with male anthropologists. Max Gluckman's research project in Zululand, for example, was effectively scuppered when the Zulu chief at Nongoma insisted that he be permanently expelled.

Other factors that explain the female dominance of the discipline in South Africa in the formative decades include their good fortune in training under male mentors who had unusually accommodating attitudes towards women intellectuals, the newness and hence relative marginality of their discipline, their location in a colonial setting in which there were enhanced research opportunities and jobs, and their ability to forge a mutually supportive network that could be sustained over decades with the two senior women scholars serving as successive 'mothers' of the discipline.

It is surely the extent and quality of their fieldwork that is the key to understanding the depth of their collective contribution to southern (and central) African anthropology. If there is one theme that connects these life histories, it is the love of fieldwork. They all found fieldwork a liberating and humanizing experience. Wilson, for instance, recalled being 'swallowed up' by the experience of cross-cultural conversation and participant observation in Pondoland, while Kuper described her experience of fieldwork in Swaziland as 'transformative'. This passion for fieldwork meant that they spent many months and years in the field. Here we might do some simple accounting. Hunter spent twenty-one months in Pondoland and the Eastern Cape in 1931–2 and (what she described as) 'only twenty months' in Bunyakyusa in 1935–7. She spent

Conclusion: a humanist legacy

another three months there in 1955. Hellmann spent thirteen months paying daily visits to Rooiyard. Richards spent fifteen months in Bembaland in 1930–1 and a further nineteen months in Bembaland in 1933–4. She did another three months in a Tswana reserve in 1939–40. Beemer spent twenty-four months in the Swaziland Protectorate in two stints, the first from 1934–5, the second in 1936–7. Krige spent three one-month vacations in the Lovedu Reserve in 1928, 1930 and 1932, and then sixteen-and-a-half months in the field in 1936–8, followed by twenty-four months of fieldwork in the early 1960s. She also spent some six months doing fieldwork in Zululand in the early 1930s and late 1960s. Even if we exclude their more 'intermittent fieldwork' of the late 1940s or 1950s,[7] we can speak of 179 months of fieldwork, 133 months (or somewhat over eleven years) of which was conducted in the 1930s. They thus averaged two years of immersed fieldwork per researcher at a very conservative estimate.

It is, however, the quality rather than the quantity of their fieldwork that was the key to the success of their ethnographies.

I have argued that their fieldwork was creative to a degree that has not been fully appreciated. Most of them entered the field with an unusually clear sense of what anthropological fieldwork involved. This was because three of them (Hellmann, Krige and Kuper) had shared a rigorous under-graduate induction into the discipline under Hoernlé. She had introduced them to fine models of ethnographic field-based research and to the func-tionalist theory that the study of African cultures was a scientific analysis of the workings of an entire social system. Four of them spent at least a year in London working with or under that self-styled revolutionary Malinowski, who promoted a specific and practical model of what they should do in the field. The other two, Hoernlé and Hellmann, attended his seminars for a semester. The new generation followed his model to the letter. This involved developing fluency in African languages. They all produced the array of field-writings that the Malinowskian model demanded, including field diaries in numerous cases, and field reports and extensive accumula-tions of field-notes in all cases, most of which have survived. They combined the use of interviews, mostly with women, with engaged parti-cipant observation, typically of rituals.

But once they had entered the field the blueprints and inspiring ethnographies had to be left behind. Each field-site presented specific difficulties: urban field-sites were dangerous, rural informants were

[7] This applies to Kuper's four years of fieldwork in Durban in 1953–7 and Richards' many months fieldwork in rural areas in Uganda during her seven years as director of the East African Institute (1949–56).

278   Pioneers of the Field

sometimes suspicious and secretive, often to an extreme degree. Establishing relations of trust required interpreters and intermediaries, but also constant adaptation, invention and innovation. So, for example, Hunter found that the best way to gather data in a remote rural field-site in Pondoland was to sit on maize bags in the trader's store and converse with local women who were buying cloth from the trader's wife. She later struck upon the idea of measuring 'culture contact' in relation to place rather than time. This took her into the towns of East London and Grahamstown, and later onto farms in the Eastern Cape frontier districts. In response to difficulties in getting into the field, due to funding constraints, teaching commitments and later family commitments, Krige developed her own highly distinctive method of data collection. She gathered information through long-term correspondence with trusted African informants, George Washington Mahlobo in Zululand and then with Simeon Modjadji in Balovedu, based on the most meticulous and extended of questionnaires, detailing across many pages precisely the kind of data she needed and generating a voluminous correspondence over years and, in the case of Simeon Modjadji, almost half a century. In urban contexts they used household surveys collected from women as a starting point in the long and patient work of building threads of trust, especially given that such information was personal.

The warmth and mutual respect of their friendships with African interpreters in the field, some lasting years, some stretching over decades, confirms my sense that their legacy is best conceived of as a form of humanism. They truly were all gifted collaborators. Their ability to collaborate with male peers beyond the field-site was also crucial to their contributions to the discipline. Indeed, my case for feminizing the foundational narrative of social anthropology in South Africa relies on recognition of the extent to which Hoernlé was able to work with male colleagues. She did this at first with Radcliffe-Brown, with whom she developed and applied, in research and teaching in the foundational years of the discipline, a rigorous theoretical model that could be applied to understanding the workings of African cultures. She did it later with his precocious student, Schapera. To him she offered moral support, shared advice, made available research materials and directed him to his future field-site. Above all, she worked with him towards the creation of a new kind of anthropology in South Africa: empirically grounded fieldwork-based ethnography. Through their joint work on the Inter-University African Studies Committee, and with the loyal assistance of her husband Alfred, they distributed the International African Institute's Rockefeller funds to these young women researchers who effected what I propose we think of as 'a revolution' in the understanding of African cultures in a time of social change.

Conclusion: a humanist legacy 279

Their most significant collaborators were their partners or husbands. Here again there is a pattern. All married or became intimately involved in a partnership when they were in their mid-twenties, usually just before or during their famous fieldwork expeditions. The patronage of their husbands would be indispensable to their careers in the long term. Following their extended years of fieldwork and the sometimes joint production of major ethnographies, they all (bar Audrey, to her life-long regret) became mothers. In all cases they viewed motherhood as no less, and perhaps more, important than their careers as social anthropologists. In ways that did not apply to male anthropologists of this period, they had to balance the considerable demands of taking care of young children and associated domestic responsibilities, embarked on relatively late when they were in their thirties, or even forties in the case of Krige, against those of earning their keep.

At the same time, they were establishing careers in universities with male-dominated employment policies and discriminatory pay scales. While they seldom complained, sexism was undoubtedly a feature of their university lives. As we have seen, Hoernlé was denied the chance of a post at the South African College (later UCT) in 1912, given the academy's view that it would be 'too great an experiment to appoint a woman'. Richards felt privately aggrieved, as did the Wilsons on her behalf, when the promises of the governor of Northern Rhodesia fell on stony ground: the all-male Board of the newly established Rhodes-Livingstone Institute refused to appoint a woman director.[8] Monica Wilson was denied a post at Wits in favour of a much inferior male candidate in 1946 and she left Rhodes University for the University of Cape Town in 1952 in part because she resented being paid less than male professors.

None of these women were active in the feminist movement from the late 1960s, nor did they embrace the feminist theory of 1970s American anthropology. Their aversion to the latter was largely due to their lifelong commitment to a broadly functionalist or structural-functionalist empirical field-based method of research and ethnography which came with a deep aversion to new-fangled theory. Yet, to return to the argument of this conclusion, a central aspect of their humanism, one that definitely sets them apart from their typically more highly esteemed male peers Isaac Schapera and Max Gluckman, is that they were all feminists in the wider sense of the term. They all believed in equality of opportunity for men and women and conducted their professional lives by this creed, in a

---

[8] Richards never got the chair she wanted in Britain, and at Cambridge was excluded by Meyer Fortes. The fact the she was a woman may not have been decisive in either case, but it certainly did not help. E-mail communication, Adam Kuper to Andrew Bank, 10 July 2015, London-Cape Town.

280   Pioneers of the Field

country where such ideas were extremely rare in the interwar years. These women anthropologists were pioneers of South African feminism in three respects.

First, and particularly when we read their contribution collectively, their ethnographies showcased southern African, and later South African Indian, women as subjects of cultural study and history for the first time. In my introductory case for rethinking the canon I highlighted the themes that their work introduced into African anthropology: nutrition, ritual and social change. In all cases their female-centred fieldwork produced female-sensitive and often female-centred ethnographies that opened up the field of women and gender studies decades before Cherryl Walker's historical research on women in South Africa.[9] Hoernlé's hidden trilogy of essays making a case for the complexity of African cultures included an extended analysis of the life-stage rituals of Nama women. The significance of Monica Hunter's work on women and sexuality has been well acknowledged in recent historical literature, but is worth restating. Through her women's networks in Pondoland and the Eastern Cape she produced essays and a classic ethnography, in which women featured as prominently as men as ethnographic subjects. Ellen Hellmann stands out as the only scholar in this early period to have focused squarely on women as her ethnographic subjects. It is no coincidence that there was a marked revival of interest among social historians of the 1980s in her study demonstrating the remarkable resilience and inventiveness of those newly urbanized women beer-brewers, who eked out their living on the very fringes of the modern South African economy and society.

Audrey Richards initiated a shift from a male-dominated focus on the sexual customs of 'primitive cultures' towards the female domain of nutrition, demonstrating that the female-centred world of African food production, circulation and consumption produced a female-centred ideology of food in different African cultures, with rich symbolic associations.

Second, they were feminists in the sense of being women leaders, and thus promoted the professional status of women in the male-dominated world of South African (and in Richards' case British) university and public life. Here Hoernlé took the lead. She was the first woman member of a Student Representative Council in South Africa (1905), one of the first women to do anthropological fieldwork worldwide (1912–13), the first woman board member of a South African scientific journal and for

---

[9] We must recall that the field of women and gender studies had not got off the ground by 1976 when Cherryl Walker began researching the subject that culminated in her landmark study and then edited collection on *Women and Resistance in South Africa* (1991). Cherryl Walker, 'Preface to the 2nd Edition', *Women and Resistance in South Africa* (New York: Monthly Review Press; Cape Town: David Philip, 2nd edn, 1991), xi.

Conclusion: a humanist legacy

281

fifteen years the only woman member (1922–37). She was one of the first women to be employed as a lecturer (and then senior lecturer) and certainly the first woman head of department in a South African university (1923–37), which she remained for fifteen years. She was the first woman to serve on the Wits University Senate. She also played important roles at a national level as the only woman representative on the Inter-University African Studies Committee (1932–6), as the first president of the National Association of South African University Women in 1938–9, and as the first woman president of the South African Institute of Race Relations in 1943.

Monica Hunter Wilson took the status of university women one step further when she was appointed as the first woman professor in a social anthropology department in South Africa at Rhodes University in 1946, being among the first woman professors in South Africa. Her distinctive contribution to promoting the role of women in South African university life is best conceived in relation to her status across fifteen years as the only woman professorial representative on the University of Cape Town Senate (1952–66), a body comprising between fifty and seventy members during these years. She was among very few South African women to have been elected to the British Academy in 1981.

Audrey Richards was an institutional pioneer on the same scale as Winifred Hoernlé. She was among the first women lecturers in social anthropology at the London School of Economics, alongside what was then an all-male staff. She played a leading role in the Nutrition Committee of the Colonial Office (1935–7) and later of its Welfare and Development Programme (1941–8), culminating in her appointment as the first director of the East African Institute based at Makerere (1949–55). It was from her Cambridge base on her return to England that her status as '*grande dame* of British anthropology' was cemented with her election as the first woman president of the Royal Anthropological Institute (1961–3), the second woman president of the United Kingdom African Studies Association (1963–5) and the head of her alma mater, Newnham College. She too was elected as a member of the British Academy.

Third, these women all played significant roles in promoting women's rights and interests in public life, both in and beyond the university. The editors of a biographical dictionary of women anthropologists published in 1988 reflect that women anthropologists have historically been far more engaged and applied in their orientation than their male counterparts.[10]

---

[10] Ute Gacs, Aisha Kahn, Jerrie McIntyre and Ruth Weinberg, 'Introduction' in Gacs et al., eds., *Women Anthropologists: A Biographical Dictionary* (New York: Greenwood Press, 1988).

282   Pioneers of the Field

This was certainly true of the generation of South African anthropologists who began their careers in the interwar years. Here again Hoernlé was the moving force. With the exception of Monica Hunter, she was able to draw her intellectual daughters, and even her heir Audrey Richards, into what the latter termed the 'feminist' network of university women involved in welfare work. They all remained involved in the anti-apartheid campaigns, including the famous Women's March of 1956 at which Hilda Kuper was arrested along with her research assistant and friend Fatima Meer.

It was, however, in their roles as university teachers and trainers of new generations of women scholars – in all cases bar that of Hellmann who followed a different career path – that their contribution as feminist public intellectuals is most apparent. We can begin with a (by no means exhaustive) roll-call of feminist scholars who were the disciples of Hoernlé's 'daughters', those we might term her 'granddaughters'. They include Monica Wilson's most famous students Pamela Reynolds and Jean Comaroff, whose ethnographies on childhood and religion in Southern Africa are internationally celebrated. Mamphela Ramphele is another strongly feminist heir of Wilson, having been drawn into university research by Monica's son Francis and then working in a university department where the methods and spirit of Monica remained very much alive. Audrey Richards trained many famous women and numerous feminist scholars, most notably the feminist anthropologists Marilyn Strathern and Jean S. La Fontaine. Hilda Beemer trained Ruth First at Wits, and Sondra Hale, Dawn Chatty and Barbara Meyerhoff at UCLA. Eileen Krige trained Diana P. Cheater, Eleanor Preston-Whyte and Harriet Sibisi Ngubane, all of whom produced feminist and women-centred scholarship.

As with their fieldwork, it was the quality rather than simply the range or quantity of engagement that stands out when reflecting on their humanist legacy. Here I am struck by the warmth and enormous respect and gratitude with which the women students above recalled their experience of working under these pioneers of the field. They spoke of sensitivity, commitment, care and depth of engagement that went far beyond the call of duty. In many cases they understood this to have reflected their mentors' interests in promoting their careers as university women, in challenging still thoroughly male-dominated intellectual institutions. This nature of their relationships with students was obviously distinctive in each case. But, without risk of gender stereotyping, there was a maternal quality about the manner of supervision and the extent of interest in the welfare of their students as women rather than only as scholars. This could include strictness, as in Pamela Reynolds' reflection on the spirit of Monica Wilson's ever rigorous supervision. It could include fun, as in

Conclusion: a humanist legacy 283

Marilyn Strathern's recollections of the irrepressible liveliness of Audrey Richards' personality. It could include the 'transformative experience' of being listened to attentively, as with Barbara Meyerhoff's reflection on Hilda Kuper's supervision. And it could be reciprocated by deep love, as was evident when Eleanor Preston-Whyte told me about Eileen Krige and what became their shared passion for social anthropology. These are but the most vivid testimonies to a profound but curiously disavowed humanist legacy.

Bibliography

Archival sources by chapter

Chapter 1

Winifred Hoernlé Papers [WHP], Witwatersrand University, Johannesburg
AU8HOE Winifred Hoernlé Papers, Witwatersrand University, University Archive.
Box 1: Correspondence, Personal Details, Diaries of Expeditions [Personal Papers]
Box 2: Correspondence, Personal Details, Diaries of Expeditions, Photographs
Box 3: 'Bantu': Lecture notes, correspondence.

R.F. Alfred Hoernlé Papers [RFAHP], Witwatersrand University, Johannesburg
AU8HOE R.F.A. (Alfred)Hoernlé Papers, Witwatersrand University, University Archive
Wooden Box containing Closed Access: Letters between RFA (Alfred) Hoernlé and Winifred Hoernlé, 1912–1915.
Box 1: Personal, Genealogical Papers, Family Testimonials etc.
Box 2: Correspondence, 1920–1929
Box 3: Correspondence, 1930–1939

Isaac Schapera Papers, University of Cape Town, Cape Town
BC1168 Isaac Schapera Papers, University of Cape Town Libraries, Manuscripts and Archives Department: including 'D: 8 letters from A. R. Radcliffe-Brown to Winifred Hoernlé, given to Isaac Schapera by Winifred Hoernle, 25.03.1924–27.07.1927'.

John Goodwin Papers, University of Cape Town, Cape Town
BC290 Goodwin Papers, University of Cape Town Libraries, Manuscripts and Archive Department: including D5 correspondence between John Goodwin and Winifred Hoernlé, 1926–1930.

Bibliography 285

Fourie Papers, Witwatersrand University, Johannesburg
AU659 Fourie Papers, Witwatersrand University, University Archive: including correspondence between Winifred Hoernlé to Louis Fourie, 1927–1933.

Chapter 2

Monica and Godfrey Wilson Collection [WC], University of Cape Town, Cape Town
BC880 Monica and Godfrey Wilson Collection, University of Cape Town Libraries, Manuscripts and Archives Department.

Catalogued materials
As listed in Lesley Hart, *BC880 Monica and Godfrey Wilson Papers: An Index Compiled by Lesley Hart* (Cape Town: University of Cape Town Libraries, 1999).

A Personal Papers
A2.2 MW Pocket Diaries, 1927.
A2.6 MW School reports, 1919.
A2.15 MW Notes: Anthropology in South Africa, recorded for Jom [*sic*] Fox, Behavioural Sciences Centre [Stanford], April 1972.

B Correspondence
B4.4 GW to and from Bronislaw Malinowski, MSS and TSS, 1934–1938.
B4.7 GW to and from Audrey Richards, 1935–1941
B5.1 Letters MW to her father (David Hunter), 1918–1944.
B5.2 Letters MW to her mother, 1931, Ntibane, 1947–8.
B6.14 Letters MW to and from Audrey Richards, 1940–1982.
B6.14 Audrey Richards to Rhodes University Appointments Committee, 'Reference for Monica Wilson', 15 June 1946, Draft version.

D Nyakyusa Research
D4 MW Missions/Christian Influences
D11 MW Correspondence with the International Institute of African Languages and Cultures including reports from the field, 1935–1939.

H Eastern Cape Research
H1.3 Reviews of *Reaction to Conquest*

N Photographs
N1 Photographs of Monica Wilson
N2 Photographs of Monica Wilson in groups

286 Bibliography

Uncatalogued materials

Uncatalogued Field-notes, Box 8 *Pondo Iintsomi Linguistic*, Correspondence between Monica Hunter and Winifred Hoernlé, Ntontela, 18 October 1932, 27 November 1932, n.d., 1934.
Uncatalogued Field-notes, Folder 'East London'.
Uncatalogued Correspondence: K, Monica Wilson/Eileen Krige. 1968–1977. Uncatalogued Correspondence: K, Monica Wilson/ Hilda Kuper. 1949–1961. Uncatalogued Correspondence: M, Monica Wilson/Archie Mafeje, 1960–1973. Uncatalogued Correspondence: S, Monica Wilson/George Stocking, 1982.
Uncatalogued CDs: Monica Wilson interviewed by Francis and Lindy Wilson, Hogsback, Eastern Cape: 'Childhood', 10 January 1979; 'Pondoland', July 1979; 'Bunyakyusa', 4 January 1982 (My transcriptions).
Uncatalogued Box labelled 'Affiliations' including folders 'Archbishop's Committee' and 'South African Association of Anthropologists'.

Chapter 3

Ellen Hellmann Papers [EHP], Witwatersrand University, Johannesburg

A1419 Ellen Hellmann Papers, Witwatersrand University, William Cullen Library.
A1419/6 Original Manuscript of Wits D.Phil Thesis of 1939, 'A Report on the Problems of Urban Bantu Youth'.
A1419/6 Photographs of Johannesburg Townships
A1419/35 Original Manuscript of Wits M.A. Thesis of 1935, 'Rooiyard'.
A1419 Photographs of Rooiyard
A1419/45 Talks.
Reviews and draft reviews; Newspaper cuttings; Proposal for Award of D.Litt. Honoris Causa, 29 August 1977 compiled by D. Hammond-Tooke and A. Dubb.

Kaplan Centre Archive, University of Cape Town

Kaplan Centre for Jewish Studies, University of Cape Town, Kaplan Centre Archive
BC949 Tape-recorded Interview with Ellen Hellmann by Riva Krut, Johannesburg, 3 June 1982.

Colin Legum Papers, University of Cape Town

BC1349 Colin Legum Papers, University of Cape Town Libraries, Manuscripts and Archives Department.
B11.38–39 Letters from Ellen Hellmann to Colin Legum, 1943–44.
B11.40 Hellmann (Koch) to Legum, 1970–71.
F1.1.1 Personal Diary, 1946.

Bibliography 287

Jewish Board of Deputies Library, Johannesburg
ARCH 809 File on Ellen Hellmann, Public Relations Committee Minutes 1944–1950.

Ruth Runciman, Private Family Photograph Album, London

Chapter 4

Audrey Richards Papers [ARP], London School of Economics, London
Audrey Richards Papers, Archives and Rare Books Collection, London School of Economics.
Richards 5/4 Makapanstad 1940–1942: 1. Report on Second Expedition to Makapanstad in September 1940.
Richards 16/36 Letters between Audrey Richards and Hilda Kuper, 1949–1984.
Richards 18/3 File 1 Letters from Audrey Richards to Dame Isabel Richards, Johannesburg, 1938–1940.
Richards 20/4 Press Cuttings.

Royal Anthropological Institute, Photographic Collection: Richards
Audrey Richards, Folder Bembaland, RAI 27731, RAI 35583.
Audrey Richards, Folder 26a Personal (South Africa), RAI001-007.
Audrey Richards, Folder 26b Urban Native Johannesburg, RAI008-RA1026.

Chapter 5

Hilda Kuper Papers [HKP], University of California Los Angeles, Los Angeles
Coll. 1343 Hilda Kuper Papers, Special Collections, UCLA Library, Los Angeles as listed in *Finding Aid for the Hilda Kuper Papers, c. 1930–1992* (Online Archive of California: California Digital Library).
Box 16, Folder 5: Interview with Hilda Kuper by Gelya Frank. June 28 1979. Rough Transcript of an Interview on *Sobhuza II* (1978).
Box 19, Folder 3: Proposal: Biography of King Sobhuza II of Swaziland. Submitted by HK to the Ford Foundation. May 1972.
Box 22, Folder 8: Anthropology and Literature. A Talk by Hilda Kuper.
Box 23, Folders 9–10: HK – Biographical.
Box 24, Folder 18: Correspondence – Sobhuza II.
Box 24, Folder 20: Correspondence – Thoko Ginindza.
Box 39, Folder 11: Correspondence with Desmond Reader, Audrey Richards.
Box 40, Folder 2: Correspondence – Pierre van den Berghe.
Box 40, Folder 6: Correspondence – *A Witch in My Heart.*

288   Bibliography

Box 40, Folder 20: Correspondence – Max Gluckman.
Box 40, Folder 22: Correspondence – Meyer Fortes.
Box 40, Folder 29: Correspondence – Adam Kuper.
Box 41, Folder 6: Unpublished Study of Western Native Township, 1945 by HK.
Box 44, Folder 1: Stories by HK.
Box 44, Folder 2: Writings, articles and clippings by Hilda Kuper, c. 1945–
Box 44, Folder 3: Short stories and articles.
Box 44, Folders 4–5: Poetry by Hilda Kuper.
Box 45, Folders 2–3: Writings by HK.
Box 45, Folder 9: Photographs – King Sobhuza with HK at Reed Dance, Lobamba, September 1981.
Box 45, Folder 7: Photographs – HK in Swaziland.
Box 48, Folder 1: Women-Wisconsin, Talk on 'What We Have in Common', April 1975.
Box 52, Folder 7: Correspondence, 1970s–1980s. Hilda Kuper to Bengt Sundkler, 1977.
Box 60, Folder 1: Photographs of Swaziland on Loose Pages.
Box 60, Folder 2: Loose black and white photographs – Swaziland.
Box 60, Folder 4: Photographs of Johannesburg.
Box 62, Folder 4: Photo album of Swaziland.
Hilda Kuper, Microfilm copy of 'Field-notes of Anthropological Research in Swaziland and South Africa, 1931–1985', Reel 1: Notebooks 2–9 (1934–5), Reel 2: Notebooks 13–19 (1935–6), Reel 3; Notebooks 20–28 (1936–1941). Selected for filming by UCLA Special Collections, 1991.

Malinowski Papers [MP], London School of Economics, London
London School of Economics, Malinowski Papers, Malinowski 7/3 Students 1932–1934: Hilda Beemer. Letters between Malinowski and Hilda Beemer, 1932–1935 including field reports from Hilda Beemer.

Jenny Kuper, Private Family Photograph Album, London

Chapter 6

Eileen Krige Papers [EKP], Killie Campbell Africana Library, University of Kwazulu-Natal, Durban
Jack and Eileen Krige Papers, Killie Campbell Library, Durban as listed in Emily-Ann Krige, *Inventory of the Eileen Jensen Krige Papers, 1927–1991* (Durban: Killie Campbell Library, 2002).
Files 1–6: Notebooks of Family Budgets from Grahamstown Locations.

Bibliography 289

File 7: Memorandum submitted to the National Health Commission by E. Jensen Krige, Social Science Department, Rhodes University College on 'Nutrition among Natives of Grahamstown Locations'.

File 14: Eileen Jensen, 'Problems of Poverty with Special Reference to Johannesburg' (unpublished M.A. thesis, Economics, 1927), 62 pp.

File 15: Eileen Krige, 'Medicine, Magic and Religion of the Lovedu' (unpublished D.Litt, Social Anthropology, 1940), 255 pp.

File 35: Correspondence and lists regarding plants, insects, and food-stuff collected by E.J. Krige and J.D. Krige in Modjadji during their fieldwork in 1937 and 1938.

Files 45–74: Simeon Modjadji: Correspondence, diaries, court-case notebooks, and answers to queries, 1938–1975.

File 187: Correspondence with Harriet Sibisi: Harriet Sibisi to Eileen Krige, 'Answers to Questions', 1966.

File 195: Dr. Eileen Krige, 'Implications of the Tomlinson Commission Report for Africans Living in the Rural Reserves in Natal', 1955.

File 257: Correspondence with Absolom Vilakazi: Absolom Vilakazi to Eileen Krige, Washington, DC, USA, 1972.

Files 229 and 230: Eileen Jensen Krige, *Social Structure and Political Arrangements of the Lovedu in the Setting of Historical Change* (HSRC Report, 1975), xvi–xxiv + 406 pp. with 46 figures, 7 diagrams, 2 tables, 13 genealogical charts and appendices. File 229 includes Monica Wilson's detailed annotations across the text.

File 417: Eileen Krige, 'Typescript draft of "curriculum vitae" prepared for her application for Chair of Social Anthropology [1960], and brought up to date in 1975'.

File 417: Copies of letters from Eileen Krige to Killie Campbell, 1959–1964.

File 418: Basic typed transcriptions of 'Writings and Jottings about Early Fieldwork Experiences', August–September 1986.

Thor and Dulcie Krige Papers [TDKP], Private Collection, Durban

Eileen's Personal Photographs, Labelled by Emily-Ann Krige, identification by Eileen Krige, c 1989.

Eileen Jensen, Diary of the General Strike, 9–15 March [1922].

Eileen Jensen, Loose Notes ('Private Diary'), Johannesburg, 18 March 1923, 20 March 1923 and 26 January 1924.

Eileen Jensen, Letters from Jack Krige before and during the time of their engagement, 1926–1928.

Eileen Krige, Letter to William Keith Hancock, Durban, 1 June 1966.

Newspaper cuttings headed 'Prof. Krige Gets Senior U.S. Science Award', *The Daily News*, 1 October 1968; 'Anthropologist back from America', *The Daily News*, 21 October 1971.

Jack Krige's books in Thor and Dulcie Krige Family Library, Durban.

290 Bibliography

Jack and Eileen Krige Photographic Collection, Iziko South African Museum, Cape Town

Jack and Eileen Krige Photographic Collection, Social History Archive, Iziko South African Museum, Cape Town.
Patricia Davison, Private Papers donated by Eileen Krige, Letters from Andreas Matatanya to Eileen Krige, Bolobedu School, 1931–1932.

Chapters 1–6

J.D. Rheinallt-Jones Papers, Witwatersrand University, Johannesburg

Witwatersrand University, William Cullen Library, AD843 Rheinallt-Jones Collection, South African Institute of Race Relations Papers.
Box 174: AD843/RJ/K6.18.1, File for the Inter-University Committee for African Studies, Letters from Schapera and Oldham to Rheinallt-Jones, 1933–1934; Applications for funding from Monica Hunter, June 1933; Applications for funding from Jack and Eileen Krige, Pretoria, 20 July 1934.
Box 182: SAIRR Papers: AD843/RJ/Kb 32.2.1.5, Bantu Affairs Research Committee, Winifred Hoernlé to Max Drennan, Chairman of the Bantu Studies Research Grant Committee, 2 May 1926. AD843/RJ, Kb32.2.1.5 'Allocation of Research Grants by the Department of Bantu Studies', 1926–1927; AD843/ RJ/Kb32.2.1.2, Bantu Affairs, Research Committees: Winifred Hoernlé, 'Application for a Grant in Aid of Research', 1927.
AD843/RJ, Kb32.2.1.5, Bantu Research Affairs Committee, 1930–1931: 'Minutes of a Meeting of the Bantu Studies Research Committee', 9 June 1931; SAIRR: Education: Wits Department of Bantu Affairs: Bantu Affairs Research Committee, 1930–1, E. Krige.
AD843/RJ/ND4.1, Minutes of a Conference on Juvenile Native Delinquency, Johannesburg, 11–13 October 1938, 1–10.

Interviews

Interview with Raymond Apthorpe, 15 May 2013, London.
Telephone interview with Gina Buijs, 26 April 2014, Cape Town-Bedford, Eastern Cape.
Interview with Lucy Dlamini, 14 July 2011, Manzini, Swaziland.
Interview with Adam Kuper, 10 May 2013, London.
Interview with Jenny Kuper, 13 May 2013, London.
Skype interview with Mary Kuper, 13 August 2011, Cape Town-London.
Interview with Thor Krige, 19 January 2014, Durban.
Interview with Dulcie Krige, 22 January 2014, Durban.

Bibliography 291

Interview with Emily-Ann Krige, 24 January 2014, Durban.

Telephone interview with Susan Middleton, 25 January 2014, Cape Town-Durban.

Telephone interview with Eleanor Preston-Whyte, 4 February 2014, Cape Town-Johannesburg.

Telephone interview with Eleanor Preston-Whyte, 11 June 2014, Cape Town-Johannesburg.

Interview with Pamela Reynolds, 15 March 2013, Cape Town.

Telephone interview with Ruth Runciman, 3 September 2011, Cape Town-London.

Telephone interview with Ruth Runciman, 5 September 2011, Cape Town-London.

E-mail correspondence

E-mail correspondence, Robert Edgar, 1 October 2014, Washington DC-Cape Town.

E-mail correspondence, Sondra Hale, 8 October 2014, Los Angeles-Cape Town.

E-mail correspondence, Emily-Ann Krige, 5 April 2014, Durban-Cape Town.

E-mail correspondence, Emily-Ann Krige, 7 April 2014, Durban-Cape Town.

E-mail correspondence, Adam Kuper, 14 September 2013, London-Cape Town.

E-mail correspondence, Jenny Kuper, 5 October 2014, London-Cape Town.

E-mail correspondence, Mary Kuper, 21 April 2014, London-Cape Town.

E-mail correspondence, Ruth Runciman, 2 February 2012, London-Cape Town.

E-mail correspondence, Michael W. Young, 15 November 2013, Canberra-Cape Town.

General titles

Ambler, Chuck and Jonathan Crush, 'Alcohol in Southern African Labour History' in Jonathon Crush and Chuck Ambler, eds., *Liquor and Labor in Southern Africa* (Athens, Ohio and Pietermaritzburg: Ohio University Press and Natal University Press, 1992).

Apter, Andrew, 'In Dispraise of the King: Rituals "Against" Rebellion in South-East Africa', *Man*, 18 (1983), 521–34.

Argyle, John, 'Eileen Jensen Krige (1904–1995)', *African Studies*, 54, 2 (1995), 112–15.

292 Bibliography

Argyle, John and Eleanor Preston-Whyte, eds., *Social System and Tradition in Southern Africa: Essays in Honour of Eileen Krige* (Cape Town: Oxford University Press, 1978).

Bank, Andrew, 'The Great Debate and the Origins of South African Historiography', *Journal of African History*, 38, 1 (1997), 261–81.

Bushmen in a Victorian World: The Remarkable Story of the Bleek-Lloyd Collection of Bushman Folklore (Cape Town: Double Storey Press, 2006).

'The "Intimate Politics" of Fieldwork: Monica Hunter and Her African Assistants, Pondoland and the Eastern Cape, 1931–1932', *Journal of Southern African Studies*, 34, 3 (September 2008), 557–74.

'The Making of a Woman Anthropologist: Monica Hunter at Girton College, Cambridge, 1927–1930', *African Studies*, 68, 1 (April 2009), 29–56.

'The Berlin Mission Society and German Linguistic Roots of *Volkekunde*: The Background, Training and Hamburg Writings of Werner Eiselen, 1899–1925' in Andrew Bank and Nancy Jacobs, eds., *Kronos: Southern African Histories, Special Issue: The Micro-Politics of Knowledge Production in Southern Africa*, 41 (November 2015) 166–92.

'Fathering *Volkekunde*: Race and Culture in the Ethnological Writings of Werner Eiselen, Stellenbosch University, 1926–1936', *Anthropology Southern Africa*, 38, 3–4 (2015), 163–79.

'*Broederbande* [Brotherly Bonds]: Afrikaner Nationalist Masculinity and African Sexuality in the Writings of Werner Eiselen's Students, Stellenbosch University, 1930–1936', *Anthropology Southern Africa*, 38, 3–4 (2015), 180–97.

Bank, Andrew, and Leslie J. Bank, eds., *Inside African Anthropology: Monica Wilson and Her Interpreters* (New York: Cambridge University Press in association with the International African Institute, 2013; Africa edn. 2014).

Bank, Leslie J., *Home Spaces, Street Styles: Contesting Power and Identity in a South African City* (London: Pluto Press, 2011).

Beard, Mary, *The Invention of Jane Harrison* (Cambridge, MA and London: Harvard University Press, 2000).

Beemer, Hilda, 'The Swazi Rain Ceremony, critical comment by P.J. Schoeman', *Bantu Studies*, 9, 3 (September 1935), 273–80.

'The Development of the Military Organization in Swaziland', *Africa*, 10, 1&2 (January & April 1937), 55–74, 176–205.

'The Swazi' in A.M. Duggan-Cronin, ed., *The Bantu Tribes of South Africa: Reproductions of Photographic Studies, Vol III, Section IV: The Swazi* (Cambridge and Kimberley: Deighton, Bull & Co. and the Alexander McGregor Memorial Museum, 1941), 9–32.

'Rank among the Swazi of the Protectorate' (Ph.D. thesis, London School of Economics, August 1942).

Beinart, William, 'Speaking for Themselves' in Andrew D. Spiegel and Patrick A. McAllister, eds., *Tradition and Transition in Southern Africa: Festschrift for Philip and Iona Mayer* (Johannesburg: Witwatersrand University Press, 1991), 11–35.

Bibliography 293

Belling, Veronica-Sue, 'Recovering the Lives of South African Jewish Women during the Migration Years, c 1880–1939' (unpublished D.Phil. thesis, University of Cape Town, 2013).

Bonner, Philip, *Kings, Commoners and Concessionaries: The Evolution and Dissolution of the Nineteenth-Century Swazi State* (Cambridge: Cambridge University Press, 1983).

Boyd, Valerie, *Wrapped in Rainbows: The Life of Zora Neale Hurston* (London: Virago, 2003).

Brokensha, David, 'Monica Wilson 1908–1982: An Appreciation', *Africa*, 53, 3 (1983), 83–4.

Brown, Duncan, 'Religion, Spirituality and the Postcolonial: A Perspective from the South' in Brown, ed., *Religion and Spirituality in South Africa: New Perspectives* (Scottsville: University of Kwazulu-Natal Press, 2009), 1–26.

Brown, Richard, 'Anthropology and Colonial Rule: Godfrey Wilson and the Rhodes-Livingstone Institute' in Talal Asad, ed., *Anthropology and the Colonial Encounter* (New York: Humanities Press, 1973), 173–97.

'Passages in the Life of a White Anthropologist: Max Gluckman in Northern Rhodesia', *Journal of African History*, 20, 4 (1979), 227–42.

Burman, Sandra and Eleanor Preston-Whyte, eds., *Questionable Issue: Illegitimacy in South Africa* (Cape Town: Oxford University Press, 1992).

Cambridge University Examination Papers: Michaelmas Term 1929 to Easter Term 1930, Vol. 54 (Cambridge: Cambridge University Press, 1930).

Carstens, Peter, 'Agnes Winifred Hoernlé (1885–1960): The Mother of Social Anthropology in South Africa', *Anthropology Today*, 1, 6 (December 1985), 17–18.

ed., *Nama Social Organisation and Other Essays: A. W. Hoernlé Centenary Volume* (Johannesburg: Witwatersrand University Press, 1985).

Carstens, Peter, Gerald Klinghardt and Martin West, eds., *Trails in the Thirstland: The Anthropological Field Diaries of Winifred Hoernlé* (Cape Town: University of Cape Town African Studies Centre, Communication Series, No. 14, 1987).

Clifford, James, *The Predicament of Culture: Twentieth-Century Ethnography, Literature, and Art* (Cambridge, MA: Harvard University Press, 1988).

Cocks, Paul, 'The King and I: Bronislaw Malinowski, King Sobhuza II of Swaziland and the Vision of Culture Change in Africa', *History of the Human Sciences*, 13, 4 (2000), 25–47.

Comaroff, Jean, *Body of Power, Spirit of Resistance: The Culture and History of a South African People* (Chicago: University of Chicago Press, 1985).

Comaroff, Jean and John L. Comaroff, 'On Founding Fathers, Fieldwork and Functionalism: A Conversation with Isaac Schapera', *American Ethnologist*, 15, 3 (August 1988), 554–65.

Comaroff, Jean and John L. Comaroff, *Of Revelation and Revolution: Christianity, Colonialism, and Consciousness in South Africa, Vol. 1* (Chicago and London: Chicago University Press, 1991).

Comaroff, John L., Jean Comaroff and Deborah James, eds., *Picturing a Colonial Past: The African Photographs of Isaac Schapera* (Chicago: Chicago University Press, 2007).

294   Bibliography

Davison, Patricia, 'Human Subjects as Museum Objects: A Project to Make Life-Casts of "Bushmen" and "Hottentots", 1907–1924', *Annals of the South African Museum*, 102, 5 (1993).

Lobedu Material Culture: A Comparative Study of the 1930s and the 1970s (Cape Town: Annals of the South African Museum, 1984).

Davison, Patricia and George Mahashe, 'Visualizing the Realm of the Rain Queen: The Production and Circulation of Eileen and Jack Krige's Lobedu Fieldwork Photographs from the 1930s' in Diana Wylie and Andrew Bank, eds., *Kronos: Southern African Histories, Special Issue: Documentary Photography in South Africa*, 38 (November 2012), 47–81.

Delius, Peter and Clive Glaser, 'Sexual Socialization in South Africa: A Historical Perspective' in Peter Delius and Liz Walker, eds., *African Studies Special Issue: AIDS in Context*, 61, 1 (2002), 27–54.

Delius, Peter and Clive Glaser, 'The Myths of Polygamy: A History of Extra-Marital and Multi-Partnership Sex in South Africa', *South African Historical Journal*, 50 (2004), 84–114.

Dubb, Allie, *Jewish South Africans: A Sociological View of the Johannesburg Community* (Rhodes University, Institute of Social and Economic Research, Occasional Paper, No. 21, 1977).

Dubow, Saul, *Illicit Union: Scientific Racism in Modern South Africa* (Johannesburg: Witwatersrand University Press, 1995).

ed., *Science and Society in Southern Africa* (Manchester: Manchester University Press, 2000).

Dubow, Saul and Alan Jeeves, eds., *South Africa's 1940s: Worlds of Possibilities* (Cape Town: Double Storey, 2005).

Du Toit, Marijke, 'The General View and Beyond: From Slumyard to Township in Ellen Hellmann's Photographs of Women and the African Familial in the 1930s', *Gender and History*, 17, 3 (November 2005), 593–626.

Eagleton, Terry, *Reason, Faith and Revolution: Reflections on the God Debate* (New Haven and London: Yale University Press, 2009).

Ellison, James, 'Transforming Obligations, Performing Identity: Making the Nyakyusa in a Colonial Context' (unpublished D.Phil thesis, University of Florida, 1999).

'Bilingual Assistants and "Tribal" Bodies in Colonial Tanganyika' (unpublished paper presented at the American African Studies Association, Chicago, 25 October 1998).

Evans-Pritchard, Edward E., *The Nuer* (Oxford: Oxford University Press, 1940).

Fardon, Richard, *Mary Douglas: An Intellectual Biography* (London: Routledge, 1999).

Ferguson, James, *Expectations of Modernity: Myths and Meanings of Urban Life on the Zambian Copperbelt* (Berkeley: University of California Press, 1999).

Firth, Raymond, 'Audrey Richards 1899–1984', *Man*, 20, 2 (June 1985), 341–344.

Fortes, Meyer, 'An Anthropologist's Apprenticeship', *Annual Review of Anthropology*, 7, 1 (1978), 1–30.

Fortes, Meyer and Sheila Patterson, *Studies in African Social Anthropology: Essays Presented to Professor Schapera* (London: New York Academic Press, 1975).

Bibliography

Fuller, Chris, 'Book Review: Ambivalence about Apartheid. Anthropology of This Century', *LSE Research Online* (October 2012).

Gacs, Ute, Aisha Khan, Jerrie McIntyre and Ruth Weinberg, eds., *Women Anthropologists: A Biographical Dictionary* (New York, London, Westport, CT: Greenwood Press, 1988).

Gaitskell, Deborah, 'Introduction', *Journal of Southern African Studies: Special Issue: Women in Southern Africa*, 10, 1 (1983), 1–13.

Gillespie, Kelly, 'Containing the "Wandering Native": Racial Jurisdiction and the Liberal Politics of Prison Reform in 1940s South Africa', *Journal of Southern African Studies*, 37, 3 (September 2011), 499–515.

Gladstone, Jo, 'Significant Sister: Autonomy and Obligation in Audrey Richards' Early Fieldwork', *American Ethnologist*, 13, 2 (1986), 338–56.

'Audrey I Richards (1899–1984)', *Bulletin of the Society for the Social History of Medicine*, 40 (1987), 115–37.

'Audrey I Richards (1899–1984): Africanist and Humanist' in Shirley Ardener, ed., *Persons and Powers of Women in Diverse Cultures* (New York and Oxford: Berg Press, 1992), 13–28.

Glaser, Clive, *Bo-Tsotsi: The Youth Gangs of Soweto, 1935–1976* (Portsmouth, New Haven: Heinemann, 2000).

Gluckman, Max, 'Analysis of a Social Situation in Zululand', *Bantu Studies*, 14 (1940), 1–30, 147–74.

'Review of *An African Aristocracy*', *Africa*, 18, 1 (January 1948), 63–4.

Rituals of Rebellion in South-East Africa (Frazer Lecture 1952, Manchester: Manchester University Press, 1954).

Gluckman, Max and Isaac Schapera, 'Dr Winifred Hoernlé: An Appreciation', *Africa*, 30 (1960), 262–63.

Golde, Peggy, ed., *Women in the Field: Anthropological Experiences* (Chicago, IL: Aldine Press, 1970).

Gordon, David M., *Invisible Agents: Spirits in a Central African History* (Athens, OH: Ohio University Press, 2012).

Gordon, Robert, 'Apartheid's Anthropologists: The Genealogy of Afrikaner Anthropology', *American Ethnologist*, 15, 3 (1988), 535–52.

'Early Social Anthropology in South Africa', *African Studies*, 49, 1 (1990), 15–48.

'"Tracks which cannot be covered": P.J. Schoeman and Public Intellectuals in Southern Africa', *Historia*, 52, 1 (2007), 98–125.

'Max Gluckman in Zululand' (unpublished seminar paper, Anthropology Southern Africa Conference, Wits University, September 2013).

Gordon, Robert, Andrew P. Lyons and Harriet D. Lyons, eds., *Fifty Key Anthropologists* (London and New York: Routledge, 2010).

Gruber, Jacob W., 'Ethnographic Salvage and the Shaping of Anthropology', *American Anthropologist*, 61 (1959), 379–89.

Haddon, Alfred Cort, 'Keynote Address', *South African Society for the Advancement of Science: Report of 1905: Transactions of Section H*, 524–25.

Hammond-Tooke, W. David, *Imperfect Interpreters: South Africa's Anthropologists, 1920–1990* (Johannesburg: Witwatersrand University Press, 1997; 2nd edn. 2001).

296 Bibliography

Handler, Richard, ed., *Significant Others: Interpersonal and Professional Commitments in Anthropology* (Madison, WI: University of Wisconsin Press, 2004).

Hansen, Karen Tranberg, 'Urban Research in a Hostile Setting: Godfrey Wilson in Broken Hill, 1938–1941' in Andrew Bank and Nancy Jacobs, eds., *Kronos: Southern African Histories, Special Issue: The Micro-Politics of Knowledge Production in Southern Africa*, 41 (November 2015), 193–214.

Hansen, Thomas Blom, *Melancholia of Freedom: Social Life in an Indian Township in South Africa* (Princeton: Princeton University Press, 2012).

Harries, Patrick, *Butterflies and Barbarians: Swiss Missionaries and Systems of Knowledge in South-East Africa* (Oxford: James Currey, 2007).

Hellmann, Ellen, 'Native Life in a Johannesburg Slum Yard', *Africa*, 8, 1 (1935), 34–62.

'Methods of Urban Field Work', *Bantu Studies: Special Issue dedicated to Winifred Hoernlé*, 9, 3 (September 1935), 185–90.

'Urban Native Food in Johannesburg', *Africa*, 9, 2 (April 1936), 277–90.

'Research into the Problems of Urban Bantu Youth' (D.Phil thesis, Witwatersrand University, 1939).

Problems of Urban Bantu Youth (Johannesburg: South African Institute of Race Relations, 1940).

'Social Services for Urban Africans', *Race Relations*, 8, 4 (1941), 1–14.

'Labour Zionism in South Africa', *The Pioneer Woman*, December 1944, 5.

'The Jewish American Scene', *Jewish Affairs*, August 1945, 4.

'"Heartbreak House": A Liberal Look at South African Native Policy', *Jewish Affairs*, April 1946.

Rooiyard: A Sociological Survey of an Urban Native Slum Yard (Livingstone, Rhodes-Livingstone Institute Papers, No. 13, 1948).

'Urban Areas' in Ellen Hellmann, ed., *Handbook on Race Relations in South Africa* (New York, Oxford and Cape Town: Oxford University Press, 1949), 229–274.

'Plea against Jewish "Isolationism"', *Jewish Affairs*, 5, 10 (October 1950), 4–6.

'The Jews Problems Cannot Be Isolated', *Jewish Affairs*, 6, 5 (May 1951), 8–9.

Sellgoods: A Sociological Survey of an African Commercial Labour Force (Johannesburg: South African Institute of Race Relations, 1953).

'The Application of the Concept of Separate Development to Urban Areas in the Union of South Africa' in Kenneth Kirkwood, ed., *African Affairs: St. Anthony's Papers, Number One* (London: Chatto and Windus, 1961), 120–46.

'Review of *The Black Man's Portion* and *Townsman or Tribesman*', *African Studies*, 21, 1 (1962), 40–3.

'Social Change among Urban Africans' in Heribert Adam, ed., *South Africa: Sociological Perspectives* (London, New York, Toronto and Cape Town: Oxford University Press, 1971), 158–76.

'The South African Institute of Race Relations, 1929 to 1979' in Ellen Hellmann and Henry Lever, eds., *Conflict and Progress: Fifty Years of Race Relations in South Africa* (Johannesburg: Macmillan, 1979).

Bibliography

Hellmann, Ellen and Quinton Whyte, 'Introduction', *Race Relations Journal: Special Issue: Homage to Winifred Hoernlé*, 22, 4 (1955), 1–5.

Hendricks, Fred, 'The Mafeje Affair: UCT, Apartheid and the Question of Academic Freedom', *African Studies*, 67, 3 (2008), 432–52.

Herle, Anita and Rouse, Sandra, eds., *Cambridge and the Torres Strait: Centenary Essays on the 1898 Anthropological Expedition* (Cambridge: Cambridge University Press, 1998).

Hoernlé, Winifred, 'Certain Rites of Transition and the Conception of !Nau among the Hottentots', *Harvard African Studies*, 2 (1918), 65–82.

'A Hottentot Rain Ceremony', *Bantu Studies*, 1, 3–4 (1922), 75–6.

'The Expression of the Social Value of Water among the Nama of South-West Africa', *South African Journal of Science*, 20 (1923), 514–26.

'The Social Organization of the Nama Hottentots of Southwest Africa', *American Anthropologist*, 27 (1925), 1–24.

'The Importance of the Sib [Clan] in the Marriage Ceremonies of the South-Eastern Bantu', *South African Journal of Science*, 22 (1925), 481–92.

'New Aims and Methods in Social Anthropology. Presidential Address to Section E of the South African Association for the Advancement of Science, 4 July 1933', *South African Journal of Science*, 30 (1933), 74–92.

'Review of *Reaction to Conquest*', *Africa*, 10, 1 (1937), 121–6.

'Foreword' to Hilda Kuper, *The Uniform of Colour: A Study of Black-White Relationships in Swaziland* (Johannesburg: Witwatersrand University Press, 1947), vii–x.

'Review of Ellen Hellmann, *Rooiyard*', *African Studies*, 7, 4 (1948), 191–2.

Hunter, Monica, 'Results of Culture Contact on the Pondo and Xhosa Family', *South African Journal of Science*, 29 (1932), 681–6.

'In Pondoland', *The Girton Review*, 92 (Easter Term 1933), 27–9.

'The Effects of Contact with Europeans on the Status of Pondo Women', *Africa*, 6, 3 (1933), 259–76.

'Review of *Valenge Women* by E. Dora Earthy', *Africa*, 7, 1 (January 1934), 110–12.

'Methods of Study of Culture Contact', *Africa*, 7, 3 (1934), 335–50.

'Effects of Culture Contact on the Pondo of South Africa' (Ph.D. thesis, Cambridge University, 1934).

Reaction to Conquest: Effects of Contact with Europeans on the Pondo of South Africa (London: Oxford University Press for the International Institute of African Languages and Cultures, 1936; 2nd edn. 1961; Cape Town: David Philip in association with Rex Collings, London, 1979, 3rd edn.; Berlin, LIT on behalf of the International African Institute, 2009: Classics in African Anthropology Series, 4th edn.).

'The Story of Nosente, the Mother of Compassion' in Margery Perham, ed., *Ten Africans* (London: Faber and Faber, 1936), 122–37.

'An African Christian Morality', *Africa*, 10, 3 (1937), 265–91.

Iliffe, John, *The African Poor: A History* (Cambridge: Cambridge University Press, 1987).

Jensen, Eileen, 'Problems of Poverty with Special Reference to Johannesburg' (unpublished M.A. thesis, Witwatersrand University, 1927).

298 Bibliography

Junod, Henri Alexandre, *The Life of a South African Tribe*, 2 Vols. (Neuchatel: A. Freres, 1912–13).

Koch, Eddie, 'Doornfontein and Its African Working Class, 1914–1935' (unpublished M.A. thesis, Witwatersrand University, 1983).

'"Without Visible Means of Subsistence": Slumyard Culture in Johannesburg, 1918–1940' in Belinda Bozzoli, ed., *Town and Countryside in the Transvaal* (Johannesburg: Ravan Press, 1983), 152–75.

Krige, Eileen Jensen, 'Agricultural Ceremonies and Practices of the Balobedu', *Bantu Studies*, 5 (1931), 207–39.

'The Social Significance of Beer among the Balobedu', *Bantu Studies*, 6 (1932), 343–57.

'Some Social and Economic Facts Revealed in Native Family Budgets', *Race Relations*, 1 (1934), 94–108.

'Changing Conditions in Marital Relations and Parental Duties among Urbanized Natives', *Africa*, 9 (1936), 1–23.

The Social System of the Zulus (London: Longmans, 1936; Pietermaritzburg: Shuter & Shooter, 1950, 2nd edition; 1965, 3rd edn. 1965).

'Medicine, Magic and Religion of the Lovedu' (unpublished D.Litt thesis, Witwatersrand University, 1940).

'Agnes Winifred Hoernlé: An Appreciation', *African Studies*, 19, 1 (March, 1960), 138–44.

'Property, Cross-Cousin Marriage and the Family Cycle among the Lovedu' in Robert F. Gray and Peter H. Gulliver, eds., *The Family Estate in Africa* (London: Routledge and Kegan Paul, 1964), 155–96.

'Girls' Puberty Songs and Their Relation to Fertility, Morality and Religion among the Zulu', *Africa*, 38 (1968), 173–98.

'Winifred Hoernlé', *Dictionary of South African Biography, Vol. 4* (Pretoria: Government Publishers, 1968), 238–9.

'Some Zulu Concepts Important for an Understanding of Fertility – and Other Rituals' in Nicolas J. Ethnological and Linguistic Essays in Honour of N.J. van Warmelo (Pretoria: Government Ethnographic Department, 1969).

'Woman-Marriage with Special Reference to the Lovedu – Its Significance for the Definition of Marriage', *Africa*, 44 (1974), 11–37.

'A Lovedu Prayer: The Light Thrown on the Ancestor Cult' in Allie Dubb and A.G. Schutte, eds., *African Studies: Special Issue on Black Religion in South Africa*, 33, 2 (1974), 91–8.

Social Structure and Political Arrangements of the Lovedu in the Setting of Historical Change (Pretoria: Report Submitted to the H.S.R.C., 1975).

'Asymmetrical Matrilineal Cross-Cousin Marriage: The Lovedu Case', *African Studies*, 34 (1975), 231–7.

'Challenges in the Social Sciences and Western Society Today' in J.V.O. Reid, ed., *University of Natal, 1977 Graduation Addresses and Citations* (Pietermaritzburg: Natal University Press, 1977), 18–25.

Krige, Eileen Jensen and John L. Comaroff, eds., *Essays on African Marriage in Southern Africa* (Cape Town and Johannesburg: Juta and Co. Ltd., 1981).

Krige, Eileen Jensen and Jack D. Krige, *The Realm of a Rain-Queen: A Study of the Pattern of Lovedu Society* (London, New York and Toronto: Published for the

Bibliography

International African Institute by Oxford University Press, 1943: reprinted 1943, 1947, 1956 and 1965).

Krige, Eileen Jensen and Jack D. Krige, 'The Lovedu of the Transvaal' in Darryll Forde, ed., *African Worlds: Studies in the Cosmological Ideas and Social Values of African Peoples* (London, New York and Toronto: Oxford University Press with the International African Institute, 1954), 55–83.

Krige, Eileen Jensen and George W. Mahlobo, 'Transition from Childhood to Adulthood amongst the Zulu', *Bantu Studies*, 8 (1934), 157–91.

Krige, Jack D. and Eileen Jensen Krige, 'The Implications of the Tomlinson Report for the Lovedu', *Race Relations Journal*, 23 (1955), 12–25.

Kros, Cynthia, *The Seeds of Separate Development: Origins of Bantu Education* (Pretoria: UNISA Press, 2010).

Kuklick, Henrika, 'Introduction' in Kuklick, ed., *Osiris: Special Issue: Science in the Field*, 11 (1996), 1–16.

Kuklick, Henrika, ed., *A New History on Anthropology* (Oxford: Wiley-Blackwell, 2008).

'Personal Equations: Reflections on the History of Fieldwork with Special Reference to Sociocultural Anthropology', *Isis*, 102, 1 (March 2011), 1–33.

Kuper, Adam, *Anthropologists and Anthropology: The British School, 1922–1972* (London: Routledge, 1973).

Among the Anthropologists: History and Context in Anthropology (London and New Brunswick, NJ: The Athlone Press, 1999).

'Isaac Schapera (1905–2003): His Life and Times' in John L. Comaroff, Jean Comaroff and Deborah James, eds., *The African Photographs of Isaac Schapera* (Chicago and London: Chicago University Press, 2007), 19–41.

Kuper, Hilda, 'Social Anthropology as a Study of Culture Contacts', *South African Journal of Science*, 41 (February 1945), 88–101.

An African Aristocracy: Rank among the Swazi (London, New York and Toronto: Oxford University Press in association with the International African Institute, 1947; 2nd edn. 1965; 3rd edn. 1981).

The Uniform of Colour: A Study of Black-White Relationships in Swaziland (Johannesburg: Wits University Press, 1947; 2nd edn. New York: Negro University Press, 1969).

'Swazi Feast of the First Fruits', *Libertas*, 71 (1947), 38–41.

'Civil Rights: U.S. and South Africa Comparisons', *Trek* (May 1949), 8–9.

'Kinship among the Swazi' in A.R. Radcliffe-Brown and Daryll Forde, eds., *African Systems of Kinship and Marriage* (London, New York and Toronto: Oxford University Press with the International African Institute, 1950), 86–110.

'An Ethnographic Description of a Hindustani Marriage in Durban', *African Studies*, 15, 1 (1956), 3–12.

'An Ethnographic Description of a Tamil-Hindu Marriage in Durban', *African Studies*, 15, 3 (1956), 207–16.

'An Interpretation of Hindu Marriage Rituals in Durban' *African Studies*, 16, 3 (1957), 221–35.

'The Amazement of Namahasha', *Africa South*, 2, 1 (1957), 102–7.

300   Bibliography

'The Indians of Natal' in Prudence Smith, ed., *African in Transition: BBC Talks on Changing Conditions in the Union and the Rhodesias* (London: Max Reinhart, 1958), 115–24.

'An Ethnographic Description of Kavady, A Hindu Ceremony in South Africa', *African Studies*, 18, 3 (1959), 118–32.

Indian People in Natal (Pietermaritzburg: Natal University Press, 1960; New York: Greenwood Press, 1974, 2nd edn.).

The Swazi: A South African Kingdom (New York, Chicago, San Francisco, Toronto and London: Holt, Rinehart and Winston, 1963; revised edn. 1985).

'Nursing' in Leo Kuper, *An African Bourgeoisie: Race, Class and Politics in South Africa* (New Haven and London: Yale University Press, 1965), 216–33.

ed., *Urbanization and Migration in West Africa* (Berkeley: University of California Press, 1965).

A Witch in My Heart: A Play Set in Swaziland in the 1930s (Oxford University Press published for the International African Institute, 1970; Zulu edn. with trans. by Trevor Cope, 1962; Swati edn. with trans. by Thembi Mthembu and Zodwa Ginindza, 1978).

'Color Categories and Colonialism: The Swazi Case' in Victor Turner, ed., *Colonialism in Africa, 1870–1960* (Cambridge: Cambridge University Press, 1971), 286–309.

'The Language of Sites in the Politics of Space', *American Anthropologist*, 74, 3 (1972), 411–25.

'A Royal Ritual in a Changing Political Context', *Cahiers d'Études Africaines*, 12 (1972), 593–615.

'Clothing and Identity', *Comparative Studies in Social History*, 16 (1973), 348–67.

'Costume and Cosmology: Animal Symbolism in the *Incwala*', *Man*, 8, 4 (1973), 613–30.

Sobhuza II: Ngwenyama and King of Swaziland: The Story of an Hereditary Ruler and his Country (London: Gerald Duckworth & Co., 1978).

Biography as Interpretation (Indiana University, African Studies Programme, 11th Hans Wolff Memorial Lecture, April 1980), 25–59.

'Function, History and Biography: Reflections on Fifty Years in the British Anthropological Tradition' in George W. Stocking, ed., *Functionalism Historicized: Essays on British Social Anthropology* (Madison, Wisconsin: University of Wisconsin Press, 1984), 192–213.

A Witch in My Heart, Short Stories and Poems (Wisconsin-Madison: University of Wisconsin-Madison, 1992).

Kuper, Hilda and Fatima Meer, *Indian Elites* (Pietermaritzburg: University of Natal Press, 1956).

Kuper, Hilda and Leo Kuper, eds., *African Law: Adaptation and Development* (Berkeley: University of California Press, 1965).

Kuper, Hilda and Selma Kaplan, 'Voluntary Associations in an Urban Township', *African Studies*, 3 (1944), 178–86.

Kuper, Leo, *Passive Resistance in South Africa* (London: Jonathan Cape, 1956).

La Fontaine, Jean S., *The Interpretation of Ritual: Essays in Honour of Audrey Richards* (London: Tavistock, 1972).

Bibliography 301

'Audrey Isabel Richards, 1899–1984', *Africa*, 55, 2 (1985), 201–6.

ed., *Cambridge Anthropology: Special Issue 'Audrey Richards: In Memoriam'*, 10, 1 (1985).

La Hausse, Paul, *Brewers, Beerhalls and Boycotts: A History of Liquor in South Africa* (Johannesburg: Ravan Press, History Workshop Topic Series, No. 2, 1989).

Lamb, Christina, *The Africa House: The True Story of an English Gentleman and His African Dream* (London: Penguin, 2000).

Lamphere, Louise, 'Unofficial Histories: A Vision of Anthropology from the Margins', *American Anthropologist*, 106, 1 (2004), 126–39.

Lau, Brigitte, *Southern and Central Namibia in Jonker Afrikaner's Time* (Windhoek: Windhoek Archives Publication Series, No. 8, 1987).

Laviolette, Patrick, 'Anthropology in the UK: Never Mind the Biographies, Here's the Reflexive Symbols', *Reviews in Anthropology*, 37 (2008), 231–58.

Leach, Edmund, 'Glimpses of the Unmentionable in the History of British Anthropology', *Annual Review of Anthropology*, 13 (1984), 1–22.

Legassick, Martin, 'Race, Industrialisation and Social Change in South Africa: The Case of RFA Hoernlé', *African Affairs*, 75, 299 (April 1976), 224–39.

Legassick, Martin and Ciraj Rassool, *Skeletons in the Cupboard: South African Museums and the Trade in Human Remains* (Cape Town: South African Museum, 1999).

Levin, Ruth, *Marriage in Langa Native Location* (Cape Town: UCT School of African Studies, 1947).

Levine, Susan, *Children of a Bitter Harvest: Child Labour in the Cape Winelands* (Cape Town: HSRC Press, 2013).

Lutkehaus, Nancy C., '"She Was Very Cambridge": Camilla Wedgwood and the History of Women in British Social Anthropology', *American Ethnologist*, 13, 4 (1986), 776–98.

Margaret Mead: The Making of an American Icon (Princeton, NJ: Princeton University Press, 2008).

Maccrone, I.D., 'A Memoir' in *Race and Reason, Being Mainly a Selection of Contributions to the Race Problem in South Africa by the late Professor R.F. Alfred Hoernlé* (Johanneburg: Wits University Press, 1945), vii–xxxvi.

Macmillan, Hugh, 'Swaziland: Decolonisation and the Triumph of "Tradition"', *Journal of Modern African Studies*, 23, 4 (1985), 643–66.

'A Nation Divided? The Swazi in Swaziland and the Transvaal, 1865–1986' in Leroy Vail, ed., *The Creation of Tribalism in Southern Africa* (Los Angeles and London: University of California Press and James Currey, 1989), 289–323.

'Administrators, Anthropologists and "Traditionalists" in Colonial Swaziland: The Case of the "Amabhaca" Fines', *Africa*, 65, 4 (1995), 545–61.

'Return to Malungwana Drift: Max Gluckman, the Zulu Nation and the Common Society', *African Affairs*, 94, 374 (1995), 39–65.

'From Race to Ethnic Identity: South Central Africa, Social Anthropology and the Shadow of the Holocaust' in Megan Vaughan and Patrick Harries, eds., *Social Dynamics: Special Issue: Essays in Commemoration of Leroy Vail*, 26, 2 (2000), 87–115.

302   Bibliography

'"Paralyzed Conservatives": W.M. Macmillan, the Social Scientists and "the Common Society", 1923–1948' in Hugh Macmillan and Shula Marks, eds., *Africa and Empire: W.M. Macmillan, Historian and Social Critic* (London: Institute for Commonwealth Studies, 1989), 72–90.

Mafeje, Archie, 'The Ideology of Tribalism', *Journal of Modern African Studies*, 9, 2 (1971), 253–61.

'Religion, Class and Ideology in South Africa' in Michael Whisson and Martin West, eds., *Religion and Social Change in Southern Africa: Anthropological Essays in Honour of Monica Wilson* (Cape Town: David Philip; London: Rex Collings, 1975), 164–84.

'A Commentary on [Sally Falk Moore's] Anthropology and Africa', *CODESRIA Bulletin*, 2 (1996), 6–13.

'Anthropology and Independent Africans: Suicide or the End of an Era?' *African Sociological Review*, 2, 1 (1998), 1–43.

Magubane, Bernard, 'The "Xhosa" in Town, Revisited Urban Social Anthropology: A Failure of Method and Theory', *American Anthropologist*, 75 (1973), 1701–15.

Magubane, Bernard M. with Mbulelo V. Mzamane, *Bernard Magubane: My Life and Times* (Scottsville: University of KwaZulu-Natal Press, 2010).

Malinowski, Bronislaw, *Sex and Repression in Savage Society* (New York: Harcourt Brace, 1927).

ed., *Methods of Study of Culture Contact in Africa* (London: Oxford University Press, 1938).

A Diary in the Strict Sense of the Term, trans. N. Guterman (London: Routledge, 1967).

Marwick, Max, 'Obituary: Professor J.D. Krige', *African Studies*, 18, 3 (1959), 146–48.

Mayer, Iona, 'From Kinship to Common Descent: Four Generation Genealogies among the Gusii', *Africa*, 35, 4 (1965), 366–84.

The Nature of Kinship Relations: The Significance of the Use of Kinship Terms among the Gusii (Lusaka: Rhodes-Livingstone Institute Papers, No. 37, 1966).

'Studies in Gusii Kinship' (unpublished Ph.D. thesis, Rhodes University, 1966).

'The Patriarchal Image: Routine Dissociation in Gusii Families', *African Studies*, 34, 4 (1975), 259–91.

Mayer, Philip with Iona Mayer, *Townsmen or Tribesmen: Conservatism and the Process of Urbanisation in a South African City* (Cape Town: Oxford University Press, Xhosa in Town Series, 1961; 2nd edn. 1973).

McAllister, Patrick A., *Building the Homestead: Agriculture, Labour and Beer in South Africa's Transkei* (Aldershot: Ashgate, 2001).

Xhosa Beer Drinking Rituals: Power, Practice and Performance in the South African Rural Periphery (Durham, NC: Carolina Academic Press, 2006).

Mendelsohn, Richard and Milton Shain, *The Jews in South Africa: An Illustrated History* (Johannesburg: Jonathan Ball, 2008).

Mills, David, 'How Not to Be a "Government House Pet": Audrey Richards and the East African Institute for Social Research' in Mwenda Ntarangwi,

Bibliography 303

David Mills and Muftata Babiker, eds., *African Anthropologies: History, Critique and Practice* (London: Zed Books, 2006), 77–98.

Modell, Judith Schachter, *Ruth Benedict: Patterns of a Life* (Philadelphia: University of Pennsylvania Press, 1983).

Mokoena, Hlonipha, *Magema Fuze: The Making of a Kholwa Intellectual* (Scottsville: University of KwaZulu-Natal Press, 2011).

Moran, Katy, 'Hilda Beemer Kuper (1911–)' in Ute Gacs, Aisha Khan, Jerrie McIntyre and Ruth Weinberg, eds., *Women Anthropologists: A Biographical Dictionary* (New York, London, Westport, Connecticut: Greenwood Press, 1988), 194–201.

Moore, Henrietta L. and Megan Vaughan, *Cutting Down Trees: Gender, Nutrition, and Agricultural Change in the Northern Province of Zambia, 1890–1990* (Portsmouth, New Haven, London and Lusaka: Heinemann, James Currey and University of Zambia Press, 1994).

Morrow, Seán, '"This Is from the Firm": The Anthropological Partnership of Monica and Godfrey Wilson' (unpublished paper presented at the Monica Hunter Wilson Centenary Conference, 24–26 June 2008).

Morrow, Seán, *Monica Wilson: A Biography* (Johannesburg: Penguin South Africa, 2015).

Murray, Bruce K., *Wits: The Early Years: A History of the University of the Witwatersrand, Johannesburg and Its Precursors, 1896–1939* (Johannesburg: Wits University Press, 1982).

Wits: The 'Open' Years, 1939–1959 (Johannesburg: Wits University Press, 1997).

'W.M. Macmillan: The Wits Years and Resignation', *South African Historical Journal*, 65, 2 (June 2013), 317–31.

Murray, Colin, '"So Truth Be in the Field": A Short Appreciation of Monica Wilson', *Journal of Southern African Studies*, 10, 1 (October 1983), 129–30.

Ngubane, Harriet, *Body and Mind in Zulu Medicine: An Ethnography of Health and Disease in Nyuswa-Zulu Thought and Practice* (London: Academic Press, 1979).

Niehaus, Isak, 'Adam Kuper: An Anthropologist's Account' in Deborah James, Evie Plaice and Christina Toren, eds., *Culture Wars. Context, Models and Anthropologists' Accounts* (New York: Berghahn Books, 2010), 170–87.

Niehaus, Isak, 'Anthropology at the Dawn of Apartheid: Radcliffe-Brown and Malinowski's South African Engagements, 1919–1940' (unpublished paper presented at the workshop 'Re-imagining Alterity and Affinity in Anthropology', University of Cambridge, 2015).

Nyamnjoh, Francis, 'Blinded by Sight: Divining the Future of Anthropology in Africa', *Africa Spectrum*, 47, 2–3 (2012), 63-92.

Parezo, Nancy, ed., *Hidden Scholars: Women Anthropologists and the Native American Southwest* (Albuquerque, NM: University of New Mexico Press, 1993).

Phillips, Howard, *The University of Cape Town, 1918–1948: The Formative Years* (Cape Town: University of Cape Town Press, 1993).

Preston-Whyte, Eleanor, 'Race Attitudes and Behaviour: The Case of Domestic Employment in White South African Homes', *African Studies*, 35, 2 (1976), 71–90.

Teenage Pregnancy in Selected Coloured and Black Communities (Pretoria: Human Sciences Research Council Press, 1991).

304   Bibliography

Preston-Whyte, Eleanor and Harriet Sibisi, 'Ethnographic Oddity or Ecological Sense? Nyuswa-Zulu Descent Groups and Land Alienation', *African Studies*, 34, 4 (1975), 283–316.

Preston-Whyte, Eleanor and Chris Rogerson, eds., *South Africa's Informal Economy* (Cape Town: Oxford University Press, 1991).

Quiggin, Allison, *Haddon, The Head Hunter: A Short Sketch of the Life of A.C. Haddon* (Cambridge: Cambridge University Press, 1942).

Radcliffe-Brown, Alfred R., *The Andaman Islanders* (Cambridge: Cambridge University Press, 1922).

Rich, Paul B., *White Power and the Liberal Conscience: Racial Segregation and South African Liberalism, 1921–60* (Johannesburg: Ravan Press, 1984).

Richards, Audrey, 'An Anthropologist in Rhodesia', *Newnham College Letter*, January 1932, 60–8.

Hunger and Work in a Savage Tribe: A Functional Study of Nutrition among the Southern Bantu (London: Routledge, 1932).

'A Modern Movement of Witch-Finders', *Africa: Special Issue on Witchcraft*, 8, 4 (October 1935), 448–60.

'The Story of Bwembya of the Bemba Tribe, Northern Rhodesia' in Perham, Margery, ed., *Ten Africans* (London: Faber and Faber, 1936), 17–40.

'Review of *Reaction to Conquest*', *London Spectator* (9 October 1936).

Land, Labour and Diet in Northern Rhodesia: An Economic Study of the Bemba Tribe (London: Oxford University Press in association with the International African Institute, 1939).

Bemba Marriage and Present Economic Conditions (Rhodes-Livingstone: Rhodes Livingstone Institute Papers, No. 4, 1940).

'The Political System of the Bemba of North-Eastern Rhodesia' in Meyer Fortes and Edward E. Evans-Pritchard, eds., *African Political Systems* (London: Oxford University Press, 1940), 83–120.

'Review of Isaac Schapera, *Married Life in an African Tribe*', *Bantu Studies*, 14, 3 (1940), 456–60.

'A Problem of Anthropological Approach. Review of E.E. Evans-Pritchard, *The Nuer*', *Bantu Studies*, 15, 1 (1941), 45–52.

'Some Causes of a Revival of Tribalism in South African Native Reserves', *Man*, 41 (July–August 1941), 89–90.

'Obituary: Bronislaw Malinowski (1884–1943)', *Man*, 63 (January–February 1943), 1–4.

'Review of *The Realm of a Rain-Queen*', *Man*, 44 (November-December 1944), 148–50.

'Review of Hilda Kuper, *An African Aristocracy*', *Man*, 48 (December 1948), 142–3.

Chisungu: A Girl's Initiation Ceremony among the Bemba of Northern Rhodesia (London: Faber and Faber, 1956).

'The Concept of Culture in Malinowski's Work' in Raymond Firth, ed., *Man and Culture: An Evaluation of the Work of Bronislaw Malinowski* (London: Routledge and Kegan Paul, 1957), 15–28.

East African Chiefs: A Study of Political Development in Some Uganda and Tanganyika Tribes (London: Faber and Faber, 1960).

'Obituary: Agnes Winifred Hoernlé: 1885–1960', *Man*, 61 (1961), 53.

Bibliography 305

The Changing Structure of a Ganda Village: Kisozi 1892–1952 (Nairobi: East Africa Publishing House for EAISR, 1966).

'Monica Wilson: An Appreciation' in Michael Whisson and Martin West, eds., *Religion and Social Change in Southern Africa: Anthropological Essays in Honour of Monica Wilson* (Cape Town: David Philip, 1975), 1–13.

Richards, Audrey and Elsie Widdowson, 'A Dietary Study in North-Eastern Rhodesia', *Africa*, 9, 2 (April 1936), 166–96.

Rotberg, Robert, *Black Heart: Gore-Browne and the Politics of Multi-Racial Zambia* (Berkeley, Los Angeles and London: University of California Press, 1977).

Russell, Margo, 'Hilda Kuper, 1911–1992', *African Studies*, 88 (1993), 145–9.

Sachs, Wulf, *Black Hamlet with a New Introduction by Saul Dubow and Jacqueline Rose* (Baltimore: The Johns Hopkins University Press, 1996; originally published 1937).

Sanjek, Roger, ed., *Fieldnotes: The Makings of Anthropology* (Ithaca, New York and London: Cornell University Press, 1990), 47–70.

'Anthropology's Hidden Colonialism: Assistants and Their Ethnographers', *Anthropology Today*, 9, 2 (1993), 13–18.

Schapera, Isaac, *The Khoisan Peoples of South Africa* (London: Routledge and Kegan Paul, 1930).

ed., *Western Civilization and the Natives of South Africa: Studies in Culture Contact* (London: George Routledge and Sons Ltd., 1934).

ed., *The Bantu-Speaking Tribes of South Africa: An Ethnological Survey* (London: George Routledge and Sons, 1937).

'The Appointment of Radcliffe-Brown', *African Studies*, 49, 1 (1990), 1–14.

Schmidt, Nancy J., 'Ethnographic Fiction: Anthropology's Hidden Literary Style', *Anthropology and Humanism Quarterly*, 9, 4 (1984), 11–14.

Schoeman, Pieter J., 'The Swazi Rain Ceremony', *Bantu Studies*, 9, 2 (June 1935), 169–76.

Schumaker, Lyn, *Africanizing Anthropology: Fieldwork, Networks, and the Making of Cultural Knowledge in Central Africa* (Durham, NC, and London: Duke University Press, 2001).

'Women in the Field in the Twentieth Century: Revolution, Involution, Devolution' in Henrika Kuklick, ed., *A New History of Anthropology* (Oxford: Blackwell, 2008).

Shain, Milton and Richard Mendelsohn, eds., *Memories, Realities and Dreams: Aspects of Jewish Experience* (Johannesburg and Cape Town: Jonathan Ball, 2000).

Sharp, John, 'The Roots and Development of *Volkekunde* in South Africa' in Terence Ranger and Colin Murray, eds., *Journal of Southern African Studies, Special Issue: Anthropology and History*, 8, 1 (October 1981), 16–36.

'Mafeje and Langa: The Start of an Intellectual's Journey' in Adebayo Olukoshi and Francis Nyamnjoh, eds., *CODESRIA Bulletin: Special Issue: Archie Mafeje (1936–2007): A Giant Moves On*, 3 & 4 (2008), 31–6.

'Serving the *Volk*: Afrikaner Anthropology Revisited' in Deborah James, Evie Plaice and Christina Toren, eds., *Culture Wars. Context, Models and Anthropologists' Accounts* (New York: Berghahn Books, 2010), 32–44.

306 Bibliography

Shepherd, Robert H., *Lovedale, South Africa, 1824–1955* (Lovedale: Lovedale Press, 1971).

Shimoni, Gideon, *Jews and Zionism: The South African Experience, 1910–1967* (Cape Town: Oxford University Press, 1980).

Smith, Prudence, *The Morning Light: A South African Childhood Revalued* (Cape Town: David Philip, 2000).

Stayt, Hugh, *The Bavenda with an Introduction by Mrs A.W. Hoernlé* (London: Oxford University Press for the International Institute for African Languages and Cultures, 1931).

Steinberg, Jonny, *Three Letter Plague: A Young Man's Journey through a Great Epidemic* (Johannesburg and Cape Town: Jonathan Ball Publishers, 2008).

Strathern, Marilyn, 'Audrey Isabel Richards 1899–1984', *Proceedings of the British Academy*, 82 (1985), 439–53.

Tilley, Helen, *Africa as a Living Laboratory: Empire, Development, and the Problem of Scientific Knowledge, 1870–1950* (Manchester: Manchester University Press, 2007).

Tucker, A. Winifred, 'Observations on the Colour Vision of School Children', *British Journal of Psychology*, 4, 1 (1911), 33–43.

Richtersveld: The Land and Its People (Johannesburg, Public Lecture of March 1913).

Tucker, A. Winifred and Charles S. Myers, 'A Contribution to the Anthropology of the Sudan', *The Journal of the Royal Anthropological Institute of Great Britain and Ireland*, 40 (January–June 1910), 141–63.

Turner, Victor W., *The Forest of Symbols: Aspects of Ndembu Ritual* (Ithaca, NY, and London: Cornell University Press, 1967).

Van den Berghe, Pierre, 'Biographical Sketch and Bibliography of Leo Kuper' in Pierre van den Berghe, ed., *The Liberal Dilemma in South Africa: Essays in Honour of Leo Kuper* (New York: St Martin's Press, 1979), 153–8.

Stranger in Their Midst (Colorado: University of Colorado Press, 1989).

Vaughan, Megan, 'Anthropologists and Others in Inter-war South-West Tanganyika' (unpublished paper presented at the Monica Hunter Wilson Centenary Conference, 24–26 June 2008).

Vicinus, Margaret, *Independent Women: Work and Community for Single Women, 1850–1920* (London: Virago, 1985).

Vigne, Randolph, *Liberals against Apartheid: A History of the Liberal Party of South Africa, 1953–1968* (London: Macmillan, 1997).

Vilakazi, Absolom, *Zulu Transformations: A Study of the Dynamic of Social Change* (Pietermaritzburg: Natal University Press, 1962).

Vincent, Kerry, 'Translating Culture: Literature, Anthropology, and Hilda Kuper's *A Witch in My Heart*', *Current Writing*, 12, 2 (2000), 113–30.

'Literature as Laboratory: Hilda Kuper's Factional Representations of Swaziland', *African Studies*, 70, 1 (April 2011), 89–102.

Walker, Cherryl, *The Woman's Suffrage Movement in South Africa* (Cape Town: UCT Centre for African Studies, Communications Series, No. 2, 1979).

Walker, Cherryl, *Women and Resistance in South Africa* (New York: Monthly Review Press; Cape Town: David Philip, 1991, 2nd edn.).

Bibliography 307

Wanless, Ann, 'The Silence of Colonial Melancholy: The Louis Fourie Archive of Bushman Ethnologica' (unpublished Ph.D. thesis, University of the Witwatersrand, 2007).

Wayne (nee Malinowska), Helena, ed., *The Story of a Marriage, Volume II: The Letters of Bronislaw Malinowski and Elsie Masson* (London and New York: Routledge, 1995).

Wayne (Malinowska), Helena, 'Bronislaw Malinowski: The Influence of Various Women on His Life and Works', *American Ethnologist*, 12, 3 (1985), 529–40.

West, Martin, 'Monica Hunter Wilson: A Memoir', *Transactions of the Royal Society of South Africa*, 45, 2 (August 1984), 205–10.

Whisson, Michael and Martin West, eds., *Religion and Social Change in Southern Africa: Essays in Honour of Monica Wilson* (Cape Town: David Philip, 1975).

Wilson, Francis, 'Monica Hunter Wilson: An Appreciation' in Monica Hunter, *Reaction to Conquest: The Effects of Contact with Europeans on the Pondo of South Africa* (Berlin: LIT on behalf of the International African Institute, 2009: Classics in African Anthropology, 4th edn.), 1–25.

Wilson, Francis and Dominique Perrot, eds., *Lovedale: Outlook on a Century: South Africa 1870–1970* (Lovedale: Lovedale Press, 1973).

Wilson, Godfrey and Monica Wilson, *The Study of African Society* (Livingstone: Rhodes-Livingstone Institute Papers, No. 2, 1939).

Wilson, Godfrey and Monica Wilson, *The Analysis of Social Change: Based on Observations in Central Africa* (Cambridge: Cambridge University Press, 1945).

Wilson, Monica, *Good Company: A Study of Nyakyusa Age-Villages* (London, New York and Toronto: Oxford University Press for the International African Institute, 1951; Boston: Beacon Press, 1963, 2nd edn.).

'Development in Anthropology', *Race Relations Journal: Special Issue: Homage to Winifred Hoernlé*, 22, 4 (1955), 1–5.

Rituals of Kinship among the Nyakyusa (London, New York and Toronto: Oxford University Press for the International African Institute, 1957; London: Oxford University Press, 1970, 2nd edn.).

Communal Rituals of the Nyakyusa (London, New York and Toronto: Oxford University Press for the International African Institute, 1959).

Divine Kings and the 'Breath of Men' (Cambridge: Cambridge University Press, Frazer Memorial Lecture, 1959).

Religion and the Transformation of Society: A Study of Social Change in Africa (The Scott Holland Lectures. Cambridge: Cambridge University Press, 1971).

'Lovedale: Instrument of Peace' in Francis Wilson and Dominique Perrot, eds., *Lovedale: Outlook on a Century* (Lovedale: Lovedale Press, 1973), 4–11.

'Review of Audrey Richards and Jean Robin, *Some Elmdon Families* (1975)', *African Studies*, 35, 3–4 (1976), 297–9.

'The First Three Years, 1938–1941', *African Social Research*, 24 (1977), 279–83.

For Men and Elders: Changes in the Relations of Generations and of Men and Women among the Nyakyusa-Ngonde People, 1875–1971 (London and

308   Bibliography

New York: Africana Publishing Company for the International African Institute, 1977).

ed., *Freedom for My People: The Autobiography of Z.K. Matthews: Southern Africa 1901 to 1968* (London: Rex Collings; Cape Town: David Philip, 1981).

Wilson, Monica and Archie Mafeje, *Langa: A Study of Social Groups in an African Township* (Cape Town: Oxford University Press, 1963).

Wilson, Monica and Leonard Thompson, eds., *The Oxford History of South Africa*, 2 *Vols.* (Oxford: Oxford University Press, 1969, 1971).

Wylie, Diana, *Starving on a Full Stomach: Hunger and the Triumphs of Cultural Racism in Modern South Africa* (Charlottesville and London: University Press of Virginia, 2001).

Young, Michael W., *Malinowski: Odyssey of an Anthropologist, 1884–1920* (New Haven and London: Yale University Press, 2004).

Malinowski, Vol. 2 (New Haven and London: Yale University Press, forthcoming).

Index

academic freedom, 99
Africa, 35, 59, 119, 140, 164, 165, 203, 251, 267
African Christianity, 82, 84, 91–4, 204, 209, 223
African history, 70, 234
  pre-colonial, 202, 206–7
African National Congress, 84, 88, 217
African nationalism, 82, 84, 88, 272
African patriarchy, 43, 215, 224–6
African sociology, 15, 39–40, 45, 51, 57, 62, 114
African Studies, 144, 181, 186, 253
African traditional cultural systems, 6, 42, *See also* kinship systems
  belief in witchcraft, 86, 93, 124, 223–7, 228, 257–8
  effect of social change on, 51, 52, 53, 54, 59, 63, 65, 76, 96, 126, 143, 183, 186, 209, 223, 238, 278, *See also* modernity:juxtaposition/conflict with tradition
  matrilineal, 158, 183, 258
  patrilineal, 87, 183
  polygamous, 215, 225–6, 228
  revival of tradition/tribalism among Tswana, 172, 184
  role of beer in, 250
  Swazi, 171, 200–2, 208, 226–8, 238, *See also* Swazi kinship systems
African urbanization, 126, 140, 144, 231
Afrikaner nationalism, 4, 17, 42, 46, 139, 176, 177–8, 235, 274–5
American Anthropologist, 168, 253
American anthropology, 1, 9, 190–1
  founding fathers of, 10
  impact of women on, 9–10, 279
  racially exclusive canon, 2
Anthropological Association
  American, 10
  British, 186

South African, 242, 269
anti-apartheid activism, 3, 100, 143, 272
  1952 Defiance Campaign, 217, 218
  and the emergence of protest politics, 141, 143, 222
  of Eileen and Jack Krige, 142
  of Ellen Hellmann, 105, 108–9, 137, 139, 142, 144, 150
  of Leo and Hilda Kuper, 217–18
  of Monica Hunter Wilson, 97, 98–100, 142
  Women's March of 1956, 236, 282
anti-apartheid politics
  and the emergence of protest politics, 217–18
anti-Semitism, 176, 216
  public/programmatic, 113
anti-Semitism in South Africa, 107, 110, 136, 137, 176–8, 193, 274
  campaign/fight against, 136, 137, 176
apartheid racial policies, 45, 65, 98, 128, 139–40, 216, 218, 261, 273, 276
  Bantu Education Act, 60, 142
  Bantustan system, 142
  Extension of Universities Act, 229
  Group Areas Act, 142, 221, *See also* forced removals
  pass laws, 128, 143, 218, 235
apartheid state repression, 137, 143, 145, 187, *See also* forced removals
Argyle, John, 241, 248, 252, 253, 261, 269

Ballinger (Hodgson), Margaret, 46, 130
Bank, Leslie, 101, 117
Bantu Studies, 120, 181, 202, 250–3, *See also African Studies*
  Publications Committee, 34, 47, 202
Bechuanaland Protectorate, 56, 58, 63, 115, 182
Behar, Ruth, 1–2, 5
Beinart, William, 106, 108
Bembaland, 159, 161–4, 277

310 Index

Benedict, Ruth, 2, 9–10, 212
Berseba native reserve. *See* native reserves: in South West Africa
Black Sash, 100, 108
Bleek, Dorothea, 55–6
Bloemfontein, 38–9
Boas, Franz, 2, 9, 194
Bourdieu, Pierre, 12, 150
Brandel-Syrier, Mia, 3, 144
British Academy, 154, 281
British social anthropological tradition, 1, 2, 8, 10, 32, 180, 191, 272
  founding fathers of, 15, 23, 32, 61, 208
  Manchester School, 8, 16, *See also* structural-functionalism
  women's contributions to, 9, 116, 153, 155, 159, 281
Bunyakyusa, 6, 65, 80, 89, 90–1, 92, 94, 121, 165, 168, 276
Bushman rock art, 26, 174

Cape Town, 22, 23–4, 26, 29, 32, 54
Carstens, Peter, 18, 101, 152
Cheater, Angela P., 264, 271, 282
colonial anthropology, 240
collaborative fieldwork, 13, 15, 19, 37, 39, 54, 58, 61–3, 161, 165
collaborative fieldwork with research assistants
  Audrey Richards and Lorna Gore-Browne, 161, 165, 179
  Eileen Krige and Andreas Matatanya, 250, 256
  Eileen Krige and George Mahlobo, 252–3, 278
  Eileen Krige and Simeon Modjadji, 253, 256, 269, 278
  Ellen Hellmann and John Chafimbira, 117–18, 125, 167
  Monica Hunter and Mary Dreyer (née Soga), 78–80, 81
  Monica Hunter and Michael Geza, 80, 81
  Monica Wilson and John Brown Mwaisumo, 94
  Monica Wilson and Leonard Mwaisumo, 90, 91–3
  Monica Wilson and the Rubusanas, 81, 82, 90
collaborative fieldwork with spouses
  Eileen and Jack Krige, 104, 121, 254–6, 270
  Monica and Godfrey Wilson, 89–92, 94, 95, 121, 165
colonial anthropology, 241, 273

colonial rule, 212
  British, 69, 90, 95, 153, 155, 156, 182–3, 207, 232, 276, *See also* German colonial rule, South West Africa
Comaroff, Jean, 101, 107, 282
Comaroff, John, 101, 266–7
Common Sense, 136, 214
Connell, Raewyn, 8
Cope, Trevor, 227, 265
cultural anthropology, 8–10, 214

Doke, Clement ('the baptist'), 46, 153, 175, 181, 202
Driberg, Jack, 71, 170
du Toit, Marijke, 122
Durban, 226, 229, 235, 256, 261, 265, 270, *See also* Kuper, Hilda Beemer, fieldwork: ethnography of Indian communities
  Hinduism in, 6, 192, 213, 221–2, 235, 238
  Indian communities of, 217–21
  Killie Campbell Library, 149, 241, 262, 268
Durkheim, Emile, 8, 34, 244
  sociological theory, 15, 23, 34, 115, 194, 270

Eiselen, Willi Werner, 4, 17–18, 203
  apartheid ideologue, 203
ethnographic data production, 5, 10, 32, 52, 117, 121, 236, *See also* writing of culture
  concept of 'ethnographic authority' in, 119, 129
  sole-authored field-based, 60, 240
ethnography, 241, 264
  'tribal', 17, 107
  modern/field-based, 13, 18, 19, 50, 51–2, 54, 59, 104, 278, 279
Evans-Pritchard, Edward E., 180, 205
  The Nuer, 180–2

feminism, 108, 154, 168, 279, *See also* women anthropologists: feminist
field diaries, 26, 29, 35, 106, 148–9, 197, 241, 245, 277
fieldnotes, 12, 26, 86, 197, 264, 277
  Bronislaw Malinowski, 164
  Eileen Jensen Krige, 241, 256, 263
  Ellen Hellmann, 106, 117, 149
  Hilda Beemer Kuper, 202–3
  Mary Soga, 80
  Monica Hunter Wilson, 80–2, 90–1, 94, 95

Index

Simeon Modjadji, 256
Winifred Hoernlé, 39, 49
fieldwork, innovative women-centred, 5–6,
  7, 13, 116, 120–1, 131–3, 165, 241,
  252, 275, 277–8, 280, *See also*
  women ethnographers
Fifty Key Anthropologists, 10–11
First World War, 8, 52, 90, 110–11, 192
First, Ruth, 3, 208, 215, 282
Firth, Raymond, 171, 177, 198
Firth, Rosemary, 164, 171
forced removals, 105, 116, 143, 146,
  259–60
Fortes, Meyer, 57, 126, 180, 192, 196, 197,
  205, 253, 266
functionalist theory, 57–8, 71, 93, 114, 120,
  121, 138, 150, 158, 181, 190, 208,
  234, 240, 250, 254, 266, 277, 279,
  See also structural-functionalism
Malinowski's charts, 198

Gandhi, Mahatma, 73, 217, 222
gender, 107, 280, 282
gender discrimination/sexism, 2, 43, 154–5,
  156, 166, 279
gender politics, 152, 154
gender relations, 5–6, 87, 179
  divide/division of labour, 156, 178,
    244, 254
  vulnerability of women, 118–19
gender studies, 263, 280
German colonial rule, South West Africa,
  22, 26, 29, 43, 177
  genocide under, 27
German diffusionist school of
  anthropology, 114
Germany, 23, 26, 110, 176
  Nazi, 100, 106, 109, 113, 136–7, 152,
    155, 176, 274, 275
Gladstone, Jo, 154–6, 158, 167
Gluckman, Max, 1, 3, 101, 167, 187, 191,
  192, 196, 228, 231, 275
  as director of Rhodes-Livingstone
    Institute, 104, 125
  fieldwork, 6, 201, 276
  friendship with Hilda Beemer Kuper,
    206, 222
  theoretical challenge to Malinowski, 16
  Wits years, 18, 46, 47, 51, 104, 194–5
Gluckman, Max, published work, 51,
  119, 140
  Rituals of Rebellion in South-East Africa,
    206, 267
  The Bridge, 16, 183
Goodwin, John, 39, 43–9

Great War. *See* First World War

Haddon, A.C., 25, 29, 30, 34, 35, 37,
  45, 212
  influence on Hoernlé's work, 23–6, 35, 61
  Torres Straits Expedition, 23–4, 25, 61
Hale, Sondra, 233, 282
Hammond-Tooke, David, 1, 4, 51, 105
  Imperfect Interpreters, 17
Harrison, Jane Ellen, 148
Hellmann, Ellen, 5, 12, 14, 167–8, 192,
  236, 241
  background and childhood, 109–10, 146,
    147, 274
  friendship with Audrey Richards, 165,
    167, 176
  friendship with Eileen Jensen Krige,
    121, 122
  friendship with Hilda Beemer Kuper, 114
  friendship/collaboration with
    Malinowski, 121, 122
  friendship/collaboration with Max
    Gluckman, 114, 125, 147
  influence of Hoernlé on, 3, 18, 47, 51,
    104–5, 109, 114, 115, 145, 147, 277
  Jewish/Zionist Socialist identity, 105,
    106, 108, 110–13, 127, 133, 134,
    136, 150, 191, 274
  legacy, 149
  social welfare activism of, 105, 127, 129,
    145, 148, 275
  Wits years, 104, 112–13, 138, 147, 194–5
Hellmann, Ellen, published work, 3, 59, 87
  anti-apartheid addresses/essays, 142–4
  *Handbook on Race Relations in South
    Africa*, 140
  misreadings of, 149–50
  on Johannesburg townships, 6, 105,
    129–31, 139, 143, 150
  on Rooiyard, 7, 53, 116, 120–6, 129, 139,
    147, 150
  on South African Jewish history and
    cultural identity, 105, 108, 136–9
  relationship between images and text,
    122, 129, 131
Hellmann, Ellen, urban African fieldwork,
  105, 114, 147, 251, 276, 280
  on education and youth culture in
    Johannesburg, 127–9, 131, 147, 148
  on factory workers, 142, 150
  on women beer brewers, Rooiyard, 6,
    104, 114, 115–20, 143, 251,
    277, 280
Hellmann, Joseph, 113, 134
Hertzog, J.B.M., 45, 50

312   Index

historical ethnography, 11, 38, 65, 189, 266
  of Pondoland, 7, 280
  of South African Indian communities,
    7, 223
  of Swaziland, 7, 191, 202, 206–8, 223
Hobart Houghton, Kenneth (Hunter
  Wilson's uncle), 78, 82
Hodson, Thomas Callan, 71, 75, 76
Hoernlé, Alfred, 17, 29, 37, 47, 49, 60, 84,
    113, 121, 253, 278
  as Dean of Arts, Wits, 47, 153
  courtship of/marriage to Winifred, 29–31
Hoernlé, Winifred, 1, 120, 172–5, 263, 275
  at Sorbonne, Paris, 23
  background and schooling, 19, 274
  Cambridge years, 22–5, 26, 34,
    61–3, 148
  collaboration/friendship with Schapera,
    2, 54, 56, 58, 59, 62, 278
  friendship with Audrey Richards, 18,
    151, 165, 166, 168
  friendship with Malinowski, 2, 52, 57–8,
    85, 87, 115
  friendship/collaboration with Radcliffe-
    Brown, 15, 32, 37–40, 45, 60, 61,
    62, 114, 278
  importance of Christianity to, 60–1,
    85, 274
  legacy, 2, 22, 35, 148
  mentorship of Eileen Jensen Krige, 18,
    241, 244, 247, 248, 249, 251, 253,
    264, 270, 275, 277
  racial politics of, 17–18, 22, 195
  relationship with Hunter Wilson, 63, 65,
    80, 84–7, 88, 91, 95
  silencing of, 17
  social welfare activism, 4, 60, 152, 166,
    168, 282
Hoernlé, Winifred, fieldwork, 5, 13, 22, 24,
    25, 26–9, 201
  Bushman communities, 26, See also
    Nama communities: Hoernlé's
    research on
  collection of artefacts, 35, 49
  Windhoek trip, 1922–3, 6, 35–7, 39,
    41–2, 44, 49, 53, 55, 62
Hoernlé, Winifred, published work, 37, 39,
    52, 59
  essay trilogy, 1923–5, 41, 42, 43–4, 53,
    55, 62, 280
  field diaries, 26
  on African ritual, 32, 56
Hoernlé, Winifred, Wits years, 3, 13, 16,
    18, 32, 35, 37, 40, 45, 46, 50, 54, 59,
    151–2, 194, 275

establishing social anthropology, 2, 18,
    37, 47, 51, 239, 281
Hogsback, Eastern Cape, 89, 102, 103
holocaust, 96, 136
humanism, 197, 234, See also women
    anthropologists: humanist legacy of
Hunter Wilson, Monica, 3, 11, 13, 41,
    103–4, 192, 206, 282
  biographies of, 4
  Cambridge years, 65, 67–76, 82–4, 274
  Christian identity of, 64–6, 72–5, 82, 85,
    97–100, 146, 274
  Collegiate Girls' High School years, 67–9
  influence of Hoernlé on, 3, 5, 18
  left-wing politics of, 64, 68, 70, 75, 275
  legacy, 101–2
  Lovedale childhood and schooling, 66–7
  LSE seminar, 76, 89, 196
  mentorship of Fort Hare anthropolo-
    gists, 101
  professorship, Rhodes University, 281
  UCT years, 67, 99, 100–1, 281
Hunter Wilson, Monica, fieldwork
  Eastern Cape and Pondoland, 65, 76–80,
    85, 90, 91, 94, 276, 278
  importance of Lovedale networks,
    76–8, 80–2
  in Bunyakyusa, Tanganyika, 6, 65, 80,
    85, 89–91, 94, 121, 165, 168, 277
Hunter Wilson, Monica, published work, 7,
    52, 59, 98, 103, 144, 147
  East London and Grahamstown
    ethnographies, 6, 53, 63
  Freedom for My People, 7, 66, 99
  Nyakyusa monographs, 94, 185
  on African farm labourers, 88
  Pondoland ethnography, 53, 63, 80, 82,
    84, 92, 280
  Reaction to Conquest, 65, 75, 84, 86–7,
    125, 168, 185
  Religion and the Transformation of Society
    (Scott Holland lectures), 97, 185
  story of Nosente, 165
Hunter Wilson, Monica, urban fieldwork
  East London and Grahamstown, 81, 88,
    117, 251, 278
  study of social groups in Langa township,
    97, 185, 222

Indian Congress, 217, 218, 225
Industrial and Commercial Workers Union
    (ICU), 70, 81, 84
International African Institute (IAI), 84, 85,
    87, 92, 147, 198–9, 228, 256, 278
Nutrition Committee, 165

Index

313

Inter-University Committee for African Studies, 18, 50, 58–9, 63, 84, 203, 252, 278, 281
Israel, state of, 107, 133, 137, 139, 146

Jewish Board of Deputies, 134–6, 139
Jithoo, Sabitha, 264, 271
Johannesburg, 1, 19, 33–4, 49, 52, 54, 57, 61, 70, 87, 110, 142, 212, 224–5, 235, 242
  Jewish community of, 109, 111–13, 193, 219
  juvenile employment in, 131, 133
  slum-yards of, 115
Johannesburg townships, 143, 214–15, *See also* township youth culture/subculture
  Orlando, 116, 128, 131, 176
  Sophiatown, 128, 131, 142, 209
Joint Councils of Europeans and Africans, 46, 127
Junod, Henri-Alexandre, 43, 44
  Life of a South African Tribe, 38, 53, 71, 87, 194

Kaumheimer, Bernard (Hellmann's father), 110, 112, 139
Kenya, 108, 211
King Sobhuza II, 171, 172, 178, 199, 200, 201–3, 204, 207, 231, 235, *See also* Kuper, Hilda Beemer, published work:*Sobhuza II*
kinship systems, 15, 38, 40, 53, 225, *See also* Radcliffe-Brown, A.R.: theory of social relationships
  cross-cultural comparison, 40, 51
  effect of social change on, 263, 268
  Herero/Nama, 35, 39, 40, 43, 55
  Lovedu, 257, 266
  Swazi, 217, 237
knowledge production, 11, 13, 52, *See also* scientific knowledge production
  collaborative nature of, 8, 61, 89, 183, 256, 278, 279
  cultural, 2, 61, 149, 256, *See also* writing of culture
Koch, Bodo, 137, 139
Krause, Marie, 248, 250
Krige, Dan (Eileen's son), 258
Krige, Eileen and Jack
  relationship and marriage, 245–8, 258, 261, 270
  teaching partnership, 261–2, 270
Krige, Eileen and Jack, published work, 53, 147, 262, 270

The Realm of a Rain-Queen, 7, 87, 187, 237, 240, 254, 257, 270
Krige, Eileen Jensen, 5, 167, 192, 271, 274, 279, 283
  background and childhood, 242
  friendship with Cato Smuts, 242, 245
  legacy, 240, 241, 263, 269, *See also under* social anthropology, southern Africa
  Natal University years, 240, 241, 264, 265, 271
  racial politics of, 240, 269
  Rhodes years, 241, 259, 261–2, 270
  romantic view of 'tribe' and tradition, 237, 241
  social welfare projects, 260–1, 275
  University of South Africa years, 241, 270
  Wits years, 2–3, 14, 18, 39, 45–6, 47, 241, 242–5, 247, 250, 258, 270
Krige, Eileen Jensen, early ethnographic encounters
  General Strike of 1922, 245
  Rain-Queen, 245, 270
Krige, Eileen Jensen, fieldwork, 47, 242
  Grahamstown, 53, 259–60
  loss of notebooks, 263, 268, 271
  Lovedu Reserve, 104, 248–9, 250, 254, 257, 263, 264, 270, 277
  Marabastad and Bethulie studies, 53, 251, 260
  methodological innovation, 241, 252, 256, 257, 278
  on African women and social change, 263, 267, 268, 271
  on magic, ritual and witchcraft, 266
  Pretoria ethnography, 6
  use of fieldwork photographs, 250
  Zulu ethnography, 251, 265, 277
Krige, Eileen Jensen, published work, 59, 242, 249
  articles and essays, 250–1, 266, 271
  Eileen Jensen Krige Papers, 241
  on Lovedu woman-marriage, 6, 267
  on Zulu women's songs, 6, 53, 267
  The Social System of the Zulus, 240, 251–4, 270
Krige, Jack, 167, 229, 240, 245, 259
Krige, Jack, published work
  on Lovedu law and marriage-cattle, 249
Krige, Thor (Eileen's son), 258, 261, 262
Kulpe, Oswald, 23, 26
Kuper, Adam, 8, 32, 56, 107, 155, 177, 184
  friendship with Schapera, 107
  influence of Hilda Kuper on, 107, 236

314   Index

Kuper, Hilda Beemer, 3, 5, 14, 167, 265,
274, 282
background and childhood, 192–3,
235, 274
friendship with Audrey Richards, 165,
176, 186–7, 197, 205, 222, 230
friendship with Monica Hunter
Wilson, 187
immigration to US, 187, 215,
229–30
influence of Hoernlé on, 18, 189,
191, 192–5, 235, 277
Jewish identity of, 190, 202–3, 219,
235, 274
left-wing politics of, 198, 212–13,
217–18
LSE years, 196, 198
Malinowski's mentorship of, 196–200,
203–4
Natal University lectureship, 229
UCLA years – teacher, mentor, role
model, 189, 230–1, 232–4
Kuper, Hilda Beemer, creative writing/
ethnographic fiction, 7, 189, 191,
192, 207, 214, 223, 227, 234–5,
236–8
A Bite of Hunger, 191, 225
A Witch in My Heart, 189, 191,
223–8, 265
as protest literature, 214, 235
poetry, 190, 209–11, 213, 232, 235
short stories, 7, 189, 191, 193, 207,
213–16, 223, 227, 235, 236–8
The Decision, 191, 225
theme of social change, 191, 213, 214,
215, 225, 235, 238
Kuper, Hilda Beemer, fieldwork, 195
ethnography of Indian communities, 6–7,
186, 192, 213, 218–22, 225–6
for SAIRR, 195
historical functionalist approach, 202,
206, 207, 236
Johannesburg mines, prisons and
townships, 6, 214
research on Johannesburg *stokvels*,
115, 208
Swaziland ethnography, 6, 53, 58, 172,
191, 194, 196, 197, 201–5, 214,
221, 230, 235, 276, 277
Kuper, Hilda Beemer,
political essays, 212–13
Kuper, Hilda Beemer, published work, 7,
51, 147, 191, 234–5
An African Aristocracy, 87, 186, 190, 191,
205, 223, 236–8

essays and articles, 203, 208, 217, 234
Indian Elites, 221
Indian People in Natal, 191, 218, 220,
221, 222
on African diet, 165
political essays, 190, 207, 216, 235
Sobhuza II, 7, 191, 230, 232, 235–8
The Uniform of Colour, 191, 205,
207–8, 238
use of fieldwork photographs, 208, 209
Kuper, Hilda Beemer, Wits years
as lecturer, 208–11
as student, 3, 46, 47, 51, 104, 194, 195,
196, 199
Kuper, Jenny (Hilda's daughter), 186, 187,
216–17, 219–20, 229, 231
Kuper, Leo, 178, 186, 191, 232
as head of Sociology Department, Natal
University, 217
defence fund for Treason Trialists, 218
marriage and family life with Hilda, 199,
207, 211, 215, 216, 234, 236
published work, 217, 229
UCLA years, 230–1
Kuper, Mary (Hilda's daughter),
187, 216–17, 219, 226, 227,
229–30, 234

La Fontaine, Jean, 154, 282
League of Nations, 36, 156
Legum, Colin, 134, 137, 145
Lestrade, G.P., 50, 85
Lewin, Julius, 167, 176
Liberal Party, 218, 229
liberalism, 17, 29, 47
liberalism, South African, 4, 99, 139, 140,
150, 244
Cape, 19, 22, 100
Christian, 72, 82, 93
left-liberal/humanist, 17, 45–6, 60–1,
105, 108, 113, 133, 139, 145, 149,
151, 152, 167, 203, 212, 213,
217–19, 229, 235, 236, 272
lobola, 67. *See under* rituals of transition,
marriage
London School of Economics (LSE), 16,
157, 166, 167, 217
Malinowski's years at, 54, 57, 71, 89, 92,
96, 115, 153, 157, 165, 166, 180,
196–7, 198, 202, 235, 253, 254

Macmillan, Hugh, 106, 200
Macmillan, William Miller, 46, 244
Mafeje, Archie, 7, 99, 101, 106, 144, 185,
222, 223, 240–1, 273

Index

Mair, Lucy, 164, 196
Malinowski, Bronislaw, 2, 9, 172, 201, 208,
   See also under London School of
   Economics
  concept of 'reciprocity', 257
  death of, 205
  friendship with Winifred Hoernlé, 52,
   57–8, 85, 87, 115, 196
  friendship/collaboration with Ellen
   Hellmann, 121, 122
  influence on Audrey Richards, 153,
   157–9, 161, 166
  influence on Eileen and Jack Krige,
   254, 257
  influence on fieldwork-based
   tradition, 51, 63, 76, 120, 121,
   197–8, 254, 277
  influence on Hilda Beemer Kuper,
   196–200, 203–4
  International African Institute
   (IAI), 59
  New Education Fellowship Conference,
   Johannesburg, 87, 121,
   164, 199
  relationship with Godfrey and Monica
   Wilson, 75, 85, 89–90, 93
  tribal model of, 16
Malinowski, Bronislaw, published work
  Argonauts of the Western Pacific, 32
  *The Family among the Australian
   Aborigines*, 57
  Trobriand monographs, 182
  Trobriand monographs – *Coral Gardens
   and Their Magic*, 196
Man, 185, 186–8, 257
Marxism, 8, 66, 149, 198, 240, 272–3
Matthews, Z.K., 7, 57, 66, 99,
  100, 196
Mayer, Iona, 107–8, 144
Mayer, Philip, 106–8, 144, 222
Mbatha, Mphiwa, 265–6
Mead, Margaret, 2, 9–10, 116, 159,
  160, 266
Meer, Fatima, 218, 221, 265, 282
Meyerhoff, Barbara, 2, 233, 282, 283
migrant labour system, 215, 235
  impact on traditional values and families,
   214, 225, 265, 267
Millin, Sarah Gertrude, 73, 176
modernity
  juxtaposition/conflict with tradition, 160,
   171, 191, 215, 225, 235
Modjadji. *See* Krige, Eileen Jensen,
  fieldwork: Lovedu Reserve
Myers, Charles, 23, 24, 25, 61

Nama communities, Hoernlé's research on,
  5, 26–9, 35–7, 38, 53–4
  ritual and beliefs, 32, 37, 41–3, 44,
   55, 280
Namaqualand, 54
  Garies, 54, 56
National Party, 133, 137, 240
National Party government, 45, 50, 100,
  139, 142, 218, *See also* apartheid
  racial policies
Native Affairs Department, 4, 229, 249
Native Juvenile Affairs Board, 128
native reserves, 6, 169, 174, 182–3, 215
  in South West Africa, 26, 36, 55
Nazism, 96, 212, 213, *See also* Germany:
  Nazi; holocaust
  in South Africa, 176–7, 275
Ngubane, Harriet Sibisi, 261, 264, 271, 282
Northern Rhodesia, 96, 156, 158, 161, 166,
  167, 168, 170, 179, 279
  Broken Hill (Kabwe), 94–5, 159, 165
  Kasama, 159, 164

oral tradition, 223
  African, 7, 206–7
Oxford History of South Africa, 7, 98–9

Paton, Alan, 218, 229
physical anthropology, 24, 46, 55
Pitje, Godfrey, 101
political power of women
  Bemba matriarch, 6
  Lovedu Rain-Queen, 258
  Pondo mother-in-law, 6
  Swazi Queen Mother, 5, 6, 172,
   203, 209
Posel, Deborah, 127, 128
Preston-Whyte, Eleanor, 229, 241, 248,
  261, 263–5, 269–71, 282, 283
Pretoria, 242, 249, 251
Progressive Federal Party, 105, 139, 149
protest literature, 191, 213–14, *See also
  under* Kuper, Hilda Beemer, creative
  writing/ethnographic fiction
psychology
  British, 23
  Gestalt, 23, 26, 27
psychology, experimental
  tests on native subjects, 25, 27, 37

racial discrimination, 193, 218
racial segregation, 19, 36, 45–6, 50, 62,
  64, 70, 75, 98, 142, 143, 212, 235,
  261, 276
  politics of, 17, 212, 273, 275

316   Index

racial types, concept of, 24, 42, 212, 273
  racial stereotyping, 42–3, 204,
    207, 212
racism, 17, 19, 143, 155, 177–8,
  212, 215–16, 235, 274
  settler, 43, 46, 96
  white brutality towards Africans,
    193, 205
Radcliffe-Brown, A.R., 1, 2, 23, 32, 34, 39,
  208, 217
  as founder/head of UCT anthropology
    department, 2, 15–16, 34, 39, 54
  critique of apartheid, 16
  influence on Hoernlé's work, 16, 35, 39,
    44, See also Hoernlé, Winifred:
    friendship/collaboration with
    Radcliffe-Brown
  legacy, 35
  'one-society' approach, 16, 239, 240
  Oxford years, 41, 180
  theory of social relationships, 15, 38,
    See also structural-functionalism
Radcliffe-Brown, A.R., published work,
  38, 52
  The Andaman Islanders, 32, 35, 41
  The Mother's Brother in South Africa,
    35, 38, 40–1, 43, 53
Read, Margaret, 164, 196
Reynolds, Pamela, 102, 148, 282
Rheinallt-Jones, J.D., 17, 46, 115, 181,
  196, 202
Rhodes University
  Anthropology Department, 99, 185, 241,
    258, 261, 270, 279, 281
  Department of Bantu (African)
    Studies, 259
  School of Social Sciences, 260
Rhodes-Livingstone Institute (RLI), 13, 16,
  95, 106, 125, 147, 166, 168, 272,
  279, See also Wilson, Godfrey: as first
  RLI director
Richards, Audrey Isabel, 2–4, 9, 76,
  96, 100, 104, 236, 274–5,
  279, 283
  as director of East African Institute,
    153, 281
  as grande dame of British anthropology,
    152, 153, 155, 281
  as Hoernlé's heir, 151, 152, 153, 184, 188
  at London School of Economics, 157,
    161, 167, 169, 257, 281
  background and schooling, 155, 274
  Cambridge years
    as student at Newnham College, 153,
      156, 184

  as teacher, mentor and role model,
    153, 156, 158, 168, 184, 281
  contribution to SA anthropology, 2, 5,
    11, 151, 152, 155, 170, 175, 184,
    187–8, 281
  ethnography of white South Africa, 178
  female friendships, 151, 165, 167, 168
    Ellen Hellmann, 165, 167, 176
    Hilda Beemer Kuper, 165, 176, 186–7,
      197, 205, 222, 230
    Lorna Gore-Browne, 161, 165, 179
    Newnham 'sisters', 157, 159
    Winifred Hoernlé, 18, 151, 165,
      166, 168
  fieldwork, 155
    among the Bakgatla, 183
    Bembaland, Northern Rhodesia, 153,
      156, 158–64, 277
    Elmdon Village study, 154, 169
    on chieftainship and political systems
      in Africa, 180
    on Tswana tribalism, 184, 277
    study of nutrition among southern
      Bantu, 116, 158, 165, 280
  friend and mentor, Malinowski, 157–9,
    161, 166, 167
  friendship with Eileen and Jack Krige,
    187, 257–8
  friendship/collaboration with Godfrey
    and Monica Wilson, 145–6, 165,
    166, 167–8, 170, 179, 180, 183,
    185–6
  London University years, 153
  published work, 155, 165
    article on Muchapi witch-finding
      movement, 164
    essays and reviews, 175, 183, 187,
      205, 257
    Hunger and Work in a Savage Tribe, 5,
      158, 177
    Land, Labour and Diet in Northern
      Rhodesia, 5, 7, 161, 165, 166, 172,
      178–80
    on Bemba, 153, 160, 164, 183
    on functionalist method and cultural
      change, 164
    on traditional political systems and
      social change, 180, 181
    Some Elmdon Families, 186
    study of Chisungu puberty rituals,
      6, 185
  published work
    essays and reviews, 180–5
  Wits years, 11, 151–2, 153, 166,
    170, 188

Index

attitude to male professors, 175–6
getting students 'into the field',
169–71, 175
work within British Colonial Office,
153, 281
Richards, Gwynneth (Audrey's sister), 156,
159, 161
Richtersveld, 22, 26, 55
rites of passage, 5, 41, 56
ritual symbolism, 6, 231, 267
rituals of transition, 32, 56, 186, 252,
See also Swazi ritual
centrality of cattle to, 44
death, 32, 174, 181
rituals of transition, marriage, 32, 43, 182,
252, 266–7
effect of social change/modernity on,
182–3, 251
lobola, 44, 251
rituals of transition, puberty, 32, 41,
56, 160
ukumetsha, 86
Zulu girls' songs, 267
Rivers Memorial Medal for Fieldwork, 182,
186, 236
Rivers, W.H.R., 23, 25, 32, 34, 61
influence on Radcliffe-Brown, 34
Roux, Eddie, 140
Labour Study Circle, Cambridge,
67–70
Royal Anthropological Institute, 153,
170, 281
Runciman, Ruth (Ellen Hellmann's
daughter), 106, 122, 127, 136, 139,
142, 145
Rungwe, Tanganyika, 89, 92–3

Sachs, Wulf, 125, 167
field trip with Ellen Hellmann, 117
Sandfontein, 29, 37, 55
Schapera, Isaac, 1, 2, 8, 57, 84, 101, 104,
192, 198
as successor to Radcliffe-Brown, 16,
17, 40
influence of Hoernlé on, 18
influence on Gluckman, 16
Wits semester, 167, 172, 194–5,
204
Schapera, Isaac, fieldwork, 5–6, 76, 115,
120, 201
on Khoisan/Nama communities, 63
studies of Tswana culture, 53, 57–9, 63,
182–3
Schapera, Isaac, published work, 55,
59, 237

Married Life in an African Tribe, 175,
181, 182
The Bantu-Speaking Tribes of South Africa,
58–9, 88, 126, 129
The Khoisan Peoples of South Africa, 55–6,
58, 63, 71
use of Hoernlé's work in, 55–6
Schmidt, Nancy J., 214, 235
Schoeman, Pieter Johannes, 202–4
Schumaker, Lyn, 13, 116
scientific knowledge production, 55, 59,
97, 117, 120, 129, 158, 160, 197,
275, 277
co-production, 38, 45, 60, 62, 89, 95,
161, 252
scientific models of knowledge, 15, 18, 24,
41, 49, 51
Second World War, 96, 134, 136–7, 155,
176, 178, 205, 209, 211
Seligman, Charles, 54, 157
sexuality, 5, 58, 147, 159, 175, 280
Malinowski on, 158, 182
Monica Hunter Wilson's work on,
87, 280
Shain, Milton, 108, 113
Simons, Jack, 57, 100, 140, 192
Smuts, Jan, 50, 87–8, 177, 240,
242, 245
Social Anthropology Department, UCT, 2,
37, 54, 67, 101
Social Anthropology Department,
Wits, 13, 16, 40, 114, 194,
253, 258
forefathers, 4
foremothers, 1–3, 5
gender politics at, 152
Museum of Ethnology, 35, 48–50,
151–2, 170
social anthropology, male-dominated
canon of, 1–2, 272, 280, *See also*
under social anthropology, southern
Africa
social anthropology, southern Africa, 10,
15, 32, 53, 166, 275–6, *See also*
urban anthropology
Africanist critiques of, 273
Eileen Krige's role in feminizing
discipline, 242, 269, *See also* women
ethnographers: Eileen Krige's role in
promoting
importance of Jewish identity in, 106–7,
177, 190
male-dominated canon of, 3, 8, 19, 52,
64, 239, 272, 280
Malinowski's influence on, 57

318 Index

social anthropology, southern Africa (cont.)
Radcliffe-Brown's role in establishing
discipline, 8, 15, 18, 32, 40, 45
Winifred Hoernlé as mother of, 3, 5, 14,
18–19, 45, 53, 167, 254, 272, 280,
282, *See also under* Winifred Hoernlé,
Wits years
women's contributions to, 3, 51, 59, 60,
153, 155, 184, 234, 272
social change, theory of, 139, 164, 180, 183,
186, 191, 223, 231, 241, 261, 263,
268, 271, 280, *See also under* African
traditional cultural systems; kinship
systems; rituals of transition,
marriage
South African Association for the
Advancement of Science, 23, 38,
58, 207
South African College, 30, 279
Hoernlé's years at, 19–22
South African Communist Party,
69–70, 134
South African Institute of Race Relations
(SAIRR), 17, 46, 60, 105, 115, 127,
129, 133, 140, 142, 144, 149, 168,
195, 196, 281
South African Party, 50
South West Africa, 34, 36, *See also*
German colonial rule, South West
Africa
Soweto Uprising of 1976, 143, 145
Stayt, Hugh, 52–3
stokvels, 124, 141, 208
Strathern, Marilyn, 154, 171, 282–3
structural-functionalism, 8, 15, 38, 41–2,
43, 180, 214, 251, 279
Swazi ritual, 202
incwala ceremony, 6, 200, 204, 206,
208–9, 231, 238
marriage, 208
rain ceremony, 202–3
umcwasho ceremony, 204, 209
Swaziland, 169, 171, 172, 202, 215,
225, 232
libutvo system, 201, 203
University of, 226, 231, 232

township youth culture/subculture, 105,
127, 130
gangs, 130–1
Transvaal School of Mines, 2, 34
Trek, 212, 213
Tucker, Winifred. *See* Hoernlé, Winifred
Turner, Victor, 6, 101, 232
Tylor, Edward B., 2, 9, 138

University of Cape Town (UCT), 19, 22,
148, 175
School of African Life and Languages,
15, 39–40, 50, 55, *See also* Social
Anthropology Department, UCT
School of African Studies, 101
University of Natal, 187, 240, 262, 265
Department of African Studies,
261, 266
Department of Sociology, 217, 232
Medical School, 223, 225, 227, 229
Social Anthropology Department, 229,
232, 240, 241, 261, 266, 270
University of Pretoria, 176, 249
University of South Africa, 229, 241, 249
University of Stellenbosch, 112, 176,
246
school of *volkekunde*, 17, 202, 203
University of the Witwatersrand (Wits), 37,
153, 245
Bantu Studies Department, 3, 45–9,
175, 249
urban anthropology, 16, 51, 53, 104, 124,
126, 144, 208, 251, 276
urban anthropology, women's pioneering
role in, 3, 6
Eileen Jensen Krige, Grahamstown
(1940–42), 53, 259–60
Eileen Jensen Krige, Pretoria (1932,
1934), 6, 53, 260
Ellen Hellmann, Rooiyard Johannesburg
(1933–4), 3, 6, 53, 104–5, 114,
115–20, 143, 251, 277, 280
Hilda Beemer Kuper, Durban (1933–7),
186, 192, 213, 222, 225–6
Hilda Beemer Kuper, Johannesburg
(1931, 1944–5), 6, 115, 208, 214
Monica Hunter Wilson, East London
and Grahamstown (1932), 6, 53, 81,
88, 117, 251, 278
Winifred Hoernlé, Windhoek (1922–3),
6, 36–7, 39, 41, 44, 53, 62

van Gennep, Arnold, 32, 56
van Riet Lowe, C., 46, 49
Vilakazi, Absolom, 261, 265–6, 271
Vincent, Kerry, 214, 226, 228, 235
volkekunde tradition, 100, 203, 272, 274,
See also under University of
Stellenbosch
role of Eiselen in establishing, 17

Westermann, Dietrich, 87, 119
Wilson, Francis (Monica's son), 96, 101,
144, 148, 282

Index

Wilson, Godfrey, 16, 65, 73, 89–90, 91–2, 96, 103, 161, 179, 180
  An Essay on the Economics of Detribalization, 95, 183
  as first RLI director, 94–6, 166, 167, 168, 183
  marriage to Monica, 72–5, 89, 96
  writing gifts of, 198
Wilson, Monica and Godfrey, joint publications
  The Analysis of Social Change Based on Observations in Central Africa, 96
  The Study of African Society, 95
Wilson, Tim (Monica's son), 96, 148
women anthropologists, 3, 10, 12, 59, 61, 159–60, 164, 165, 188, *See also* women ethnographers
  feminism of, 1–2, 10, 167, 226, 264, 279–82
  humanist legacy of, 64, 72, 231, 273, 275, 276, 278, 279, 282, 283

Jewish, 107–8, 167, 176
marginalisation of, 4–5, 8, 10–11, 147, 166, 183, 236
women ethnographers, 3, 5, 34, 52, 242, *See also* fieldwork, innovative women-centred
  Eileen Krige's role in promoting, 242, 263–5, 271
  writing/narrative gifts of, 7, 121, 198
working class, 141, 150
  culture/subculture, 6, 104, 123, 126, 136, 144, 146, 149
World Council of Churches, 99–100
writing of culture, 2, 5–6
  women's contributions to, 2
Wundt, Wilhelm, 23, 26

Zionism, 108, 109, 134, 135
Zionist Socialist Party, 105, 133–4

Titles in the series

50. MAXIM BOLT: *Zimbabwe's Migrants and South Africa's Border Farms: the roots of impermanence*
49. MEERA VENKATACHALAM *Slavery, Memory, and Religion in Southeastern Ghana, c. 1850–Present*
48. DEREK PETERSON, KODZO GAVUA, and CIRAJ RASSOOL (eds.) *The Politics of Heritage in Africa: economies, histories and infrastructures*
47. ILANA VAN WYK *The Universal Church of the Kingdom of God in South Africa: a church of strangers*
46. JOEL CABRITA *Text and Authority in the South African Nararetha Church*
45. MARLOES JANSON *Islam, Youth, and Modernity in the Gambia: the Tablighi Jama'at*
44. ANDREW BANK and LESLIE J. BANK (eds.) *Inside African Anthropology: Monica Wilson and her interpreters*
43. ISAK NIEHAUS *Witchcraft and a Life in the New South Africa*
42. FRASER G. MCNEILL *AIDS, Politics, and Music in South Africa*
41. KRIJN PETERS *War and the Crisis of Youth in Sierra Leone*
40. INSA NOLTE *Obafemi Awolowo and the Making of Remo: the local politics of a Nigerian nationalist*
39. BEN JONES *Beyond the State in Rural Uganda*
38. RAMON SARRÓ *The Politics of Religious Change on the Upper Guinea Coast: iconoclasm done and undone*
37. CHARLES GORE *Art, Performance and Ritual in Benin City*
36. FERDINAND DE JONG *Masquerades of Modernity: power and secrecy in Casamance, Senegal*
35. KAI KRESSE *Philosophising in Mombasa: knowledge, Islam and intellectual practice on the Swahili coast*
34. DAVID PRATTEN *The Man-Leopard Murders: history and society in colonial Nigeria*
33. CAROLA LENTZ *Ethnicity and the Making of History in Northern Ghana*
32. BENJAMIN F. SOARES *Islam and the Prayer Economy: history and authority in a Malian town*
31. COLIN MURRAY and PETER SANDERS *Medicine Murder in Colonial Lesotho: the anatomy if a moral crisis*
30. R. M. DILLEY *Islamic and Caste Knowledge Practices among Haalpulaar'en in Senegal: between mosque and termite mound*
29. BELINDA BOZZOLI *Theatres of Struggle and the End of Apartheid*
28. ELISHA RENNE *Population and Progress in a Yoruba Town*
27. ANTHONY SIMPSON *'Half-London' in Zambia: contested identities in a Catholic mission school*
26. HARRI ENGLUND *From War to Peace on the Mozambique–Malawi Borderland*
25. T. C. MCCASKIE *Asante Identities: history and modernity in an African village 1850–1950*
24. JANET BUJRA *Serving Class: masculinity and the feminization of domestic service in Tanzania*

23. CHRISTOPHER O. DAVIS *Death in Abeyance: illness and therapy among the Tabwa of Central Africa*
22. DEBORAH JAMES *Songs of the Woman Migrants: performance and identity in South Africa*
21. BIRGIT MEYER *Translating the Devil: religion and modernity among the Ewe in Ghana*
20. DAVID MAXWELL *Christians and Chiefs in Zimbabwe: a social history of the Hwesa people c. 1870s–1990s*
19. FIONA D. MACKENZIE *Land, Ecology and Resistance in Kenya, 1880–1952*
18. JANE I. GUYER *An African Niche Economy: farming to feed Ibadan, 1968–88*
17. PHILIP BURNHAM *The Politics of Cultural Difference in Northern Cameroon*
16. GRAHAM FURNISS *Poetry, Prose and Popular Culture in Hausa*
15. C. BAWA YAMBA *Permanent Pilgrims: the role of pilgrimage in the lives of West African Muslims in Sudan*
14. TOM FORREST *The Advance of African Capital: the growth of Nigerian private enterprise*
13. MELLISSA LEACH *Rainforest Relations: gender and resource use among the Mende of Gola, Sierra Leone*
12. ISSAC NCUBE MAZONDE *Ranching and Enterprise in Eastern Botswana: a case study of black and white farmers*
11. G. S. EADES *Strangers and Traders: Yoruba migrants, markets and the stage in northern Ghana*
10. COLIN MURRAY *Black Mountain: land, class and power in the eastern Orange Free State, 1880s to 1980s*
9. RICHARD WERBNER *Tears of the Dead: the social biography of an African family*
8. RICHARD FARDON *Between God, the Dead and the Wild: Chamba interpretations of religion and ritual*
7. KARIN BARBER *I Could Speak until Tomorrow: oriki, women and the past in a Yoruba town*
6. SUZETTE HEALD *Controlling Anger: the sociology of Gisu violence*
5. GÜNTHER SCHLEE *Identities on the Move: settlement and survival in Membwe villages, Zambia*
4. JOHAN POTTIER *Migrants No More: settlement and survival in Mambwe villages, Zambia*
3. PAUL SPENCER *The Maasai of Matapato: a study of rituals of rebellion*
2. JANE I. GUYER (ed.) *Feeding African Cities: essays in social history*
1. SANDRA T. BARNES *Patrons and Power: creating a political community in metropolitan Lagos*

Printed in the United States
By Bookmasters